KNOW YOUR RIGHTS

A SURVIVAL GUIDE FOR NON-LAWYERS

RONALD M. BENREY, JD

STERLING

New York / London
www.sterlingpublishing.com

DEDICATION

This book is for Janet, for too many reasons to mention.

STERLING and the distinctive Sterling logo are registered trademarks
of Sterling Publishing Co., Inc.

Library of Congress Cataloging-in-Publication Data

Benrey, Ron, 1941-
Know your rights : a survival guide for non-lawyers / Ronald M. Benrey.
    p. cm.
Includes index.
ISBN 978-1-4027-6391-5
1. Law--United States--Popular works. I. Title.
KF387.B39 2011
349.73--dc22
                            2010024253

2 4 6 8 10 9 7 5 3 1

Published by Sterling Publishing Co., Inc.
387 Park Avenue South, New York, NY 10016
© 2011 by Ronald M. Benrey
Distributed in Canada by Sterling Publishing
℅ Canadian Manda Group, 165 Dufferin Street
Toronto, Ontario, Canada M6K 3H6
Distributed in the United Kingdom by GMC Distribution Services
Castle Place, 166 High Street, Lewes, East Sussex, England BN7 1XU
Distributed in Australia by Capricorn Link (Australia) Pty. Ltd.
P.O. Box 704, Windsor, NSW 2756, Australia

Manufactured in the United States of America
All rights reserved

Sterling ISBN 978-1-4027-6391-5

CONTENTS

CHAPTER 13

BUYING A CAR

CHAPTER 14
TRIALS IN SMALL CLAIMS COURT

CHAPTER 15
YOUR CONSTITUTIONAL RIGHTS AND FREEDOMS

ACKNOWLEDGMENTS

A venerable legal maxim teaches that "the well-trodden path is the safest." That's why so many contracts, wills, and familiar legal documents seem so similar. Many publishers choose the "safe route" for the legal guides they offer. I thank Meredith Hale, who launched this project, and her management colleagues at Sterling Publishing, for having the determination to avoid the trodden path. They gave me the freedom to write the book I've dreamed of writing since I graduated from law school.

Another oft-heard legal adage affirms that "no one can properly understand any part of a thing till (s)he has read through the whole again and again." I know this was the case for Kate Zimmerman, my editor, and Scott Amerman, my production editor. Their willingness to read and reread my manuscript made the editorial process painless for me.

Yet another maxim instructs: "He who does a thing by an agent is considered as doing it himself." While this is a truism in the law of agency, a good literary agent routinely accomplishes things a writer can't do by himself. Cheers for Marilyn Allen, my literary agent, for her support throughout the long development process.

And one final legal aphorism proclaims: "There is no obligation under law to do impossible things." Perhaps not, but my wife, Janet, often did impossible things to help me complete this book. I'm truly grateful for her patience and forbearance.

Ron Benrey
New Bern, North Carolina, 2011

+⫝̸ ⫝̸+

CHAPTER 1

KNOW YOUR RIGHTS
UNDER THE LAW

W HAT ARE MY RIGHTS?
Chances are you asked that very question the last time you faced a
challenging legal problem. Perhaps you wanted to get out of the lease
on your apartment. Or possibly your neighbor owned a pack of noisy dogs that
kept you awake all night. Or you may have wondered if it made any sense to fight
a recent speeding ticket. Or you might have felt compelled to file a suit against a
local contractor in small claims court.

I assume that you *shouted* "What Are My Rights" if you were required to
deal with a more complex legal issue. For example, a serious automobile accident caused by another driver's carelessness. Or the decision to sign a prenuptial
agreement before you got married. Or an employer who discriminated against
you by withholding a plum promotion. Or the need to bail a relative out of jail.
Or the painful procedure of filing for bankruptcy.

This Book Is a "Survival Guide" for Non-Lawyers

The chapters that follow will help you know your rights when commonplace
legal issues arise in your daily life, in your home, in your car, and at your job.
Sometimes, you'll find enough information to be able to deal with an issue
yourself; other times you'll need the assistance and counsel of an experienced
attorney.

No book can replace a knowledgeable lawyer when you need comprehensive
legal advice, but it can be difficult to appreciate the need for professional legal
counsel without some understanding of the basic issues and the risks you may
face if you delay talking to a lawyer. Moreover, there are a number of common
legal chores—suing someone in small claims court, for example—that you can
handle yourself without a lawyer. That's why this book has three goals:

1. To reduce the panic factor by helping you understand the
   fundamental legal principles that are at the heart of the legal
   problems we face most often. ("The law" varies from state to state,
   but similar legal principles apply everywhere. Some date back
   hundreds of years; others were applied in Ancient Rome and even
   Biblical times.)

2. To make you familiar with enough specialized legal language so that you'll be able to talk sensibly and productively with an attorney—and also be able to find more information in your local law library and on the Internet. (Each chapter explains important legal terms in context.)

3. To overcome some of the familiar misconceptions about law and our legal system. One of the most popular misbeliefs is the idea that the laws that underpin everyday legal issues are based on "common sense." For example, the renter of an apartment may think it sensible not to pay rent to a landlord who hasn't fixed a plumbing problem. However, a small claims court judge is not likely to agree, because the law pertaining to landlords and tenants was designed to balance many competing interests. (*See* Chapter 8.)

How I Organized the Content

There are many ways to carve up the list of common legal issues. For example, I could have put all the topics related to your home—from buying one to dealing with a noisy neighbor—in a single chapter called "Your House." But I chose a different approach. I grouped topics together that apply similar legal principles. Consequently, you'll find all kinds of accidents (from someone slipping on your driveway to a fender-bender in your automobile) in Chapter 4. And, you'll read about all manner of crimes—including speeding tickets—in Chapter 17. This approach let me use hypothetical scenarios to illustrate and illuminate the law in action.

Hypotheticals for Fun and Learning

I also chose an unusual strategy for presenting the essential legal principles that you need to know. It's not enough to merely explain the law, because it's important that you understand how these legal principles are actually *applied* in everyday situations. And so, most chapters in this book are built around detailed *hypothetical scenarios*—*stories* based on the kinds of legal situations that real people face every day. I've supplemented the hypotheticals with sidebars and notes that present specific details you need to know about each subject area. And, several chapters end with sections labeled "Other Things Worth Knowing about . . . " that further flesh out the information contained in the hypotheticals.

A NOTE ABOUT THE *HYPOTHETICAL SCENARIOS* IN THIS BOOK

Many law schools test student knowledge with end-of-the-term exam questions based on improbable hypothetical situations that may even seem cartoonish at times. Some take place in states you won't find on most U.S. maps: *the State of Confusion, the State of Uncertainty, and the State of Ruin.* As one professor explained to me, this isn't done to poke fun at situations that may be tragic (there's nothing funny about an automobile accident, on-the-job discrimination, a lengthy child custody battle, or a serious injury caused by someone's negligence) but rather to focus attention on the legal principles involved. I've assembled far-fetched circumstances in many of the hypothetical scenarios in this book for much the same reason. Consequently, when *Wanda,* a house cat who liked to roam, triggered an unlikely chain of events (see Chapter 4) that ended in mayhem and destruction, you don't have to be concerned that real people have been injured or lost everything. This makes it easier to identify—and understand—the various torts (legal wrongs) that have been committed.

The use of hypotheticals is a fine, old tradition among attorneys. Many generations of law professors and law students have found that fictional scenarios communicate important legal principles more effectively than paragraphs of "bare" facts and complex definitions. Where appropriate, I constructed the hypotheticals to be entertaining as well as enlightening. Why not have fun while you're learning to think like a lawyer?

Thinking Like a Lawyer

Decades ago, *The Paper Chase* was a popular TV series (based on a popular movie) that depicted the challenges of attending law school. The commanding voice of stern Professor Kingsfield would begin each episode with, "You come here with minds full of mush—and leave thinking like a lawyer."

What does it mean to *think like a lawyer?* Well, while lawyers need to think clearly and logically (a requirement of many other occupations), clients often ask lawyers to anticipate legal consequences. To do this, a lawyer must reason from the known to the uncertain. Let me illustrate what I mean with our first hypothetical.

To set the stage: a law student named Earl Lee Riser learns that pointing a loaded gun at someone is a legal wrong called *assault*. It's also considered a crime in most places. We'll examine both the legal wrong and the crime of assault in greater detail later, but for now, let's define *assault* as putting a person in reasonable fear of immediate violence.

But what if the gun being pointed happens to be unloaded?

This simple change of facts requires Earl Lee to "fill in the gap"—from a known situation (pointing a loaded gun) to an uncertain situation (pointing an unloaded gun).

A bit of legal thinking convinces him (and should convince you) that the gun itself—loaded or not—is sufficient to create fear and, consequently, to *complete* the assault. Looking at it another way; it's reasonable for a person staring down the barrel of a gun to presume it's loaded and to fear immediate violence. This is the law virtually everywhere.

Let's spin the fact wheel once more: This time, we'll make the "gun" a realistic non-firing replica that resembles an actual weapon. Can pointing a *toy gun* at someone be assault?

Yes! A fake weapon that looks real can be just as threatening under the right circumstances, which is why many pointers of toy guns have been charged with the serious crime of *assault with a deadly weapon* (known as *aggravated assault* in some states).

Now comes our hypothetical: Decades later, Earl Lee (now an experienced attorney) is hired to watch over the legal affairs of the Blackacre Summer Theater. The fabulous Ima Starr—the company's lead actress—visits Earl Lee and says:

"I play Mrs. Plum. The director wants me to point a toy gun at Colonel Gray during the second act of our upcoming production, *Murder Most Foul*. Will I commit assault with a deadly weapon in front of 500 people? Specifically, will I be in legal jeopardy if I wield a gun on stage?"

What should Earl Lee tell Ima? And why?

Earl Lee will probably explain that Ima's action *won't* be considered an assault because the actor playing Colonel Gray *fully expects* Ima to point a toy gun at him as part of the performance. Consequently, he won't be put in reasonable fear of immediate violence.

You'll find many more examples of reasoning from the known to the uncertain on the pages that follow—each designed to sharpen your thought process, so that you better understand the relevant legal principles when you do your own research or when a lawyer explains them to you.

"The First Thing We Do, Let's Kill All the Lawyers"

Those are well known words from *King Henry VI, Part II*, one of William Shakespeare's historical plays. They're spoken in Act IV, Scene ii by an unsavory character named Dick the Butcher, a follower of Jack Cade, a leader of an ill-fated rebellion against the king.

A surprisingly large segment of America's population might applaud Dick's suggestion today. If you ask them why they dislike lawyers, you'll probably hear things such as "lawyers use technicalities to put their dangerous clients back on the streets, enabling obvious criminals to commit more crimes." Or, "lawyers file goofy lawsuits that earn millions of dollars for people who aren't bright enough to take personal responsibility when a waiter puts a cup of hot soup in front of them."

Opinion surveys consistently show that lawyers—and the legal profession—are not highly regarded in the United States. Here's what a much reported survey conducted several years ago by Columbia University's Law School found:

⇥ 39 percent of Americans think that lawyers are dishonest.

⇥ 60 percent of Americans feel that lawyers are overpaid for the work they do.

⇥ 41 percent of Americans believe that lawyers do more harm than good by filing lawsuits that may raise the cost of doing business.

These unhappy statistics explain why jokes about lawyers have become a staple with comedians:

Q: How can you tell when a lawyer is lying?

A: His lips are moving.

Q: Why won't sharks bite lawyers?

A: Professional courtesy.

Q: What's the difference between a good lawyer and a bad lawyer?

A: A bad lawyer can drag your case out for ten years. A good lawyer can make it last even longer.

And my personal favorite:

The trouble with the legal profession is that 99 percent of America's lawyers give the rest a bad name.

Yes, these jokes are painfully funny. And nobody laughs more at them than practicing attorneys. But the people who tell lawyer jokes usually have much in common with the people who participated in the survey conducted by Columbia. The large majority of the respondents had no recent experience working with a lawyer. Less than a third had used the services of a lawyer for any purpose within the previous year. Simply put, their downbeat opinions were based largely on negative stereotypes and the "bad" lawyers portrayed on some TV shows and in some movies.

Lack of hands-on experience with lawyers is a good thing. Lawsuits, trials of any kind, and brushes with the law are rare events for most people. And few of us need the advice of an attorney on a regular basis. But that doesn't mean that lawyers and the law don't impact our everyday lives.

The truth is, if lawyers didn't exist, we'd have to create them. That's because the vital (but unglamorous) work that the majority of lawyers do escapes the attention of most people. Only a small percentage of attorneys—fewer than 20 percent in most areas of the country—show up in courtrooms to prosecute or defend criminals, or press medical malpractice claims, or handle personal injury lawsuits, or work as divorce attorneys.

What do the other lawyers do? If you asked that question in a crowd, you'd probably get a lot of vague stares. Press harder and one or two people in the crowd might remember their high school civics class and say that lawyers guide their clients through the intricacies of the legal system, advise clients about their legal rights and obligations, and help to protect personal rights and liberties.

In fact, the real answer is much less fancy. The majority of attorneys practicing law today—and most of the lawyers you're likely to deal with during your lifetime—specialize in contracts, real estate conveyances, wills and estates, financial transactions, bankruptcy, business transactions, and matters related to these things. These lawyers spend their work days surrounded by paper rather than witnesses because the bulk of legal issues that crop up every day are largely concerned with money, the goods and services people buy and own, and real estate. These are the chief ingredients of the routine legal stew. People have been dealing with—and getting into conflict over—money, things, land, and houses since the dawn of recorded history.

It's not by accident that the majority of the chapters in this practical guidebook to common legal issues involve the making and enforcing of different kinds of contracts—for purchases of goods and services, personal loans, insurance, apartment leases, real estate purchases and sales, real estate covenants, and even prenuptial agreements.

But times are changing and so is the nature of "commonplace" legal issues. The old contract-based goulash is being spiced up with immigration issues, questions about the free exercise of religion and the rights of students in schools, identity theft, invasion of privacy, and many other contemporary legal questions. And so, I've included other areas of law that you're likely to run into without really trying.

When You Really Need a Lawyer

I often hear my friends—especially my well-educated friends—say, "Learning the foundational legal principles is fairly simple. Besides lots of books, there are loads of resources available on the Internet that *seem* to cover almost every topic. When do I *really* need a lawyer?"

They expect me to start my answer with that old cliché: A person who acts as his own lawyer has a fool for a client.

That's not what I say. My usual answer is: It's fairly obvious, fairly quickly, to most people when their own knowledge of the law is not sufficient for the situation they find themselves in. Consequently, I've never met a person who didn't know when he or she "really needed" a lawyer—although I've met several who decided not to get one when they needed one. They invariably came to regret their decision.

The obvious occasion when you absolutely, positively need a lawyer in your corner is whenever you find yourself up against an attorney acting in an adversarial role—typically at a trial or hearing in other than small claims court. Doing adversarial law yourself is equivalent to going to war unarmed because there's bound to be a lot you won't know about current law, legal procedure, and rules of evidence. Your lack of knowledge in these areas will help the other attorney turn you into courtroom roadkill.

We have an *adversarial legal system*. That sounds nasty because *adversary* is an unfriendly word and because the underlying concept harks back to medieval trial by combat. The fundamental idea is to have two opposing lawyers vigorously advocate the opposing positions and zealously test witnesses and the other evidence. When this is done, proponents claim, the *fact finder* (a jury or judge) will be in the best position to determine guilt or innocence (in a criminal trial) or legal responsibility (in a civil trial).

Fortunately, most common legal issues *don't* involve true examples of the adversarial system. You may see opposing attorneys sparring during a divorce, for example, and in personal injury cases. I say "may see" because few routine legal disputes end in an actual trial anymore, thanks to the greater use of alternative dispute resolution (ADR) methods, such as a mediation and arbitration. (You'll find the details of ADR covered in Chapter 2.) And most civil lawsuits that seem to be headed for litigation are settled—with the judge's encouragement—before the trial begins.

These are happy trends because trials can be dramatic, expensive, and not all that pleasant for the people involved. About a hundred years ago, Ambrose Bierce, the American journalist and satirist, included the following definition in his *Devil's Dictionary*: "Lawsuit: A machine which you go into as a pig and come out of as a sausage."

One actual legal battleground where you won't find opposing attorneys is small claims court. The rules in many states prevent claimants from having an attorney to press their cases. Instead the judge asks questions of both parties in an effort to surface and understand the causes of their dispute and ultimately reach an appropriate decision.

Two Opposing Lawyers Are Not Necessarily Adversaries

Some legal issues that look adversarial at first glance really aren't. When you buy a house, for example, both you and the seller may be represented by different attorneys—with both attorneys looking after their client's specific interests. But neither the buyer's lawyer nor the seller's attorney is trying to convince a judge or a jury that his client is right and the other party is wrong. The chief reason to have your own attorney there is to help you understand the meaning of the different clauses in the papers you are signing and to help make certain that your desires are expressed in the documents. Your lawyer serves as your counselor and adviser rather than an advocate for your position.

Many routine transactions involve attorneys—although you may not see any lawyers at work. The insurance company that writes a policy will have an attorney draft the paperwork—as will the bank that hands you a loan form to sign, the rental agent who invites you to sign a "standard" lease, and the investment firm that invites you to sign up for an account.

Many people in these situations argue they don't "really need" a lawyer to look after their interests, that they can figure out the arcane legal language by themselves. Maybe so, but over the years countless others have come to wish they had had an expert legal adviser on their side when they signed documents that created unforeseen legal problems—possibly *years* later.

Because our daily affairs involve a flood of documents, several of the topic area chapters specifically highlight the legal language you're likely to find in the documents you're asked to sign. My purpose here is to help you understand what "the other side" is trying to accomplish.

Beware of Half-Baked Legal Information

The oft-heard idea my friends expressed—that the world is awash in legal information—is true, but this is not necessarily good news, because much of what you'll find out there is half-baked at best. Happily, there are many useful sources of basic legal information—including free websites. Despite the availability of accurate information, a surprising number of people get their legal "facts" from less credible sources:

→ Friend-of-friend experiences

→ Miscellaneous anecdotes recounted by relatives

→ Self-taught legal "experts" who dispense legal advice on Internet blogs and mailing lists

→ Law-related TV shows and movies (This would be funny if it weren't true.)

Law is truly one of those activities where a little bit of knowledge can be a dangerous thing. Well-meaning friends usually don't know what they don't know about the law. The wrong word in a will . . . the incorrect response to a legal document . . . misinterpretation of the fine print in a contract . . . any of these "little mistakes" can cause significant difficulties later on. Keep in mind that the prohibition against practicing law without a license isn't a make-work scheme for lawyers; it is an important protection against costly problems. Bad legal advice can be much worse than no advice at all.

One Final Point of Introduction

The best time to read this book is long *before* you have a legal problem. Many (and perhaps most) people dealing with unpleasant legal issues got into their predicament because they didn't think about the consequences of their actions or inactions. For example:

> + You have a responsibility to read—and understand—contracts and other important papers *before* you sign them.
> + You have a responsibility to think about purchases *before* you make them.
> + You have a duty to exercise caution and care about the safety of other people.
> + You have a duty to obey all the traffic laws and to control your temper.

This book sets forth and explains dozens of commonplace legal responsibilities and duties in important areas ranging from contracts, to marriage, to landlord-tenant relationships, to getting along with neighbors. Understanding these things can be the key to avoiding everyday legal problems.

A Final Caveat

What would a book written by a lawyer be without some fine print? Understand that this is not a legal textbook. This is a friendly guidebook to *"everyday law."* (I'll use that term as a catchall label for the various commonplace legal issues that are most likely to touch our daily lives.) Students in law schools are exposed to an endless stream of *what-ifs*—facts that continuously change the circumstances. I've had to simplify many key concepts of everyday law to keep them understandable and fit them inside one volume. I'll never lead you seriously astray, but I'll also never tell you the whole story.

Other Things Worth Knowing about Everyday Law

Civil Law vs. Criminal Law

Everyday law can be divided into two major categories: civil law and criminal law. Civil law is designed to resolve private disputes between people or between people and entities, such as companies, banks, shops, or hospitals. The most common goal of a case in civil law—what most of us call a *lawsuit*—is to reimburse the harm suffered by one party because of the other party's actions. The *plaintiff* (the person bringing the suit) believes that the *defendant* (the person being sued) broke a contract, failed to repay a debt, was responsible for an accident, shouldn't have kept a found object—or did something (or failed to do something) that harmed the plaintiff in some way. If the plaintiff wins in court, the judge will order the defendant to pay appropriate *money damages*.

The overwhelming majority of attorneys practice some aspect of civil law.

Although criminal law is a relatively small corner of everyday law, it is typically more dramatic than civil law because the plaintiff in a criminal trial is the government, acting as the representative of other citizens. Here too, the plaintiff believes that the defendant did something (or failed to do something) that caused harm—but there's a significant difference. A criminal defendant who loses his or her case can be ordered to pay a fine, can be sentenced to a term of imprisonment or probation, and in some extreme circumstances can be executed. These sanctions punish criminals and deter others from committing similar crimes. We'll look closely at criminal law in Chapter 17.

Different Burdens of Proof

Civil and criminal trials can look much the same, take place in the same courtroom (at different times, of course), and be presided over by the same judge. Another thing they have in common is that the plaintiff in a civil and the government in a criminal prosecution both have the burden of actually proving that the defendant did wrong. As you might expect, this *burden of proof* is more stringent in a criminal trial. Specifically, the government must prove that a criminal defendant is guilty *beyond a reasonable doubt*. In fact, the defendant is presumed to be innocent until the very moment that the jury (or judge in some cases) determines that he or she is guilty.

By contrast, most civil plaintiffs will win if they make their case with a *preponderance of the evidence*. This means that it's slightly more probable than not that the defendant did wrong. You've probably seen drawings or sculptures of Justitia, the Roman goddess of justice, blindfolded (because justice is blind) and holding a scale (to weigh the evidence). A preponderance of the evidence tips the scale slightly toward one side, while proof beyond a reasonable doubt swings the scale completely away from the defendant.

We'll touch on both standards in greater detail in the hypothetical scenarios.

Your Right to a Jury Trial

The Sixth Amendment to the U.S. Constitution provides that

> [in] all criminal prosecutions, the accused shall enjoy the right to a
> speedy and public trial, by an impartial jury of the State and district
> wherein the crime shall have been committed . . .

JUDGMENTS VS. VERDICTS

Although the following terms both refer to the outcome of a case,
a *judgment* is the decision announced by the judge, whereas a
verdict is the decision reached by a jury. Consequently, a jury
trial may end with a *judgment of conviction* following the jury's
guilty verdict.

This has been interpreted (by the U.S. Supreme Court) to apply to criminal
trials in state and federal courts for "serious" offenses—these are crimes that are
punished with prison terms of six months or longer. Your state may choose to
provide jury trials for less-serious prosecutions, but it is not required to do so. A
jury operates as a *trier of fact* at a criminal trial; it determines guilt or innocence
(a fact). The right to a jury trial does not impose a jury on a defendant. He or she
can waive a trial by jury and be tried by the court without a jury. In that event,
the judge becomes the trier of fact.

The Seventh Amendment establishes the right to a jury trial for civil suits
in federal courts that seek money damages but does not apply to state courts.
Nonetheless, many states have included in their constitutions the right to jury
trial for some categories of civil cases. Here too, the jury acts as a trier of fact; it
answers such questions as "Who owns a specific piece of property?" (a fact). One
important civil exception is suits *in equity* rather than *in law* (*see* below). Claims
that require a determination of fairness rather than facts are resolved by judges.

Common Law vs. Civil Code

One of the reasons—perhaps the most important reason—you're reading this
book is to understand "the law." And that raises two interesting questions: First,
who makes the law? Second, how do we know what the law is?

You've probably heard that the United States is a *common-law country.* That label
provides important partial answers to the two questions I just posed. We inherited
the so-called common law from England, where it grew and developed over many
hundreds of years. It's impossible to provide a precise history because the essence

of common law is the idea that we do things today in the way that people have "always" done them. English common law originally dealt with laws relating to the possession, use, and inheritance of land. Because ownership of land was so important, people needed to understand who owned land under different circumstances—and what were the rights of people who owned land against others.

These laws weren't collected in a code of specific rules and regulations. Rather, they could be found by reading the opinions written by different judges when they decided cases. People came to rely on the notion that the legal principles used by judges to resolve disputes yesterday would be applied to similar disputes today, even if the case was heard by a different judge. This made the law of property predictable—an essential requirement for any practical legal system.

Over the years, common law grew to encompass disputes involving contracts, personal property, and *legal wrongs* done by one person to another. But the idea of looking to what was done by earlier courts remained a fundamental feature. This evolved into the doctrine of *stare decisis*—"let decided things stand"—the principle on which the decisions of higher courts must be followed by lower courts. Consequently, when a lawyer wanted to advise a client about a specific question of law, he or she would look at appropriate earlier decisions—confident that a trial court today would apply the law outlined in those same cases. In circumstances where there is no prior decision—no authoritative statement of the law—judges will make new law by creating new precedents for others to follow in the future.

Civil Code Countries

The need for predictability and consistency of the law is just as obvious in countries that didn't "borrow" English common law. The trial courts in these countries honor the much older tradition of looking to imperial edicts, express legislative acts, scholarly essays, and other forms of written law, rather than to the precedents established by higher courts. The principles of everyday law are often codified in documents called *civil codes*.

In theory, trial judges—and the judges of higher courts—have different roles to play in common-law and civil code systems. When faced with a new legal issue, a common-law judge tries to follow judicial precedent and apply established principles to the new circumstances. When faced with a similar challenge, a civil code judge tries to interpret the intent of codified law and apply it to the new circumstances.

Forty-nine of the fifty states have common-law-based systems. The sole exception is Louisiana. Because French law is based on a civil code, and because Louisiana was originally a French colony, the state of Louisiana still follows the civil code approach in much of its law.

In practice, however, the differences between common-law legal systems and civil code ones are shrinking every day. All forty-nine common-law states have codified statutes and regulations in important areas of everyday law. And in Louisiana, *jurisprudence* (as Louisianans refer to judge-made decisions) is recognized as an important source of law.

"Cases in Equity" vs. "Cases in Law"

Who hasn't heard the biblical story (told in 1 Kings 3:16–28) of how two women petitioned King Solomon to decide which one of the two was the true mother of a baby. Solomon applied his legendary wisdom and offered to split the baby in two and award half to each woman. One woman agreed, while the other abandoned her claim—enabling Solomon to identify the "true mother"—the one who had the baby's best interests in mind.

Solomon resolved the kind of family law dispute that could easily end up in court today. Although he used unusual evidence to tell which woman was lying, the outcome was fair and just—and vindicated the right woman's claim—even though no money changed hands after the trial.

Previously, I said that the most common goal of a civil *lawsuit* is to reimburse (with money damages) the harm suffered by one party because of the other party's actions. This is true of many, but not all, lawsuits. A plaintiff may also come to court in the hope that the judge will resolve a dispute by ordering the defendant to do something—or *not* do something else.

This is an example of a *case in equity*, as opposed to a *case in law*.

To understand the differences, you need to look back at the beginnings of English common law—some seven centuries ago. The king's courts of the day could hear a narrow range of kinds of cases on specific legal issues. Someone with a dispute that didn't fit within the rigid boundaries of common law couldn't ask for a remedy "in law."

However, like Solomon, the English kings also dispensed justice. Practically speaking, this meant seeking a remedy from the king's chancellor—an adviser on spiritual matters who often acted as "the keeper of the royal conscience." The chancellor—and his *courts of chancery*—weren't bound by inflexible common-law principles. They could resolve disputes according to equity (or fairness).

Two separate legal systems—law and equity, each specializing in different kinds of disputes—evolved in England. Equity took over only when there was no adequate remedy at law and when a party would be irreparably harmed without equity's intervention.

The wall between law and equity carried over to the United States. In the nineteenth century, however, states began to merge law and equity in single court systems. The federal court system completed the merger in 1938.

Today the same judge can provide remedies *in law* and remedies *in equity*—depending upon what the plaintiff seeks. As I've noted, the most common remedy *in law* is an award of money damages. By contrast, remedies *in equity* often involve the judge directing the defendant to do something:

If Bob breaches a contract to sell Bill a unique antique car, Bill may not want money damages—he wants the car. A judge can impose the equitable remedy of *specific performance*: He orders Bob to deliver the unique car to Bill for the agreed-upon price.

Perhaps the most important equitable remedy is the *injunction*—a court order that requires a person to act (mandatory injunction) or to refrain from acting (prohibitory injunction)—possibly under the threat of prison if he or she disobeys.

Another difference between law and equity is that *in law* cases often involve circumstances where the plaintiff has been injured, whereas in many *in equity* cases the plaintiff wants the court to intervene to prevent injury or stop it before it does significant damage.

I'll include several examples of *in law* versus *in equity* remedies in the scenarios that follow. An important point to keep in mind is that judges—never juries—fashion equitable remedies.

Why Are There So Many Different Courts in the United States?

We're a country full of courts. There are hundreds of different courts in the United States. Why do we have so many courts? There are three simple answers. On the one hand, people have many different kinds of legal issues to resolve. On the other hand, people who lose in court want and expect another bite at the apple—and so we need courts of *appeal*. On the third hand, we have fifty states, each with its own legal system.

The fact is, the Constitution of the United States limits the role (the *jurisdiction*) of federal courts to specific kinds of disputes and crimes. The lion's share of lawsuits, legal matters, and criminal prosecutions are handled by state courts. Should you run into a significant legal issue that can't be solved by negotiation, mediation, or arbitration, it will probably be adjudicated in a state court.

State Court Systems

Over the years, state courts have become complex "legal systems" in their own right, with a rich assortment of component parts. Although no two state judicial systems are alike, I can provide an outline of the various courts you'll find in a typical state. The details in your state *will* be different, but the general "architecture" is likely to be the same three-layer structure:

1. State supreme court (the state's highest court)
2. Intermediate appellate court
3. Trial courts of general jurisdiction and trial courts of limited jurisdiction

Trial Courts of General Jurisdiction

If you run afoul of the law in your state—or have a dispute that requires taking legal action—you'll get involved with your state's court system at the trial court level. A state's trial courts of general jurisdiction are the courts most people envision when imagining full-blown criminal or civil trials before a judge and jury. Because state court systems evolved independently, different states will have different names for their courts of general jurisdiction: superior court, circuit court, court of common pleas, and (confusingly in New York State) supreme court. Courts of general jurisdiction try both civil and criminal cases. In some states these courts hear appeals from trial courts of limited jurisdiction (*see* below).

Trial Courts of Limited Jurisdiction

As the name suggests, these trial courts are the "specialists" who deal with narrow areas of everyday law. Judges (and sometimes lower-level judicial officers called magistrates) hear cases without juries. These are common areas of responsibility:

→ *Probate*—Probate judges administer the estates (*see* Chapter 19) of *decedents* (deceased persons).

→ *Family law*—Family court judges hear cases involving adoption, annulments, divorce, distribution of marital property, child custody and visitation rights, child support, alimony, and related issues.

→ *Juvenile justice*—Specially trained judges hear cases involving delinquent children and possible child neglect and abuse.

→ *Small claims*—Small claims courts resolve disputes in which a relatively low dollar amount is in controversy, less than $5,000 in many states.

→ *Business issues*—Specialized courts have the expertise to handle cases involving corporate and commercial law.

→ *Minor crimes*—Judges (and sometimes magistrates) try *misdemeanor* and *infraction* cases.

→ *Criminal justice*—Judges or magistrates issue arrest and search warrants, oversee *initial appearances* of defendants charged with serious crimes (to schedule a preliminary hearing and set bail), and hold subsequent *preliminary hearings* (to establish reasonable belief that the suspect committed a crime).

Intermediate Appellate Court

Criminal defendants convicted of crimes and civil-suit parties unhappy with the outcome of a trial have a right to appeal the trial court's decision. In the majority of states, these appeals are heard by an *intermediate appellate court*—so labeled because they sit above trial courts of general jurisdiction in the organization in the state court hierarchy, but fall below the state supreme court, the highest court in the state. Many are called, logically enough, the *court of appeals*, although some states reserve that name for their highest appeals court.

Appeals are typically heard by panels of three appellate judges. They rarely consider fresh evidence or challenge the "facts" determined by the judge or jury during a trial. Rather, they look for errors in interpretation of relevant law—and mistakes in procedure—that might have caused an unjust result at the trial.

State Supreme Court

The top of the judicial pyramid in all states is the state's highest court—usually called the *supreme court*. In most states, the supreme court is the third "layer" of courts. A panel of judges called *Justices* (typically seven or nine) hear appeals that usually involve interpretation of state law. Most of the cases arriving at a state's supreme court are there because the Justices agreed to hear them. There's generally no right to an appeal in the state supreme court; rather, a convicted criminal defendant or the losing party in a civil suit must petition the court for a review. Most state supreme courts automatically review criminal cases involving capital punishment. Some look at any case that caused a dissent (disagreement) among the judges in the intermediate appellate court.

The U. S. Court System

Article III of the U.S. Constitution states that "[t]he judicial power of the United States, shall be vested in one Supreme Court, and in such inferior courts as the Congress may from time to time ordain and establish."

A page or so earlier, Article I states that "Congress shall have the power to . . . constitute tribunals inferior to the Supreme Court."

Article III Courts

The core of the U.S. court system is a three-layer "cake" of so-called Article III *courts of general jurisdiction:*

1. *U.S. Supreme Court*—The highest court in the nation; most of its cases require the nine Justices to resolve fundamental questions about the Constitution or federal law. Most cases reach the Supreme Court because one of the parties files a *Petition for a Writ of Certiorari.* The court grants "cert" (agrees to consider the issues involved) for only about 2 percent of the petitions it receives.

2. *U.S. Circuit Courts of Appeals*—These are the nation's intermediate appellate courts (*see* above); panels of judges review verdicts and judgments made in U.S. district courts.

3. *U.S. District Courts*—These are the federal trial courts (also known as *courts of original jurisdiction*). The lion's share of federal civil and criminal cases begins in U.S. district courts.

Two other special courts are attached to the district courts:

1. *Magistrate Judges*—The first judicial officer a criminal defendant sees after an arrest is typically a U.S. magistrate judge, who takes care of *preliminary matters* in criminal cases, including the *initial appearance*, bail review, and *preliminary hearing*. Magistrates also hear pretrial motions in civil cases, conduct trials for misdemeanors and petty offenses, and perform other judicial proceedings to expedite the civil and criminal cases moving through U.S. district courts.

2. *U.S. Bankruptcy Courts*—These are specific courts to handle cases that arise under U.S. bankruptcy laws (*see* Chapter 20).

There are also two Article III *courts of special jurisdiction:* the U.S. Court of Federal Claims (that hears claims against the U.S. government for monetary damages) and the U.S. Court of International Trade (that hears claims involving customs law disputes and questions international trade).

Article I Courts

In addition, the U.S. court system includes several special Article I (or *legislative*) courts established for special purposes. Their names are almost self-explanatory:

→ *U.S. Court of Appeals for the Armed Forces*—This is the final court of appeals for military personnel convicted of crimes under the *Uniform Code of Military Justice.*

→ *U.S. Tax Court*—At this court, taxpayers can dispute tax deficiencies assessed by the Internal Revenue Service *before* paying the disputed amount.

→ *U.S. Court of Veterans Appeals*—At this court people can appeal the denial of veterans' benefits if their claims are rejected by the Board of Veterans' Appeals, part of the U.S. Department of Veterans Affairs.

A Short Course in U.S. Court Geography

One of the most confusing aspects of TV and newspaper reports about U.S. court trials and decisions is the geography of lower-level Article III courts. The U.S. Supreme Court is, naturally enough, in Washington, D.C. However, U.S.

district courts are located in one of ninety-four districts. Every state has at least one district court—for example, Montana is home to the U.S. District Court for the District of Montana. States with large populations may have as many as four district courts. California, for example, is broken into the Northern District, Eastern District, Central District, and Southern District. The official name of each court ends with the district; for example, United States District Court for the Southern District of California.

So far, so good. But U.S. Circuit Courts of Appeals change the naming scheme dramatically. Judicially speaking, the United States is carved into eleven *circuits* (*see* the table on page 21). The First Circuit (the smallest circuit) includes the states of Maine, Massachusetts, New Hampshire, and Rhode Island, and the self-governing Commonwealth of Puerto Rico. The massive U.S. Court of Appeals for the Ninth Circuit includes California, Idaho, Montana, Oregon, Nevada, and Washington.

Reporters rarely use full official titles when writing (or talking) about appellate decisions. You'll often see (or hear) things like, "The Fifth Circuit held today . . ." or "A decision by the Second Circuit . . . ." Whenever you hear the word *circuit* think U.S. Circuit Court of Appeals.

To put a cherry on the cupcake of potential confusion, there are actually *twelfth* and *thirteenth* circuit courts, although they doesn't have numbers: the U.S. Court of Appeals for the Federal Circuit, which sits in Washington, D.C., and hears appeals from those courts of special jurisdiction that I mentioned, along with appeals about patents, copyrights, trademarks, federal government contracts, and other issues regulated by federal law; and the U.S. Court of Appeals for the District of Columbia Circuit, which also sits in Washington, D.C., and deals with challenges to the rules and decisions made by federal agencies.

The Limits of Federal Court Jurisdiction

A court's *jurisdiction* establishes the boundaries of the kind of cases it can handle. The jurisdiction of federal courts—even *courts of general jurisdiction*—is limited by the powers granted to the federal government under the U.S. Constitution. This means that most crimes—from drunk driving to murder—are the bailiwick of state courts. The chief exceptions are crimes that violate a federal law, such as tax evasion, drug trafficking, kidnapping, tapping a telephone, or vandalizing federal property.

When it comes to civil disputes, U.S. courts have strict limits on the kinds of cases they can hear. Four kinds of lawsuit allowable in federal courts might fall within my definition of everyday law:

1. Lawsuits where both the plaintiff and defendant are citizens of different states (these invoke what is called *diversity jurisdiction*) *if* the amount in controversy exceeds $75,000

2. Lawsuits disputing federal questions that arise from a federal statute (for example, a lawsuit charging that the plaintiff's civil rights were violated)

3. Lawsuits in which the U.S. government is a party (perhaps following a traffic accident involving a federally owned vehicle)

4. Lawsuits in which one of the parties is a state (perhaps a challenge, in federal court, to a state criminal conviction)

One of the most significant categories of everyday law issues that *can't* be taken to federal courts is what the U.S. Supreme Court labeled *domestic relations law*. Even if the parties live in different states, U.S. courts won't do the following:

→ Grant a divorce decree (*see* Chapter 6)

→ Distribute marital property at or after divorce

→ Award or modify separate maintenance (*alimony*)

→ Determine or modify child custody (*see* Chapter 7)

One reason for this is that marriage and divorce have long been seen as matters of state law (*see* Chapter 5). Another is that state courts are presumed to have more experience in resolving family-law disputes and are supposedly better equipped to enforce compliance with custody, child support, and alimony orders. But there's probably important practical consideration lurking in the background: Adding domestic relations to federal court dockets might overwhelm an already too-busy court system.

Class-Action Suits

You've probably received at least one mailing in recent years announcing that unless you *opted-out*, you would be a *member* of a *class action* suit. A class action is a single lawsuit on behalf of a large group (possibly thousands) of people who all allege they've been injured by a single defendant. Recent class actions have involved the following claims:

→ A credit card company charged inappropriate fees to thousands of card holders.

→ An injectable drug, contaminated with bacteria, caused many illnesses and deaths.

→ A major employer systematically discriminated on the basis of sex when hiring and promoting employees.

→ A technology corporation misrepresented the size of available memory in the digital memory cards it sold to consumers.

→ A university used an inappropriate admission "points system" that gave unfair advantage to minority applications, at the expense of Caucasian applicants.

A class-action suit can be more efficient than multiple repeated lawsuits that involve virtually identical claims and evidence. Class-action suits can be brought both in state and federal courts, depending on whether a particular court has *jurisdiction* based on the subject matter, the amount of money in controversy, and the locations of the plaintiffs and defendants.

A class-action suit begins when a few named plaintiffs file a lawsuit on behalf of a much larger proposed class of plaintiffs who have similar claims against the defendant. Next, the named plaintiffs file a motion to have the class *certified*. When courts decide whether or not to move ahead with a class action, they consider the following:

→ If the large number of plaintiffs makes individual suits impractical

→ Whether the plaintiffs have legal and/or factual claims in common and meet the legal requirements to be certified as a class

→ Whether the defenses the defendant raises against the representative parties are typical of the defenses against all plaintiffs

→ If the representative parties will protect the interests of the class members

→ Whether a class action, rather than individual litigation, is the best way to resolve the disputes between the many plaintiffs and the common defendant

When a class is certified, members are notified so that any member who chooses to can opt out and proceed with their own lawsuits against the defendant. The members of the class will also be notified in the event of a proposed settlement.

If the parties don't reach a settlement, the trial goes forward much like a single-plaintiff lawsuit. Courts can generally award both actual damages (to compensate the plaintiffs' losses) and punitive damages (to punish the defendant's behavior). In most cases members of the class don't receive equal compensation; rather they receive shares of the total damage award that reflect their individual losses.

The plaintiffs' attorneys often work on a *contingency* basis: they receive a percentage of the eventual damage award (sometimes as high as 40 percent), but are not compensated if the plaintiffs lose.

FEDERAL CIRCUIT COURTS

1st Circuit
- Maine
- Massachusetts
- New Hampshire
- Rhode Island
- Puerto Rico (and U.S. Virgin Islands)

2nd Circuit
- Connecticut
- New York
- Vermont

3rd Circuit
- Delaware
- New Jersey
- Pennsylvania
- U.S. Virgin Islands

4th Circuit
- Maryland
- North Carolina
- South Carolina
- Virginia
- West Virginia

5th Circuit
- Louisiana
- Mississippi
- Texas

6th Circuit
- Kentucky
- Michigan
- Ohio
- Tennessee

7th Circuit
- Illinois
- Indiana
- Wisconsin

8th Circuit
- Arkansas
- Iowa
- Minnesota
- Missouri
- Nebraska
- North Dakota
- South Dakota

9th Circuit
- Alaska
- Arizona
- California
- Hawaii
- Idaho
- Montana
- Nevada
- Oregon
- Washington
- Guam
- Northern Mariana Islands

10th Circuit
- Colorado
- Kansas
- New Mexico
- Oklahoma
- Utah
- Wyoming

11th Circuit
- Alabama
- Florida
- Georgia

United States Court of Appeals for the Federal Circuit

United States Court of Appeals for the District of Columbia Court

CHAPTER 2

┿╾ ╼┿

THE LAW OF CONTRACTS

C ONTRACTS PLAY SUCH A SIGNIFICANT ROLE IN EVERYDAY LAW THAT MOST people have a feel for the essential concepts even if they aren't familiar with the lawyerly terminology of contract law. A contract is involved when you make a purchase at a store; when you buy or sell a home; when you buy, sell, or lease a car; when you rent an apartment; when you order cable TV, Internet, or cell phone service; when you load new software into your computer; when you get any kind of loan; when you co-sign for someone else's loan; when you purchase insurance; when you're cared for by a doctor or dentist; when you buy an airplane ticket; when you make a hotel reservation; when you rent a car; and even when you place a bid at a live or Internet auction. The list goes on and on.

Our daily lives are so full of contracts, in fact, that most of us simply can't spend much time thinking about their legal ramifications. Alas, the commercial companies on the other ends of these contracts do lots of thinking, which is why a lion's share of common legal problems concern people who want to get out from under contracts they wish they hadn't entered into.

The Case of the Big-Screen TV

The time has finally come, you decide, to buy that large-screen, high-definition TV (HDTV) set you've wanted for so long. You fire up your trusty computer and discover that TVs R Me, a local TV dealer, has a website. The big banner at the top of the page proclaims "Internet Specials: Save Money by Ordering Online" and lists dozens of different HDTVs. There's a tiny thumbnail photo next to each model number. When you click on the thumbnails, a new web page appears that describes the features and specifications of each HDTV and its price. At the bottom of each page is a button that reads, "Click to Buy Me."

You're mightily impressed by the Kudzo LCD 48, an obvious bargain at only $1,200 including sales tax, free delivery, and set-up in your home. It has all the bells and whistles you'd ever want and an impressive two-year warranty. So you click the "Click to Buy Me" button.

A new web page appears that spells out terms and conditions for the sale. The most prominent of these is "All Sales Are Final." The page explains that a TVs R Me truck will deliver the Kudzo LCD 48 to your home within ten calendar days. You will pay for the TV at time of delivery with a cashier's check for $1,200. A form on the page asks for your name and address and your e-mail address. The web page has a button on the bottom that reads "Click to Complete Purchase." A note beneath the button says, "By Clicking This Button You Confirm Your Intention to Enter into a Binding Contract to Purchase the Above Mentioned TV set from TVs R Me."

You provide the requested information, take a deep breath, and click the "Click to Complete Purchase" button.

Blink! A pop-up screen says, "Congratulations, You've Purchased a Kudzo LCD 48 HDTV."

More than that, you've entered into a contract—which may surprise you. Most people think a *contract* is a piece of paper, laden with confusing words, which two parties sign at the bottom.

In reality, a contract is a special kind of promise. What makes it special is that a court will enforce it. You make dozens of promises each day: "I'll call you tomorrow." "I'll help you bake cookies." "I'll buy you a sweater like mine for your birthday." "I'll love you 'til the end of time." The people to whom you made these promises may become upset if you don't follow through, but they'll never be able to convince a judge to do something about it.

The promise you made to TVs R Me is different. Should you decide not to keep it, a judge will likely do something to change your mind.

Mutual Promises

Actually, your contract with TVs R Me involves *two* promises. The store promised to deliver a Kudzo LCD 48 HDTV, and you promised to pay for it by handing over a cashier's check for $1,200.

Most contracts involve *mutual* promises. The two promises are voluntary—they're arrived at without coercion or duress—and reflect a meeting of the minds. Consider your purchase. Both parties agree that the fair price for a Kudzo LCD 48 is $1,200. You've agreed to buy one; TVs R Me agreed to sell you one and deliver it to your home.

How can a court know when a meeting of the minds has happened? After all, a judge can't look inside the parties' heads to verify that a meeting of the minds actually happened. In a courtroom situation, one of the parties might deny that they made promises to each other.

Over the years, judges have learned to look for four indicators that the parties reached a meeting of the minds and voluntarily entered into a contract that created legal obligations:

1. Offer
2. Acceptance
3. Consideration
4. Terms

An *offer* is just what the name suggests. One party (called the *offerer*) communicates that he is ready to enter a contract. For a judge to take notice, an offer must plainly make clear the following criteria:

→ The identity of the offerer

→ What is being offered (called the subject matter)

→ The quantity offered and the price

You found a valid offer on TVs R Me's website. TVs R Me offered to sell and deliver one Kudzo LCD 48 for $1,200, including sales tax.

An *acceptance* is typically equally straightforward. An acceptance happens when the second party to the contract communicates his unqualified agreement and assent to the offer:

→ He agrees to enter a contract with the offerer.

→ He agrees to the offer's subject matter.

→ He agrees to the terms of the offer.

You made a valid acceptance of TVs R Me's offer when you agreed to purchase one Kudzo LCD 48 for a delivered price of $1,200, paid by cashier's check.

Offer and acceptance seem obvious—and logical—requirements for a contract, but what on earth is *consideration*? No, it doesn't mean that the parties to a contract have to care about each other. However, their promises must involve the exchange of *something of value* to each party.

Consideration is what each party agrees to give up when entering a contract— it is what induces the parties to make a binding agreement. Countless contracts involve the exchange of goods or services for money. In our hypothetical purchase, you agreed to hand over $1,200 in consideration for receiving a Kudzo LCD 48 delivered and installed in your home. As seen from the other side of the transaction, TVs R Me agreed to deliver a Kudzo LCD 48 in consideration for your payment of $1,200.

Last, but certainly not least, are the *terms* of the offer—the rules of the game that the offerer puts forward at the start of the contracting process. In our example, as I noted above, TVs R Me proposed two principal terms: payment by cashier's check and "All Sales Are Final." Real contracts often involve many more terms—those many items you find in the *small print*.

In theory, everything is up for negotiation in a contract. A true meeting of the minds can't take place until both parties are satisfied with all aspects of the deal they've made. In practice, though, many of the purchases we make involve "take it or leave it" offers. We don't have much opportunity to negotiate. Instead, if we don't like the offer from one shop, we look elsewhere until we find an offer more to our liking.

Where's the Piece of Paper?

One unusual aspect of our hypothetical transaction is that it's *paperless*. We're so conditioned by the concept that contracts must be on paper that it's worth asking, how can we have a contract without a paper document? I noted earlier that the promise, not the paper, is the contract. An obvious question then is, what is the document that most of us think of as a contract? A popular legal name for the paperwork is *memorandum of contract*. Simply put, the memorandum—the *written contract*—memorializes (captures) all the particulars of the mutual promises, including the following:

→ A recitation of the parties' intent to create a contract
→ A description of the offer
→ A description of the acceptance
→ Details about the consideration
→ A list of all the terms and conditions that were agreed to by the parties

We've all laughed at the old joke that an oral contract isn't worth the paper it's printed on. This may be funny, but it's not true. A valid oral contract is binding and will be upheld by a court—if the key aspects of the contract (offer, acceptance, consideration) can be proved in court by the party seeking to enforce the promise. Therein lies the fundamental challenge of oral contracts: proving they exist and providing evidence of the terms. A memorandum of contract signed by both parties eliminates much of the potential confusion.

In most states, a promise to buy an item of significant value—an HDTV, for example—requires some sort of memorandum of contract. This is also true of promises to buy and sell real estate or promises that require a long time (say more than a year) to accomplish.

"Some sort of memorandum" are the words to pay attention to. In many situations, an acceptable memorandum of contract need not be a printed document labeled CONTRACT in bold black letters. A handwritten note summarizing the agreement can be a valid memorandum of contract. So can an exchange of e-mails. Capturing the details of an agreement in web-based forms (the way TVs R Me did) will also suffice.

Excuse Me! I've Changed My Mind

Soon after ordering your Kudzo LCD 48 you have dinner with you brother-in-law, an expert on all things electronic, who tells you that the Kudzo LCD 48 received abysmal ratings when tested by two different consumer organizations. He convinces you that you have just ordered the absolutely worst large-screen HDTV ever built.

Naturally, you phone TVs R Me, explain that you've changed your mind, and try to cancel your order. Equally naturally, the customer service representative you talk to reminds you that "All Sales Are Final." It won't do any good to point out that the Kudzo LCD 48 is not worth the price you agreed to pay for it. The HDTV that TVs R Me agreed to deliver to you is more than sufficient consideration to support the contract. The law of contract has no interest in stopping you from making a bad deal. In most cases, a court doesn't care if the price you agreed to pay is fair or reasonable. Judges presume that you accepted the offer only after you decided that you'd reached a worthwhile bargain.

In desperation, you threaten to tear up the so-called contract. "I won't have a cashier's check ready when TVs R Me tries to deliver the Kudzo LCD 48," you say. In turn, TVs R Me threatens to sue you for breach of contract.

Keep in mind that one of the purposes of a contract is to bring as much certainty as possible to a business transaction. In most dealings, neither the buyer nor seller wants the other party to change the agreement.

At this point you begin to look for what are called *defenses to contract*. Simply put, should the case end up in court, you want to convince the judge that you don't have a binding contract with TVs R Me.

Your first defense attacks a fundamental requirement of every contract. Formation must begin with an offer. Perhaps you can argue that the web page describing the Kudzo LCD 48 wasn't an actual offer. The page might merely be an *advertisement*—an expression of TVs R Me's intent to sell HDTVs and an invitation to negotiate the specific details of a sale. Courts and consumers both know that an advertisement doesn't qualify as an offer that can be accepted to create a contract.

Nice try, but it won't work. A court might decide that many commercial websites are advertisements, but the TVs R Me website was designed in such a way that a *reasonable person* would conclude that the Kudzo LCD 48 web page made a complete offer to you. On the one hand, it clearly communicated that TVs R Me was ready and willing to enter into an agreement to sell you an HDTV. On the other hand, the page plainly spelled out the subject matter, quantity, and price.

A Short Detour to Reasonableness

Lawyers and judges often talk about the *reasonable person*. Do you know any reasonable people? Probably not—because the reasonable person is a legal fiction. There are no such creatures; although he or she has helped to resolve countless legal disputes.

A reasonable person does the right thing under the circumstances, makes the right decision given the available information, and reaches the right conclusion given what he or she can know from the facts on hand.

Although we've never met a reasonable person—and can't even describe one in detail—judges and juries routinely use them as standards of behavior. I'll say much more about the reasonable-person standard in Chapters 3 and 4.

The bottom line: If a reasonable person browsing TVs R Me's website would conclude that the Kudzo LCD 48 page presented a valid offer, the judge will hold you to the same standard and not let you claim that you thought the page was nothing but a fancy advertisement.

But Our Minds Never Met

Undaunted in your battle with TVs R Me, you try another tack. Perhaps you can argue that the two parties never had a true meeting of the minds. After all, the transaction in question took place on the Internet, without any face-to-face interaction. How can there have been a meeting of the minds when the parties never met?

As a game show host might say after honking his horn, "Wrong! Wrong! Wrong!" The whole idea of Internet commerce is that buyer and seller don't have to meet face to face. The website you accessed served in lieu of a live salesperson. And, as I noted above, the resulting transaction clearly encompasses TVs R Me's offer, your acceptance, and sufficient consideration (your $1,200 for a Kudzo LCD 48).

Fraud: The Big Gun

A court can void a contract if one party commits fraud against the other party. Fraud occurs when one party tells a material untruth that the second party relies on. *Material* means that the second party might not accept the offer if he knew the truth. The court will ask whether it was reasonable of the second party to rely on the misrepresentation.

You immediately revisit the Kudzo LCD 48 web page and discover the following statement: "The Kudzo LCD 48 is an excellent HDTV that you'll be proud to own."

Ah-ha! You clearly relied on these words. You'd never have clicked the "Click to Complete Purchase" button had TVs R Me told you the truth about the Kudzo LCD 48—that it scored miserably in two consumer magazine tests.

Maybe not—but TVs R Me didn't commit fraud. For starters, the statement that the Kudzo LCD 48 "is an excellent HDTV that you'll be proud to own" is the seller's opinion—an example of *sales puffery* that a reasonable person would know better than to take at face value. The company didn't tell an outright lie about the Kudzo LCD 48 (nor did it have an obligation to tell you about the negative consumer magazine tests—which are, after all, just other opinions).

Bring in the Technicalities

Few people like legal technicalities until *they* need them to help resolve a legal dispute. Let's see if we can think of a contract technicality or two to invalidate your alleged contract with TVs R Me.

Here's an interesting possibility. In most states a contract to buy or sell an item of significant value requires a signed contract. But you never actually put your signature on anything.

TVs R Me will argue, of course, that your second click (on the "Click to Complete Purchase" button) served as your signature. A judge will probably agree.

The signatures on a paper contract are often handwritten, but a stamped signature, or even a simple X mark, is sufficient. What matters is that a *signature* (whatever its form) is authorized by the person making it and that he or she intends the signature to *authenticate* the written contract (signal the signer's acceptance of the offer).

WHEN THE PARTIES MAKE MISTAKES

Because forming a contract presumes a meeting of two minds, what happens if one or both parties make significant mistakes during the negotiations? In limited circumstances, a court will find that a contract was never created.

For example, a contract will be voided when both parties make a *mutual mistake* about the same *material* fact. The classic case used to illustrate this principle is a Michigan case that dates to 1887. It involves a supposedly barren cow named Rose. Walker sold Rose to Sherwood for little more than the cost of beef, but before Walker delivered Rose, he discovered that Rose was pregnant—and worth much more money. He refused to go through with the transaction. The court agreed that because both parties thought the cow barren, there was sufficient mutual mistake to conclude that true offer and acceptance never occurred.

Everyone who watches *Antiques Roadshow* dreams of buying a scruffy old painting at a garage sale for five dollars, only to discover that it's the work of a famous painter—and worth millions. Most courts will *not* void this contract after the fact, probably because both parties got what they bargained for at the time—a scruffy painting and a five-dollar bill. Also, courts will not void contracts where one party has mistakenly exercised poor business judgment and bought something he or she didn't need, or agreed to pay too high a price.

In fact, TVs R Me seemed to go the extra mile to explain the impact of clicking the second button. A reasonable Internet consumer—even an inexperienced one—would understand the significance and purpose of the "Click to Complete Purchase" button.

Because you despair that you'll ever find a valid defense to contract, you decide it's time to reach for straws. One of the important requirements for the formation of a valid contract is the subject of the promise and the consideration must be illegal. If the Kudzo LCD 48 is as awful as your brother-in-law claims, perhaps the U.S. Consumer Product Safety Commission banned its sale in the United States. If so, a local court could hardly enforce your promise to buy one. However, a bit of late-blooming research proves that while the Kudzo LCD 48 is a terrible HDTV, it's not dangerous to use.

You've finally reached the bottom of the barrel. Your final possible technicality is a claim that you didn't agree to the contract's terms and conditions. Once again, sorry! The two chief terms were detailed on the Kudzo LCD 48 web page. If this were a real sale, rather than a hypothetical, the web page would probably provide a long list of terms and conditions—and a check box that affirms you've read them. (Every computer user is familiar with the "click-wrap" screens that pop up when loading new software. They enable the user to review the terms of use and then accept or reject them.)

CLICK-WRAP AGREEMENTS

Although click-wrap agreements have become a standard feature of software installation, there hasn't been much litigation about them. However, courts seem willing to enforce them—*if* the customer truly receives an opportunity to read the contract's terms and conditions before clicking the "I Agree" icon. This kind of "take it or leave it" agreement is known as a *contract of adhesion* (see "Other Things Worth Knowing about Contracts," *below*).

A Short Detour to Conditionville

Although *condition* is sometimes used as a synonym for *term*, a condition is really a different kind of contract item. A condition is something that has to happen—or must not happen—before the parties must perform as they've promised to under the contract. One of the most familiar examples of a condition can be found in most agreements to purchase a house. The buyer is likely to condition the purchase agreement on his ability to secure a mortgage to finance the new house. If, after making a good-faith effort to apply for a mortgage, he can't arrange financing, then the buyer no longer has an obligation to complete the purchase transaction.

Onward to a Bigger Screen

In the end, you resolved your dispute with TVs R Me by adopting a *win-win* strategy. The store happily let you out of your contract to purchase a Kudzo LCD 48 when you offered to buy a highly rated WowScreen 64 for $1,800. A binding contract can always be voluntarily renegotiated by the parties involved. In this case, you've both agreed to additional consideration. TVs R Me will deliver a bigger, more expensive HDTV, and you will hand over a heftier cashier's check.

But then, a few days before your WowScreen 64 is delivered, you get a curious letter from TVs R Me: "Because the salaries of service technicians increased in recent months, we've had to increase the delivered price of the WowScreen 64 to $2,000. This modest price increase will enable us to provide a two-year warranty on your new HDTV."

Whoa! The moment you read the letter, you know that something's wrong—it doesn't seem right for TVs R Me to set a new price after the deal has been finalized, but you can't put your finger on what's bothering you.

Well, the problem in a nutshell is that TVs R Me seeks to charge you more money for doing what they agreed to do under the original contract: deliver a WowScreen 64 with two-year warranty. In lawyerly language they are not offering additional consideration, because TVs R Me's "new" promise obligates them to do exactly what they are already required to do.

You wisely point out to your favorite customer service representative that TVs R Me has offered no new consideration to justify a price increase and that before entering the current contract, they should have thought about the possibility of labor cost increases and adjusted their offer price accordingly. You enjoy the opportunity to take a little dig: "It's not my job to shelter your company from business risk." After some hemming and hawing, the rep agrees that the original agreement remains in effect.

Your Family Loves Your New HDTV

The WowScreen 64 is the perfect addition to your home, but Junior, your fifteen-year-old son feels more than a little left out because his video-game console is an antique and not designed to connect to an HDTV. He knows that one of the newer models would create really fabulous images on the huge screen.

And so, one afternoon, he switches on your computer, visits the TVs R Me website, and finds to his delight that the company stocks an impressive assortment of top-of-the-line HDTV game consoles. One of them—the Dazzle 600—catches his eye and his fancy. What's more, it's on sale: The complete package costs only $549, including sales tax and shipping.

Without thinking about your reaction, Junior clicks the "Click to Buy Me" button. Much to his surprise, when the final screen appears, the form is already filled out with your name, address, and e-mail address. He spots something on the screen about a cashier's check, but doesn't worry about it. He's confident that you too will be delighted with a new Dazzle 600.

There's nothing more to do except finalize the purchase, which he does by clicking the "Click to Complete Purchase" button. The pop-up screen offers its congratulations: "You've Purchased a Dazzle 600."

The first time you learn about this supposed transaction is when you read an e-mail from TVs R Me reminding you to prepare a cashier's check in anticipation of the Dazzle 600's delivery to your home.

You're furious at Junior, but you're madder yet at TVs R Me. How dare they accept an order from a fifteen-year-old?

That's a question worth asking. Because there must be a meeting of the minds to form a contract that courts will enforce, both parties must be capable of understanding the consequences of what they're doing. As a result, contract law includes the concept of *capacity to contract*. Broadly speaking, minors are not presumed to have the capacity to understand the offer, its terms, and any conditions. As a result, courts in most states allow minors to void contracts they've entered into. One notable (and obvious) exception is a "student loan."

As Junior's parent, you're well aware that he barely knows what day of the week it is. You breathe a sigh of relief, place a call to the customer service rep you've come to know on a first-name basis, and request that the latest purchase contract be voided.

You're amazed when he says, "No. We assume that *you* placed the order. It arrived with your information—the same information we received from you when you purchased an HDTV."

"But, but, but, . . ." you begin to argue, but you stop when you realize that because Junior used your computer to buy the Dazzle 600, TVs R Me had no way of knowing they were doing business with a minor.

There's nothing to do but reach for your checkbook—and configure your web browser so that it no longer fills out forms automatically (or captures credit card numbers and other financial data).

Look on the bright side, you may come to enjoy playing video games.

Other Things Worth Knowing about Contracts

Contracts Statutes of Limitations

Every state sets time limits for filing lawsuits. These are called *statutes of limitations*; they ensure that a defendant to a legal action doesn't have to respond to a *stale* claim long after evidence and witnesses have vanished. The period of time in which a lawsuit can be launched varies from state to state and typically depends on the kind of claim being made. States commonly require *personal injury lawsuits* involving negligence (*see* Chapter 4) to be brought within one to three years after the injury is discovered. But the period for filing a lawsuit for breach of contract is usually much longer: possibly four, six, even ten years from the date of the breach. (The terms of some sales contracts establish shorter statutes of limitation.)

The practical effect is that anyone who enters a contract should keep—for at least the contract statute of limitations period in his or her state—records documenting the fulfillment of the terms. Simply put, keep all the paperwork and receipts related to house and car purchases and leases; other major transactions; house, appliance, and car repairs and warranties; and other big-ticket agreements. You might need them *years* after you thought the deal was over.

Detrimental Reliance Instead of Consideration

On rare occasions, a court will enforce a promise that doesn't involve the usual contract triad of offer-acceptance-consideration. These are situations where someone has *relied* on a promise to his or her detriment. The doctrine of *detrimental reliance* often goes by the odd name of *promissory estoppel.* This means that the person who made the promise is estopped (barred) from denying the validity of the promise.

Imagine that your favorite rich aunt made a promise out of the blue: "I'm going to pay your son's college tuition this year." In reliance on her promise, you use the tuition money you've saved to make repairs to your house that you'd intended to defer. But, when the time comes to pay, she says, "Sorry . . . I've changed my mind."

Because you feel boxed in by impossible circumstances, you decide to file a lawsuit. You argue in court that you *reasonably relied* on your aunt's promise. She's known to be generous with her money, has plenty of it, and likes your son. Moreover, because of your reasonable reliance on her promise, you detrimentally changed your position (you spent the money you saved for tuition). With both of these factors present, the court *might* decide that injustice can be avoided only by enforcing the promise. Your aunt will be ordered to pay the money she promised to pay.

Contracts of Adhesion

A contract of adhesion is a form contract prepared by one party and offered to the other party on a "take it or leave it" basis. Common contracts of adhesion most of us sign are application forms required by credit card companies, the preprinted agreements at car rental kiosks, the standard form leases used by most landlords, and the array of forms a real estate agent puts in front of you when you commit to buy a house.

In fact, it would be impossible for many businesses to operate if they had to rewrite their contracts with every transaction. Many of the terms in a residential lease, for example, are controlled by state law. Consequently, a standard form lease ensures that the landlord follows local regulations—even though the contract terms typically favor the landlord.

The chief problem with a contract of adhesion is that the parties have significantly unequal bargaining power. This may tempt the stronger party to take advantage of the weaker party and fill the form contract with a supposedly standard non-negotiable *boilerplate*—almost always in small print— written in complex legal language. There's not much any of us—even practicing attorneys—can do when faced with complicated forms, unless we are willing to postpone a transaction late in the game. It's not really practical *not* to rent that car . . . and there may be other potential buyers competing for the same house. And so, we sign— with little certainty about the commitments we've made.

Fortunately, most courts are willing to apply the doctrine of *unconscionability* (*see* below) to contracts of adhesion, and other courts examine contracts of adhesion with special scrutiny that looks for contract terms *outside the reasonable expectations* of the party who didn't write the contract. In other words, would a reasonable person find an onerous term out of bounds—given the term's impact, the way it was hidden in the small print, and the pressures to sign the contract quickly? If so, the term will not be enforced. Of course, there are no guarantees that a court will agree with your contention that a specific term is outside reasonable expectations.

Specific Performance Instead of Money Damages

The usual remedy for breach of contract is money damages. If a party fails to keep his promise, he knows that a court will award compensatory damages— typically the *cost of the breach* to the plaintiff. Given the commercial nature of most contracts—and the universality of money—this seems appropriate.

But some breaches don't have price tags. English courts ran into this situation hundreds of years ago when faced with breached agreements to sell land. A piece of land is unique. If I agree to buy Blackacre from you, but you abruptly decide not to sell, how does a court measure my loss? In any case, money damages don't truly compensate me because there is no other Blackacre I can buy instead.

Courts of *equity* (*see* Chapter 1) came up with a *remedy in equity* called *specific performance*. Rather than order compensatory money damages, the judge orders that the specific terms of the contract be performed by both parties. In our example, I get Blackacre; you get the agreed-upon price. Specific performance is available today, but is fairly uncommon, because money damages *do* resolve the overwhelming majority of contract disputes.

Unconscionable Contracts

There are some contracts that shouldn't be enforced as written. The terms are so unfair that no court in good conscience will impose them on the party that has breached the contract. In cases like this, the judge can apply the *doctrine of unconscionability* and refuse to enforce especially harsh or unfair agreements— that were probably one-sided contracts of adhesion from the get-go.

Unconscionability is a doctrine that emerged from actions in *equity*. A court can refuse to enforce an otherwise valid contract, to echo words of explanation that have been repeated in many decisions at trial involving contracts:

→ "If there's an absence of meaningful choice on the part of one party due to one-sided contract provisions;

→ If contract terms are so oppressive that no reasonable person would make them and no fair and honest person would accept them."

Because unconscionability comes from equity rather than from common law, a judge—not a jury—decides if and when a contract is unconscionable. It's not enough that the complaining party failed to read a contract before signing it, or misunderstood the terms of the agreement, or later decides that it's not a "good deal." A contract is unconscionable only if it includes terms that are grossly unfair. For example: terms that surreptitiously eliminate warranty protection, or impose significant hidden transaction fees, or place a lien on the customer's house for a relatively small purchase on credit. A claim of unconscionability is difficult to sustain in routine contract disputes.

Choice of Law and Forum Selection Clauses

If you've read the small print of a contract you signed recently, you might have wondered about the purpose of a straightforward clause that said something like, "This agreement shall be interpreted under the laws of the New York State. Any litigation under this agreement shall be resolved in the trial courts of Suffolk County, New York State."

The first sentence in this clause is the so-called *choice of law clause*. You have agreed that all of the terms in the contract will be interpreted—and enforced—according to the law of contracts in New York State.

Surprising to many non-lawyers, a court, for example, in Anchorage, Alaska, will determine the rights and duties under a contract using another state's law if that's an aspect of the agreement the parties to a contract reached. So it's quite possible to sign a form contract in Alabama that specifies that the contract will be interpreted using the law of North Dakota. This might have happened in our contract hypothetical if TVs R Me is a corporation headquartered, let's say, in Bismarck, North Dakota. Because they operate all over the country, TVs R Me prefers "local" North Dakota law—statutes and precedents it understands—to control all the contracts it offers to customers.

An even more likely reason for a choice of law clause is that something about the law in the chosen state is more favorable to the party who wrote the contract. Many insurance contracts apply New York law for this reason.

Courts are more likely to enforce a choice of law clause in contracts between two commercial companies than in a standard form contract given on a "take it or leave it" basis to a consumer. This is because a consumer who blindly agrees to the clause may unknowingly waive rights established by his home state's consumer protection statutes.

The second sentence in the short contract clause, above, is known as a *forum selection clause*. When a plaintiff (the person alleging a breach of contract) files a lawsuit in a specific county in a specific state, he or she has chosen a specific *forum* to be the legal battlefield. Traditionally, the plaintiffs choose the forum for a lawsuit—and most often select their home county. This means that a national company like TVs R Me could find itself defending lawsuits all over the United States.

Enter the forum selection clause. It takes the forum choice away from would-be plaintiffs and specifies the only allowable forum. TVs R Me will probably try to make its forum Bismarck, North Dakota. This is good for TVs R Me, but not so good for you—particularly if you live on the other side of the country.

Because courts usually enforce a forum selection clause, they can raise the cost and complexity of filing a lawsuit—and discourage a potential plaintiff who contemplates legal action.

Mandatory Arbitration and Alternative Dispute Resolution

Many contracts between consumers and businesses (stock brokers, banks, car dealers, telephone companies, credit card companies, stores, and others) include clauses that require *binding arbitration* in the event of a contract dispute.

Arbitration is one of three common forms of alternative dispute resolution (ADR) that can be used instead of filing a lawsuit for breach of contract:

1. *Negotiation*—The parties (and typically their attorneys) try to work out a compromise that satisfies everyone. This often works if the parties can remain civil to each other. Unfortunately, contract conflicts tend to become overheated—*quickly*.

2. *Mediation*—An impartial third party, the *mediator*, attempts to facilitate a win-win compromise between both parties and may even propose a formula designed to resolve the dispute. Some contracts call for mediation, and in certain kinds of disputes, a court may order a try at mediation. The actual mediation process, though, remains voluntary—and can fail to produce results (although studies have shown that the majority of disputes submitted to mediation are resolved). The benefits of successful mediation are much reduced costs and stress for everyone involved.

3. *Arbitration*—A third party, the *arbitrator*, acts as a "private judge and jury" and determines an outcome for the dispute, which can range from voiding the disputed contract, to awarding damages to one of the parties, to ordering *specific performance* by one

party. When the parties to a contract agree to arbitration, the outcome is usually binding—the parties agree to be bound by the arbitrator's decision. In most states, an unhappy party can't appeal the unfavorable decision in court unless the results are truly unconscionable or there's solid evidence that the arbitrator was biased toward the winning party.

An arbitration clause in a contract typically establishes the ground rules for a required arbitration (often that it will follow the rules of the American Arbitration Association), specifies how the arbitrator will be chosen, and usually states that the arbitrator's fees will be split between both parties. The clause may also include some potentially expensive fine print, such as "the prevailing party shall be reimbursed for filing fees and related administrative costs."

The advocates of binding arbitration argue that the process is faster, more informal, more flexible, and less costly than a full-blown contract lawsuit. And, unlike a public trial, the arbitration process is private and confidential. In theory, neither party needs to be represented by an attorney during an arbitration hearing, although companies are almost always represented by lawyers who specialize in arbitration.

While arbitration is fast, flexible, and relatively informal, going through the process can be unexpectedly expensive for consumers—typically many thousands of dollars. The bottom-line: The cost of binding arbitration can be higher than the actual damages of a contract breach—making it impractical to pursue a claim that you might have taken easily and quickly to small claims court.

The opponents to arbitration clauses in consumer contracts also argue that

- → arbitration tends to favor defendants (which is why companies insert arbitration clauses into contracts);
- → many arbitrators come from the "company side" of disputes and may be biased against consumers;
- → the outcome of arbitration is often unpredictable because, unlike a judge, an arbitrator isn't required to follow state law and legal precedents when reaching a decision;
- → some arbitration clauses are one-sided: The consumer agrees to binding arbitration to resolve disputes while the company reserves the right to sue the consumer.

On balance, it's probably wise to reject binding arbitration clauses in the contracts you sign, but in the real world most consumers don't have the clout to rewrite standard contracts. The only answer—admittedly, not a good one—is to avoid dealing with companies that impose binding arbitration.

CHAPTER 3

⇥ ⇤

INTENTIONAL LEGAL WRONGS

L EGAL WRONGS ARE KNOWN AS TORTS—WHICH SOUNDS LIKE A KIND OF cake, but actually comes from an Old French word meaning "wrong" that grew out of the Latin word *tortum*, "to twist." (The official written language of early English law was French, and many French words became part of the language of English common law—the ancestor of America's legal system.) A person who commits a tort is called a *tortfeasor*.

Over the years, the law has recognized a variety of different legal wrongs. If you are the victim of a tort, you can bring an action (file a lawsuit) in a civil court. If you win, the judge will order the person responsible to pay monetary compensation for the damages you've suffered. These can include the cost of damaged property, medical bills, lost wages, other related costs, monetary compensation for your physical pain and suffering, and sometimes compensation for your emotional distress.

You'll often find information about tort law—and lists of lawyers who specialize in it—under the heading "personal injury law." This is because the majority of tort lawsuits—and the biggest tort judgments—involve claims of physical injury to someone's person. Think of *personal injury* in broader terms. You're personally injured when a baseball shatters your living room picture window and causes several hundred dollars of damage.

In this chapter, we'll look at *intentional torts*—legal wrongs that result from intentional actions. In Chapter 4, we'll move on to *negligent torts*—legal wrongs that result from a lack of care.

To illustrate the difference: Someone who purposely lobs a baseball through your front window commits the intentional tort of *trespass*. However, if the same person plays baseball next to your house and accidentally shatters the same window with a carelessly misdirected line drive, he'll probably be found to be negligent. In either case, the court will require him to pay the cost of repairing your window. And therein lies a key principle of tort law: A tortfeasor is *liable* for the harm he has done; he has the obligation to *make his victim whole again* by paying appropriate compensation for the damage he caused.

The War of the Roses

Botanically speaking, a rose is a member of the *Rosales* order, the *Rosaceae* family, the *Rosoideae* subfamily, and the *Rosa* genus.

Iona Wynner was only vaguely aware of these facts and knew nothing else about the science of horticulture; but her undeniably green thumb—and the affection she lavished on her beloved rosebushes—enabled her to grow what many people considered the most beautiful roses in town. This state of affairs greatly annoyed April Schauer, Iona's next-door neighbor. April, a Master Gardener and founder of the local Rose Club, was determined to display the rose at this year's Garden Show that would win the Gold Medal. Alas, April's rosebushes gave no sign they would yield winners.

April watched Iona's bushes grow, until finally on Easter Sunday, she could stand it no more. She poked the nozzle of her high-pressure power washer through the hedge that separated her land from her neighbor's and took aim at the buds on Iona's biggest rosebush. Alas, April was a terrible shot. Her blast of water soared above the rosebush just as Fuller Payne—Iona's next-door neighbor on the other side—was leaving for church. The high-pressure water jet whooshed over Fuller's picket fence, slammed into Fuller's antique satin top hat (the hat he wears every year in the Easter pageant), and sent it flying into the water feature next to Fuller's bird feeder. The priceless Payne family heirloom was ruined.

As April will discover when she learns about the lawsuit filed by Fuller, she has been charged with the intentional tort of *battery*.

PLAINTIFF AND DEFENDANT

When Fuller sues April, he will be the *plaintiff,* the party that launches a lawsuit in court. The label comes from an Old French word that means "aggrieved." The process begins when the plaintiff files a *complaint* (sometimes called a *petition*)—a legal document that explains the plaintiff's claim against the *defendant* (the party alleged to have caused harm). April will be named as the defendant in the complaint.

Battery is an old word that traces its roots to the Latin word *batuere*, which means "to strike." To succeed in a lawsuit for battery, the plaintiff must prove that the defendant's intentional act resulted in *harmful or offensive contact* with the plaintiff's person.

Harmful contact includes all kinds of contacts, from a poke in the snoot, to a blow from a stick, to being struck by a jet of water—but what makes contact *offensive*? To find out, we need to *query* the hypothetical *reasonable person* we met in Chapter 2. Contact that would offend a reasonable person's sense of personal dignity is deemed offensive. Our reasonable person has ordinary sensitivity and understands what is considered acceptable (nonoffensive) touching at the time and place the contact is made.

Touching a stranger's shoulder in an airport line to get his attention is not battery, nor is being jostled by the person next to you while walking into a crowded movie theater. These kinds of everyday touchings don't offend a reasonable person's sense of personal dignity. But intentionally patting a stranger's backside while in line or inside a theater would be battery, because a reasonable stranger would be offended if touched in this way.

Similarly, tripping a stranger in an airport line, or shoving a fellow theatergoer out of the way, would likely be offensive to a reasonable person.

What if April says, "*Whoa!* The tort of battery seems to require contact with a live *person*. I never actually touched Fuller; I merely knocked a hat off his head."

Sorry April! The tort of battery is *complete* when the defendant causes harmful or offensive contact with a person or to something closely associated with the person (a hat, a purse, a parcel held tightly against the person's body). Again, a reasonable person finds contact with these items an affront to his or her dignity.

HARMFUL AND UNPLEASANT CONTACT COMES IN MANY FLAVORS

Contact doesn't necessarily mean "touching." A person who spikes someone's drink with drugs or tampers with Halloween trick-or-treat candy commits battery. So does a surgeon who operates on the wrong body part.

April tries another defense. She insists, "I didn't intend to hit Fuller's hat with my water jet. I didn't even see him leave his house!"

For starters, a person who acts *intentionally* doesn't need to have the specific harmful consequences of his or her act in mind. Although she didn't set out to hit Fuller's hat, she *did* want to hit Iona's rosebush with the water jet. That was April's purpose when she intentionally pulled the nozzle's trigger.

In legal language, she intended to damage a *chattel*—an item of personal property. Had she succeeded, she would have committed the intentional tort of *trespass to chattel* (*see* below). And so, the law will *transfer* her intent from what April meant to hit to what she actually hit. This is called the *doctrine of transferred intent.*

If April had merely been careless with her power washer—if she'd been trying to clean her fence and the nozzle had jumped out of her hand and blasted the hat—Fuller could still sue April, but now the legal wrong would be *negligence* (*see* Chapter 4). As you can see, tort law is extremely flexible: Its general principles are able to adapt to the most unlikely circumstances. It's probable that no one else in the history of American law ever blasted someone's heirloom top hat with a high-pressure washer—neither judges nor legislators could have predicted April's legal wrong—and yet, the law of intentional torts can resolve the dispute and award monetary damages to the person who was harmed.

Awarding Damages for Harm Done

A central focus of tort law is to make the party who has suffered harm *whole again* by making a wrongdoer pay compensatory damages. Consequently, the court will order April to pay Fuller the value of his ruined top hat. But what if the antique hat had not been harmed? What if Fuller had been able to wipe it dry, pop it back on his head, and go to the Easter pageant?

Suffering actual harm is not necessary to move ahead with an intentional tort claim. Seemingly trivial offensive contact can be battery. Think of the person I mentioned earlier, who reasonably found an uninvited pat on the backside offensive. That person was the victim of a legally significant battery even though he or she was not physically injured.

Courts can award three kinds of monetary damages to plaintiffs injured by the defendant's legal wrong:

1. *Compensatory damages*—This award is designed to make whole the economic harm that the plaintiff suffered. These may include monetary compensation for losses that don't have an actual price tag, including pain and suffering and mental distress.

2. *Nominal damages*—This is a symbolic award (perhaps as small as one dollar) that vindicates the plaintiff's claim that tort was committed, although no actual harm occurred. Seeking nominal damages—making a claim in tort as a matter of principle—was common years ago when legal fees and court costs were lower.

3. *Punitive damages*—This kind of award is intended to punish and deter particularly egregious conduct (such as that unwelcome pat on the backside).

A NOTE ABOUT PUNITIVE DAMAGES

The primary goal of a tort damage award is to compensate a victim for the injury he or she has suffered. A secondary goal is to deter other potential tortfeasors from engaging in similar harmful behavior. One way courts do this is by awarding a few victorious plaintiffs *punitive damages* (sometimes called exemplary damages) that significantly exceed the dollar value of the actual harm done.

Punitive damages punish the defendant for his misconduct and set an example for others: Pay attention; doing this kind of legal wrong will cost you a lot more money than fixing the harm you cause.

Some states leave the amount of punitive damages up to juries (who can punish especially outrageous torts with multimillion-dollar punitive damage awards). Other states set specific limits, say three times the actual damages.

MONEY ISN'T ALWAYS EVERYTHING

Practically speaking, it usually makes little sense to file a tort claim these days if compensatory damages will be small and the tortfeasor's conduct is not sufficiently reprehensible to warrant an award of punitive damages. However, there are a few circumstances when seeking nominal damages still makes sense. Consider the case of a homeowner who finds his next-door neighbor's odoriferous pig pen a *nuisance*—an activity that unreasonably interferes with the use and enjoyment of the homeowner's property (see Chapter 10). The goal of the lawsuit is to convince the judge to order the neighbor to dismantle the pig pen. The homeowner may not have suffered any actual money damages.

Did April Also Assault Fuller?

Here's an interesting question: When April wielded her high-pressure water nozzle, didn't she also commit the intentional tort of *assault*? A defendant commits assault by causing the plaintiff to reasonably apprehend an imminent unpleasant or harmful *touching* (a battery). And, a reasonable person would expect being touched by a 2,000-pound-per-square-inch blast of water to be harmful.

True! But Fuller *never* apprehended the likelihood of an imminent battery. His first clue that he'd been the victim of a legal wrong was when his top hat went flying. Consequently, April *didn't* commit assault. The unexpected pat on the backside I mentioned above is another example of battery without a preliminary assault.

Similarly, assault can be committed without a subsequent battery. That's why assault and battery stand as independent legal wrongs; although, most of us say "assault and battery" as a single phrase. A tortious assault is *complete* even if the unpleasant or harmful touching never actually occurs. It is necessary, though, that it's actually possible for a battery to occur imminently. Shaking a menacing fist at someone across a river is not assault. Neither is a threat to shoot someone next week. However, under the right circumstances either of these actions could support a claim for *intentional infliction of mental distress* (*see* below).

Also, there are some visible *threats* that don't count as assaults. Do you remember the stage actor I introduced in Chapter 1? He'll lose if he claims that Ima Starr committed the tort of assault when she pointed a toy gun at him on stage. The court will conclude that he can't *reasonably apprehend* an imminent unpleasant or harmful *touching* from a prop aimed by a fellow actor.

INTENTIONAL TORTS VS. CRIMES

Some intentional torts, as I've noted, are also crimes—a source of considerable confusion to many first-year law students. Although both a tort and a crime are *legal wrongs,* it's best to think of them as completely different creatures. This is because the plaintiff in a lawsuit—and the prosecutor in a criminal trial—have to prove different things (and have different *burdens of proof*) to win their respective trials. If you are the victim of a tort, a court will order the tortfeasor to *make you whole again* by paying you compensatory damages. Compensation is the central focus of tort law. But, if you are the victim of a crime, the court will order the perpetrator to pay a fine or spend a term in prison or under supervised probation. These sanctions are designed to punish criminals and deter similar antisocial behavior by others. In the tort case, a legal wrong you suffered is being righted. In the criminal case, justice is done to benefit society as a whole.

A person who threatens you with a loaded pistol commits the intentional tort of assault and *also* the crime of assault with a deadly weapon (or aggravated assault). He will be punished by the state, and you can file a lawsuit that demands monetary compensation for any damages you suffered. Many victims of crimes seek recompense in civil lawsuits after the state has convicted and sentenced the persons who committed the crimes.

Defenses to the Intentional Tort of Battery

A defendant facing a battery lawsuit can raise different defenses to the claim that he or she committed a legal wrong. For example, imagine that a man performs CPR on a woman who then wakes up and begins to scream. If she claims that he committed battery, he will reply that touching her was a necessity under the circumstances. Also a prize fighter can't complain that his opponent's knockout punch was a battery. He consented to be hit by the other man in the ring. Incidentally, the fighter need not say, "I give you permission to hit me." Legally speaking, his consent can be actual or *apparent*. Apparent consent exists when a reasonable person would understand the plaintiff's words, deeds, or even silence as an indication of consent. By stepping into the ring, the fighter gave his consent for potentially harmful contact to his jaw.

All intentional torts have potential defenses that plaintiffs can raise.

Can Iona Also Sue April?

When April shot her blast of water across Iona's yard, April committed the intentional tort of *trespass to land*. This happens when the defendant enters the plaintiff's land without permission, or causes something else to enter the land. Driving on the plaintiff's land, shooting a bullet across it, or directing a high-pressure water spray across the land all qualify as trespass to land.

However, when it comes time to claim damages for this particular trespass, Iona will be at a loss. The jet of water hit nothing on Iona's side of the fence and caused no injury whatsoever. Moreover, the alleged trespass to land lasted a few seconds, at most. All in all, this seems too small a tort for a court to trouble about.

April Attacks Again

When April Schauer decides to do something, she'll stick to her guns until the job is done. And so, when April realized that she'd missed Iona's prize rosebushes with the high-pressure water jet, she conceived Plan B: A few ounces of weed killer judiciously applied to the ground around the bottoms of the rosebushes would completely eliminate them from competition.

Bottle of weed killer spray in hand, April made her way into Iona's garden. As she tiptoed through the tulips, she heard a noise come from Iona's garden shed. The door was closed, but just to make sure she wouldn't be disturbed, April swung the hasp shut and secured it with a thick stick.

Almost immediately, April heard Fuller Payne begin to holler. "Hey! It's me! You locked me in the shed—let me out!"

Rats! April immediately realized her mistake, but she didn't want a witness while she disposed of the rosebushes. She let Fuller out and waved a long pair of garden shears at him. "Shut up and don't move. Stay put next to the shed, or I'll prune you like a stunted arborvitae."

With Fuller out of the way, April doused the bottom of each rosebush with enough weed killer to terminate an oak tree. They immediately begin to wilt.

We've just witnessed April commit three (possibly four) intentional torts:

1. False imprisonment
2. Assault

3. Trespass to chattel

4. Conversion

Let's look at them in the order April committed the legal wrongs.

Fuller's False Imprisonment and April's Assault

Poor Fuller Payne! He'd stepped into Iona Wynner's shed in the hope that he might find something he could use to clean his top hat. Imagine his surprise when he discovered that someone had locked the door and that he was trapped inside.

At that moment of discovery, April became liable for the tort of false imprisonment. She had intentionally confined Fuller within a *bounded area* (in this case a small shed) with a *physical barrier* (a locked door). Most courts require the victim to be aware of his imprisonment. The fact that she eventually released Fuller doesn't change her liability—especially because she immediately committed the tort a second time.

It's perfectly true in everyday law that "stone walls do not a prison make, nor iron bars a cage." However, Fuller was falsely imprisoned again when compelled to stand next to the shed (a bounded area) by *force or the threat of force*. April completed the tort when she restrained (confined) Fuller by threatening him with her garden shears.

She also committed an obvious assault. A reasonable person would feel threatened by garden shears—even if not completely certain about the battery involved in being "pruned like a stunted arborvitae."

You might think the tort of false imprisonment rather unusual. In fact, more than a few lawsuits are filed each year by customers who are restrained in some way by store security personnel—typically because they are suspected of shoplifting. Many states have laws that allow store personnel to detain a suspected shoplifter for a reasonable period of time to investigate the situation. The *victim* can't recover for false imprisonment if the store can show evidence of *reasonable suspicion* that the shopper committed a crime.

Attempting to make a so-called citizen's arrest—even grabbing someone's arm to stop them from walking away—can leave you liable to a claim of false imprisonment. If you see a person commit a *felony* (*see* Chapter 17) or other serious crime, you can, under the law of most states, *detain* the person (not truly arrest him or her). But be wary—because making a mistake may expose you to lawsuits and even criminal charges.

Trespass to Chattel and Conversion

When April intentionally damaged the rosebushes, she became liable for *trespass to chattels*—a tort that's survived from the heyday of old English common law. It provides appropriate damages when a defendant intentionally interferes with the right of possession of a plaintiff's personal property. *Chattel* means an article of *movable* personal property; it comes from the same Old English root word as *cattle*. We'll look at the key aspects of personal property law in Chapter 11.

The defendant can intentionally interfere with the plaintiff's right of possession in three different ways:

1. By damaging the chattel
2. By making it impossible for the plaintiff to use the chattel for a substantial period of time
3. By ending the plaintiff's possession of the chattel—say by stealing it or by completely destroying it

In many states, trespass to chattels requires some kind of actual physical damage to the article, although a chattel doesn't need to be destroyed. April quite clearly intentionally damaged rosebushes—and it may well be that her actions will lead to their total destruction.

IS E-MAIL SPAM TRESPASS TO CHATTELS?

A few courts have held that overloading computer systems with sufficient e-mail to impact productivity constitutes trespass to chattels. Other courts have been unwilling to make the leap, on the theory that spam doesn't actually cause physical damage—a requirement for a successful trespass to chattels claim in many states.

The intentional tort of *conversion* overlaps trespass to chattels, although they are two separate legal wrongs. Like trespass to chattels, the central idea of conversion is that a defendant interferes with a plaintiff's right to possess a chattel. But this time, the defendant exercises so much *dominion and control* that justice requires him to pay the full value of the chattel to the plaintiff. Only serious harm to the property—or serious interference with the plaintiff's property rights—constitutes conversion.

Whether April committed trespass to chattels or conversion will likely depend on the fate of the rosebushes. If the weed killer April applied merely damages the rosebushes superficially, she'll be liable for trespass to chattels. But if they die or are so badly injured that they no longer produce competitive roses, she'll be liable for conversion.

In either case, the judge will order appropriate monetary damages—including punitive damages if the jury concludes that April's behavior was reprehensible enough to warrant punishment.

Iona Suffers Mental Anguish

At the very moment April began to pour weed killer on the rosebushes, Iona looked out of her bedroom window. She realized immediately that April was up to no good and raced to her garden. "What are you doing to my roses?" she yelled.

"Making sure that my roses win the prize this year," April said, with a laugh. She poured the last of the weed killer into the soil, then lobbed the empty bottle toward Iona.

Iona caught the bottle, read the label, and then screamed. She fainted straight-away and collapsed on her damp lawn.

Given these circumstances, there's little doubt that April committed the fairly new legal wrong (it dates back to the start of the twentieth century) of *intentional infliction of mental distress*. A defendant becomes liable for damages when he or she intentionally or recklessly causes a victim severe mental distress by engaging in extreme and outrageous conduct.

A definition of *extreme and outrageous conduct* used in many states is behavior which is "beyond all possible bounds of decency and to be regarded as atrocious, and utterly intolerable in a civilized community."

The plaintiff must prove that the defendant acted with the intent to cause emotional distress, or else did something intentionally with reckless disregard that his or her behavior would cause emotional distress for the victim.

In this hypothetical, we know that April intentionally damaged the rose-bushes, but we can't be as certain that she wanted to cause Iona emotional distress. Nonetheless, her reckless disregard of the mental pain her behavior would cause seems more than sufficient to make her liable for damages. After all, April knew how much Iona cared about her roses. We (and the members of the jury) can easily imagine the kind of mental pain that Iona felt when she watched her next-door neighbor—a fellow rose grower—poison her beloved rosebushes.

When applying these rules, courts will look at the relationship of the victim to the defendant (for example, was the defendant in a position of power?) and the *vulnerability* of the victim (for example, did the victim lack the power to repel the abuse?). Courts have held defendants liable for intentional infliction of emotional distress in a variety of unpleasant circumstances:

+ A prankster notifies a man that his wife was killed in an automobile accident.
+ A thug makes repeated threats of violence.
+ A supervisor unceasingly humiliates an employee.
+ A railroad employee heaps demeaning insults on a passenger.
+ A hotel desk clerk impugns the morals of a guest and orders him to leave.

What Did You Say about Me?

Fuller Payne heard the thump when Iona Wynner fainted and tumbled to the ground. He ignored April's command to stay put, ran to Iona, and helped his neighbor stand up. When Iona began to cry, Payne wrapped his arms around her. His concern further outraged April.

"Ha!" April shouted, "I knew it! You two are an 'item.' Iona Wynner is having an affair with Fuller Payne." When April saw Iona gasp, she went on shouting: "Your infidelity doesn't surprise me. It's time the world knew that your first husband filed for divorce when he discovered you were fooling around with Willie Wynner—the man you eventually married."

April did more than shout; she bellowed loud enough for Willie to hear her rants inside the Wynner kitchen. Five other close-by neighbors—all members of the straight-laced church that Iona and Willie Wynner attend—also heard April's statements.

As it happens, April was wrong; Iona was not having an affair with Fuller. (April had seen them together on a few occasions and jumped to the wrong conclusion.) However, April's assertion about Iona and Willie Wynner is perfectly true—although both Iona and Willie have worked hard to keep their ancient history a secret.

April probably committed two more intentional torts:

1. *Defamation*—Specifically, she *slandered* April by making a defamatory oral statement that reached the ears of other people. Under traditional tort law concepts, a defamatory statement is one that holds the victim up to scorn, ridicule, or contempt. The only real defense is for the defendant to prove that the statement is substantially true. April will not be able to do this because her statement was false.

2. *Invasion of privacy*—April disclosed embarrassing private facts about Iona and Will that, while true, are not *newsworthy* (not of legitimate public interest). If a reasonable person would find the disclosed information highly offensive, April will be liable for the damages caused by her invasion of Iona and Will's privacy. The court will look very closely at whether the disclosed facts were truly private. For example, April did not commit the tort if the details of Iona and Will's *indiscretion* were part of the public record of her divorce.

Defamation is a lively topic of everyday law that often makes the evening news. The Internet has made it remarkably easy to defame others and be defamed one's self. However, defamation law has become achingly complex because it has been constitutionalized by several U.S. Supreme Court decisions that blended the intentional tort of defamation with constitutional principles about freedom of speech and freedom of the press found in the First Amendment (*see* Chapter 15).

Because of defamation's significance, I've included a discussion of defamation in the "Other Things Worth Knowing about Intentional Torts" section, below.

Other Things Worth Knowing about Intentional Torts

Intentional Torts by Children

Many people are surprised to learn that minors are held responsible for their intentional torts—unless a court concludes they are too young to have the required intent. For example, a young boy can be liable for a battery if he yanks a chair away when an adult is about to sit down. Even a seven-year-old boy can form the required intent: *Pull chair . . . grown-up will try to sit down . . . grown-up hits ground.*

The boy's thoughts are probably too childish to realize that the fall will injure the adult—but that understanding is not a concern to most tort courts, because tort focuses on compensation rather than punishment. Most states don't set a fixed age at below which a child is seen incapable of forming tortious intent, but it's unlikely—for example—that a four-year-old child would be considered able to intend the battery just described.

Where a child's tort involves negligence, some states do set minimum ages, on the theory that a young child doesn't have the judgment to assess the risks of his or her acts. (*See* "Other Things Worth Knowing . . ." at the end of Chapter 4.)

The Details of Defamation

The law of defamation evolved centuries ago in England, driven by the societal importance of personal reputation. Injuring someone's reputation with a falsehood that exposed a person to scorn, ridicule, or contempt was a truly serious legal wrong—so serious in fact that the law of defamation turned usual tort procedure on its head. A defendant who *published* a statement of a defamatory nature was presumed to have harmed the plaintiff and was liable for damages.

A communication was seen as defamatory if it was detrimental to the plaintiff's reputation by decreasing respect for the plaintiff or by causing hostile, disparaging, or disagreeable opinions about the plaintiff. It's no defense that the statement was intended as a joke. If only one person believed it, the joke became defamation.

Published doesn't mean that the statement is on paper—rather, a defamatory statement is published when it reaches at least one person other than the plaintiff. Common law did, however, recognize a distinction between oral and written defamation:

> ✦ *Slander* is a spoken statement (the kind that April Schauer made in our hypothetical).

> ✦ *Libel* is a more permanent expression—typically a statement in print.

April published her defamatory statement because Iona's husband and five neighbors heard the falsehood. April could have called Iona an adulterer to her face, but she committed slander because other people heard the remark.

Repeating a defamatory statement publishes it again—and may create a new defendant. For example, if one of Iona's neighbors had telephoned a friend and shared the news, her "Let me tell you what I just heard about Iona . . ." conversation would represent a fresh legal wrong. Iona could file a defamation suit against the gossiping neighbor, even if she attributed the statement to April Schauer.

These days, it's all too easy to republish potentially defamatory statements in e-mail messages, text messages, blog responses, and other new media. Merely "letting people know" can make the author or poster liable for defamation initiated by someone else.

To escape liability under common law, the defendant had to prove that the statement was *substantially true*. (Common law also acknowledged a few *privileges* to making possibly false defamatory statements. The idea is that courts did not apply the law of defamation in a few limited situations where falsehoods were often "published." For example, comments about the qualifications of public officials were usually privileged; so were statements by witnesses in court and critiques of an artist or writer.)

For hundreds of years, libel and slander were the province of state law. The situation changed dramatically in 1964, when the U.S. Supreme Court constitutionalized the tort of defamation by incorporating free speech and freedom of the press principles. The basic notions of slander, libel, damage to reputation, and publication still apply—and truth is still the best defense for a defendant charged with defamation.

However, so many new rules have been added that analyzing a charge of defamation is confusingly tricky. However, current defamation law makes the most sense if you keep your eye on *who* claims to be harmed by a defamatory statement.

Defamation of a Public Official

A public official is an elected official (for example, president, governor, senator, member of congress, or mayor) and non-elected government employees who have substantial responsibility or control over public affairs (for example, cabinet secretary, judge, or police chief). Broadly speaking, a public official has the power to determine public policy.

When a public official is the *target,* the First Amendment protects an individual's right to free speech and expression—*even if the expression is defamatory.*

This means that a public official won't win a defamation lawsuit unless he or she shows clearly and convincingly that the defendant

→ knew the statement was false (intentionally defamed the public official);

→ recklessly disregarded the possibility that the statement was false (entertained serious doubts as to the truth of the statement).

Either of these circumstances demonstrates that the defendant acted with *actual malice* when making the false statement. A defendant charged with actual malice can defend himself by showing that he acted in good faith and made reasonable efforts to verify the truth of the statement.

Because actual malice is a very tough fault standard to prove in court, public officials have little chance of prevailing in an action for defamation.

Defamation of a Public Figure

The U.S. Supreme Court subsequently extended similar free-speech protection to a defendant who makes a defamatory statement about a *public figure*. A public figure won't win a defamation lawsuit unless he or she can prove that the defendant acted with actual malice. The Supreme Court made it more difficult for public figures to challenge defamatory statements on the theory that a public figure has easy access to the media and can rebut libelous or slanderous communications.

Although this sounds straightforward, it's often not easy to know who is a public figure. There are two kinds:

→ *All-purpose public figure*, who has a *continuous and powerful influence* on public matters (most celebrities qualify as public figures)

→ *Limited purpose public figure*, who voluntarily thrusts himself or herself into a particular public controversy and is thereby deemed to be a public figure only for purposes of that controversy

This *limited purpose* category is highly fact specific. Although courts understand that classifying a plaintiff as a public figure may end any chance of recovering damages for a reputational injury, a judge can find a relatively ordinary person to be a limited purpose public figure if he or she voluntarily assumes a role of special prominence in a public controversy. For example, if Alice organizes a campaign to fight local property tax increases, she'll probably be considered a limited purpose public figure should someone make defamatory comments about her own tax-paying history.

When the Plaintiff Is a Private Person

A private person is a plaintiff who isn't found to meet any of the public official or public figure tests. Iona Wynner, the victim in our hypothetical, is a private person. In most states, she'd be able to recover *actual damages* for the proven impairment of her reputation and standing in the community, personal humiliation, and mental anguish and suffering—and probably also punitive damages.

I say "probably," because just when it looked like things had become simple, the U.S. Supreme Court tossed in another wrinkle. The judge has to look at whether April was addressing an issue of public concern. If so, Iona may have to prove actual malice on April's part to collect punitive damages or *presumed damages* (I'll explain them *below*).

None of this should represent a problem for Iona. Her morals are not an issue of public concern. Even if they were, April seems to have acted with actual malice.

Personal Opinion

Courts have long recognized a difference between personal opinions and statements of fact. An opinion is a particular judgment or sentiment which one mind formed about persons or things. My opinion may not reflect reality but that does not make it a falsehood, because it *is* my opinion. Consequently, many states accept opinion as a defense against defamation. Simply put, if a defamatory assertion is shown to be an expression of opinion rather than a statement of fact, the defendant is not liable.

Convincing a court that a statement is opinion isn't as easy as it seems. Suppose Jim's high school English teacher says, "In my opinion, Jim is a liar and a cheat." Although apparently expressed as an opinion, most listeners would assume that Jim's teacher really knows the truth about Jim and has made a factual statement. Most courts will evaluate whether a reasonable person would understand an alleged opinion to be a statement of verifiable fact (an assertion that can be proven right or wrong). "I hated every minute I taught Jim" is not such an assertion; the original comment made about Jim is.

The U.S. Supreme Court has held that the First Amendment doesn't require that expressed opinions receive special protection in defamation lawsuits. Accordingly, a growing number of courts look beyond the artificial distinction between fact and opinion and zero in on the statement's defamatory power.

Consent as a Defense

A defendant can sometimes assert that the plaintiff consented to defamation. This happens most often when the plaintiff has previously released the defendant from liability for statements made about the plaintiff. Here's a simple example: David applies for a new job and wants Linda, his former supervisor, to write a reference letter. Linda knows the laws of defamation, so she asks David to agree not to sue her for defamation if she shares her opinions about David. He signs, she sends—David doesn't get the job. His waiver precludes a claim that her opinions were defamatory statements (*see* above), no matter how unflattering.

Retraction as a Defense

In a few states, publishing a timely retraction of an allegedly defamatory statement provides protection from a lawsuit; in others, a plaintiff who doesn't seek a retraction must show actual damages (*see* below) or he or she can't ask for punitive damages. The concept of retraction makes more sense when applied to libel rather than slander. The general rule is that a retraction must be "substantially as conspicuous" as the original allegedly defamatory statement.

The Need to Prove Actual Damages Up Front

Many states still honor the old common-law principle that some statements are so obviously defamatory that the plaintiff does not have to prove that he or she experienced actual damages to move ahead with a libel or slander lawsuit. This concept is easier to understand from the other side of the coin.

Imagine that a newspaper publishes the following statement, "Roger is president of an organization that teaches the Earth is flat." You, I, and most judges might find this a rather benign criticism, even if untrue. But what if Roger also produces proof that because this falsehood was published, he lost his job as an instructor in Orbital Mechanics at a local technical college?

If a statement is not defamatory on its face, a plaintiff is required to prove that the statement caused actual damages. On the other hand, if the statement is *defamatory per se*—Latin for "defamatory by itself"—the court will presume that the plaintiff's reputation has been damaged.

Here, for example, is how some judges instruct jurors: "Certain written defamatory statements are considered to be so harmful in and of themselves that the person to whom they relate is entitled to recover . . . damages for injury to reputation. *Libel per se* is a type of libel in which the defamatory meaning is apparent on the face of the statement. When the defamatory words are *libel per se,* the law conclusively presumes that there is injury to the plaintiff's reputation. The plaintiff is not required to prove that his [or her] reputation was damaged. The plaintiff is entitled to recover damages for the injury to his [or her] reputation and for the humiliation and mental suffering caused by the libel."

Whether or not a publication is libelous per se (or slanderous per se) is a matter of law for the court. The judge ultimately decides and instructs the jury accordingly.

It's difficult to predict how a court will react to April Schaeur's statement about Iona. In years past, impugning a single woman's chastity was per se defamatory, but given today's anything-goes attitudes, it may be difficult for Iona to argue that a lie about her fidelity triggers the presumption of a damaged reputation. A judge may require Iona to prove that she suffered actual damages because of April's false statement.

Trade Libel

People who post negative reviews about products and services on Internet websites and blogs can potentially commit the tort of *trade libel* if they intentionally or recklessly include false information.

Trade libel resembles the tort of defamation, but is actually a different legal wrong. In most states, the plaintiff must prove that the intentional or reckless falsehoods disparaged the company's products or services in a way that caused actual financial damage. (As in defamation, *recklessly* means that the poster had serious doubts about the truth of the posted information.)

Statements which compare one product to another—"Brand A is a better value than Brand B"—won't make a defendant liable. Neither will personal opinions, as long as they do not merely camouflage statements of fact.

While a few upset companies have sued customers who posted negative reviews, producers of products and services are more likely to threaten legal action against the website or blog that "hosts" the review. Nonetheless, it's a bad idea to take revenge on a company by blasting its products and services online with postings full of falsehoods.

CHAPTER 4

NEGLIGENCE AND ACCIDENTS

C HANCES ARE YOU'VE LAUGHED ALONG WITH ME AT THE BUMPER STICKER, "Life is uncertain, eat dessert first." One reason we recognize the wisdom in this modern-day maxim is that we've all experienced life's uncertainties—including many different *accidents* in our homes, on the road, and while we're at work. Our daily lives seem chock full of unusual, unforeseen events that happen by chance (to offer a common definition of *accident*).

A moment's thought will convince you that this definition is incomplete. We all know that some accidents don't happen by mere chance—that someone is to blame, although they didn't intend to do harm. Perhaps you were sideswiped on the road by a car whose driver was paying more attention to her mobile phone than to the cars around her. The other driver didn't set out to ding your fender, but nonetheless, her careless conduct directly led to a traffic accident that damaged your car. The event may be called an accident, but the damage didn't happen by pure chance.

Everyday law offers a comprehensive approach for dealing with "not-quite" accidents.

Careless conduct that results in harm is considered to be a legal wrong: the tort of *negligence*. A judge will order the person responsible to pay the cost of the damages done. Negligence is different than the intentional torts we considered in Chapter 3, because it focuses on acts that—if done carefully—are not reasonably likely to cause harm. Chatting on a cell phone is routine behavior: an act performed many millions of times each day in the United States. Had the driver pulled to the curb to complete her call, the fender bender she caused never would have happened because her complete attention would have been given over to the task of driving.

But making the call took her eye off the ball, so to speak. She owed other drivers on the road a duty of care—to keep alert for the cars ahead of her. This is how any reasonable driver at the wheel of a moving automobile would behave.

Consequently, a jury will probably decide that the driver's negligence—her failure to act reasonably under the circumstances—is the legal cause of the minor collision that damaged your car.

Negligence law is another example of *legal flexibility*. Negligent torts come in unlimited variations and can never be cataloged in advance, because who knows when someone's lack of reasonably required care will cause harm to another person? Courts deal with the endless variety by applying a few key principles to all negligence cases.

Finally, negligence law is complex and highly situation specific. Moreover, successfully pursuing a claim against a potential defendant often involves the promise of going to trial if a settlement isn't forthcoming. For both of these reasons, recovering damages for negligent behavior is definitely not a do-it-yourself chore. Find a good lawyer the moment you discover that you've been personally injured by someone's lack of care.

I'm Dreaming of an Icy Christmas

All that poor Brighton Early hoped for was a merry Christmas. Unhappily, fate—or was it his negligence?—intervened and transformed his Christmas story into a tale of good intentions gone bad. The only silver lining in sight is that Brighton's experiences taught him lots about the law of negligent torts. Unfortunately, he'll have to pay a substantial tuition for his education—in the form of hefty attorney fees and (possibly!) monetary damages awarded to his next-door neighbor, Mona Lott.

It all began a few days before Christmas, when Brighton Early completed an elaborate display of lights, plastic Santa Clauses, illuminated reindeer, and other seasonal symbols.

Although impressive (the countless lights shone brightly enough to illuminate the neighborhood), Brighton was a bit disappointed because it had neither rained nor snowed in the State of Regret for several weeks. He'd hoped that a normal helping of winter snow or ice would add that extra Christmas touch to his display.

Brimming with good intentions, he got out his garden hose one freezing evening and sprayed his display with water—watching icicles form on the angels, the elves, Santa's sleigh, and even the wiring for the outdoor Christmas lights. Brighton was so full of Christmas spirit (actually brandy-laced eggnog) that he didn't notice the water bounce off of a reindeer's bulbous nose and fall on Mona Lott's covered back porch, forming a thin coating of ice on the decking.

An hour later, Mona, wearing her leather-soled moccasins, stepped out on the dimly lit porch to let Wanda, her cat, go for a walk. Alas, Mona slipped on the ice, came down with a thud, and suffered a painful injury to her shoulder.

A Duty of Care

Mona (and her attorney) feel strongly that Brighton caused the accident that injured Mona—and that fairness dictates that he should pay her medical expenses, the money she lost by being unable to work, and the other costs she encountered. But how will they convince a judge that everyday law gives the court a reason to award damages to Mona?

This seems like a simple question—but it isn't, because negligence is a slippery subject. Legally speaking, negligence is enmeshed with the concept of a *reasonable person* (*see* Chapter 2). It may strike you as weird for anyone to water his

Christmas display, but a key question here is how would the hypothetical reasonable person have created icicles on his or her plastic reindeer?

A court may conclude that Brighton had a duty to spruce up his display in the way that a reasonable person would have done it—presumably a careful way that wouldn't have coated Mona's back porch with ice.

Courts use the reasonable person as a standard of comparison. A reasonable person takes reasonable care to protect others from harm. If Brighton didn't act carefully—using a reasonable person as a yardstick—if he failed to exercise what lawyers call his *duty of care*, then he probably acted negligently.

TRUE ACCIDENTS DO HAPPEN

Each year, many people are injured in true accidents, where no one can be said to have acted negligently. The law calls them *unavoidable accidents*. They are, as one court noted, "inevitable occurrences that can't be foreseen or prevented by vigilance, care, and attention and are not caused by (or contributed to) by an act or omission of the party claiming the accident was unavoidable." If a jury concludes that a plaintiff was injured by an unavoidable accident, it will find for the defendant—the plaintiff will bear the cost of his or her injuries.

Why the weasel words: *may, presumably, if,* and *probably?*

Because none of this happens automatically. Mona's lawyer will have to convince a judge that Brighton had such a duty of care to Mona. The judge will likely base his decision by asking himself whether a reasonable person would have recognized the potential for danger and taken what precautions were necessary not to create a layer of ice on Mona's porch. If the judge agrees there is such a duty, the trial will move ahead; if not, the judge will dismiss Mona's complaint—and end the lawsuit. This is only fair: If a reasonable person could not have foreseen the problem—and taken care to prevent it—it would be unjust to hold a defendant to a stricter standard.

However, should the judge let the trial go forward, Mona will have two more major hurdles to get over: She (actually her lawyer) has to convince the jury that

→ Brighton's careless behavior breached the duty of care—in short, that he acted negligently;

→ Brighton's negligence is the *legal cause* of the injury she experienced.

The second item—*legal cause*—deserves some explaining. We know so far that the redirected spray from Brighton's hose coated Mona's porch with ice.

And we know that Mona fell and was injured. But what if she'd tripped on the door sill, or what if she had fallen over Wanda. In either of those events, Brighton's negligence—even if proved—would *not* have been the cause-in-fact of her banged-up shoulder.

A common legal rule-of-thumb is to ask whether the harm would have occurred *but for* the negligence. In other words, would the plaintiff have suffered an injury if the defendant had not acted negligently. If the answer is *yes*, then the negligence can't be the legal cause of the plaintiff's injury. In this case, we are fairly certain that Mona would have had a painless evening but for Brighton's decision to add ice to his Christmas display.

SLIP-AND-FALL ACCIDENTS

A fairly common kind of tort lawsuit involves slip-and-fall accidents, where the plaintiff slipped on ice, a wet floor, a piece of torn carpeting, or some other hazard. These are often called *premise liability* suits. Most (but not all) are filed against commercial property owners and landlords.

Plaintiffs fall into two categories: *invitees* (visitors, such as customers, whose presence on the property benefits the defendant) and *licensees* (social guests and others who are said to enter the property for their own purposes). The general rule is that the premises' owner owes the highest duty of care to an invitee. A supermarket owner, for example, has a duty to periodically inspect the floors for spilled liquids and broken bottles—they pose obvious hazards.

Licensees are treated differently. A property owner has a duty to warn a licensee of a dangerous condition *if* the owner knows about it *and* the licensee is unlikely to discover the hazard before it causes injury. In most states, the neighbor does not have a duty to inspect his property for hazards nor to repair the problems he knows about. Warning his guests is sufficient.

In most states a homeowner is not responsible *under tort law* for keeping the sidewalk in front of a house free of snow and ice hazards (although local laws may require prompt snow shoveling).

There's another aspect to the notion of legal cause which goes by the legalese moniker of *proximate cause* (*proximate* means "close in space and time"). This idea of nearness can be important at times. Imagine that Mona had a boyfriend, Mike, who purchased two non-refundable tickets to a local play. The ticket he bought for Mona will go to waste because her injury—caused by Brighton's negligence—will prevent her from going to the theater. Will Mike be able to sue Brighton for the cost of the ticket?

No! Mike's injury is *too far away* from Brighton's negligent act. A stranger's wasted theater ticket is not a foreseeable consequence of carelessly wielding a water hose in winter. In legal speak, Brighton's negligence is not a proximate cause of Mike's loss.

What will the judge and jury do in Mona's suit?

That's always difficult to predict in tort cases. If I were the judge, I'd agree that a reasonable person would have foreseen that cold water sprayed on a chilly winter evening would create ice—and taken appropriate care to avoid dousing Mona's porch. But you might see things differently. And, if I were on the jury, I'd also conclude that Mona made her case that Brighton was negligent—but that's a closer call. Ask yourself if a reasonable person could *really* foresee that a plastic reindeer snout would redirect water at the house next door. Some members of the jury might decide that Brighton had taken appropriate care, had not acted negligently under the circumstances, and that Mona's fall was an *unavoidable accident*.

Mona Also Has to Act Reasonably

When Mona took that first step onto her back porch, she also had a duty of care—*to herself*. Brighton's attorney will almost certainly assert that Mona's own negligence contributed to the accident: A reasonable person would have anticipated ice outdoors in winter and would have exercised appropriate care by

- ➔ providing ample lighting so that any ice on the dark porch would be easily visible;
- ➔ wearing proper outdoor footwear, not leather-soled moccasins.

Again—although we can't be sure what a jury will decide, I think that both arguments will fail because a reasonable person would probably not foresee a coating of ice on the decking of a covered porch after a long stretch of dry weather. It stretches credulity to think that a reasonable neighbor would anticipate a spray of cold water from a carelessly handled hose.

When Brighton claims that Mona might be partially responsible for her accident, he is invoking a legal defense called *contributory negligence:* "I may have been careless, but so was Mona."

At one time, the law in most states was that even a smidgen of plaintiff responsibility would end any chance of recovery from the defendant. So, in our hypothetical, if the jury concluded that Mona was 1 percent responsible for her injuries because she *negligently* wore leather-soled moccasins outdoors, she'd be barred from collecting damages even though Brighton's negligent icicle-making was 99 percent responsible for her injured shoulder.

Only a handful of states still enforce this doctrine (Alabama, Maryland, North Carolina, and Virginia—and the District of Columbia). The forty-six other states have switched to *comparative negligence*—a defense against a charge of negligence that produces less harsh results. Here, the jury will weigh the responsibilities of both plaintiff and defendant. There are several formulas in use, but the essential idea is to reduce the plaintiff's damage award proportionally to the plaintiff's responsibility. Thus, if a plaintiff is 20 percent responsible for causing an accident, his or her damage award is reduced by 20 percent. Typical contributory negligence formulas pay the plaintiff nothing if he or she is found to be 50 percent or more responsible.

Wanda on the Loose

When Mona slipped and fell, she lost sight of Wanda, her all-too accurately named cat. Instead of trotting into the Lott back garden, the large feline immediately headed for the festival of red and green lights in Brighton Early's front yard. The object she found most intriguing was a giant plastic candy cane that reached to Brighton's roof. The coating of imitation snow provided perfect traction for Wanda's claws. In no time, she had scampered up to the roof and—for reasons no one has ever explained—began to chew on the thick extension cord that carried power to the elves and sugarplum faeries that decorated the eaves of Brighton's home.

Wanda bit through the insulation, giving herself a powerful electric shock and causing a short in the wires. Happily, a circuit-breaker tripped before Wanda had used up all her nine lives. She rolled off the roof and fell stunned into an artificial snow bank made of Styrofoam packing peanuts.

However, an instant before the circuit breaker turned off the power, a shower of sparks from a junction box ignited the fuses of a partially completed fireworks display atop Brighton's roof—a special treat that he had planned for the neighborhood New Year's Eve celebration. Most of the rockets soared harmlessly into the night sky, but one of them flew in a devilish loop, smashed through Mona's picture window, penetrated an expensive leather armchair, and exploded with a shower of batting—but no further damage.

Meanwhile, Mona was slowly coming to her senses on the back porch. She couldn't quite understand the flashes of light she saw in the sky or the sound of breaking glass she heard. Despite the severe ache in her shoulder, she pushed herself into a sitting position and looked around for Wanda.

She murmured, "Where did that silly cat go?"

Strictly Liable

The purpose of tonight's accidental fireworks display is to introduce the concept of *strict liability*—the legal doctrine that holds a defendant responsible for the damage the plaintiff suffers even if the defendant does nothing negligent.

A plaintiff must still show that the defendant's actions or behavior was the legal cause of his injuries, but the plaintiff doesn't have to prove that the defendant didn't meet the reasonable person standard of care.

Strict liability was invented to handle situations where a defendant performs activities that are inherently hazardous even when done with great care—such as demolishing a building or storing large quantities of flammable materials. Everyday law recognizes that a plaintiff may be harmed even though the defendant did everything a reasonable person would do to anticipate and prevent harm. And so, a defendant can't escape the obligation to make a plaintiff whole by pointing at his reasonable precautions.

Looked at the other way around, the defendant—not the people around him—bears the risk of damages should something go wrong.

Placing fireworks on the roof of a home in a residential neighborhood is an activity that cries out for the doctrine of strict liability. There's little doubt that a court will find Brighton liable for the damage done to Mona's picture window and leather chair.

Brighton won't be able to shift the blame to Wanda by arguing that the unfortunate fireworks incident wasn't his fault. Strict liability requires that a person performing inherently dangerous activity shoulder the costs for any damage the activity causes.

But isn't this an unfair result? After all, Mona let Wanda loose—and Wanda chewed the extension cord and created the short circuit that made the sparks that ignited the fuses. Why doesn't Mona bear some of the liability for the damage to her home?

The answer is simple: Brighton is wholly liable because the court applied the doctrine of strict liability, which looked beyond Brighton's negligence to the dangerous nature of the activity itself. Everyone agrees that Brighton exercised all possible care when he set up his fireworks display—everyone accepts that Brighton had good-faith intentions to be safe and took reasonable safety precautions—everyone acknowledges that he did nothing wrong to cause the accidental launch of the rockets—and everyone knows that Wanda caused the sparks that sent the rockets flying.

But none of this makes any difference, because strict liability doesn't base Brighton's liability on his duty to act carefully. Therefore, the court has no reason to measure Mona's comparative negligence. Brighton is legally responsible for *all* damage caused by his inherently dangerous activity.

What about Wanda?

Strict liability is also applied to some situations that may not strike most people as inherently dangerous: owning a pet, for example. In most states, a dog owner is strictly liable for any damage the dog does—from the dog digging up a neighbor's yard, to biting the mailman, to injuring another pet dog.

But Wanda is a cat—which can make a world of difference under everyday law.

Curiously, many states do not require that cats be leashed or make owners liable for the damage they do. This seems to be a recognition that cats traditionally were kept as rodent-catchers, and needed to be loose. Also, cats are less likely to cause serious injuries to people. But the growing population of cats (there are upwards of 90 million pet cats versus 75 million pet dogs) has prompted some local governments to enact leash laws for cats.

THE ANCIENT "ONE-FREE-BITE" RULE

A minority of states still use a negligence approach for dog damage that goes back to old English common law. Only after a dog bites someone (or does damage) is the owner put on *notice* that the dog can be dangerous. At that point, the owner has a responsibility to prevent any future injury or damage.

Because the State of Regret still allows cats to wander—and still follows the old no-liability rule for cats—Mona will not have to pay for the damage Wanda did to Brighton's extension cord (or fireworks) during her late-night jaunt.

The Havoc Continues

Brighton knew something was wrong the moment he noticed that his Christmas display had gone dark, so he guessed that something unfortunate and electrical had happened. Although he still felt a bit tipsy from the brandy he'd consumed earlier that evening, he decided to go outside to investigate. His first discovery was a limp, slightly singed, cat lying next to a choir of plastic angels.

"Good heavens! It's Wanda."

Brighton cradled the still-stunned cat in his arms and walked to Mona's back porch, knowing that he was likely to find her behind the back door, in her family room. He climbed the five steps and was about to tap on the back door when Mona startled him by saying, "What's wrong with Wanda?"

Brighton hadn't expected Mona to be sitting at his feet. He reacted by dropping Wanda, thus squandering the last of her nine lives. Mona screamed and fell into a dead faint.

Brighton immediately dropped to his knees and tried to revive Mona. Unfortunately, the sight of Brighton looming over Mona greatly disturbed Bowser, Mona's oversize St. Bernard, who had come to the rear window in response to hearing her scream. Bowser leaped through the window—scattering pieces of glass in all directions—and chomped down hard on Brighton's left foot, ruining a pricey boot and causing several puncture wounds.

Fortunately, at this point, Mona regained consciousness and realized that poor Wanda was still breathing. She ordered Bowser away from Brighton and shooed the dog back into her house. Brighton looked around, took stock of the situation, and decided that he, Mona, and Wanda required medical assistance. Rather than call the paramedics, Brighton helped Mona and Wanda to his car. "I insist! We'll drive to the veterinary clinic. Once Wanda is taken care of, we'll drive to the emergency room at the hospital."

Mona could see that Brighton's eyes were bloodshot and glassy—and she could smell alcohol on his breath. She realized that he was in no condition to drive, but she knew that arguing with Brighton would be futile. Besides, she wanted to get Wanda to the clinic as quickly as possible. So she ignored her throbbing shoulder and asked Brighton for his car keys. She would drive to the clinic and then on to the hospital.

I wish I could report that Brighton's day of excitement was over. Unfortunately, while Mona was driving to the vet, she decided to telephone her insurance agent and discuss the coverage available under her homeowner's policy. While speaking on her cell phone—she held her mobile phone up to her ear—Mona managed to sideswipe your car. The resulting delay at the accident scene proved too long for poor Wanda. Moreover, the bouncing around during the drive caused additional damage to Mona's shoulder.

My, How the Torts Roll In!

You might want to pause a moment and try to find the different legal wrongs that I *may* have included in this closing hypothetical. I'll give you a hint. I'm about to discuss four could-be negligent torts, one possible intentional tort, and one strict liability tort.

What to Do about Wanda

Mona and her attorney decided not to charge Brighton with *malicious injury of a pet*, a new tort in some states, including the State of Regret. Pets were tradition-ally covered by the old tort of trespass against a *chattel* (an item of personal prop-erty, *see* Chapter 11), but damages were limited to the dollar value of the pet—in Wanda's case, a paltry sum. The new malicious injury tort recognizes that pets are seen as members of the family and that their untimely death can cause serious emotional distress. As an appellate court in the State of Washington wrote, "we hold malicious injury to a pet can support a claim for, and be considered a factor in measuring a person's emotional distress damages."

NEGLIGENT INFLICTION OF EMOTIONAL DISTRESS

Many states allow courts to award damages for *negligent infliction of emotional distress*. This tort is built atop the still-controversial notion that people have a legal duty to use reasonable care to avoid causing emotional distress to other individuals. This yardstick is significantly less stringent than the *reckless disregard* standard applied in the tort of intentional infliction of mental distress (see Chapter 3). The plaintiff must prove that the defendant engaged in negligent conduct . . . that a reasonable person would foresee that the conduct would cause the plaintiff severe emotional distress . . . and that the plaintiff suffered real emotional distress as a result of the defendant's conduct (typically manifested by real physical symptoms, such as weight loss or blackouts).

Negligent conduct that might qualify includes a funeral home accidentally loses the corpse of a loved one; a mother sees her child maimed in a gruesome accident; or a negligently caused injury results in a woman's severe disfigurement.

Mere indignities and/or *upsetting conduct* are not enough; these things are inevitable in our complex society. People are expected to cope with everyday hurts and unpleasantness. This tort requires misconduct that is universally recognized as severe enough to cause emotional distress.

Mona's lawyer explained to her: "The law defines *malicious* as acting with illegal motives. Brighton Early may have been careless when he dropped Wanda, but he didn't *intentionally* act maliciously toward her. Brighton actually wanted to help the cat, but he was careless. If we charge him with negligence, we'll be back to using Wanda's value as the yardstick for damages."

But Brighton Was Drinking!

Mona wondered if the law might take special notice of the fact that Brighton had been full of Christmas cheer. "He was sozzled when he picked up poor Wanda. Doesn't that make a difference?"

"It does indeed," the lawyer said, "but not in the way you might think. Brighton can't claim that he *accidentally* dropped Wanda because he was intoxicated. Simply put, a voluntarily intoxicated person is held to the same standard of care as a sober person. This is because the law typically looks at the defendant's conduct—not his or her mental condition—to gauge negligence. A person who chooses to drink alcohol—or use drugs—is expected to act as carefully as a person who doesn't."

INTOXICATION AND NEGLIGENCE AS A MATTER OF LAW

One familiar situation where a defendant's intoxication does translate into more-or-less *instant negligence* is causing a traffic accident when driving while intoxicated. Because an intoxicated driver violates a statute designed to enhance public safety, a decision to drive drunk is considered negligence as a matter of law (*negligence per se* in legalese). This presumption of negligence means that a plaintiff need not present evidence of how a reasonable person would have avoided causing an accident. Of course, the plaintiff still must prove that the defendant's presumed negligence legally caused the harm he or she suffered.

The same rule applies to plaintiffs also. He or she can't point to voluntary intoxication as an excuse for behavior that contributed to the injuries he suffered—but, being intoxicated isn't evidence that he or she was automatically negligent. A plaintiff must act reasonably under the circumstances, drunk or sober.

The Bowser Factor

When Mona sued Brighton, he and his attorney looked at the possibility of filing a *counterclaim* against Mona. They decided that they didn't have a case based on her negligent release of Wanda the cat (in the State of Regret, as I explained above, a cat owner isn't liable for the damage done by his or her pet). Bowser, though, is a pet of a different color. Brighton wondered if Mona is strictly liable for the damage the big dog did to his foot and boot.

The lawyer explained that strict liability for a dog bite has two exceptions. The first is that the government is not liable for bites inflicted by dogs used to apprehend criminal suspects (that is, K-9 police dogs) or dogs used in the investigation of a crime (possibly drug-sniffing dogs who become overly excited). The second exception is when a dog is provoked by the victim. "Mona will argue" the lawyer went on, "that you provoked Bowser when you approached his master on a darkened porch after she screamed."

"That doesn't seem fair," Brighton said, "I didn't threaten Mona in any way."

COUNTERCLAIM

Think of a counterclaim (occasionally called a *countersuit*) as a tit-for-tat lawsuit that the defendant launches against the plaintiff—usually to offset the plaintiff's original claim. For example, a store sues a customer for an unpaid debt. The customer counterclaims that the store used fraudulent sales tactics to close the deal. If the court considers that both claim and counterclaim are closely related, both will be resolved in a single lawsuit.

"Yep. I think the jury will feel that way, too. We probably have a good case in strict liability against her."

Brighton frowned. "I just remembered—Bowser jumped through a window to reach me. Mona wasn't careless with her dog. She kept him locked up inside her house. Won't the jury conclude that she took reasonable precautions to prevent Bowser from biting anyone?"

The lawyer smiled. "The doctrine of strict liability isn't concerned with the care she did—or didn't—take. Mona is strictly liable for the damage her dog does."

DOGS AND HOMEOWNER'S INSURANCE

The liability for dog bites is usually covered by homeowner's insurance, but the soaring number of lawsuits has encouraged some insurers to exclude certain breeds of dogs from coverage—or to set premiums based on a pet's propensity to bite. (At least two states forbid companies to refuse to write homeowner's insurance because an insured owns a specific breed of dog.) Although the industry doesn't publish an official "don't-insure-this-dog" list, your insurance agent will know if the breed you have in mind will raise your rates. Among the breeds that seem to concern insurers are Akita, German Shepherd, Chow Chow, Doberman Pinscher, Husky, Pitbull, Rottweiler. Staffordshire Bull Terrier, and Wolf Dog (wolf/dog hybrid).

Was Brighton Negligent for Not Calling the Paramedics?

This is a potential tort you might not have identified. Would a reasonably prudent person faced with similar circumstances have dialed 911 and asked for a paramedic? If so, perhaps Brighton acted negligently when he insisted on using his car to convey Mona to a hospital? And perhaps his negligence is the legal cause of the additional pain and suffering she experienced when driving around aggravated her shoulder injury?

This would make an interesting question on a law-school torts exam. Brighton has two replies: First, Mona *assumed the risk* of any subsequent injury when she took over the chore of driving Wanda to the veterinary clinic in Brighton's car. Second, that the jury should look at what a reasonable person would have done facing a similar *emergency situation*. Brighton will argue that given the need to get Wanda to the clinic as soon as possible, his decision to drive was completely reasonable. (I doubt that Mona will insist that Brighton was wrong to consider the injuries to her cat more pressing than the injuries to her shoulder.)

Mona's Automobile Accident

Personal injury claims following automobile accidents represent the single largest category of negligence-tort lawsuits. You'll undoubtedly want to recover the cost of repairing your car's bodywork from Mona, and you have a reasonable chance of succeeding. In some states, speaking on a conventional mobile phone while driving is an infraction that may trigger the *negligence per se* doctrine I described earlier. (Of course, you'll need to provide evidence of Mona's law-breaking.)

Even if not negligence as a matter of law, Mona was not exercising the degree of care expected from a reasonable driver. The bottom line: You should have no difficulty convincing a court that Mona is liable for the damage done to your car by the fender-bender she caused.

But whom will you sue? Mona was at the wheel, so she is a possible defendant. In many states (including the State of Regret), you also have the option of suing the owner of the car. These are states with so-called "permissive user" statutes that make the owner liable for damage caused by the negligence of another driver who drives with the owner's permission. This is an example of what lawyers call *vicarious liability*. *Vicarious* means that the owner bears the liability that the driver deserves.

Permissive user statutes also make parents responsible for traffic accidents caused by their children. In addition, some states apply the *family purpose doctrine*, which makes the owner of a car used by family members liable for any damage they negligently cause while driving. The idea is that a family car is owned for *family purposes*.

Why worry about suing Brighton? Because you may not be able to recover money damages from Mona. If Mona owned her own car—she doesn't!—her automobile insurance policy would probably cover any liabilities she incurred when driving another car with the owner's permission. Consequently, Mona will have to pay any damages awarded by the court out of her own pocket. But many defendants—possibly including Mona—have so little resources that they are *judgment proof*—you may win your case, but you won't be able to collect the damages the court awards. Simply put, Brighton (or more correctly, his automobile insurance company) has the "deep pockets" to pay when you win.

NEGLIGENT ENTRUSTMENT

Negligent entrustment is the legal doctrine that lets a plaintiff sue a car owner if the owner carelessly entrusts a *dangerous instrumentality* (his car) to a person who should not have been allowed to drive. At first glance, negligent entrustment resembles vicarious liability, but it's actually quite different. A plaintiff seeking damages under a permissive user statute must show that the driver was negligent. The car owner becomes liable for damages merely because he or she owns the car.

But a charge of negligent entrustment requires the plaintiff to prove that a reasonable car owner would never have turned the car keys over to the driver who caused the accident—perhaps because he or she doesn't have a license, is intoxicated, or is otherwise impaired. In our case, for example, Mona's injured shoulder may have made it impossible for her to drive safely.

Most negligent entrustment suits stem from automobile accidents, but the action might arise if a defendant let an unqualified person use a firearm or allowed a child to operate a dangerous power tool.

Judgment proof defendants are all too common. We'll look at the realities more closely when we talk about bankruptcy (*see* Chapter 20). For now, recognize that your ability to file a lawsuit against a potential defendant doesn't mean that it makes sense to do so. Few personal injury attorneys will move ahead against an uninsured, financially insolvent defendant who lacks the resources to pay a judgment. Simply put—why engage in an exercise in futility that wastes time and costs money?

Other Things Worth Knowing about Negligence

Punitive Damages

Negligence is carelessness—doing something (or not doing something) that a reasonable person would do in a similar circumstance. A court will make you pay for the harm caused by your carelessness, but it won't add punishment—in the form of punitive damages—for a routine mistake or lapse in judgment.

However, when behavior becomes *grossly negligent*—when it involves outrageous conduct that the defendant knew posed an extreme risk of harm to others—a plaintiff can ask for punitive damages (*see* Chapter 3). A plaintiff seeking punitive damages must prove that the defendant acted recklessly—with *conscious indifference* to the substantial likelihood that an injury would result. Someone who fires a gun indoors, not caring that a bullet can travel through adjacent walls and strike a next-door neighbor, is grossly negligent. So also is an intoxicated surgeon who operates on a patient.

Statute of Limitations

We explained the idea of a statute of limitations for contract lawsuits in Chapter 2. Every state also sets a specific number of years in which you must file a lawsuit to recover damages caused by a defendant's negligence. The time periods vary widely—some as short as one year, others as long as four years. Many states give you more time to file a lawsuit for a negligent tort than for an intentional tort. This is because it may take some time to discover the extent of injuries done during an accident. Keep in mind that most statutes of limitations are "hard" deadlines—miss the one that applies to your case, and your negligence lawsuit will almost certainly be thrown out of court.

Everyday law recognizes that it may take a long time for certain latent negligent injuries to become visible—the use of wrong construction materials by a house builder, for example—and so many courts implement the so-called discovery rule in appropriate circumstances. The plaintiff can file a lawsuit for a short period of time after the damage is recognized, even though the statute of limitations for tort claims has run out.

Wrongful Death

Under traditional notions of tort law, a tort victim's claim for compensation died when he or she did. Practically speaking, this meant that there was no one to sue the tortfeasor if negligence or an intentional act resulted in death.

To get around this unfair result, all states enacted *wrongful death statutes* that allow a narrowly defined group of survivors to seek monetary damages if a legal wrong causes a victim's death. Here's a typical list of eligible plaintiffs: the victim's spouse, child, or parent; then any person who is related by blood or marriage to the victim and who was substantially dependent upon the victim. (Some states specifically exclude the victim's siblings and unadopted stepchildren.)

A claim for wrongful death requires that the defendant negligently or intentionally caused the victim's death, or is strictly liable for it. Common causes of wrongful death include automobile accidents, defective products (*see* Chapter

12), medical malpractice (*see* Chapter 18), construction accidents, and intentional torts (such as battery) inflicted during crimes.

More on the Reasonable Person

The reasonable person is an essential aspect of negligence tort law because this hypothetical individual provides an objective yardstick to evaluate a defendant's behavior. Over the years, thousands of courts have written the reasonable person's "biography." Here are some details worth knowing:

→ A reasonable person is well-informed, alert, aware of the law, and attuned to the riskiness—the likelihood of harm to others—of any action he or she might contemplate.

→ A reasonable person isn't an *average person* who behaves like most of the people in a community behave; rather he or she behaves in a way that reflects the community's standards of safe behavior. For example, most people in a community may drive above the posted speed limit and jaywalk on city streets. The reasonable person does neither.

→ A reasonable person knows all of the things commonly known in the community—that ice is slippery, that it's more difficult to see at night than during the day, that children are likely to follow a ball into the street when playing, that women do not want to be touched by strangers, that drinking alcohol impairs judgment and driving ability.

→ A reasonable driver possesses the skills, knowledge, experience, judgment, and common sense to operate a motor vehicle in a way that avoids accidents and harm to other people. *Anyone* who drives a car is held to this standard—even a newly licensed driver who has only hours behind the wheel, and even a joyriding teenager without a license.

→ A reasonable person sees what is visible and hears what is audible. Consequently, a reasonable driver sees a stop sign and hears a warning horn sounded by an adjacent car (a reasonable deaf driver takes into account that he or she will not hear nearby horns).

→ A reasonable person takes his or her physical limitations into account. For example, a reasonable blind person will not attempt to drive a car.

→ A reasonable person prepares for foreseeable emergencies, understands that unexpected things can happen, and recognizes that people often act unpredictably. The reasonable owner of a cruise ship will provide lifeboats, the reasonable owner of a movie theater will provide emergency exits, the reasonable manufacturer of a dangerous product provides detailed safety warnings, and the reasonable owner of a residential swimming pool will take precautions to prevent neighborhood children from accidentally drowning.

Negligence by Children

Because the negligent acts of children are measured against the yardstick of a *reasonable child* of the same age, intelligence, and experience, young children can't be negligent because they simply can't recognize the risks that a reasonable adult person would foresee. Because it keys on age and experience, the standard of care applied to children's behavior is fairly subjective and tends to be a moving target. Most states recognize that children above a certain age—often six or seven years old—can behave negligently to some extent.

Although older children can be suited for tortious conduct, they are usually judgment proof unless a state statute makes parents responsible for a child's negligent acts. Hawaii was the first state to enact such a law (the statute actually dates back to Hawaii's days as a territory). It imposes unlimited parental liability for both negligent and intentional torts by children. Most other state parental responsibility laws set upper bounds on the dollar amount of a parent's liability.

When Government Employees Are Negligent

Under the hoary legal doctrine of *sovereign immunity*, the king could do no wrong and could not be called into court and sued without his express permission. This doctrine passed through common law into the United States' legal system. Consequently, federal and state governments are immune against lawsuits for legal wrongs done by government employees who are doing their jobs at the time. Both federal and state governments have waived much of this immunity by passing statutes that impose some liability for torts committed by government employees.

One important exception is that governments don't waive immunity for injuries that result when a government employee exercises *discretionary power to enforce the law*. While you can usually sue the government if a police officer driving a police car negligently rear-ends you on a busy street or falsely imprisons you (*see* Chapter 3) during a routine traffic stop, you can't sue because the same officer failed to arrest the person who later burgled your home.

The important point is the government must give you the permission to sue in an appropriate statute. If the kind of claim you want to make isn't included in the law, you won't be able to file suit.

Tort claim statutes usually cap the damages you can recover from the government and may not allow punitive damages. They also compel a plaintiff to follow detailed rules for launching a lawsuit. A typical required first step is to file a *notice of claim* shortly after the injury (possibly within only sixty days). If the claim is denied, you are free to file a traditional lawsuit or sue in small claims court.

Consequently, personal injury attorneys advise plaintiffs to file a notice of claim—even multiple notices of claims to different agencies—whenever the government *might be* liable for damages.

CHAPTER 5

╺╾╼ ╺╾╼

MARRIAGE AND PRENUPTIAL AGREEMENTS

E VERYONE UNDERSTANDS THE MEANING OF *MARRIAGE*. YOU QUITE possibly are married yourself; if not, you certainly have married friends and relatives. You've read books about married people, seen plays and movies about marriage, listened to news reports and sermons, and talked to other people about the topic—maybe even took part in marriage counseling.

So, you should know the answer to a simple question: How do you define *marriage?*

Marriage

My *simple question* is anything but. The more you think about what *marriage* is (or means), the harder it becomes to explain in a few well-chosen words.

Here's a definition from a dictionary published about a hundred years ago: "Marriage is a legal union of a man and a woman for life, as husband and wife."

An even older definition says, "Marriage is a voluntary union for life between one man and one woman to the exclusion of all others."

Here's a more recent dictionary definition: "Marriage is the state of being united to a person of the opposite sex as husband or wife in a consensual and contractual relationship recognized by law."

And here are two other definitions I recently came across: "Marriage is a social, religious, spiritual, or legal union of individuals." And, "Marriage is a social contract between two individuals that unites their lives legally, economically, and emotionally."

Are you still awake? All five of these explanations are remarkably bland. They convey the concept that marriage is a *union* (whatever that means), but none seems to capture the heart of the matter. And, though most introduce the notion that law is somehow linked to marriage, none conveys the extent that government regulates the *institution* of marriage.

The "Are They Legally Married" Game

Her name is Mary, his name is John. She's twenty years old, he's twenty-one. They meet, they fall in love, and John proposes marriage. Mary accepts his proposal. They set a date and, with plenty of time to spare, complete the required formalities in their state:

> ❖ They take a blood test because they live in one of the few remaining states that still requires tests for sexually transmitted diseases and/or rubella (German measles).

> ❖ They apply for and receive a marriage license.

> ❖ They exchange vows in a ceremony at their local church; the *officiant* (the person who officiates at a marriage ceremony) is Pastor Smith, who baptized both of them as babies.

Are John and Mary legally married?

They certainly are! By every standard, they are more than merely married—they are really most sincerely married.

Each year, more than two million couples follow the rules and regulations in their states and walk down the aisle—metaphorically if not literally. Few of these people ever ask why state governments enact laws that seek to regulate marriage.

Here's what the U.S. Supreme Court wrote in 1888, in a decision named *Maynard v. Hill*:

> [Marriage] is an institution, in the maintenance of which in its purity the public is deeply interested, for it is the foundation of the family and of society, without which there would be neither civilization nor progress. Marriage, as creating the most important relation in life, as having more to do with the morals and civilization of a people than any other institution, has always been subject to the control of the legislature. That body prescribes the age at which parties may contract to marry, the procedure or form essential to constitute marriage, the duties and obligations it creates, its effects upon the property rights of both, present and prospective, and the acts which may constitute grounds for its dissolution.

In other words, state governments (actually, governments all over the world) exercise considerable control over many aspects of marriage because of the foundational importance of marriage to society.

Round 2: An Informal Marriage

The game goes on with Len and Lena, two devoted joggers in their late twenties, whose paths cross one day. They fall in love and decide to get married—but feel put off by all the *unnecessary formalities.*

And so, Len and Lena decide to short-circuit the official marriage process. They begin to live together as husband and wife, immediately tell people they are married, and rent an apartment together as a married couple.

Are they legally married?

The answer is *Yes*, in the relatively few remaining states that still recognize common-law marriage (sometimes called an *informal marriage*). Len and Lena are married because

→ both consented to be married;

→ both were of legal age to be married;

→ they lived together as husband and wife;

→ they "held themselves out" to the world as married.

THE INTENSIFYING BATTLE OVER SAME SEX MARRIAGE

Three of the definitions of marriage I presented above presume that the very heart of the concept is a union between one man and one woman. The two more recent definitions I came across don't contain this presumption— a clear tip of the head toward the idea that same-sex marriage has become acceptable to many. Advocates against same-sex marriage warn that it undermines the ancient institution of marriage, while proponents argue that the right to marry whomever one chooses—even a member of the same sex— is a fundamental civil right. This is clearly an aspect of everyday law that is changing, but no one can predict the eventual outcome.

Relatively few states currently allow same-sex marriage, but the number seems to be increasing. On the other hand, the federal Defense of Marriage Act (DOMA), signed into law in 1996, explicitly states that for all aspects of federal law, "'marriage' means only a legal union between one man and one woman as husband and wife, and the word 'spouse' refers only to a person of the opposite sex who is a husband or a wife." The DOMA further eliminates any requirement that sister states must recognize the marriage of a same-sex couple from another state. In short, states are free to recognize or ignore same-sex marriages. Of course, the DOMA could be repealed by Congress as easily as it was passed—and many of the act's detractors are working toward that end.

STATES THAT RECOGNIZE COMMON-LAW MARRIAGES

Alabama, Colorado, Kansas, Rhode Island, South Carolina, Iowa, Montana, Oklahoma, Texas, and the District of Columbia recognize common-law marriages. In addition, Georgia, Idaho, Ohio, Oklahoma, and Pennsylvania recognize common-law marriages that were established before a specific date. For example, the critical date in Pennsylvania is January 1, 2005.

The fourth item is absolutely essential—the key factor that transforms an engaged couple into husband and wife. There's a widely held misconception that a man and woman automatically become common-law spouses by living together as husband and wife for a lengthy period—seven years is an oft-heard number. In fact, cohabitation by itself is not enough to establish a common-law marriage; the couple must behave as if they want the world to view them as married.

Today, Len and Lena could establish their common-law marriage in only nine of America's fifty states. For example, if they did the four things listed above in Colorado, they would be married. But if they did them in, say, California, they would not be considered married.

What If Len and Lena Move?

Let's assume that Len and Lena have established a valid common-law marriage in the state of South Carolina. After a few years of wedded bliss, they decide to relocate to a new home in North Carolina.

Are they legally married?

Once again, the answer is *Yes*.

Even though North Carolina is not among the few common-law-marriage states, the *full faith and credit* provision of the U.S. Constitution requires every state to recognize *most* marriages that are validly established under the laws of another state.

I've stressed "most," because states have long had the power to reject marriages that violate their strongly held public policies—for example, a marriage of a significantly underage person or a marriage between close *blood relatives*. (Some states will permit marriages between first cousins while others refuse to recognize them.)

Len and Lena's common-law marriage in South Carolina circumvented state formalities, most notably the familiar requirement to apply for a marriage license, but in other regards their marriage honored public policy. Thus, it seems appropriate (and logical) for other states to recognize their marriage.

OTHER EXCEPTIONS TO FULL FAITH AND CREDIT RECOGNITION

Some states refuse to recognize a marriage between a couple that travels to another state for the sole purpose of escaping their local marriage regulations. And, many states refuse to recognize the same-sex marriages permitted in some states. These areas of everyday law vary from state to state and are subject to rapid change; check with a local attorney specializing in family law to verify the current regulations in your state.

A Fundamental Freedom

Most engaged couples treat applying for a marriage license as one more minor pothole on the journey to the altar—a less onerous detail than deciding which friends not to invite to the wedding reception. Almost everyone ignores the legal implication behind the word *license*: the state gives you *permission* to get married. The marriage license application procedure is designed to ensure that the state's established regulations on who can and can't get married are enforced.

Some states believe an amorous couple should take the time to ponder the commitments that marriage entails; their application processes include waiting periods.

The application's questions about age verify that the bride and groom meet the state's minimum age requirements. Questions about current domestic status reflect the rule enforced everywhere in the United States that a husband or wife can only have one legal spouse at a time. And, questions (if any) that ask if the applicants are related to each other are related to prohibitions against marrying close blood relatives.

While states do have the power to impose reasonable regulations on how marriages are formed and dissolved, the U.S. Supreme Court has held that the right to marry whomever one chooses is a fundamental freedom that states' can't limit in the absence of a compelling reason. For example, states can prevent bigamous and underage marriage, but have no compelling reason for prohibiting interracial marriages (as some states once did).

Two Closing Questions about Len and Lena

We'll reverse the situation we just looked at. This time, Len and Lena have lived together in North Carolina—seemingly as man and wife. They then decide to move to South Carolina.

Are they legally married?

Not yet! Because Len and Lena didn't form a valid marriage under the laws of North Carolina, they arrived in South Carolina as a cohabiting couple, not as a husband and wife. Living together for years—holding themselves out as married—*didn't* create a common-law marriage in North Carolina.

However, things work differently in South Carolina. If Len and Lena continue to make others believe they want to be (and are) husband and wife, they will likely establish a common-law marriage in South Carolina.

Incidentally, a brief visit to South Carolina probably isn't sufficient to achieve a common-law marriage—although this is a murky area of everyday law.

We've talked a lot about Len and Lena—but before we leave them, let's ask one more question: Who cares whether they are legally married?

At first glance, their precise domestic status seems unimportant—a big to-do about nothing. Well, consider what would happen if Len unexpectedly died. The probate judge—the judge who'll distribute Len's property after his death—would have a tough decision to make: Should the court view Lena as Len's spouse or merely as a good friend? Chapter 19 explains why Lena will care mightily about the choice the judge makes.

Because more and more states want to eliminate this kind of uncertainty, fewer and fewer states permit common-law marriages.

Round 3: Not Quite the Truth

Bill and Sue, both professional storytellers in their early twenties, fall in love at a book festival and agree to marry. They duly apply for a marriage license and are wed a week later in the chapel of The Church of What's Happening Now. The officiant is Pastor Izzy Shady, the church's founding pastor.

After two years of wedded bliss . . .

> → Bill discovers that Sue fibbed on their marriage license application—it seems she'd been previously married and divorced.

> → Sue realizes that Bill also fibbed—he was only seventeen, not twenty-one as he claimed.

> → They both learn that Pastor Shady downloaded his religious credentials from a website on the Internet.

Are they legally married?

Almost certainly. Making false statements on a marriage license application is a crime—in some states, a crime treated as seriously as perjury—but is not in itself a reason for most state family courts to grant an *annulment* (declare that an otherwise valid marriage is null and void).

Of course, had Sue still been married to her first husband when she applied for a marriage license, her subsequent marriage to Bill would have been void from the get-go—and Sue would be guilty of the crime of bigamy. This would be true even if Sue somehow managed to terminate her first marriage by a late-breaking divorce or annulment after her supposed marriage to Bill.

Everyday law works a bit differently for Bill's fib. He was only seventeen when the wedding took place—although their state required both parties to be at least eighteen years old. (This is a common requirement; some states allow sixteen- and seventeen-year-olds to marry with parental permission.) Had Sue brought the fact of Bill's underage to a court's attention when Bill was still seventeen, a judge would have granted an immediate annulment. But Sue discovered the truth two years later, when Bill was nineteen years old. Because the parties continued to live as husband and wife, their *voidable marriage* (*see* Chapter 6) is now considered valid.

Moving on to Reverend Shady . . .

The *officiant* at a marriage ceremony generally has two roles to perform:

1. Administer the marriage oath (whatever its form)

2. Notify the appropriate state record-keeping agency that the marriage was solemnized (often done by signing and returning a portion of the marriage license called the *Certificate of Marriage*)

State law establishes requirements for marriage officiants, but the rules vary enormously from state to state:

In Maryland, for example, "the rites of marriages may be performed by any minister, or official or other member of a religious group so authorized by the rules and customs of the group, or for a fee, by any clerk or designated deputy clerk of the Circuit Court of any county . . . ."

In Kansas, any ordained clergyman of any religious denomination or society may perform marriages. However, ministers are required to file credentials of ordination with the judge of a probate court before performing marriages.

And in Arizona, marriages can be performed by "duly licensed or ordained clergymen—any minister who has been licensed by their church."

These somewhat vague specifications tend to be loosely enforced because state governments are ill-equipped to determine the legitimacy of a particular cler- gyperson within his or her church or denomination. This is true even in states that require clergy to register in advance of the wedding. (Kansas is one.)

Sue and Bill now suspect that Reverend Shady didn't meet their state's statu- tory requirements when he spoke, "I now pronounce you man and wife."

If they're right, Pastor Shady may be liable for a stiff fine—and possibly a stay in prison—but the pair remains genuinely married. The rule in most states is that a marriage is valid even if a person without legal authority performed the ceremony. (Some states also add the requirement that the couple believed that the officiant had legal authority at the time of the wedding.)

Any other approach would place an unfair burden on couples getting married: They would have to validate the credentials of the clergyman or official they choose to perform the ceremony.

THE CONSUMMATION CONUNDRUM

There was a time when a marriage wasn't considered valid until the couple had completed their first act of sexual relations after exchanging wedding vows. Today, most states deem a man and woman to be legally married at the moment the wedding ceremony is complete. However, in many states, an intentional failure to consummate the marriage—or an inability (for example, impotence or physical disability)—will support a request to have the marriage annulled.

Round 4: Married Afar

Carl met Celine in the picturesque Duchy of Grosse Fenwick, a tiny country in Europe that's been described as a fairytale kingdom. Carl proposed after a whirlwind romance. The adventurous couple, both in their thirties, were married in a mountaintop ceremony officiated by a local *Grand Guide*—the Fenwickian term for village mayor—after both Carl and Celine performed the required Engagement Yodel, as specified in the Grosse Fenwick Code of Civil Law.

Curiously, the little nation has never required marriage licenses, although Grand Guides register all marriages in the National Hall of Records. This seems a money-saving aspect of Fenwickian law, because frugal Fenwickians can have as many as ten spouses. Now that the newlyweds are living in the United States, Carl's curious mother wonders:

Are they legally married?

Indeed they are married! Broadly speaking, a *registered* marriage legally performed abroad, which is valid according the laws of a foreign country—and meets all of its formalities—is considered to be valid everywhere in the United States. One important qualification is that the parties would have been able to marry legally in the United States. Consequently, a polygamous Fenwickian marriage by Celine to Carl will not be considered valid in the United States, even though she could legally have two (or more) husbands in the Dutchy of Grosse Fenwick.

Similarly, U.S. states will look to their laws that limit marriages between blood relatives and set minimum marriage ages when evaluating the validity of a Fenwickian marriage.

The marriage formalities in the foreign country don't have to match U.S. state law. The replacement of a marriage license with an engagement yodel won't impact the marriage's validity.

Incidentally, I emphasized the word *registered* above because there will certainly come a time when Carl and Celine will need to provide proof of their marriage—at the very least when one or both applies for Social Security, and possibly also for insurance and employment. A marriage certificate issued by Grosse Fenwick's National Hall of Records will generally be accepted as proof of marriage, although some requesters may want a detailed English translation accompanying the document.

Anyone contemplating a marriage abroad should determine if

> → local law permits a registered marriage by a noncitizen or nonresident;

> → local law limits registered marriages to civil ceremonies (in some countries, a religious wedding is not considered a registrable marriage).

Prenuptial Agreements

A prenuptial agreement—a *prenup* to its friends—is a contract that two engaged persons enter into before they are married. Some people use the label *antenuptial agreement*, others *premarital agreement*. A prenup changes the rules for carving up the *marital property* pie should the marriage fall apart in the future.

Most of us know an unfortunate someone who's gone through a messy divorce. Chances are, the lion's share of the mess involved a battle over money—specifically the *marital property* that the husband and wife acquired during their marriage. We'll dig deeply into the details of marital property in Chapter 6. For now I'll illustrate the concept with a simple hypothetical:

Honey (a traveling salesperson who flies more than one hundred airline round trips per year) and Sonny (a freelance editor who works out of a home office and never travels) decide to divorce. One of the first questions that Honey asks her divorce lawyer is, "Will I get to keep the several million frequent flyer miles I accumulated during our five-year marriage?"

The lawyer thinks a moment, then sighs. "Most of the property acquired by a husband and wife during their marriage is called marital property. Each spouse shares in the ownership of marital property. Our state, like all others, has a *marital property distribution* scheme built into state law that judges apply in the event of divorce. Our specific scheme treats 'your' frequent flyer miles as part of marital property. Consequently, they will be divided between you and Sonny when you divorce."

Honey groans, then says, "That's not fair! I earned those miles in hundreds of different airplanes. My butt sat in those seats, not his."

The lawyer shrugs. "This is one of the ways that our legislature prescribes the duties and obligations marriage creates and its effects upon the property rights of husband and wife." He smiles hesitantly. "I borrowed those words from a U.S. Supreme Court decision written in 1888. As for fairness . . . our state's property distribution laws try to balance the interest of both spouses."

Although Honey is unhappy to learn her miles are marital property, Sonny admits to his attorney that he finds the state's approach eminently reasonable.

Enter the prenuptial agreement!

Had Sonny and Honey created a prenup before their wedding, they could have shaped the distribution of marital property (including her precious frequent flyer miles) in the event of divorce (or death) of either spouse.

In years past, many divorce courts refused to enforce prenuptial agreements, viewing them as attacks on marriage. In the middle of the twentieth century, for example, a judge in Wisconsin wrote, "any contract which provides for, facilitates, or tends to induce a separation or divorce of the parties after marriage, is contrary to public policy and is therefore void." Today, however, properly drafted prenups that meet the key requirements you'll learn about below are enforced across the United States. In many other countries, however—England is one example—divorce courts aren't bound to enforce a prenup but may give it consideration when dividing marital property.

THE CHANGING FACE OF PRENUPS

You're not alone if prenuptial agreement conjures up an image of an octogenarian billionaire with a twenty-year-old starlet on his arm. However, the picture is rapidly changing, and non-wealthy, non-celebrity folks are creating prenups—not to thwart a gold-digging spouse, but to simplify their lives in the event of a divorce. There aren't any solid statistics on the number of prenups created each year, but one oft-repeated estimate projects that about 5 percent of people marrying for the first time have prenups. The estimate jumps to 20 percent for people marrying a second and third time.

Consequently, prenups are becoming increasingly popular—particularly among individuals contemplating a second (or third) marriage—although it's still true that the vast majority of engaged couples wed without a prenuptial agreement. One reason is the cost of preparing an effective prenup (even a simple prenup can involve sixteen hours of two lawyers' time). But even more important is the widely held belief that a contract that looks forward to divorce starts a marriage off on the wrong foot—with a focus on doubt rather than trust, commitment, and love.

I won't take sides in this argument, but I will note a few considerations:

→ Sadly, roughly half of all marriages end in divorce—and many divorces involve bitter fights over marital property.

→ There's no evidence that prenups increase the likelihood of a couple divorcing. (To the contrary, a 2007 study revealed that the exercise of working with attorneys to construct a prenup acts as a kind of premarital counseling that might actually strengthen a marriage.)

→ Another study of recently divorced people who didn't have prenups found that half of them wished they had created a prenuptial agreement.

→ Not having a prenup means that marital property distribution will be solely determined by state laws that themselves "look forward to divorce."

A Prenup in Action

Justin Case and Lou Pole are engaged to be married in four months. Although they are deeply in love, and hope to stay married forever, both have heard horror stories from their divorced friends about "nuclear battles" fought over marital property. Moreover they realize that they are likely to accumulate significant assets in the years ahead, because Justin owns a successful day spa and Lou is a busy dentist.

With the help of two attorneys—one representing Justin, the other Lou—they reach a simple agreement:

Justin Case and Lou Pole, who plan to get married under the laws of the State of Grace, have created this prenuptial agreement because both of them want their present respective business and professional interests to remain the same after their marriage. Now, therefore, they agree as follows:

1. *Case's Rays Day Spa* belongs solely to Justin and shall forever be part of his personal estate. This includes all assets *and all profits which may accrue from the business.* Lou Pole agrees that if the couple separate or divorce in the future, she will not make any kind of claim against *Case's Rays Day Spa* and that Justin will have, at all times, the full right and authority, in all respects (the same as if he had not married Lou Pole), to operate, sell, enjoy, gift, and convey the business.

2. The dental practice owned by Lou Pole, DMD, belongs solely to Lou and shall forever be part of her personal estate. This

includes all assets *and all profits which may accrue from the dental practice.* Justin Case agrees that if the couple separate or divorce in the future, he will not make any kind of claim against Lou Pole's dental practice and that Lou will have, at all times, the full right and authority, in all respects (the same as if she had not married Justin Case), to operate, sell, enjoy, gift, and convey the dental practice.

3. In the event that Justin and Lou separate or divorce in the future, their joint savings account shall be split equally between them. All other marital property after their marriage shall remain subject to division, either by agreement or through judicial determination.

4. In the event that Justin and Lou separate or divorce in the future, they shall have no right against each other by way of claims for alimony, spousal support, or separate maintenance.

LEARN FROM THESE WORDS . . . DON'T COPY THEM

The contract clauses in this chapter are purely educational. Please don't adopt—or adapt—them if you ignore my later advice and try to draft your own prenuptial agreement.

The Divorce Judge Nodded

Alas, Justin and Lou's marriage broke down after ten years. When they were divorced, the judge agreed to honor the property distribution clauses in their prenup. The day spa remained Justin's property, the assets of the dental practice Lou's property. The judge *equitably* divided (*see* Chapter 6) their marital property, including a house, a vacation cottage, and a joint bank account.

Everyone in the courtroom noted the judge's relief. Trying to divide a business or professional practice can require the wisdom of Solomon. Although it's a general principle that property belonging to a man and a woman before they are married does not become part of marital property, this can be a difficult precept to implement. Justin's business probably increased in value during his ten years of marriage to Lou. The increased value is usually treated as marital property. Lou would have been entitled to a portion of it. The same would be true for the increased assets in Lou's dental practice.

Justin's and Lou's prenup would be useful even if they were able to reach their own *property settlement* (*see* Chapter 6) without the "help" of a judge. Because they have already determined a property split that each considers fair, the prenup may well be the template for a property settlement that will satisfy both of the spouses.

But What If It's Unfair Today?

Prenuptial agreements attempt to predict the future—a difficult thing to do well. What would happen to Justin and Lou's prenup if his day spa had gone out of business a year after their wedding? Let's also assume that he spent the next nine years as Lou's office manager—and helped grow her one-chair office into a dental "super practice" with six other offices? Should the divorce court care about these significantly changed circumstances?

Surprisingly to many, the judge will probably enforce the prenup as written—and *not* include the value increase of Lou's dental practice as part of the couple's marital property.

But . . . doesn't it seem unfair to enforce an agreement created a decade earlier that ignored the possibility of changing values? Poor Justin is left out in the cold with nothing to show for his efforts?

Well, no judge will enforce a prenup—or any other contract—that is truly *unconscionable* in the sense that provisions are so onerous that no reasonable person would willingly agree to them (*see* Chapter 2). *But*—and this is a big *but*—most courts will scrutinize the fairness of a prenup at the time the engaged couple made the agreement rather than second-guess its negative impact today.

Ten years ago, it seemed perfectly fair to everyone involved for Justin to keep his spa and for Lou to own the assets in her practice should they divorce in the future. This was what they wanted when they made their agreement; this was what the court gave them when their marriage ended.

The logic behind this is twofold: First, people enter into contracts with the expectation that courts will enforce them. Second, almost every time a prenup is enforced, one the spouses "loses," in the sense that he or she received less property than if the judge had followed the state's marital property distribution scheme. But, the key purpose of a prenup is to override the scheme. That's why it doesn't make sense to use the state's marital property distribution scheme as the yardstick of the agreement's fairness.

If Justin complains, the judge might gently remind him that he and Lou could have amended (revised) their prenuptial agreement during their marriage to recognize their changing circumstances.

Marital Misconduct

Some prenups set conditions for marital property division that change property distributions in the event of marital misconduct. For example, Justin and Lou might have added a clause that split their joint savings account equally between them *unless* one of them had been unfaithful. It that event, the entire savings account would go to the faithful spouse. Here too, courts will enforce provisions that don't lead to grossly unfair distributions.

Note that unless a prenup specifically addresses the issue, marital misconduct will not invalidate the agreement or modify the terms.

POSTNUPTIAL AGREEMENTS

A prenuptial agreement *must* be executed before marriage to be valid, but two spouses can agree to overrule their state's property-division scheme at any time during their marriage by creating a *postnuptial agreement*. Divorce courts treat postnups and prenups pretty much the same. One important difference is that judges look with even sharper eyes for potentially unjust results because of the possibility that the stronger spouse (in most cases a dominant husband) had enough leverage to pressure the weaker spouse into a one-sided agreement.

Despite greater scrutiny, postnups can be useful when one spouse launches a business or professional practice later in the marriage or begins to earn a significantly larger salary.

About That Alimony Clause . . .

There was a time when divorce courts would automatically reject a provision like Clause 4 (*above*), for fear that a waiver of separate maintenance (alimony) in a prenuptial agreement might, as one judge put it, "cast an indigent spouse on public charity."

These days, an increasing number of states allow spouses to waive their rights to separate maintenance after a divorce—although courts look closely at the provisions and refuse to honor them if the outcome seems unjust—for example, the end of a long-term marriage that will leave an unemployed spouse with insufficient income if an alimony waiver is enforced to the letter.

Our judge might well conclude that Justin—who now has significantly lower earnings than Lou—has a right to receive spousal support despite Clause 4.

Did I Mention the Kids?

Justin had been married before he met Lou and fathered a son name Slip. Lou and Justin soon had two children of their own: Chris and Anita. The couple decided to provide for Slip and anticipate additional children in their prenuptial agreement:

5. The stamp collection begun by Justin Case during his childhood shall forever be part of his personal estate. This includes all stamps added during his marriage to Lou Pole and any increase in value of previously purchased stamps. Lou acknowledges that Justin intends, in the event of his death, to bequeath the collection to Slip Case. She further agrees that if the couple separate or divorce in the future, she will not make any kind of claim against the collection.

6. The college savings fund established by Justin Case for Slip Case shall be part of Justin's personal estate until distributed to Slip Case. Lou agrees that if the couple separate or divorce in the future, she will not make any kind of claim against the fund or contributions made during the marriage.

7. The collection of antique fishing gear bequeathed to Justin Case by his father shall forever be part of his personal estate. Lou acknowledges that Justin intends, in the event of his death, to bequeath the collection to Slip Case. She further agrees that if the couple separate or divorce in the future, she will not make any kind of claim against the collection.

8. Justin and Lou agree that if the couple separate or divorce in the future, she will become the primary custodial parent of any children born during the marriage. Justin and Lou further agree that neither will be required to make payments for the support of any children born during the marriage.

The Judge Smiled Three Times . . . Then Frowned

The judge wondered if Lou also has an expensive hobby, but he cheerfully honored Clause 5. Few can blame Justin, a devoted philatelist, for wanting to keep his growing stamp collection intact—no matter what. Perhaps the judge is also a collector.

Slip's college fund won another smile from the judge, because the prenup resolved an increasingly common (and troublesome) property division issue. Ten years of contributions can grow into a sizable marital property asset.

As for the antique fishing gear—well, Clause 7 is an example of prenup overkill. The collection, bequeathed to Justin, is not part of marital property. Lou has no claim on it during or after the marriage.

But Clause 8 took the smile off the judge's face. No court will honor an agreement between parents that seeks to establish child custody in the future or tries to limit child-support payments. Public policy dictates that these things must be determined at the time of a divorce—with each child's best interest uppermost in the judge's mind.

Who Takes Out the Trash?

Justin and Lou reasoned that since they were investing in a prenup they might as well also clarify other details that can cause conflict in a marriage. Although most prenups zero in on money issues and property distribution, in most states an engaged couple is free to contract to "any other matter, including their personal rights and obligations," to use language from Connecticut's prenup law as an example. And so, Justin and Lou add the following clauses to their prenuptial agreement:

9. Justin Case agrees to buy a term life insurance policy with a face value of one million dollars that names Lou Pole as sole beneficiary, and Lou Pole agrees to buy a term life insurance policy with a face value of one million dollars that names Justin Case as sole beneficiary. Both parties agree to keep these policies in effect as long as their marriage continues.

10. Justin and Lou agree to purchase a house (their principle residence) together, each making equal dollar amount contributions to the down payment, mortgage, and upkeep.

11. Justin and Lou agree to file joint income tax returns as long as their marriage continues.

12. Justin and Lou agree to have a single savings account for their joint savings, with each having the right to make deposits and withdrawals.

13. Justin agrees to be responsible for removing trash from the family residence, to not smoke cigars inside the family residence, and to set aside a minimum of twenty-one days each year for vacations with Lou.

14. Lou agrees to be responsible for cooking meals, for caring for any pets she decides to acquire, and for keeping the family residence in a "shipshape condition."

This Time the Judge Winced

The judge had no problems with Clauses 9, 10, 11, and 12. Insurance policies, home ownership, bank accounts, and how taxes will be handled are all standard fare for prenuptial agreements. But the personal responsibility items in Clauses 13 and 14 are problematic. Although they *can* be part of a prenup, they aren't promises that a judge can enforce from a bench. Moreover, their presence in the document adds a note of frivolity that may cause the court to doubt the *gravitas* of the whole prenup. For this reason, most experienced family lawyers suggest that future spouses work out these relationship details between themselves—or if they must transform their mutual promises into a contract, to prepare a separate agreement.

A PRENUP IS A CONTRACT

A prenup, like other contracts, can be enforced in civil court even if a couple does not divorce. Consequently, it would be possible (though not probable) for Justin to file suit against Lou if she suddenly canceled the life insurance policy she agreed to purchase. However, failing to follow key provisions can cast doubt on the intentions of the two parties. In extreme cases, a judge might invalidate the whole prenup.

How to Create a Protest-Proof Prenup

Many celebrity divorces prove the point. Oftentimes, the spouse who comes out second best if a prenup is enforced is likely to claim that the agreement is invalid. Prenups are often challenged because divorce lawyers know that courts aren't shy about throwing away a questionable prenuptial agreement. This, in turn, is because judges know that many prenups aren't the products of arm's-length negotiations between parties who have equal bargaining power. Too often, one party gives in to the other's unfair demands so that the wedding can move ahead.

Consequently, courts watch carefully for signs of overreaching, fraud, and duress. These will get a prenup invalidated at first motion—even if the "signs" signal carelessness rather than bad faith.

The best way to ensure that a prenup will survive an unhappy spouse's protest is to keep every aspect of its creation fair and aboveboard and to meet all of the state's formal requirements for marital agreements.

A No-Fraud Prenup

The quickest way to encourage a judge to invalidate rather than enforce a prenup is for either party to make a false or incomplete financial disclosure when the agreement is being crafted. Hiding bank accounts, "forgetting" to disclose a family heirloom, failing to disclose valuable personal property, or misrepresenting net worth is almost certain to backfire years later in divorce court, when the judge concludes that the prenup is tainted by fraud.

Ensuring and documenting full disclosure is one of the reasons that

→ prenuptial agreements should be drafted by experienced attorneys;

→ both parties should be represented by independent attorneys (simply put, each spouse-to-be should have his or her own lawyer).

A Voluntary Agreement

These are the two common challenges to a prenup: "The legal gobbledygook was so complicated for me that I couldn't understand the agreement," and "I thought the property clause meant something else and that I would get much more if we divorced."

One of the fundamental underpinnings of contract law is that a contract—including a prenup—is a *voluntary* agreement. For this to be true, both parties must know what they're getting into—how the prenup works and what will happen if the terms are enforced.

Once again, the most certain way to ensure complete understanding is to have two independent lawyers who can fully—and separately—explain the implication of the agreement to each spouse-to-be. Also, a prenup should be written in as close to plain English as possible, with a minimum of legalese.

No Duress

Duress means threat or coercion that pressures a person to do something he or she otherwise wouldn't do. Divorce judges often hear things such as "I didn't like the prenup, but everyone pushed me to sign it so that the wedding wouldn't be delayed."

It's wise to complete a prenuptial agreement *at least* a month before a wedding. Given the time it takes to prepare one, you should begin three months in advance—perhaps even earlier if the prenup will significantly limit one spouse's rights under the state's marital property distribution scheme.

And although you're tired of reading it, independent attorneys make a successful duress claim much less likely.

Cross the T's and Dot the I's

Every state requires a prenuptial agreement to be in writing and signed by both future spouses. Some states add the requirement that witnesses be present or that the signing take place before a notary.

Many family lawyers recommend making a video of the actual signing—showing witnesses, notary, and both parties represented by attorneys. A good movie can nip many prenup challenges in the bud.

An Aside: What If the Pair Weren't Married?

What if Justin and Lou had not married but had merely lived together? State-mandated property distribution schemes for married couples—and in a minority of states for *registered domestic partnerships* or civil unions—do not apply to two single people who live together, acquire property as a couple, and then break up.

This can represent a huge "land mine" for two people who are together long enough to acquire significant property—say buy a house together.

When a court is forced to deal with a lawsuit between a formerly cohabiting couple, the judge typically looks for an agreement between the parties that describes who owns the property that each acquired while they lived together. If the two people did not create a formal written agreement (few do), the judge may consider evidence of an *implied contract* based on the pair's behavior and actions. Incidentally, the judge in question is probably not a family court judge; contract disputes are resolved by a court of general jurisdiction (*see* Chapter 1).

An agreement—express or implied—is the central concept of *palimony*, a word used by journalists, not judges. Consequently, a couple that lives together is wise to create an express written contract that sets forth the property rights and obligations of each partner. Much like preparing a prenuptial agreement, both parties should be represented by independent attorneys to avoid future arguments about who pressured who into signing the agreement.

A good agreement will be sufficiently comprehensive to encompass the property-division topics that are covered by marital property distribution statutes:

> → How will income earned and debt acquired during the
>   relationship be shared?

> → Which property will be separately owned and which will be
>   jointly owned?

> → Will jointly owned property be owned in equal shares by both
>   partners, or will one person own a greater percentage?

> → Will the parties use a dispute resolution mechanism such as
>   mediation to resolve property battles?

> → How will big-ticket items be titled? (For example, the deed to
>   a house might record ownership as *joint tenants with rights of
>   survivorship, see* Chapter 9.)

→ Who will keep what in the event the relationship is terminated?

→ Who will pay attorney fees if one party challenges the agreement in court?

"Put it in writing" is equally sound advice when one partner of a living-together couple wants the other to inherit property in the event of his or her death. State *intestate statutes* (*see* Chapter 19) don't recognize an informal domestic partner as the equivalent of a spouse if a person dies without a will.

␥ ⩳ ⩲ ␥

CHAPTER 6

SEPARATION AND DIVORCE

T HE CHANGE CAME SLOWLY AND WITHOUT ANY FANFARE, BUT MOST states now use the term *dissolution of marriage* for what used to be called *divorce*. And so, the official name for the court order that ends the union between two spouses is typically "Decree of Dissolution of Marriage." Of course, the name change hasn't stopped the rest of us—including attorneys—from talking about *divorce*, so I'll stick with the familiar moniker in this chapter.

The first thing you need to know about divorce is that the U.S. Constitution doesn't give a married couple a *right to divorce*. Neither has the U.S. Supreme Court ever found such a right implied as part of our broader rights. Consequently, it's up to individual states to dissolve—or not dissolve—marriages. The consequence is that divorce law varies considerably from state to state. What is universally true across the United States is that it's surprisingly easy to establish a marriage, but much more of a hassle to terminate one:

→ The state government that didn't ask about finances, or property, or even if either party had children before the wedding, now looks exceedingly closely at all of these things when granting a divorce.

→ The state government that didn't require any "how to stay married" training may now require the spouses to take part in counseling designed to save the marriage.

→ The state government that let a couple get married on the day that they met may now insist that they spend a considerable time apart (perhaps a year or two) before allowing a *no-fault* divorce.

→ The state government that never asked the reason a couple wanted to get married (or even fully defined what marriage means) now may invoke a short list of precisely specified reasons for ending their union.

→ Finally, the state government that said "Congratulations!" when two of its residents married abroad during a weekend jaunt may now refuse to recognize a quickie divorce granted by authorities in the same foreign country.

The maxim "easy marriage, hard divorce" was coined in the nineteenth century, when few states required marriage licenses and many made divorce almost impossible. Times have changed, but most couples seeking a divorce find this an annoyingly realistic description of the state of everyday law.

To be fair to state legislatures, the legal complexity of dissolving a marriage is largely a reflection of the fact that a marriage union becomes increasingly complicated as a couple has children, acquires possessions, and faces many different state-imposed obligations. Consequently, it's not that surprising that ending a marriage is a fairly involved process.

Three things happen during a typical divorce proceeding:

1. The couple's money, property, and debt are appropriately divided between the divorcing spouses—and one spouse may be ordered to provide *separate maintenance* (alimony).

2. The custody of the couple's minor children is determined—along with visitation rights and child support.

3. The court issues a "divorce decree" that dissolves the marriage—terminating spousal obligations and allowing the parties to remarry, if they choose to.

The "Are They Still Legally Married" Game

Eddie and Teddie established a valid *common-law marriage* in the State of Confusion—a common-law marriage state—(*see* Chapter 5) by holding themselves out as married to their friends and family, and by buying a house together as husband and wife.

After a decade of slowly decreasing marital bliss, they decided to part. They sold their house, Eddie moved to the State of Regret, and both he and Teddie began to hold themselves out as *unmarried* individuals.

Are Eddie and Teddie still legally married?

Yes! There is no such thing as *common-law divorce*. As the U. S. Supreme Court noted in *Maynard v. Hill*, in 1888:

> The consent of the parties is of course essential to its existence, but when the contract to marry is executed by the marriage, *a relation between the parties is created which they cannot change.*
>
> Other contracts may be modified, restricted, or enlarged, or entirely released upon the consent of the parties. Not so with marriage. The relation once formed, the law steps in and *holds the parties to various obligations and liabilities.*

I highlighted the 19 words in the Supreme Court's observation that are most important when you read this chapter: Unlike other contracts, the parties to a marriage can't change the terms on their own. Moreover, the state imposes obligations on both husband and wife. Here, for example, is a succinct statement from Delaware law: "The duty to support a spouse rests upon the other spouse."

If Eddie and Teddie want to end their marriage they will have to seek either a divorce or an annulment—legal procedures that will dissolve their union or declare it void—but which may impose a new set of ongoing obligations on him or her.

Let's Get an Annulment

Eddie is willing to seek a divorce, but Teddie worries there is still a stigma attached to divorcing—she would rather have their marriage *annulled*. After all, she reasons, they never really exchanged vows in front of a pastor or a state official, so perhaps they qualify for an annulment. They go to an Internet site that offers do-it-yourself annulments, fill out the required legal complaints, and file the paperwork at their local courthouse.

Will they soon be free of each other?

Probably not—although they may give a local judge a chuckle or two.

Annulments are available in all states, although the advent of *no-fault* divorces has dramatically reduced their use. The key to understanding annulment is to zero in on the heart of the word: the three letters *nul*. This comes from the Latin word *nullus* that means "not any"—in short, nothing.

An annulment declares that the union between two people is *nothing*—that it never existed. Over the years, courts have identified two kinds of marriages that can be annulled:

1. *Void marriages*—These are unions that never existed, most often because one party was already married, or is mentally incompetent, or because the two parties are too closely related.

2. *Voidable marriages*—These are unions that a court could declare void but which will remain intact if no one challenges their validity. Most voidable marriages become completely valid as time passes. We looked at one example of a voidable marriage in Chapter 5: A judge will void a marriage where one or the other party is underage—*if* the validity of the marriage is challenged while age is still an issue. But if the parties quietly cohabit until both are older than the legal age to marry, their marriage becomes fully valid. (It is no longer voidable.) Another example of a voidable marriage is a union formed under duress—the classic shotgun wedding. However, if the groom doesn't complain within an allowable period of time (which varies from state to state) the marriage is considered fully valid because he has *ratified* the union.

ARE MARITAL OBLIGATIONS ALSO ANNULLED?

In the event a marriage is annulled, any children of that marriage are considered legitimate offspring, fully entitled to the same rights, protections, and parental financial support they would have received had the couple divorced.

In some states, however, a decree that a marriage never existed also voids any spousal responsibility to provide separate maintenance (alimony)—although most courts can order *temporary alimony* (see below) during the legal proceedings and order that the spouses' marital property be distributed appropriately.

Many states, though, treat all dissolved marriages the same; a judge granting an annulment or a divorce has the same ability to award spousal support.

Teddie had read enough about annulments to realize that their best chance of getting a judge to grant one lay in claiming her marriage to Eddie was based on fraud that goes to the very essence of their marital union. In other words, one of them will have to prove that the other party intentionally concealed or misrepresented a fact that is so *vital to the relationship* that had the deceived party known the truth, he or she would not have consented to the marriage. A few possibilities:

→ One party conceals sterility or other impediment to having children.

→ One party conceals his or her intentions not to have sexual relations after the wedding.

→ One party intends to continue an ongoing sexual relationship with another person after the marriage.

→ One party conceals a record of past felony convictions.

→ One party conceals a serious infectious disease such as HIV.

→ The woman falsely claims she is pregnant or falsely states that she is not pregnant by another man.

Teddie also knew that many deceptions are *not* considered serious enough to justify an annulment on the basis of fraud. Because the law of annulment tries to preserve marriage when possible—few judges are willing to hold that the *very essence of the marital union* is shattered if any one of the following occurred:

> One party concealed his or her nasty temper, alcoholism, or unpleasant medical condition (for example, incontinence)

> One party misrepresented his or her true wealth, occupation, or education

> One party falsely promised to seek a job after the wedding

> One party "changed" after the wedding—becoming less caring, less polite, even cold

> One party concealed an intention to "let him- or herself go" after the wedding and subsequently became less attractive

After a bit of thought, Teddie concludes that she never would have agreed to their common-law marriage had Eddie told her the truth about the large credit card debt he owed. She offers proof of her assertion: an *affidavit* executed by Eddie that admits he didn't disclose his credit card debt to Teddie.

Will her argument convince the judge? I tend to doubt it because Teddie and Eddie seek the annulment of a supposedly voidable common-law marriage that took place in another state. Even if concealing a debt is sufficient fraud, how can the judge be sure that Teddie and Eddie didn't hold themselves out as married *after* she learned about his proclivity for plastic? If so, Teddie can't claim to have been deceived by Eddie before their marriage.

Legal Separation

Teddie has made her peace with getting a divorce, but Eddie insists that they file for a *no-fault divorce* (*see* below) that doesn't assign blame for the break-up to either spouse. In the State of Regret, this requires that the spouses live apart for more than a year. One of the couple's friends suggests that they get a legal separation in the interim—so Eddie researches the possibility.

A legal separation doesn't terminate a marriage. The couple remains legally married—and so neither party can remarry—but the two live apart under the terms of a *decree of legal separation* that outlines the rights and responsibilities of each spouse. Generally speaking, the usual obligations of marriage end, and the parties no longer acquire marital property or take on joint debt. The court creates (or preferably approves) a *separation agreement* that defines how marital property, debts, and tax obligations will be divided—and sets the terms of spousal support (alimony). Some states allow the separation agreement to address child custody, child support, and visitation schedules. Others require a separate *parenting plan agreement*.

Why would a couple choose legal separation rather than divorce? In fact, a few states don't even provide the option. Most states do, however, because of the following:

→ Some couples don't want an *absolute divorce*—sometimes for religious reasons, other times because dissolving their marriage will end spousal health insurance coverage or preclude certain spousal pension or social security benefits that require ten years of marriage.

→ A couple may not meet the strict residency requirements for a divorce, but have resided in the state long enough to qualify for a legal separation.

→ A couple may hope to eventually reconcile—and see legal separation as a way to "cool off" their conflict.

→ Many divorcing couples see a legal separation as an intermediate stopover point on the road to absolute divorce—a way to protect their individual property interests before the marriage is actually dissolved. (A judge is likely to use a separation agreement as the template for final property distribution during a divorce.)

DIVORCE FROM BED AND BOARD

Some states provide for a *divorce from bed and board*, which is really a legal separation on steroids. The parties are economically divorced for the long haul but remain legally married. This locks in the advantages and disadvantages of a legal separation for people who don't want to divorce for religious reasons or have been married for many years and have no intentions to remarry. Some states impose fault requirements (see below) on a divorce from bed and board.

Let's Get a "Quickie Divorce"

When Eddie and Teddie decide that a legal separation isn't for them, the helpful friend offered another suggestion: "You don't have to wait a year for no-fault divorce. You can get a divorce in a few days—and have a great vacation at the same time."

Their friend gave them an illustrated brochure that seems an answer to their prayers. "Why Wait to Get a Divorce?" the headline proclaims. "Come to the Duchy of Grosse Fenwick," the sales pitch goes on, "and solve all your problems in three glorious days of fun and enchantment. Our unique weekend package program includes deluxe rooms for you and your soon-to-be-ex spouse at separate Fenwickian casino resorts, full-day spa treatments, guided tours of our fairy-tale countryside, admission to two dinner shows, and the world's easiest divorce.

"You don't need a lawyer. Our friendly English-speaking judges come to your rooms and deal with the formalities quickly and painlessly. You'll leave Grosse Fenwick with a stunning divorce decree that's suitable for framing—an 11-inch by 14-inch document, hand calligraphed on the finest parchment, embossed with the national seal of Grosse Fenwick to attest its authenticity."

Eddie and Teddie were wise enough to check with Conrad, a lawyer friend, who explained. "A high-speed Grosse Fenwick divorce is granted via a special legal process that is available only to foreigners who enter the country on a tourist visa. Simply put, the Duchy set itself up as an overseas *divorce mill*. The State of Regret (and most other states) decline to recognize the validity of a Fenwickian divorce granted to anyone other than the legal residents of Grosse Fenwick.

"A person has to live in Grosse Fenwick for 90 days—and hold an immigrant visa—to be considered a valid resident. He or she can apply for a no-fault divorce after residing in the Duchy for at least 180 days. The State of Regret will recognize that form of marital dissolution—although we reject the quickie kind."

Teddie jumped in. "But the brochure says . . ."

"That you'll receive a divorce decree . . . and you *will*. Trouble is, it won't be worth the parchment it's written on. The *full faith and credit* provisions in the U.S. Constitution don't apply to divorces granted by Grosse Fenwick, although the State of Regret will usually honor the principle of *comity*. We extend to Grosse Fenwick the courtesy of recognizing their legitimate judicial decrees—and Grosse Fenwick recognizes ours in return. However, we draw the line at money-making schemes."

To be perfectly frank, there are a few states that will recognize quickie divorces from certain overseas countries. A local family lawyer is likely to know which decrees will be recognized and which will not. Keep in mind, though, that a *legal* quickie divorce may dissolve a marriage but will probably leave the complex issues of property distribution, spousal support, child custody, and child support up in the air.

Fault-Based and No-Fault Divorces

When Eddie and Teddie run out of alternatives, they'll need to file for a divorce. With the possible exception of wills, there's no topic of everyday law that receives more attention in books and on websites aimed at non-lawyers This is not surprising given the vast numbers of people at any given moment who are going through a divorce or pondering the possibility. Eddie and Teddie compare notes and verify that *divorce* is the process through which a marriage is dissolved and a new set of legal rights and obligations are determined (regarding marital property, spousal support, child custody, and child support). Every state provides for the divorce of its residents. Some states make the process simple enough to complete without a lawyer, if both parties agree to the divorce (an *uncontested divorce*), there are no property distribution issues, and (usually) there are no children of the marriage who are still minors.

While this is true of some divorces, many dissolutions involve disputes over property, money, and children. Fighting during these more complex divorces seems inevitable, considering that the chronic inability to agree about essential things is a key factor that prompts many couples to dissolve their marriages. For this reason, it usually makes sense—despite the cost—for each party to be represented by an independent lawyer.

Speaking of cost . . . you may have seen the bumper sticker: Marriage is grand, but divorce is a hundred grand. Happily, that's an exaggeration unless one or the other spouse has lots of assets to fight over and the legal battles turn into "family nuclear wars." The best way to control the cost of a divorce is for the parties to work out as many of the issues as possible by themselves.

A Divorce Based on Fault

Not that many decades ago, most states granted divorces only when one of the parties behaved in a way that could be said to have destroyed the marriage. In other words, there was sufficient fault by one spouse to warrant freeing the innocent spouse from the bonds of matrimony. The following were the most common traditional grounds for divorce:

- → Adultery
- → Cruelty (either physical or emotional)
- → Desertion

In some states, the "guilty" spouse was forbidden to marry again—at least in the state that granted the divorce. At the very least, the alleged spousal wrongdoing was revealed in a public proceeding that could easily become a media circus if the parties were well known.

It was never easy to prove fault if the accused spouse decided to contest the divorce or defend him- or herself. However, in most fault-based cases, the allegedly guilty spouse often helped to provide *evidence* of fault, which was fabricated to facilitate the divorce. Sham fault was the easiest way out when two spouses no longer wanted to live together.

The Switch to No-Fault

This was one of the realities that prompted most state legislatures to adopt no-fault divorce procedures. *No-fault divorce* is a generic name given to any marriage dissolution process that allows the court to grant a divorce because the parties no longer want to be married and there's *general incompatibility* or *irreconcilable differences* between the spouses.

Neither spouse is required to prove that the other spouse did something wrong. Some states require little more than mutual legal filings from both spouses agreeing that their marriage has failed and is beyond repair; other states require that the spouses live apart for a statutory period of time—typically from six months to two years. In a few states, living apart is, by itself, a sufficient legal reason (possibly the only legal reason) to justify a no-fault divorce. The period of separation required by law is often less if both spouses agree to the divorce.

If only one party wants a no-fault divorce and leaves the marital residence, there's little the other spouse can do to stop an eventual divorce—although he or she can slow the process down by invoking the full period of separation.

Note that while a no-fault divorce simplifies the process of granting the decree that dissolves the marriage, it doesn't magically distribute marital property, award spousal support, or determine child custody and support. These things often require a hearing or trial to resolve.

COVENANT MARRIAGE

A few states permit *covenant marriage*—a legally different kind of marriage that can't be dissolved by a no-fault divorce (at least in the states that have covenant marriage), have a limited number of grounds for a fault-based divorce, and require premarital counseling before the wedding ceremony. The proponents of two-tiered marriage laws argue that making both marriage and divorce more difficult will reduce the divorce rate. To dissolve a covenant marriage, an injured spouse must typically prove adultery or significant abuse. A divorce will also be granted if one spouse is convicted of a felony punished by a prison sentence. However, states that do not recognize covenant marriages have no obligation to honor these restrictions and will apply their own divorce statutes—including no-fault divorce.

Why Fault-Based Divorce Survives

Some states have retained fault-based grounds for divorce, although few divorcing couples choose this option. It's almost always more expensive, invariably generates more ill will, and usually offers no advantages to an "innocent" spouse. There are two exceptions: The first is divorce in a state that has a long period of separation (although living apart is often simpler and cheaper than proving fault). The second exception is when an innocent spouse wants the judge to take the other spouse's bad behavior into account when determining child custody, property distribution, or alimony. In some, but not all, no-fault states, excluding fault from the divorce also excludes considerations of fault when dividing property and debt, evaluating child custody, and determining spousal support.

What Happens When?

Eddie and Teddy live apart for a full year. The next day, they can take the first steps to dissolve their marriage with an uncontested no-fault divorce.

Divorce proceedings begin when one spouse files a petition for dissolution of marriage (still called a *complaint* in some states) with the division of the state court that handles divorces. This may be the trial court of general jurisdiction (*see* Chapter 1) or a special domestic relations court or family court. In the State of Regret, Teddie's lawyer filed the petition in family court. In legal-speak, Teddie is called the *petitioner*, while Eddie is known as the *respondent*.

The petition names both spouses, states when and where they were married, sets forth why the petitioner is entitled to a divorce (either fault grounds or no-fault grounds allowed by state law), and declares that the required separation period—if any—has been fulfilled. Teddie's lawyer also attached a copy of a *marital settlement agreement* that details the arrangements the couple worked out to divide their property, bank accounts, debt, and tax liabilities—and the solution they propose for separate maintenance (alimony).

Although most states don't require filing an agreement as part of the petition for dissolution, a well-crafted agreement that covers all the bases (it's even possible to propose child custody and support) will probably be approved by the judge—and applauded as a time and work saver for the court. Like a prenuptial agreement (*see* Chapter 5), a marital settlement agreement is best negotiated and written with the help of independent attorneys.

A few states require divorcing spouses who have unresolved disputes to participate in one (sometimes more) mediation sessions. This is a last-ditch effort to get the parties to make decisions between themselves before the court is forced to intervene.

UNCONTESTED VS. CONTESTED DIVORCES

Practically speaking, an *uncontested divorce* doesn't require the two parties to agree up front on every issue—few divorcing spouses do. Rather, it means that they (and their lawyers) have been able to resolve thorny disputes outside of a courtroom—possibly with the help of a mediator—without a judge making decisions for them. When a divorce becomes a contest, cost, stress, and emotional turmoil all skyrocket. Although everyone involved knows this, the dynamics of a divorce often make it impossible for the parties to seek the most sensible solution at the time.

Once the petition is filed, the clerk of court takes over and *serves* Eddie with *divorce papers*—a *summons* or *citation* that informs him that he is now within the jurisdiction of the court for the possible dissolution of his marriage along with a copy of Teddie's petition. *Service of Process* is a formal personal delivery procedure (performed in the State of Regret by a sheriff's deputy, and in other states by a law-firm employee, a licensed process server, or even by certified/registered mail).

This procedure is designed to ensure that the respondent is notified of the petitioner's request to dissolve the marriage and that the court is moving ahead. However, Eddie does not intend to contest the divorce and is fully aware of Teddie's intentions, so he *waives service* to save the cost of formal service of process. Instead, Teddie's lawyer hands Eddie a copy of the summons and the petition.

The ball is now in Eddie's court. He has a statutory period of time—often thirty days—to respond to the petition. Eddie's reply—filed through his lawyer—is an *Affidavit of Consent*. This acknowledges that he has read and understands the complaint, that he agrees with the declarations that Teddie made about their marriage, and that he consents to the divorce.

In the Interim

Although not a problem for Eddie and Teddie, the interval between filing the petition and the entering of the decree of dissolution leaves critical issues up in the air for many divorcing couples. For example: Who has to move out of the marital residence? Who has custody of the minor children? Who can access which bank accounts? Does one spouse need to keep paying for the other's health insurance? Who drives which car? How will a nonworking spouse pay routine living expenses? Who pays for car maintenance? And the monthly mortgage? And for the kids' orthodontic care? Or for visits to the vet for the family dog?

These questions will be answered in the marital settlement agreement that will be approved by the court and incorporated into the divorce decree—but that day of certainty can be months or years away if a judge has to resolve spousal disputes.

MARITAL AND SEPARATE PROPERTY IN THE INTERIM

Even though divorcing spouses are still legally married until the court enters the decree of dissolution, in some states any property acquired by either party after the filing of a divorce petition is considered separate rather than marital property. However, in other states, divorcing spouses acquire marital property up to the moment the judge enters the final decree. This can be a highly confusing aspect of getting a divorce.

Certain aspects of the before-divorce status quo may be preserved by *standing orders* in some states that spring into effect when a divorce petition is filed. These typically prevent either spouse from taking minor children out of the state, selling marital property, borrowing against land, cars, or other items that can be used as collateral for loans, and canceling insurance policies that benefit the other spouse.

In the interim, the court can also issue *temporary orders* that require each spouse to take certain actions, or refrain from taking certain actions. It's common for one spouse to ask for *alimony pendente lite*—spousal support for the duration of the pending litigation. Temporary orders often cover such things as child custody, visitation, and support; payment of specific obligations and debts; payment of attorneys; the possession of different real properties (for example, the primary residence and vacation homes), the use of major items of personal property (such as cars), and the continuing payment of premiums for health and life insurance policies. The court can also prevent one or the other spouse from withdrawing savings from joint bank accounts.

If necessary and appropriate, the court can also issue a temporary restraining order that keeps a possibly aggressive spouse from harassing the other.

Temporary orders are legally binding—and taken seriously by courts. A party who blatantly ignores an interim order will be found in contempt of court. Judges punish contempt with fines and sometimes jail terms.

The End of the Story

Because Eddie and Teddie mutually consented to the dissolution of their marriage—and worked out a marital settlement agreement satisfactory to both parties—their divorce will move ahead more or less "on autopilot." The State of Regret requires a brief hearing before the judge who will issue the decree of dissolution. Only the petitioner has to attend, although it's not uncommon for both spouses to be there. Some states have eliminated the requirement for a formal hearing; courts simply notify the parties when the decree of dissolution has been entered.

When you read about divorce in older books, you'll come across the term *interlocutory decree.* This was an initial divorce decree that would become final after a period of time. The idea was to give the parties an opportunity to reconcile before a divorce became absolute. Although this two-step process has been abolished, many states have a statutory waiting period—a *second* delay that is unrelated to the living-apart period necessary to file for a no-fault divorce.

The second clock begins ticking when the petition is filed (or sometimes when the respondent is served). It counts down the minimum number of days between the initiation of divorce proceedings and the date a divorce may be granted. (The State of Regret mandates 60 days; the periods in other states vary from 20 days to 180 days.) The goal of this cooling-off period is to allow the petitioner to rethink divorce and perhaps cancel the proceedings; in fact, few divorcing spouses use the waiting period to reconcile.

Coming to the end of the statutory waiting period doesn't guarantee that the court will immediately grant an absolute divorce. The family court's workload can add an unpredictable delay—though usually not a long one.

A WAIT TO REMARRY

A few states require divorced persons to wait a period of time before they can remarry (the waiting periods ranges from thirty days to six months). The clock begins to run on the date a judge signs the divorce decree.

I'll See You in Court

All timing bets are off, however, if a divorcing couple can't reach a marital settlement agreement and relies on the court to resolve major property, financial, and child custody disputes. The judge—sitting without a jury—will hear both sides of the case (including any witnesses the parties offer) and then reach a decision that encompasses all open issues.

A true adversarial divorce can easily add a year or two to the proceedings— much of the time consumed in gathering information and preparing for a trial on the issues. Some spouses in adversarial divorces have been known to intentionally cause even more delay by impeding information collection, postponing hearings, and refusing to attend required mediation or parenting classes (required by some states if the couple has minor children). Although a judge can compel compliance, going through the sanction process may pile additional months onto the divorce proceedings.

Moreover, the divorce clock doesn't necessarily stop ticking when the trial judge enters a final decree. Either spouse can file a *motion for relief from the final judgment*—essentially asking the judge to reconsider the decision.

If the motions are denied, the unhappy party can appeal to the state's appellate court. This succeeds fewer than 10 percent of the time with divorce judgments. Appellate courts don't try to evaluate the evidence presented by the spouses; they are chiefly concerned with whether the trial judge applied the state's divorce laws and property distribution scheme (*see* Chapter 5) correctly. Moreover, the appellate court won't change a marital settlement agreement that the trial court approves. The only way to change its terms is to file a *motion to modify* the divorce decree with the trial court (*see* below).

For most divorcing couples, adding a year of courtroom angst is a huge waste of time and money. As a rule, only about 10 percent of all divorce cases actually make it to trial. Because judges push hard to encourage battling spouses to settle their own disputes, it makes sense for both parties to forge an agreement as soon as possible. Why delay the almost inevitable?

Marital Property and Spousal Support

Lester and Hester also live in the State of Regret. He is forty-three, she is thirty-eight. They've been married fifteen years. Lester and Hester have two children Nestor, eleven, and Esther, nine. They own a mortgaged four-bedroom house on Sylvester Street and a three-year-old Golden Retriever named Jester.

Hester earns a good salary as the manager of the local "big-box" store; Lester is a stay-at-home dad. They have a joint checking account, a joint savings account, and six credit cards (all with substantial balances). Hester has a vested pension and 401(k) retirement plan.

The couple owns (more accurately, they and the credit union own) a Volvo sedan and a Chrysler minivan. They are also the landlords of a mortgaged rental property (a condominium apartment) on Fester Lane.

Hester and Lester have just decided to get a divorce. The couple also decided that Hester will file the petition for dissolution.

The Challenge of Dividing Marital Property

When Lester and Hester's case reaches family court, one of the judge's primary responsibilities will be to ensure that each receives an *appropriate* share of their marital property. (The judge will also need to address the custody, visitation, and support of Nestor and Esther, but I'll wait until Chapter 7 to consider the couple's children.)

If Lester and Hester can't reach a marital settlement agreement (*see* above) between themselves, the judge will make an *appropriate* distribution of their marital property—including Jester. I chose the word *appropriate* with care. Most people are aware that two different schemes for marital property division are used in the United States:

1. Arizona, California, Idaho, Louisiana, Nevada, New Mexico, Texas, Washington, and Wisconsin are *community property states* (in Alaska, a married couple can agree to have their property treated as community property). These states follow the simple approach of giving each spouse an equal share of the marital property—a straightforward 50-50 split.

2. The other states (including the State of Regret) apply *equitable property distribution*. Equitable distribution often begins with the equal division of marital property, but then the judge adjusts the final balance after taking the totality of the spouses' circumstances into account.

Over the years, both methods have proved effective at dividing marital property. Before I explain the two schemes in detail, let me answer an obvious question.

What Is Marital Property?

Simply put, marital property is anything that belongs to both husband and wife. Now before you say "Duh!" let me add that although the concept is simple, judges often have to struggle mightily to figure out whether a particular item is marital property or whether it should be treated as *separate property* (nonmarital property).

- → Marital property generally consists of everything earned, acquired, or accumulated during a marriage—no matter which spouse did the earning.
- → The wages earned by either spouse during the marriage are marital property—even if only one spouse had an income.
- → A house bought during the marriage is marital property—even if only one spouse's name is on the deed.
- → Savings accumulated during the marriage are marital property—even if the account is only in one spouse's name.
- → The stamps acquired for a stamp collection during the marriage are marital property—even if only one spouse is a philatelist.
- → Employment-related assets accumulated during the marriage are marital property, including a pension, the growth of a 401(k) investment plan during the marriage, stock options, unused vacation time—and even frequent flyer miles.

What Is Separate Property?

Separate property belongs to a single spouse and will not be divided during a divorce:

- → Property owned by a spouse before the marriage is separate property—if it was kept separate (not *commingled, see* below) during the marriage.
- → Gifts and inheritances a spouse received during the marriage is separate property—if they are not commingled during the marriage.
- → Damages awarded to one spouse following a personal injury suit are treated as separate property—again unless they have been commingled during the marriage.
- → Property defined as belonging to one spouse in a valid prenuptial or postnuptial agreement (*see* Chapter 5).

As you can imagine, the realities of married life make it difficult to determine where separate property ends and marital property begins. To illustrate a common source of property-division friction, imagine that Lester used his separate property (savings he accumulated long before marriage) to make the down payment on the four-bedroom house that he now owns jointly with Hester.

In many situations like this, a divorce judge can identify the equity in the house that is attributed to the down payment and can also apportion some of the appreciation of the house of value to the down payment. If so, it's easy to calculate the separate property that still belongs to Lester.

But, what if Lester and Hester took a large home-equity loan a few years after they were married and used the money to buy a boat? Even if they subsequently repaid the loan, and restored the home's equity, it's no longer possible to identify Lester's original down payment.

This is called *commingling*. Separate property was combined with marital property in a way that makes it impossible to identify one from another.

Another example of commingling: Hester inherits a tidy sum from her great aunt's estate and deposits the money into the joint checking account that receives her paychecks and which she and Lester use to pay routine bills. After a few years of money coming and going, not even Solomon could sort out "her money" from "their money."

In some divorces, spouses fighting over what is and isn't separate property have to hire accountants to track the history of disputed property. This is because most states require the spouse who claims that a specific piece of property is separate to provide clear and convincing evidence that the asset should not be treated as marital property.

Is Lester's stamp collection separate property? Some stamps are, but some aren't. The stamps he owned before he married Hester are separate property; so is any increase in their value during the years that he and Hester were wed. However, the stamps he added to the collection while they were married are marital property.

And what about Lester's old savings account? Again the answer is, it depends!

→ If he maintained it as an individual account in his name, the money deposited in it before the wedding is separate property, although deposits made since the wedding—along with the interest accumulated during their years of marriage—are marital property.

→ But, if Lester transformed the account into a joint savings account after the wedding, everything in it will be considered marital property.

Many of the most difficult issues about separate vs. marital property arise when one of the spouses began a small business before the marriage. If either of the spouses subsequently made an *economic contribution* to the business, the resulting increase in value is marital property. However, if neither of the spouses made such a contribution, the small business remains separate property—along with the *passive* increase in value.

To illustrate the complexities, let's assume that Lester had bought the rental condo as an investment before his marriage to Hester. After the wedding, however, Hester took over the chores of managing the property and finding new tenants. She also worked with Lester to refurbish and repaint the interior. Moreover, the couple used all of the profits to pay down some of the mortgage on the property. And, both enjoyed the benefits of tax deductions related to the property when they filed a joint income tax return.

You get the point! The divorce judge will have a hard time deciding how much of the current value of the condo—if any—remains Lester's separate property.

Let's have one last example. Imagine that Hester received an award of damages following an automobile accident and that she deposited the money in an individual savings account (solely in her name). The portion of the award that made good her pain and suffering is separate property. But, the compensation she received for lost wages and medical expenses will probably be considered marital property.

Community Property Distribution

In a community property state, marital property is divided equally between divorcing spouses—unless the spouses have worked out another arrangement in a prenuptial agreement, postnuptial agreement, or marital settlement agreement. The court doesn't consider such factors as a poorer spouse's financial needs and his or her ability to earn income when dividing marital property during a divorce. (Of course, the judge does consider these things when making decisions about spousal support.)

THE INFLUENCE OF CIVIL LAW

It's not by accident that most community property states are in the southwest. The legal systems in these states were influenced by "civil law" principles institutionalized in France and Spain. The civil law system traces its roots back to Roman law—and is used in many more countries than common law.

"We each get half" or "we each pay half" is the way that people instinctively resolve everyday property disputes. Many divorcing couples who don't live in community property states automatically choose to follow a 50-50 approach when they negotiate their own marital settlement agreements. And many judges in "equitable distribution states" use equal division of marital assets as the starting point of a fair and just distribution.

In most real-world property distributions, it's neither practical nor possible to demand the strictly equal division of every marital asset, because this would require the sale of many assets and the subsequent division of the proceeds. A judge will be reluctant to order the sale of a family home when one of the spouses and the couple's children are living in it. And selling the couple's cars is likely to disrupt both spouses' lives. The same holds true for most of the family-owned items in daily use. Moreover, the forced sales of used personal property will almost certainly yield significantly less money than the replacement costs.

Consequently, community property state judges shape marital property distributions that give each of the divorcing spouses the same total dollar value. This works *if* the various items of marital property (other than money) are accurately valued. And therein lies two potential sources of considerable conflict: Who values marital properties, and how are values estimated? A popular solution is for each party to hire a divorce property appraiser. The spouses typically agree to use the average of the values provided by the two appraisers as the presumed value for each item of significant value.

Of course there's nothing to stop two spouses from establishing their own valuations as part of a marital settlement agreement—and this almost is a practical necessity when dividing the small items of marital property. Another useful technique is *alimony in lieu of property division* (a kind of alimony which has nothing to do with spousal support). One spouse pays monthly payments for an agreed-upon period of time to the other spouse in lieu of his or her 50 percent share of a marital asset. This is often done when dividing family businesses, but it can be used when any marital asset is difficult to split, or when a forced sale to recover the equity is otherwise impractical.

Equitable Property Distribution

Equitable means fair and just—but don't think of the name as a dig at the community property approach. *Equitable distribution* replaced old-fashioned property distribution schemes that traditionally gave marital property to the spouse who paid for it—the spouse who earned the money (most often the husband)—without adequate recognition of the stay-at-home wife's non-monetary contributions to marital property, or that the spouses might face significantly different economic conditions after the divorce.

Many courts, as I said, begin the equitable distribution process by presuming that marital property belongs equally to both spouses. Then, the judge shifts the balance one way or the other in response to a long list of considerations:

- → The age and health of the respective spouses
- → How long they have been married
- → The employability and future earning capacity of both spouses
- → Their relative contributions to the accumulation of marital property
- → The spouses' individual and joint debts
- → Whether one of the spouses has significant obligations arising from a previous marriage (for example, child support and/or alimony)
- → Whether one spouse will receive child custody and child-support payments
- → The value of each party's separate property
- → Whether one spouse "dissipated" marital property during the marriage
- → The pension and retirement rights of each spouse
- → The tax consequences of the property allocations after the divorce
- → Sometimes, whether one spouse's bad behavior caused the divorce

It's actually impossible to come up with a full list of equitable distribution considerations, because in most states, judges have enormous discretion and can consider almost any factor that circumstances require in the search for a fair and just division.

In many cases, *equitable* turns out to be a 50-50 split of marital property—especially for a childless couple, both of whom have good jobs and good long-term economic prospects.

During the seventeenth century, one English law judge complained that "equity varies with the length of the Chancellor's foot." In other words, there's no predictability to equitable decisions—the parties can't be sure in advance what solution a particular dispenser of equity will see as *fair and just.*

The same complaint can be made of many equitable property distributions in modern family courts. There's no telling how a judge will divide marital property—and it's almost impossible for an unhappy spouse to successfully appeal the court's distribution after the fact. This fact of judicial life is one more reason why it makes good sense for divorcing couples to resolve property-division disputes on their own.

Because there's no "formula" the family court judge will apply to Lester and Hester's situation, we can't do more than come up with guesstimates of what a judge might do with some of their marital property, assuming (as we'll "determine" in Chapter 7) that Lester will receive custody of Nestor and Esther:

→ Rather than give Lester the family residence outright (or require a sale so that the equity can be divided), the judge might order that Lester will have *use and occupation* of the house until Esther is eighteen. In the meantime, both Lester and Hester will continue to jointly own the house, but she will be responsible for making mortgage payments. When Esther is no longer a minor, the pair can sell the house and split the equity—say 40 percent to Lester, 60 percent to Hester. (This solution is practical in this case because Hester has a substantial income and neither party needs a share of the equity for routine expenses. Note that some states do not permit a use and occupancy award that lasts longer than three years.)

→ The judge might award the small balance in the checking account and 70 percent of the savings account to Lester, in recognition of Hester's higher future earnings capacity.

→ And, the judge might issue a Qualified Domestic Relations Order (*see* below) that transfers a portion of Hester's vested pension and 401(k) retirement plan.

→ Finally, the judge might transfer ownership of the Volvo sedan to Hester and the Chrysler minivan to Lester—and build the car payments to the credit union into the *temporary alimony* payments that Lester seeks (described below).

The Confusing World of QDROs

A Qualified Domestic Relations Order (QDRO—commonly pronounced *cue-dro* or *quad-roe*) is a legal document that transfers an interest in a *qualified retirement plan* (401(k) or pension plan) to an *alternate payee*—the spouse, former spouse, child, or other dependent of the plan participant.

The family court will issue a QDRO to divide a pension or 401(k) as part of a divorce decree or court-approved property settlement.

Broadly speaking, federal law prevents the assignment to other parties of the benefits owed to a pension plan participant. One important exception is an assignment made by a *domestic relations order* related to "child support, alimony payments, or marital property rights of an alternate payee." Because there are specific legal requirements for a Qualified Domestic Relations Order, they are best left to experienced attorneys.

Division of Marital Debt

In our age of "plastic finance," appropriate division of debt during a divorce can be just as important—and challenging—as the division of property. Most states divide debt the same way they distribute property. Marital debt (debt that benefited both spouses) is

→ divided equally in community property states;

→ apportioned equitably in equitable distribution states.

It's often more practical to assign an entire debt to one of the spouses (so that he or she can keep making payments). In that event, the spouse taking on the full debt will be given additional property as compensation.

Nonmarital debt (typically a debt that one spouse incurred before marriage) usually remains the responsibility of the debtor. A common exception in some states is a student loan. Although one party borrowed the money years earlier, both spouses subsequently benefited from the income made possible by his or her education. Consequently, it's reasonable to treat the loan as marital debt.

Complete Financial Disclosure Is a Must

It's a simple truism that no property distribution scheme can work if one or the other spouse tries to hide assets. The law in all states—community property and equitable distribution—requires both parties to the divorce to make a full and complete financial disclosure to each other to facilitate the court's property division.

If necessary, a judge will compel full disclosure—but the party who forces a judge to take action has made a serious mistake. In most states, a judge can make "reasonable inferences" against the spouse who fails to disclose—don't be surprised if the judge reaches conclusions that strongly favor the other spouse.

Separate Maintenance

It goes by several names—*separate maintenance, spousal support,* and the familiar standby, *alimony*—but most adults understand the idea: The divorcing spouse with more resources (and better economic prospects) pays a *sum certain* (usually on a monthly basis) to the other spouse. A court may order separate maintenance in addition to child support (*see* Chapter 7).

Alimony is not punitive. Different courts explain the purpose of alimony in different ways. These are most common reasons given:

→ To prevent the less affluent spouse from requiring public assistance (welfare)

→ To maintain, as much as possible, the standards of living that both spouses enjoyed while they were married

→ To correct a significant economic imbalance in the earning capacities of the divorced spouses

> ⇥ To give an economically dependent spouse the opportunity to become economically self-sufficient

All of these purposes flow from the universally applied principle that spouses have a responsibility to support each other financially.

Before a court awards alimony, it is supposed to carefully consider one party's financial needs and the other party's ability to pay—although many former spouses paying alimony believe that the judge truly ignored both before awarding separate maintenance. Because of this widespread belief, divorcing clients often arrive at their attorneys' desks fearful of alimony—and ready to fight.

Most calm down a bit when the attorney explains that even *permanent alimony* can be changed after an award, and that court-ordered alimony is usually tax-deductible for the party paying it—making the bottom-line cost of spousal support less than it first seems. In any case, divorce courts will award alimony when necessary to achieve the purposes listed above.

There are four kinds of spousal support:

1. *Alimony pendente lite*—This supports a spouse during the divorce proceedings (also called *temporary alimony*).

2. *Rehabilitative alimony*—This type is awarded for a relatively short period of time (typically three to four years maximum) so that the recipient spouse can get back on his or her feet financially.

3. *Permanent alimony*—This type of spousal support is paid for an indefinite period of time (as long as the recipient spouse requires it).

4. *Reimbursement alimony*—This kind is awarded by some states to compensate one spouse for the *economic sacrifices* he or she made during the marriage to raise the other spouse's earning capacity. In most cases, this means that one spouse supported the other during college, graduate school, law school, or medical school. The court will tailor a reimbursement alimony formula—possibly fixed payments for several years—to repay the working spouse's "investment" in the other spouse.

The Case of Hester and Lester

In our hypothetical example, Lester requests the first three forms of alimony:

1. He asks for temporary alimony during divorce proceedings—enough money to pay usual household expenses.

2. He asks for relatively high rehabilitative alimony for a period of two years so that he can take refresher courses necessary to renew his teaching credentials, so that he can apply for a teaching job.

3. He asks for smaller permanent alimony after that because he doubts that he'll ever be able to earn as much as Hester.

We'll assume that Hester and Lester couldn't agree between themselves about separate maintenance. So the divorce judge will award—or not award spousal support—based on several considerations:

→ The length of their marriage

→ The estimated length of time between the filing of the petition and the entering of a final divorce decree

→ Hester's and Lester's ages

→ Their education

→ The contributions each made to the well-being of the family

→ The standard of living that both *became accustomed to* while married

→ Their current salaries

→ Income, if any, from separately owned property

→ Their employability—and their comparative abilities to be self-supporting

→ Their health

→ The long-term disparity between their future financial prospects (in some states, if one spouse will have three or four times the income of the other, the difference is seen to warrant spousal support)

→ The fact that Lester stayed out of the workplace to care for the couple's children

→ Hester's and Lester's respective fault in causing the marriage to fail

→ The likelihood that one of the other will be ordered to pay child support

Although some courts try to ensure that both spouses are able to maintain their standard of living after the final divorce decree, this is usually possible only when one spouse is wealthy. Most divorces *lower* both parties' standards of living—typically for several years, potentially even longer.

While it's impossible to foresee what family court in the State of Regret will do, I suspect that the judge will award Lester temporary alimony and rehabilitative alimony. The judge may also award a modest amount of permanent alimony—confident that Hester will ask for a modification (*see* below) once Lester is established in a good paying job.

In years past, the spouse who paid spousal support was almost always the husband. That has changed. Today, courts look at the financial resources of both spouses. Consequently, many more women pay alimony, and male recipients don't feel the "recipient stigma" that once existed.

The End of the Obligation

An obligation to pay permanent alimony typically ends when

→ the paying spouse retires;

→ the receiving spouse enjoys a significant increase in his or her income;

→ the receiving spouse remarries or begins to live with another person in a marriage-like relationship.

In many states, the death of the paying spouse ends spousal support; in other states, alimony becomes an obligation of the paying spouse's estate. Many divorce settlements call for the paying spouse to also pay for a life insurance policy on his or her life—a policy typically owned by the receiving spouse, who is also the beneficiary.

Courts use their contempt powers to enforce the payment of spousal support. A spouse who fails to bring delinquent alimony up to date can be fined or even jailed. All states have passed some form of the *Uniform Reciprocal Enforcement of Support Act*, which makes it relatively easy to enforce support orders if the paying spouse moves to another state.

A Property Settlement in Lieu of Alimony

I described *alimony in lieu of property division* above. It's also possible to have a *property settlement in lieu of alimony*. For example, Lester might be awarded the entire income of the rental property—and full ownership—as a fraction of the spousal support provided by Hester. Most courts will also approve agreements wherein the parties agree to a lump-sum alimony settlement rather than periodic payments.

Modifying Property Division and Separate Maintenance

Times change—and so do former spouses' financial circumstances and ability to pay alimony. If Lester finds that he needs more support or Hester's bright financial picture darkens, either party can request the family court to change the spousal support order. (Child custody, visitation, and support orders can also be modified, when necessary—*see* Chapter 7.) In theory, divorced spouses can also request a change to the way marital property was divided. In practice, courts rarely modify property distribution decrees—and almost never redo the distribution established by both parties in a marital settlement agreement. By contrast, courts often reexamine separate maintenance.

The first step is for Hester or Lester to file a *motion to modify* the divorce decree. Either party can ask for a *permanent modification* (perhaps Lester's developed a chronic medical condition that makes it impossible for him to take a full-time job) or a *temporary modification* (maybe Hester was laid off and is searching for a new job).

In the event of changed circumstances, the parties can agree between themselves to modify spousal support. At this point, they must file a motion to modify that includes a *stipulation* of the revised agreement. The court can then modify the original decree to reflect the new agreement.

There's a common misconception that a revised support agreement becomes enforceable if the two former spouses sign it in front of a notary. In fact, a judge must incorporate the changes into a modified decree. This requires a trip back to family court via a motion to modify.

Another point worth mentioning: Courts have the power to modify spousal support if the recipient spouse discovers after the fact that the wealthier spouse didn't fully disclose his or her financial circumstances during the divorce. As with other requested changes, the adjudication process begins when the unhappy spouse files a motion to modify.

CHAPTER 7

ADOPTION, CHILD CUSTODY, AND CHILD SUPPORT

A LTHOUGH THIS CHAPTER BEGINS WITH A HAPPY TOPIC (ADOPTION), THE subjects that follow represent two of the most challenging and painful areas of everyday law: child custody and child support. (The chapter ends with a brief discussion of juvenile justice.) Dealing with custody and support issues can involve enormous stress and mental anguish—and significant legal expenses. You'll watch them develop in the ordinary lives of two people—Jack and Jill—a couple who ran into all-too-common marital problems.

One of the serious mistakes they made during their divorce proceedings was to take revenge via their children. Using child custody and child-support processes to punish a former spouse multiplies the inherent pain and confusion, making a bad situation even worse—and increasing the burden on the children. As is often said, no one wins that game—not even the lawyers.

The law relating to child custody and support is highly complex. Moreover, judges make decisions that impact lives and bank accounts for decades. This is one corner of everyday law where you definitely need the counsel of an experienced attorney to guide you through the legal minefields and protect your rights.

Jack and Jill Adopt a Child

Jill Stem met Jack Christie while skiing on a hill. The pair fell head-over-heels in love (both figuratively and literally) and married days later. The Stem-Christies settled in the State of Confusion and bought a house in Muddy City. Several years later—after their own attempts to have children didn't work—the couple decided to adopt a child.

Jack and Jill began by finding Paula, an attorney who specializes in family law. State law and regulations govern the adoption process in every state. The laws vary, are often complex, and can be unforgiving if parties make procedural mistakes. Many friends had cautioned Jack and Jill that an experienced attorney can help smooth the process.

Paula explained that most adoptions in the State of Confusion are arranged by adoption agencies licensed by the state. "However," she added, "an increasing number are private or independent adoptions arranged by attorneys and physicians.

It's not unusual in a private adoption for the birth mother to take an active role in selecting the adoptive parents and to require, for example, that the child be raised in a certain religion. The adoptive parents often pay the birth mother's medical expenses, her living expenses during pregnancy, and all legal fees—but state law prohibits any other payments (that might imply the baby is being 'bought' by the adoptive parents).

"We also have *adoption facilitators*—some are individuals, some are organizations—who locate adoptable children for adoptive parents, but are not empowered to 'place' them, as an adoption agency can. Adoption facilitators can't charge fees in this state, but they can in some other states.

"A fourth, increasingly popular, option is international adoption. Adoptive parents adopt a child of foreign nationality—in a foreign court—following the laws and legal procedures of the foreign country.

"Adoption is not inexpensive. Costs vary enormously, beginning at a few thousand dollars and ranging beyond $50,000 for some international adoptions [*see* below] which require international travel. However, the federal Adoption Tax Credit can take a big bite out of adoption costs, and many large corporations provide adoption benefits to employees, which may include adoption cost reimbursement. The fees published by many adoption agencies are designed to recover their costs; many agencies scale their actual fees to the family incomes of adoptive parents. Additionally, grants and low-interest adoption loans are offered by certain adoption agencies and organizations."

Adoption Creates a New Parent/Child Relationship

The adoption process creates a new parent/child relationship that transforms an adopted child into the legal equivalent of a natural offspring. Some courts say "as if born to" to describe the relationship after adoption, for these reasons:

→ The adoptive parents gain full parental rights ("the fundamental liberty interest of natural parents in the care, custody, and management of their children," to quote the U.S. Supreme Court).

→ The adoptive parents have all of the responsibilities they would if they were the child's biological parents—including the duties to nurture and provide financial support.

→ The legal relationship between the child and its biological parents is severed, terminating their responsibilities, their parental rights, and all rights of custody and visitation (*see* below).

→ The adopted child gains the same rights of inheritance as the adoptive parents' natural children and typically loses the right to inherit from a biological parent who dies without a will (*see* Chapter 19).

"This is a significant shift from the way things were before the adoption," Paula went on, "especially the severing of an existing parent/child relationship—and so legislatures created a slow-moving process that protects the rights of the biological parents and ensures that the new relationship is in the best interest of the child."

Who Can Adopt?

"In the State of Confusion," the lawyer continued, "we have no specific requirements for adoptive parents other than that they be 'fit parents' at least twenty-one years old and capable of providing a loving, safe, and permanent home. However, different adoption agencies and facilitators may have definite destination preferences for the children they have available for adoption. (If agencies don't, biological parents often specify distinct wants.) Whatever the driving force, preferential treatment may be given to the following people:

→ Married parents (compared to single people or unmarried couples)

→ Childless couples (compared to people parenting other children)

→ Parents without serious disabilities

→ Couples without prior divorces

→ Adoptive parents younger than forty

→ Heterosexual adoptive parents

→ Adoptive parents of the same race (and possibly religion) as an available child

"These preferences—biases, if you prefer—are often revealed in questions designed to test the prospective adoptive parents' fitness. A single person, for example, may be asked this:

→ Why he or she hasn't married

→ To describe his or her strategy for simultaneously supporting and caring for a child

→ What will happen to the child should he or she marry in the future

→ Whether he or she has considered the impact of a child on a single person's social life

"The bottom line: Although times are changing, *traditional adoptive couples* still find it easier and quicker to adopt a child. Nontraditional adoptive parents can often move to the top of the waiting list by agreeing to adopt a *special needs* child (an older child, part of a sibling group, or one who has physical, mental, emotional, or learning disabilities)."

The Adoption Process

"Once a 'match-up' is made by an adoption agency, attorney, or physician," Paula, the Stem-Christie's family lawyer, explained, "or with the assistance of anadoption facilitator, adoption becomes a legal process in the appropriate state court. Depending on the state, this may be family court, a designated juvenile court, the probate court that handles wills and estates, the domestic relations court, the surrogate court; or a court of general jurisdiction: superior court or district court. In the State of Confusion, *orders of adoption* are entered by family court judges.

ADOPTING AN ADULT

Most states allow one adult to adopt another adult—when the adoptee consents (many states also required the consent of the petitioner's spouse; some require notification of the adoptee's natural parents). Why would anyone adopt an adult? There are three common reasons. First, it gives the adoptee automatic inheritance rights. Second, it makes the adoptee eligible under the petitioner's insurance and benefit programs. Third, some children become stepchildren after age eighteen (when their parents remarry) ; a petitioner may want to adopt all of his or her stepchildren—young or adult.

"The process begins when I draft and file a *petition for adoption* with family court. Because you're married, state law requires that we file a joint petition. (Some adoption agencies that handle all aspects of adoption will file the petition.) A typical petition for adoption in this state does the following:

- ⇥ Identifies the adoptive parents and the child to be adopted
- ⇥ Specifies the relationship, if any, between the adoptive parents and the child (for example, a stepparent adopting a stepchild)
- ⇥ Explains why the biological parents' parental rights can be terminated as part of the adoption process. In most adoptions, the reason stated is that the birth parents "gave the child up for adoption" and consented to the termination of their rights; in a few adoptions, the court is asked to order involuntary termination of the biological parents' parental rights. (Common justifications for involuntary termination are abandonment, failure to support the

child, or a finding of parental unfitness based on abuse
or neglect.)

↣ Asserts that the adoptive parents are fit parents who have the
resources to care for the child

↣ Asserts that the adoption will be in the best interest of the
child (not every state includes this in its petition, although the
requirement is always uppermost in a judge's mind)

↣ Requests the judge to order that the child's name be changed

"The judge will hold a hearing at which he or she will terminate the natural
parents' parental rights, approve (or, if the adoptive parents make a poor showing,
deny) the petition for adoption, and change the child's name."

"Home Study"

"You may see it called a *home study*, a *preplacement assessment*, or a *family assessment*," Paula said. "It's a detailed investigation—performed (at your expense) by
social workers employed by a licensed adoption agency—that evaluates all the
aspects of your fitness as adoptive parents. The home study generates a compendium of information that will be used by adoption agencies, government officials, and ultimately the judge when he or she determines whether or not to allow
you to adopt a child. Here's what the typical home study includes:

↣ Interviews with all of your household members

↣ Review of your home environment

↣ Confirmation of your physical and mental health, age, marital
status, income, employment, and financial obligations

↣ Confirmation of an adopted child's coverages under employment
benefit programs and other insurance programs

↣ Summaries of comments made by personal references

↣ Review of any court orders, judgments, or pending legal proceedings
that might be relevant to the welfare of an adopted child

↣ Criminal and abuse history record checks

↣ Documentation of other facts or circumstances that raise concerns
about the fitness of the adoptive parents

"The home-study report prepared by the adoption agency typically includes a
finding by the agency about the fitness of the adoptive parents and the suitability
of their home—in short, a recommendation (positive or negative) to the judge who
makes the final decision. Most courts also want to know the fees that the adoptive
parents will pay to agencies and other parties during the course of the process.

OPEN AND CLOSED ADOPTIONS

Some states permit two kinds of adoptions: open and closed adoptions. An *open adoption* enables the birth mother to approve her child's adoptive parents and remain involved, to some extent, in the child's upbringing. This definition is intentionally vague because there are as many variations on the theme as there are open adoptions. The chief common denominator is that an adopted child can maintain some kind of relationship with its birth mother (and possibly its birth siblings) despite a full parental relationship with adoptive parents. The nature and degree of the extra relationship invariably depends on the people involved—and may or may not "work." A *closed adoption*—the traditional kind—empowers an adoption agency to conduct the selection process, results in the birth mother relinquishing all rights over the child, and typically forecloses future contact.

"The agency preparing the home study will need access to many of your most personal files, documents, and papers. Many agencies will also ask you to write a brief autobiography—often based on a set of 'leading' questions. All of this seems highly invasive to many adoptive parents, but it's the way adoptions are done throughout the United States. It's wise to ask the agency if anyone other than the judge will see the information (and why). In some circumstances, birth parents may be shown portions of the home study.

ADOPTING A STEPCHILD

Some states don't require—or allow a judge to waive—a home study when a stepparent adopts a stepchild with the consent of the absent biological parent and the custodial natural parent who is married to the petitioner. This is one aspect of the somewhat streamlined stepchild adoption process found in many states.

"The process of completing a home study typically takes two to six months from start to finish," Paula said. "Many of my clients begin the study long before being matched to a child; I recommend that you commission a study immediately. That will allow your home study to wear 'two hats.' You'll be able to submit the study to adoption agencies to help them determine the best child for their circumstances. A home study has a typical 'shelf life' of about eighteen months; after that, it has to be brought up to date to verify that the information is still current."

Consent to Adopt

Although the lion's share of adoptions are unchallenged, contested adoptions are often opposed on the basis of lack of consent to the adoption by the child's biological parents.

"Written consent by the birth parents is irrevocable in a few states," Paula said. "In others—the State of Confusion is one—birth parents have the right to withdraw consent to the adoption for any reason for a brief period of time (typically ten to thirty days). The 'change of mind' period lengthens if consent was obtained fraudulently, through duress, or if maintaining the natural parental relationship is in the best interests of the child. In almost all states, consent becomes irrevocable once the court terminates the original parental relationship, typically at the adoption hearing.

"More than a few lack-of-consent battles have been triggered when birth fathers discovered that their children were given up for adoption by the birth mothers acting on their own. (Some of these mothers claimed that they didn't know the fathers' identities, others that the fathers didn't care about the children.) Consequently, it's essential to identify the adoptee's biological father and obtain his valid consent.

"In many states, biological parents must receive form notice of the adoption hearing (they may be allowed to waive notice in the written consent). Some courts have the statutory power to insist that at least one birth parent appear and testify that the written consent was voluntarily executed. This is often the case when a stepparent seeks to adopt a stepchild. Consent can become a sticky issue in stepchild adoptions, because severing the former spouse's parental relationship also breaks the legal ties between the child and other family members—former grandparents, aunts, uncles, and cousins.

"Finally, if you decide to adopt an older child, you would also need his or her consent to be adopted. That's true almost everywhere, although the minimum age at which consent is required varies from state to state: fourteen years old in many, twelve years old in a few. The judge will ask for the child's consent at the adoption hearing."

Custody Pending Adoption

"In most states," Paula explained, "courts can authorize the *temporary place-ment* of a child in the petitioners' home pending the completion of the adoption process. In fact, many states require a period of residence in the adoptive home—a sort of *trial adoption*—before the final decree of adoption is entered. State laws often mandate that the home study be completed before a judge grants custody pending adoption.

"In this state—and in others—there are two kinds of temporary placements:

1. In a direct adoption, the petitioners can be granted true custody of the adoptee—they acquire the right to legal and continuing physical custody of the adoptee and become fully responsible for the care and support of the adoptee.

2. In an agency-managed adoption, the agency may allow the petitioners to receive the adoptee into their home. The agency continues to have legal custody and control of the child and remains responsible for care, maintenance, and support. However, the agency delegates some of its authority and responsibilities to the adoptive parents.

"Unhappily, custody before adoption can become a time of stress and anxiety for adoptive parents. On the one hand, they bond with their soon-to-be-adopted child; on the other hand, they worry that the adoption process is not finalized and might fall apart for many different reasons (for example, last-minute revocation of consent by one or the other birth parent).

The Adoption Hearing

"An adoption hearing is a civil proceeding," Paula said. "The petitioners and the child usually must appear at the hearing, which is typically confidential and held in the judge's chambers, rather than an open courtroom.

"The petitioners must show that that adoption is in the child's best interests. Their *burden of proof* [*see* Chapter 1] is by a preponderance of the evidence (the 'scales of justice' tip a smidgen to the petitioner's side). A petitioner who seeks to terminate a biological parent's parental rights without his or her consent [*see* below]—as can happen when a stepparent fights for the right to adopt a stepchild—must prove by *clear and convincing evidence* (a much tougher burden of proof) that the termination is in the child's best interest.

"Few adoption hearings turn out to be unpleasant events for participants. Most tend to be brief, simple, and upbeat. The judge grants the petitions, issues a decree of adoption that finalizes the new parent/child relationship, and signs a second order that changes the child's name. I predict that your hearing will be a piece of cake. We'll follow the petition process carefully, ensure there'll be no objections to the adoption, and let the mountain of favorable information about you in your home study make the case for you."

OPENING ADOPTION RECORDS

Should an adopted child have access to his or her adoption records—including the identity of his or her biological parents? Most states still honor the traditional notion that adoption records are permanently *sealed* and that the relationship between child and biological parent is forever severed. It generally takes a court order to pierce the veil of secrecy. However, many states allow an adopted child to get *nonidentifying information* about birth parents—such details as general appearance, ethnicity, religion, race, education, and occupation, along with the name of the agency that arranged the adoption, and information about the nature and cause of the adoption. Other states operate *registries* (that allow an adopted child and his or her birth parents to express a mutual desire to establish contact) or have a *confidential intermediary* program (an independent third party who tries to locate a birth parent at the request of an adopted child, then informs the person that the child wants to make contact). Neither a registry nor an intermediary program guarantees that a birth parent will be willing to establish contact with a child given up for adoption.

A Change of Geography

Six months later, Jack and Jill were back in their attorney's office. "Paula—we talked to several domestic adoption agencies," Jill explained, "and they all had long waiting lists. So we'd like to consider an international adoption."

Paula nodded. "There are many reasons to choose an *intercountry adoption*, to use the increasingly popular name, but here are the big three:

1. *Speed*—Adoptable children are available *now*.
2. *Certainty*—There's no likelihood of the adoption ever being challenged.
3. *Compassion*—There are children in need of parents across the world.

"Intercountry adoptions changed dramatically on April 1, 2008—the date when the United States became a full participant of the Hague Convention on

Intercountry Adoption. The Intercountry Adoption Act (IAA) is federal law that implements the provisions of the Hague Convention in the United States.

"The Convention itself is an international agreement among more than seventy-five participating countries (including Brazil, Bulgaria, Chile, China, Ecuador, Mexico, Panama, Paraguay, Peru, Romania, Russian Federation, Slovakia, South Africa, Sri Lanka, and Turkey) that establishes international standards for intercountry adoption and

> → formally recognizes intercountry adoption as a means of providing a permanent home to a child when a suitable family has not been found in the child's country of origin (the Convention requires that *proper effort* be given to arranging a local adoption);
>
> → ensures that the best interests of children are considered with each intercountry adoption;
>
> → works to prevent the abduction, exploitation, sale, or trafficking of children;
>
> → implements *best practices* for processing intercountry adoptions;
>
> → ensures that adoptions under the Convention will generally be recognized and given effect in other Convention countries.

"Although you still can adopt children from a non-participating country—Haiti, for example—the process carries more risk, involves more red tape, and requires slightly different procedures and requirements.

"The Hague Convention requires signatory nations to establish a *Central Authority*—the authoritative source of information and the chief point of contact in that country. The U.S. Department of State is our Central Authority. The Department of State is responsible for ensuring that the requirements of the Convention and the IAA are followed. You can find current information by visiting: http://adoption.state.gov.

"For example, the department maintains the list of *accredited* adoption agencies that are allowed to manage Hague Convention adoptions. You must have a home study [*see* above] performed by either an accredited agency or a *supervised provider* working under an accredited agency. The agency you choose must also be licensed by the state.

"Although Russia is on the Hague Convention list, the Convention doesn't yet control adoptions of Russian children. Russia has established its own list of U.S. adoption agencies that have a *Russian Permit for Adoption Activity*. These agencies are supervised by Russian authorities and are allowed to arrange adoptions in Russia. Many large U.S.-based adoption agencies are Hague Convention accredited *and* have a Russian Permit. The important thing to keep in mind is that these are two separate permissions to arrange adoptions and are not interchangeable.

"A Hague Convention accredited adoption agency performs six functions:

1. Identifies a child for adoption in a foreign country and arranges for an adoption.

2. Secures the consent to terminate parental rights.

3. Performs a home study [*see* above] on prospective adoptive parents and obtains a background report on the child.

4. Determines the child's best interests and whether adoptive placement is appropriate.

5. Monitors the case after a child has been placed until the adoption is final. (This may be only a few weeks for a typical adoption in a foreign country.)

6. Assumes custody of a child (provides childcare and any required services) in the event the process is disrupted."

Adoptions vs. Legal Guardianship

"The laws of adoption vary widely overseas as they do in the United States," Paula said. "Some Convention countries allow full and final adoptions in their courts, but others grant legal guardianship of a child to adoptive parents—and permit the child to travel to the United States. In that event, the child's adoption is finalized under the laws of the adopting parents' state of residence."

Hague Convention Home Study

Paula went on, "The first significant chore you'll undertake under the Hague Convention process is to ask the U.S. Citizenship and Immigration Services (USCIS) to declare you eligible to adopt a child under the Hague Convention. You will complete Form I-800A (Application for Determination of Suitability to Adopt a Child from a Convention Country), a fairly detailed—though not hard to understand—application, and submit it along with the completed home study.

"Keep in mind that your home study must meet a host of requirements and be acceptable to the State of Confusion, the USCIS, and foreign officials. Accordingly, a knowledgeable agency or provider—one with experience with the country of your choice—is essential (accredited agencies often specialize in a few countries). You'll each also need ten hours of parenting education and an FBI fingerprint-based clearance against criminal and child-abuse registries, along with a state criminal records check. The documentation and clearances will be sent—typically by your agency—to the Central Authority in the Hague Convention country you've chosen."

Your Country of Choice Takes Over

"The next steps happen in the Convention country where you plan to adopt. Local officials will review your I-800A and home study report and—unless something negative slipped past State Department scrutiny (unlikely!)—will accept you as a prospective adoptive parent.

"The country then matches you with an appropriate child and forwards a report on the child's medical and social history—called an *Article 16 Report*—to your adoption agency. You'll have at least two weeks to accept the match. Should you reject the match, the country will try to identify another suitable child."

The Critical, Essential *Article 5 Letter*

"The Department of State emphatically warns adoptive parents," Paula went on, "*to not* short-circuit the next steps. Although people want to rush overseas to take legal custody—or even adopt—the matched child they've accepted, you must first do this:

→ File Form I-800 with USCIS. This is the Petition to Classify Convention Adoptee as an Immediate Relative. USCIS reviews the I-800 and the Article 16 Report to make certain that the child qualifies as a Hague Convention adoptee. Minor ineligibilities can be resolved by requesting a waiver.

→ Submit an 'Immigrant Visa Application' (Form DS-230) to the U.S. Embassy or Consulate in the Convention country along with the child's birth certificate and three full frontal photographs (these will be provided by your adoption agency). A consular officer will review the application and verify that the child qualifies for the visa.

"The idea of course is to cross the t's and dot the i's of visa formalities *before* the child is adopted—and uncover any unresolvable issues that could bar a child from emigrating to the United States. The consular officer is required to reject the I-800 petition if the petitioner completed the adoption of the child, or acquired legal custody of the child for purposes of emigration and adoption, before the provisional approval of the Form I-800. At that point, the adoption or legal custody must be vacated, voided, or annulled, so that the process can begin again and follow the prescribed order.

"When the consular officer determines that the matched adoptee qualifies for an immigrant visa, he or she will notify the Convention country's Central Authority. This notice is called an *Article 5 Letter* that formally notifies the Convention country that you are suitable adoptive parents and that the child you selected will be able to enter and reside permanently in the United States. You'll be notified that the letter has been sent."

Proceed with Adoption or Legal Custody

Paula leaned back in her chair. "Your long journey is nearly over. You can now adopt or take legal custody of the child according to the laws of the Convention country. Local authorities will issue an *Article 23 Certificate*—typically an adoption or custody decree that also certifies that the adoption or grant of custody complies with the Hague Convention."

Final Visa Interview

"The last overseas formality is an interview at a U.S. Embassy or Consulate. The child must appear before the consular officer and possess a birth certificate and passport. The officer will issue either an

- → IH-3 visa to a child who was adopted (this automatically gives U.S. citizenship to any adopted child under the age of eighteen as soon as they enter the United States);
- → IH-4 visa to a child who will be adopted later in the United States (this visa doesn't grant immediate U.S. citizenship; the parents must complete another application and pay an additional fee)."

Re-adoption

"It may seem strange," Paula said, "but after completing an intercountry adoption, it makes good sense to *re-adopt* the child according to your state law. Here are the three most important reasons:

1. Re-adoption gives the child a domestic birth certificate (in English)—that will simplify all of the many activities that demand a birth certificate, from getting a driver's license to applying for social security benefits.
2. The child's name can be legally changed during the re-adoption process.
3. Every state must recognize a domestic adoption, but not all honor foreign adoption decrees.

"The complexity of the re-adoption procedure varies from state to state. Here in the State of Confusion, re-adoption involves the same procedure as an ordinary adoption—with one important difference: The foreign adoption decree proves that the birth parents have consented to the adoption."

Post-placement Reports

"Certain Hague Convention countries," Paula said, "require *post-placement* status reports about the adopted child's health, development, and adjustment to life in a new country. (Similarly, many domestic adoption agencies require post-placement counseling for the new family and reserve the right to observe the child's acclimation to the new home.)

"The Department of State (DoS) points out that the reports provide assurance to political leaders and adoption officials in Convention countries that children they place in the United States are receiving appropriate care and protection. As a result, the DoS encourages adoptive parents to comply with post-adoption reporting requirements and warns that a failure to provide post-adoption reports could put intercountry adoption programs at risk."

Non–Hague Convention Intercountry Adoptions

The process for adopting a child from a non–Hague Convention country is similar in most respects, with two key exceptions:

1. The child must be classified as an *orphan,* according to the detailed definition in the U.S. Immigration and Nationality Act. (The fact that the child is an *orphan* according to the laws of his or her country is not sufficient.)

2. The adoptive couple *does* legally adopt the child or gain legal custody in the foreign country *before* applying for the child's immigrant visa.

These differences raise the frightening possibility that a newly adopted child might not be allowed to enter the United States. For this reason it's imperative to arrange a non–Hague Convention adoption through a reputable—and highly experienced—adoption agency.

Jack and Jill Tumble into Divorce

The Stem-Christies adopted two children from Hague Convention countries: Mack (from China) and Lil (a special needs child from Brazil). All went well for several years, but then Jack and Jill fell off their marital hill. Alas, their relationship deteriorated to the point that they fought about every aspect of their divorce—including their children. They were in the small minority of divorcing couples who could not work together to create a marital settlement agreement (*see* Chapter 6) or a parenting plan. The judge's encouragement failed, so did court-ordered mediation, and so did their lawyers' attempts to facilitate a mutually acceptable compromise.

In the end, their divorce resembled the Battle of Stalingrad during World War II: two relentless foes, fighting for every inch of "territory," each insisting that "defeat" is not an option. The family court judge who had to unravel the details of their broken marriage could be seen to wince when Jack and Jill walked into her courtroom.

Paula, their previous attorney refused to represent either Jack or Jill, because she knew and liked both parties. Jack hired Tom to represent him; Jill chose Tina as her divorce lawyer.

TODAY'S KINDER, GENTLER LANGUAGE

I've used the familiar terms *custody* and *visitation* throughout this book, because they are words in use every day. However, many recently written statutes replace custody with *allocation of parental responsibilities and parental decision-making,* and visitation with *child timesharing* schedules and *parenting time plans.* Advocates argue that the old terms didn't convey the idea that communication and cooperation are essential between divorced spouses who are raising a child.

The Battle for Custody

As Tina explained to Jill, "Courts traditionally honored the *tender-years doctrine,* the presumption that *a child belongs with its mother,* but today, judges award custody based on *the best interest of the child.* The court will begin by looking at the child's

→ age;

→ gender;

→ mental and physical health;

→ relationships with siblings (if any);

→ emotional bonds with parents;

→ current living pattern and daily routines—including home, school, community, and religious activities;

→ expressed preference (in many states, a child older than ten or twelve has a voice in the custody decision; in most states, judges will consider his or her preferences);

→ current care-giving arrangement (for example, the person caring for the child now, if one of the spouses has left the marital home).

JOINT CUSTODY

The term *joint custody* (sometimes seen as *shared custody*) confuses many parents, because it can have two elements: *Joint legal custody* enables both parents to share decision-making for the child, including education, health care, and religious upbringing. This can work when the divorced spouses are willing to communicate and cooperate. *Joint physical custody* of a child (which is possible, cumbersome to orchestrate, and demands an even more cordial relationship between the divorced spouses) enables shared custody that can approach 50 percent of the time with each parent (but is typically less).

"Next, the court will examine each of the parent's capacities to meet the child's needs. The commonly considered factors about each parent are

> ❖ mental and physical health;

> ❖ occupation and work responsibilities;

> ❖ ability to provide the child with food, shelter, clothing, and medical care;

> ❖ ties to the community and local extended family;

> ❖ ability to give the child guidance;

> ❖ lifestyle;

> ❖ moral fitness (for example, criminal record, drug use, record of child abuse);

> ❖ current relationship with the child (whether the parent has maintained contact after leaving the marital home);

> ❖ willingness and ability to facilitate and encourage a relationship between the child and the *other* parent (most judges believe that a good relationship with both parents is in the best interest of a child)."

Tom explained to Jack, "Gathering a mass of information about the parents is usually much easier than choosing which of two parents will provide the child with the more stable environment—and provide continuity in education, neighborhood life, religious institutions, and peer relationships. It's not by accident that courts want parents to work out a sensible parenting plan. Judges often modify the plan—in the children's best interest—but it's a foundation for the court to build upon. The fact is, both you and Jill *look* equally qualified to provide for your children's welfare and well-being."

"That's not true!" Jack said. "She smokes at home. Our kids live inside a cloud of second-hand smoke. A few more years around Jill will ruin their health. I want the judge to know that."

"I'll make sure that she does—and Jill's lawyer will tell the judge you were cited twice for transporting Mack in your car without a properly fitted child safety seat. Jill will argue that's proof of child abuse, and that you can't be trusted to care for Mack or Lil."

"EVERY OTHER WEEKEND"

It's almost an everyday legal cliché: Lawyers expect to find the phrase *every other weekend* somewhere in the first sentence of the order that establishes visitation for noncustodial parents. Then comes the usual additions: one weeknight evening, alternate major holidays, half of the child's school breaks, and several weeks in the summer. In fact, judges will vary *typical visitation schedules* significantly depending on the age of the child, the preferences and work schedules of the parents, whether the noncustodial parent lives close to the child, and the post-divorce relationship of the parents (their willingness to cooperate in the child's best interest).

Tom interrupted when Jack tried to reply. "The point I started to make is that you and Jill are forcing the family court to resolve a thousand interrelated disputes based on paper dossiers and noisy cross-claims. I doubt that either of you will be happy with the final results. However, when it comes to custody of Mack and Lil, the judge will work hard to identify the parent who'll provide the best environment and upbringing for the children. She'll see that as her Job One."

"And your Job One is to zero in on the most important custody factor in the judge's mind. That's where I'll blow her out of the water."

Tom sighed. "We'll know the deciding factor when the judge announces it. As I keep reminding you, every custody case is different." He shook his head. "And don't forget that a court may grant custody to the parent who's more likely to encourage a good relationship between the child and the non-custodial parent."

IS TEMPORARY CUSTODY
REALLY TEMPORARY?

Temporary custody orders issued by a judge determine child custody and visitation during the sometimes lengthy legal proceedings of a divorce. In theory, the fact that one spouse receives temporary custody doesn't impact who receives final custody. In practice, the *temporary* order often sets the stage for the final order made a year (possibly two) later. At the very least, a judge may prefer not to upset the children's stability by breaking the custody/visitation routine that's been established. For this reason, many experienced divorce attorneys challenge any proposed temporary custody scheme that their clients can't live with over the long haul.

The Judge's Custody Decision

At the end of the day, the judge sought to maximize the stability of Mack and Lil's lives in the face of their parents' ongoing arguments. She awarded custody of the children to Jill and also awarded Jill the family home, so that the children would remain in their familiar environment.

The judge ignored Jack's request to split up the children and award him custody of Mack and Jill custody of Lil. As Tom explained, "There's a long tradition in the United States of keeping siblings together, absent some clear and compelling reason for separating them. For example, courts will sometimes separate siblings if they are far apart in age, have a record of conflict, or if the preferred custodial parent is unable to provide proper care for all the children."

Although Jill asked for spousal support, the judge refused to award any, citing Jill's significant income (almost as much as Jack's) and recent inheritance. The judge did, however, order Jack to pay child support calculated according to State of Confusion's child-support guidelines. The number was almost exactly what Tom had estimated it would be in the event that Jack didn't gain custody of the children.

Unlike many other aspects of everyday law, child support is fairly easy to predict. This is because federal law requires every state to establish—and publish—guidelines for child support. Having well-defined guidelines ensures that child-support awards are not arbitrary or unfair. Federal law also requires that the guidelines be reviewed every four years.

WHY SHOULD I PAY CHILD SUPPORT?

Some divorced spouses have fought orders to pay child support on the ground that he or she doesn't want to have a parental relationship with the child of a failed marriage. The judges explained (presumably patiently) that a child's right to receive financial support from parents exists—and will be enforced—whether or not a parent wants to take a role in parenting. (Note that the parent can escape liability for support by consenting for the child to be adopted by a stepparent.)

Child-support guidelines are often in the form of a formula that considers a number of well-defined factors such as the incomes of each parent, spousal support (if any), which parent will be responsible for health insurance, the number of jointly parented children, the number (if any) of separately parented children, and each parent's "parenting time."

The State of Confusion, like many other states, has a web-based calculator that people can use to estimate child-support awards. When actual awards differ significantly, it's typically because the court adjusted—up or down—the parental incomes used in the computations.

When both parents are required to pay child support, the custodial parent typically pays less, because the guidelines recognize the inherent expenses associated with having custody. On occasion, a wealthier custodial parent may be required to pay child support to a noncustodial parent with limited financial resources to fund the child's visitation.

The Fight Goes On

Tina and Tom knew it was inevitable that Jack and Jill would continue their bickering after the judge entered the divorce decree and the order. Jill escalated the war by withholding the visitation privileges the court had ordered. "I see no reason to let the jerk spend so much time with the kids," Jill said to Tina. "The judge gave Jack more visitation than he deserves; I'm merely correcting her obvious mistake."

Jack immediately retaliated. "Why should I pay child support if I can't see the kids?" Jack said to Tom. "It's only fair to withhold my payments until Jill stops fooling around."

Both Jack and Jill are wrong. In most states, child custody and visitation are individual rights and obligations—wholly separate and independently enforceable. This means that visitation must be allowed whether or not court-ordered child-support payments are made—and that child-support payments must be made whether or not visitation goes according to the quarterly schedule. Although many divorced parents have played the tit-for-tat punishment game, they risk civil sanctions in most states and criminal penalties in a few.

Interference with Visitation

Tina reminded Jill that courts typically have three options when the custodial parent prevents the noncustodial parent from visiting his or her child:

1. Modify the visitation order—typically adding more terms and conditions that will ensure future compliance by the custodial parent.
2. Award court costs and legal fees to the noncustodial parent.
3. Hold the noncustodial parent in contempt of court. (However, courts have traditionally been reluctant to use their contempt powers to enforce visitation orders, because jailing or fining a custodial parent is rarely seen as being in the best interest of a child.)

Tina also advised, "In some states, a noncustodial parent can request the assistance of the police to enforce a routine visitation order. But in most jurisdictions, the police will not get involved unless a judge has issued an *enforceable order* that compels visitation. That can happen in the State of Confusion.

"Moreover, here, and in several more states, unlawful visitation interference is a crime. Again, judges are reluctant to punish custodial parents because the penalties may impact the children as much as the parent. But egregious behavior can push any judge to the 'jailing point.'"

Can Jill Move to Another State?

Probably—with the court's agreement. Because of the unrelenting hostility between Jack and Jill, Tom wisely requested the judge to include a provision in her custody order that prevents the custodial parent (Jill) from moving out of the State of Confusion without first obtaining the court's permission. Tina warned Jill that violating this requirement would be industrial-strength contempt of court—a breach that often results in permanent loss of custody.

Broadly speaking, if Jill has a legitimate reason for moving (say she received a promotion that requires her to move to another state) the judge will allow her to relocate children. But if Jill's goal is to make it more difficult for Jack to exercise his visitation rights, her request to take the children out of the jurisdiction will be denied.

Parental Kidnapping

Parental kidnapping happens when one divorced parent takes a child to an unknown location for the purpose of preventing custody by the custodial parent (or visitation by the noncustodial parent). The court will typically issue an arrest warrant for the absconding parent and issue other orders (say, an emergency custody order) to protect the child until the issue is resolved.

But—note that the failure to make a child available for a scheduled visitation, or the failure to bring a child back home immediately after a scheduled visitation, or moving a child to another state without the court's permission don't automatically qualify as examples of parental kidnapping. Legally speaking, these unfortunate but commonplace happenings are initially deemed *interference with court orders*. However, if the blameworthy parent ignores follow-up court proceedings initiated by the aggrieved parent and fails to produce the child in response to subsequent court orders, that behavior may well be treated as parental kidnapping and trigger the involvement of the F.B.I.

Failure to Pay Child Support

Paying child support is essentially a *no-matter-what* obligation that continues *no matter how* contentious a divorce becomes, *no matter* how the divorced spouses use the children to punish each other, and *no matter* if the custodial parent interferes with court-ordered visitation.

Tom reminded Jack that the family court judge had many ways to compel payment of child support, including the following:

→ Embarrassing him by publishing his photograph on state websites

→ Seizing tax refunds

→ Taking away his driver's license

→ Garnishing his wages

→ Sending him to jail for contempt of court

The general public tends to be unsympathetic when deadbeat spouses complain, because not paying child support throws the burden on state welfare programs. Consequently, noncustodial spouses who avoid their child-support obligations are often jailed for contempt.

The Federal Child Support Enforcement Program

At one time, a noncustodial parent could escape his or her liability for child support by moving to another state and "beginning a new life." These days, the Federal Child Support Enforcement Program—a partnership between the Federal Office of Child Support Enforcement (OCSE) and many different state and local child-support agencies—makes escape impossible for most would-be deadbeat spouses.

The OSCE is chiefly a computer-based information clearinghouse that draws data from the Internal Revenue Service, the Social Security Administration, the Department of Defense, and the National Directory of New Hires—all with an eye toward locating missing parents who have avoided their child-support obligations. (The OCSE also has the power to prevent individuals with outstanding child-support debt from obtaining a passport from the Department of State.)

The OCSE provides parental location data to state and local child-support enforcement agencies—they do the actual collecting of unpaid child support.

A custodial parent can't access OCSE resources directly; he or she must work through the state or local partnership agency responsible for enforcing child-support orders.

Jack and Jill Refuse to Let the Grandparents Visit Mack and Lil

Before the divorce was finalized—during the bitterest days of the battle—Jill's parents, Billie and Millie, became worried about Mack and Lil. They tried to gain legal custody of their grandchildren, and they made it known that they considered both Jack and Jill to be unfit parents.

After the divorce, Jack and Jill were able to agree on one point: Billie and Millie were no longer allowed *any* contact with Mack and Lil.

Billie and Millie spoke to their attorney: "Can we do anything in family court to force Jack and Jill to change their minds? Don't we have 'grandparents' rights' in the state?"

"Yes, but mostly no," the lawyer said, glumly. "This is one area of family law where a U.S. Supreme Court decision—reached in the year 2000—has had a major impact. The decision affirmed that fit parents have a fundamental right to raise their children in the way they think best—and that the state can interfere only to prevent harm to the children.

"That case involved grandparents' rights; the grandparents were allowed some—very limited—visitation by the parents. The grandparents tried to argue that more visitation was in the children's best interest. The Supreme Court concluded that even if the best-interest argument was valid, a state can't intervene unless there is a significant reason for upsetting the parent's decision not to allow extensive contact.

"The courts in the State of Confusion are willing to consider petitions from grandparents who have been denied any access, and who have had a previous relationship with the children that rises to the level of a genuine *bond*. But we'll still have to convince the judge that Mack and Lil are being harmed by lack of contact with their grandparents."

"No problem! They used to spend lots of time with us," said Millie. "We have—*had*—a great relationship. An arbitrary decision to isolate the children from their grandparents has got to cause harm."

"Although many people will agree with you, the law in the State of Confusion requires that we show that the lack of contact has *significantly impaired the children's physical health or emotional well-being.*

"This is a very tough standard to meet. It's not enough that the children are *sad* because they miss their grandparents. They must suffer actual harm before the court will overrule parents' wishes."

Things Worth Knowing about Juvenile Justice

The *juvenile justice system* has much in common with the adult criminal justice system (*see* Chapter 17) although there's greater emphasis on the rehabilitation of offenders, in addition to the goals of protecting society and holding lawbreakers accountable for their criminal conduct.

Different states—even different communities in states—have different ways to "process" juveniles who enter the juvenile justice system. What follows is a guide that applies to most states. For convenience, I've used the term *Juvenile Justice Department* as a label for the decision-making authorities responsible for the various processing activities.

Who Is a "Juvenile Offender"?

A good working definition of a juvenile offender is any person charged with criminal behavior who is of an age that fits within the jurisdiction of juvenile court:

- ✦ The upper age in most states is eighteen years (a person stops being a juvenile on his or her nineteenth birthday and will be tried in adult criminal court); however, a handful of states set the upper age at sixteen years and other states set it at seventeen years. (One state—Wyoming—has an upper age of nineteen years.)

- ✦ Most states set a lower age limit of six or seven years, on the theory that children younger than that can't have the intent—the requisite guilty mind—to commit a crime.

Juvenile Offenses

Broadly speaking, juvenile offenders enter the juvenile justice system because they have committed either a delinquent offense or a status offense.

- ✦ A *delinquent offense* is an illegal act for which an adult would be prosecuted in criminal court—for example, shoplifting, automobile theft, or burglary.

→ A *status offense* is a wrong that only a juvenile can commit—truancy, curfew violations, and running away from home. Many status offenses are ultimately resolved through the efforts of social service agencies rather than juvenile court.

The Role of Law Enforcement in Juvenile Justice

Almost all adult offenders begin their journey through the justice system when they are arrested by police or other law enforcement personnel. Only about half of juvenile offenders are initially arrested by police. The other half enters the juvenile justice system through referrals to the state's Juvenile Justice Department. A *referral* is a report alleging the commission of a crime or violation of a court order. It can come from child welfare agencies, schools, probation officers, crime victims, parents—and of course, law enforcement agencies.

When the police arrest a juvenile, they typically have broad discretion to decide what to do next. Upwards of 20 percent of arrested juveniles are subsequently released by police after they talk to the juvenile, the victim, and the parents and review the juvenile's prior involvement with the juvenile justice system.

The Intake Decision

The intake decision is the determination by the Juvenile Justice Department about how a referral will be handled. It may decide to handle the matter informally or to formally prosecute the offender in juvenile court.

Handling the matter informally can range from dismissing the case to negotiating a series of conditions with a young offender who admits his or her wrongdoing. The conditions may call for victim restitution, school attendance, psychological counseling, drug counseling, community service, or a curfew (or other behavior modifications).

The Waiver Process

Waiver refers to the process whereby a juvenile defendant is transferred from juvenile court to adult criminal court. This can happen when an older child is accused of committing an especially serious or violent crime. In a few states, prosecutors have the discretion to file serious cases involving a juvenile offender in adult criminal court from the start; in other states, a juvenile court judge must agree before a juvenile defendant can be tried as an adult. (Some states define a list of serious crimes that can only be tried in criminal court, whether the defendant is juvenile or adult.)

Adjudication in Juvenile Court

A juvenile offender is not *tried, convicted*, and *sentenced*. Rather, he or she receives an *adjudication hearing* before a judge, who may determine that the juvenile committed a *delinquent act*—not a *crime*—and will then decide on an appropriate disposition. This is the outcome that the judge believes is in the child's best interest and is most likely to achieve rehabilitation.

Some adjudicated delinquents are committed to juvenile detention centers; more than half are placed on probation that includes other requirements: counseling, community service, and victim restitution.

Institutionalized juveniles are typically ordered into a period of aftercare after their release (monitored probation similar to adult parole). During this period—which in some states can extend to age twenty—the juvenile is under supervision of the court or Juvenile Justice Department.

CHAPTER 8

RENTING A
HOME

Whenyou rent an apartment or a house, you and your landlord enter into a kind of contract called a *lease* (or a *rental agreement*). Although a lease has the essential aspects of the contract we talked about in Chapter 2, the specific terms you'll find are typically regulated by state (and occasionally city) law. Because of this, most landlords use pre-formatted rental agreements tailored for specific communities. These are available via the Internet and sold in office supply stores. Although these standard forms honor local lease requirements, they are invariably designed to protect the landlord's interests. For starters, they leave a prospective tenant little or no opportunity to make changes. The "take it or leave it" attitude will be even stronger during periods when your community has a shortage of available rental units.

The Rental on Elm Street

I call this hypothetical the *Rental on Elm Street . . .* and Yes!, it is a horror story—but only because landlord/tenant issues got out of hand and escalated into monster problems. It didn't have to happen that way. Landlords and tenants have been battling for millennia—too often because they start their relationship as near-adversaries, anticipating fights to come. The far better approach—as many wise tenants and landlords have found out—is to understand each others' rights and duties under everyday law.

A Big, Big Mistake

Our story begins (cue the scary music) when a married couple named Les and Penny Wise decided to rent an apartment. They found what they thought was an ideal apartment on Elm Street in a building owned and managed by Evan Slicker.

Every horror flick has a scene when one of the characters—known among horror movie fans as the *stupid victim*—does something incredibly foolish, like walking down a dark staircase into a pitch-black basement where everyone knows the killer is hiding behind the furnace. Well . . . Les and Penny Wise did something just as foolish: They signed a lease they didn't understand.

Always Read the Lease

A *residential rental agreement*—simply a *lease* to most people— is a legally binding contract that describes the property being rented, names the landlord and tenant, and specifies the terms of the rental—including the length of the rental period and the amount of rent—and also details the essential rights and responsibilities of both landlord and tenant.

Alas, the lease that Evan Slicker handed to the Wises was written in complex legalese. Moreover, the "original" that Les and Penny signed was a fifth-generation photocopy that was barely legible—many clauses they tried to read were indecipherable.

As a result, the Wises never noticed that the document was chock full of things they had to do—and couldn't do—as tenants.

Two Kinds of Rentals

The lion's share of residential leases fall into one of two categories that depends on the kind of *rental tenancy* the lease creates. *Tenancy* in a rental context (*see* Chapter 9 for tenancies in land ownership) is the possession and use of real estate owned by another party. These are the two common tenancies:

1. *Fixed-term tenancy* (also called a *tenancy for years*) lasts for a definite period of time—anything from a week to ninety-nine years. The rent—typically payable each month—remains the same for the duration of the lease (unless the parties agree to other arrangements). Neither party has to give notification at the end of the lease. The lease expires automatically at the end of the definite time period.

2. *Periodic tenancy* (also called a *month-to-month lease*) continues from period to period—renewing automatically for another period—until either the landlord or tenant gives *timely notice* to end the lease. The most common periodic leases are *by the month* and *by the week*. If the lease document doesn't define *timely notice*, it's typically thirty days for a by-the-month lease and seven days for a by-the-week lease. The landlord can increase the rent for future periods any time, upon the same timely notice as a lease cancellation.

The Wises signed a two-year—twenty-four month—fixed-term lease. They wanted a shorter lease, but Elm Street is a highly desirable neighborhood and Evan Slicker wasn't willing to negotiate a shorter term.

Put It in Writing!

Most states require that a fixed-term lease for longer than one year be in writing. Short-term leases and by-the-month or by-the-week leases can be oral—and are as binding as written leases. But the terms of an oral agreement are always subject to "I said/You said" disagreements if disputes develop about duties and responsibilities—and oral leases can be difficult to enforce in court. Consequently, all leases should be in writing.

Most landlords use pre-prepared standard lease forms, which, as I noted earlier, usually favor landlords. This makes it even more important for a tenant to read the document carefully and understand its different clauses and terms. Even when a landlord offers a "take it or leave it" lease, the tenant who takes the time to peruse the document will understand from the get-go what the landlord has committed to do—and not to do.

Few tenants take advantage of the opportunities they have to gain an early familiarity with the kind of lease they'll likely be offered. Standard leases for many parts of the United States can be read for free on the Internet. Use a search engine to look for "residential lease [CITY] [STATE]." You're likely to find several that meet local requirements. Chances are good that your future landlord will use one of them.

DISCRIMINATION IN RENTING

A landlord is a businessperson who is free to accept or reject tenants on the basis of valid business criteria—for example, a good credit rating, positive references, stable employment—that indicate the tenants will pay rent on time and take good care of the rental property. However, these criteria must be applied equally to everyone who seeks to rent. Federal law makes it illegal to discriminate against prospective rental tenants on the basis of race, religion, national origin, sex, familial status (including having children or being pregnant, except in certain *senior-only* housing), or mental or physical disability. Some state and local anti-discrimination laws add age, marital status, and sexual orientation to the list. Landlords are forbidden to falsely deny to some applicants that a rental unit is available, set more restrictive standards (for example, higher income) for some renters, or discriminate by specifying different terms in rental leases.

Surprise: The Condition of the Wise's New Apartment

Les Wise distinctly remembered reading the following phrase in the lease: "Tenants acknowledge that the rental unit he and she are renting is in good condition without damage or problems." This recitation was certainly true of the *model apartment* they saw before the Wises signed the lease. Unfortunately, their apartment proved to be full of minor problems—and a few serious deficiencies.

The lesson: The Wises should have conducted a *walk-through* of the apartment before signing the lease—and check systems, appliances, doors, windows, and decor items.

WHERE'S MY PAINTBRUSH?

Most residential leases forbid tenants to make significant changes to a rental unit without the landlord's permission— including redecorating with new paint and wallpapering, or adding *fixtures* (things permanently attached to walls, floors, or ceilings). When a landlord gives permission to install shelves or closet storage units, he or she is likely to require that they become his or her property and will be left in the apartment. Hanging pictures with simple picture hooks is generally allowed, but hanging a heavy mirror with wall anchors (or similar heavy-duty hardware that requires drilling holes in walls) is probably not. The tenant will be responsible for the cost of repairing the wall at the end of the lease.

Any defects discovered during a walk-through—from minor cosmetic problems to malfunctioning appliances—should be presented to the landlord in writing. The tenant should ask for a signed copy in return—along with a promise (ideally also in writing) that serious defects will be repaired within a reasonable period of time. Tenants who've lived through disputes with landlords recommend taking photos of all existing defects (an easy job with a digital camera or a cell phone with a built-in camera). A picture can be worth much more than a thousand words when shown to a judge.

Surprise: Some Utilities Not Included

The ad in the paper said "utilities included." Had Les and Penny read the lease that Evan Slicker—wearing a big smile—slid across the desktop, they would have discovered that water, sewer, and trash collection *are* included, but that gas or electricity are specifically excluded from the list of provided utilities.

Different landlords have different policies; so it's wise for the tenant to request that the lease *clarify* what's included in the rent. An assigned parking space in the complex's garage? Use of the pool and gym room? Use of washers and dryers? A central office to receive packages delivered during the day?

Surprise: Some Rights Are Built into Every Lease

Not all the "news" was bad for Les and Penny Wise. Two important benefits are built into a lease by the action of state law even though they're not explicitly mentioned in the document: The *right of quiet enjoyment* and the *warranty of habitability*.

The Right of Quiet Enjoyment

We're talking here about legal *quiet*—the right of a tenant to use his or her rental property without *interferences* that deprive the tenant of expectations under the lease (and probably reduce its value). For example:

→ A landlord rents the same apartment to two tenants (both can complain that their rights of quiet enjoyment have been violated).

→ A landlord renovates the apartments on either side of the tenant's unit, filling the air with dirt and dust, the smell of paint, and the sounds of heavy machinery.

→ A neighbor's vicious dog—though on a chain—represents a constant threat every time the tenant enters or leaves the apartment.

→ A landlord places a dumpster next to the tenant's apartment— causing foul odors and noise at all hours of the day and night.

→ A landlord tries to drive a tenant out of his or her apartment by various kinds of intimidation.

Courts have long held that a landlord covenants (promises) quiet enjoyment to a tenant. A breach of quiet enjoyment must be more than a minor annoyance—it must be a serious inconvenience that fundamentally interferes with the tenant's use of the rental property.

WHEN A LANDLORD FACES FORECLOSURE

One significant blow to quiet enjoyment may occur during an economic slowdown. The landlord loses his property through a foreclosure proceeding because he falls behind in mortgage payments—and the tenant is suddenly, and unexpectedly, evicted from the house or apartment. Until May 2009, tenants were out of luck—the bank (or foreclosure-sale buyer) could evict the tenant even though the lease had not terminated. This changed with the Protecting Tenants at Foreclosure Act of 2009. A lease now *survives* a foreclosure. A term-lease tenant can remain until the end of the lease; a month-to-month tenant is entitled to ninety days' notice that the lease is being terminated (a significantly longer period than the usual thirty days' notice). The exception in the law: If foreclosed property is bought by a buyer who intends to live in the house or building, the new buyer may terminate the lease with ninety days' notice.

Warranty of Habitability

In most states, every lease has an implied *warranty of habitability*—the landlord's presumed promise that the rental unit will remain fit for human beings to live in during the life of the lease. This is not luxury living—or an aesthetically pleasing residence—but rather a minimum standard for decent, safe, sanitary housing.

The definition of *habitability* varies from state to state. Some are broad and include such factors as no torn or loose carpeting, faucets that don't leak, and air conditioning that works. In other states, a rental unit must merely *substantially* comply with those building and safety code standards that materially affect tenants' health and safety. This can be little more than an apartment that's free of vermin, does not pose any fire or health hazards, and has a working toilet.

The landlord is responsible for making repairs necessary to bring a rental unit up to habitability standards when he or she knows about the deficiency. This requires that the tenant notify the landlord about nonobvious defects. In turn, a tenant is required to take reasonable care of the rental unit and to keep it clean. Tenants are generally responsible for damage caused by their neglect or abuse.

Surprise: An Expensive Pet Policy

On the day Les and Penny moved into their apartment, Evan Slicker dropped by to announce the Wises' rent had just increased by $50 a month. Because they hadn't read the lease carefully, they hadn't noticed a clause that required "tenant to pay $50 'small pet fee' for any month in which a dog or cat resides in the apartment for more than eight hours." Another clause explained that no pets are permitted in the apartment without the landlord's written consent, but that such consent would be given—on a month-by-month basis for "small cats and dogs" upon payment of a "small-pet fee."

Is it legal? Yes—if a landlord charges *pet rent* to all tenants with small pets. Landlords justify the additional fee by arguing that maintenance and management costs increase when tenants' own pets. The Wises didn't think that made much sense—few tenants do—but they agreed to pay a small-pet fee.

Surprise: Exorbitant Late Fees

The Wises also agreed to add a hefty late fee if they don't pay the rent on time. Their lease calls for a 15-percent fee after a five-day grace period. *Reasonable* late fees are generally enforceable—after all, legislatures and courts recognize that landlords need to be paid on time and that a late fee provides tenants with an incentive to honor their financial duties under the lease (and also covers the additional costs of dealing with late-arriving payments). Some states have statutory definitions of *reasonable*—for example, North Carolina allows a maximum late fee that is the greater of either $15 or 5 percent of the rental payment.

However, the late fees called for in many rental leases have no relation to the landlord's real costs and effectively punish the tenant. Although they are unenforceable in court, the landlord is likely to withdraw unpaid late charges from the tenant's security deposit—or even threaten to evict the tenant. Consequently, most tenants simply pay the exorbitant fees and avoid the tumult of a court battle with their landlord.

Surprise: A Promise to Pay Evan's Legal Fees

One of the standard clauses in the lease that the Wises signed—a clause found in most rental leases—makes the tenant responsible for the landlord's attorney's fees if Evan has to take legal action should the tenant *default* (fail to comply with their duties under the lease). Many states limit the clause: The landlord can recover attorney's fees only if he or she wins in court. Other states impose reciprocity to an attorney-fees clause: The landlord must pay for the tenant's lawyer if the tenants win a lawsuit brought by the landlord.

Surprise: Too Much "Right of Entry"

Every rental lease gives a landlord the right to enter a rented dwelling upon *reasonable notice* to make inspections and repairs—and typically also to show the apartment to prospective tenants at the end of the lease. A landlord can enter the apartment without notice in the event of an emergency (say, a burst pipe). However, a landlord who abuses his right of entry by repeatedly entering at unreasonable times, without reasonable notice, and without a valid emergency can be sued for trespass—or for breaching the tenant's right of quiet enjoyment (*see* above).

Reasonable notice is often twenty-four to forty-eight hours, although some states allow the landlord to specify required notice time in a lease. Les and Penny Wise soon discovered that Evan Slicker had defined *reasonable notice* as a mere eight hours—and that state law allowed him to do so.

Even worse, Evan had inserted the following sentence: "Tenants agree that 'convenient time' ('reasonable time') to enter their apartment shall be any hour between 7:00 a.m. and 11:00 p.m." This too passed legal muster, because state law allowed the parties to a lease to decide the meaning of *convenient*.

Surprise: The Wises Are Responsible for Many "Routine" Repairs

Landlords are generally responsible for maintaining the premises and making necessary repairs—fixtures, heating equipment, air conditioning, and other major systems. A landlord also has the responsibility to repair appliances that are "included" in the lease.

I emphasized *included* because Evan Slicker placed the following sentence in the lease that the Wises signed: "Tenants acknowledge that the washing machine and dryer currently in the apartment are not 'included' appliances that the landlord must maintain. Tenants are free to use both appliances and to keep them in working order, as they wish."

A few clauses below, the lease also provided: "Tenants acknowledge that they have received a 10 percent reduction from the usual rent charged for their apartment. In exchange for this reduction in rent, tenants agree to maintain easily accessible plumbing and electrical devices, including faucets, flush toilet mechanisms, light switches, light-bulb sockets in lighting fixtures, and all light bulbs. At the end of the lease period, tenants agree to professionally clean the carpeting in the apartment at their expense."

Can the Wises challenge these clauses? Probably not.

Even in a community with tenant-friendly laws and courts, people are allowed to set reasonable terms in a residential lease. There's nothing unreasonable about excluding nonessential appliances or trading lower rent payments for certain maintenance responsibilities. Courts are unsympathetic to people who don't take the time to read the documents they sign.

Evan Slicker's lease affirmed—as most leases do—that the landlord will make repairs that are the responsibility of the landlord within a reasonable period of time. The tenant is responsible for notifying the landlord that repairs are necessary. What *reasonable* means depends on the facts of the situation. A broken water line, a failed heating system in winter, or a faulty air conditioner in the height of summer demands quicker action from the landlord than a jammed garbage disposal.

TENANT-CAUSED DAMAGE

Tenants are generally held responsible—under the lease and under state law—if they intentionally or negligently destroy, deface, damage, or remove any part of the premises. On occasion, the bill to repair tenant-caused damage exceeds the security deposit. If so, the landlord can bill the guilty tenant for the excess and, if necessary, bring a lawsuit for the balance. Many leases require that any tenant-caused damage be repaired by professionals rather than the tenant. This is to ensure that the quality of the repair—or more likely the lack thereof—doesn't adversely impact future residents of the apartment or other tenants in the building.

Surprise: A Festival of Breakdowns

In quick succession, the roof began to leak, the air conditioning stopped working (it was summertime), and an infestation of ants made life difficult—and itchy. The Wises notified Evan Slicker per the requirements of the lease (at this point in their tenancy, Les and Penny had read the document so many times that they almost knew the terms by heart). Unfortunately, Evan replied with a long list of excuses, but no repair people. The Wises wondered if they could force Evan to live up to his responsibilities under the lease by refusing to pay rent.

RENT STRIKES

A *rent strike* is a protest against poorly maintained rental units by a group of tenants who place rent in a special bank account rather than pay it directly to their landlord. Rent strikes are not legal in much of the country because the traditional rule is that a tenant who stays in an apartment has a duty to pay rent. The tenants can then take advantage of a local "repair and deduct" provision or seek damages from the landlord in small claims court. Where rent strikes are legal—California, for example—the landlord must have materially breached the implied warranty of habitability by failing to correct serious housing code violations. Most maintenance issues don't justify a rent strike.

More than a few tenants reach this point in their relationship with their land-lords—but as a general principle, a tenant's duty to pay rent flows from the lease he or she signed and continues even if the landlord fails to meet his or her maintenance obligations under the lease. However, this general principle has been modified by law in many states, giving unhappy tenants two powerful weapons to counteract a nonresponsive landlord:

1. *Repair and deduct* statutes (also called *self-help for minor defects* laws) empower a tenant to redirect a rent payment to pay for essential minor repairs that a landlord ignores. But the tenant typically must notify the landlord of his or her intention to deduct rent money to pay for a repair. There are typically limits on the amount of rent a tenant can deduct (often a maximum of one month's rent); most laws require the work to be done by a licensed contractor; and the landlord must have a reasonable time (which obviously will depend on the nature of the problem) to respond to the notice.

2. *Termination of the rental agreement* laws empower a tenant to terminate a rental lease in the event that the landlord is in *material noncompliance* with the terms of the lease. Failure to maintain the rental unit in a habitable condition qualifies as material noncompliance. Statutes generally require a tenant to give the landlord adequate notice of termination—typically fourteen days—unless the noncompliance impacts health and safety (violations here will shorten the notice requirements).

If a landlord wrongfully ignores his or her responsibility to supply such essentials as heat, hot water, air conditioning (in some locations), water, or working toilets, some states allow a tenant to move to reasonable substitute housing until the problem is corrected—and redirect rent payments to cover the cost of the substitute apartment.

Also, a tenant can sue the landlord to recover the diminished value of the rental because of the landlord's failure to maintain the apartment or because a problem (such as a leaky roof) caused damage to the tenant's personal property.

Les and Penny Wise—tired of dealing with Evan Slicker—decided to terminate the rental agreement. Evan didn't challenge their decision, but when the time came to return their security deposit he took . . . *forever.*

UNFAIR AND DECEPTIVE TRADE PRACTICES

Some states provide another remedy to tenants when landlords fail to maintain a rented residence in a fit and habitable condition but continue to collect rent. The landlord can be sued for engaging in an "unfair and deceptive trade practice." Losing can be expensive for a landlord because he or she becomes liable for triple (treble) damages—the tenant's actual damages are multiplied by three, to punish the landlord's willful bad behavior.

Surprise: How Do We Get Our Security Deposit Back?

In most states, a landlord can request a security deposit to cover such costs as abnormal wear and tear on the apartment, unpaid rent, late charges, and actual damages caused by the tenant's breach of the lease. Many states set statutory limits to the amount a landlord can collect as a security deposit (typically one and one-half times or two times the monthly rent). But, a landlord may also be able to collect other front-end fees and deposits: application fee, cleaning fee, pet damage deposit, key deposit, and an advance rent deposit.

The lease that Les and Penny Wise signed left the decision of what is *normal wear and tear* to the landlord's discretion and determination. Simply put, it's what Evan Slicker says it is. Not surprisingly, he compiled a list of damaged items that totaled the full amount of their deposit. The Wises have the right to contest his decision to keep their whole deposit, but they have little evidence to present to a small claims judge because they never made an initial walk-through or documented the apartment's existing problems.

Normal wear and tear is a vague concept that can mean many things to many people. Bare patches on an old carpet may be the result of normal wear and tear, but they can also be caused by heavy, inappropriately placed furniture. On the other hand, most people recognize that certain kinds of damage don't count as normal wear and tear:

- → Gouges in walls
- → Pet stains on carpets
- → Burn marks on counter tops
- → Broken windows and glass door panels

→ Lost keys that force the landlord to rekey the locks

→ Clogged drains caused by misuse of sinks or toilets

→ Infestations of fleas caused by tenants' pets

→ Excessive mildew accumulation on bathroom tiles (the tenant has a responsibility to keep the apartment reasonably clean). Note that some leases try to make tenants responsible for any mold accumulation in the apartment, which can be exceedingly expensive to repair.

In many states, security deposits must be kept in a segregated bank account, with interest accruing to the benefit of the tenant. A landlord generally has a reasonable period of time to return the deposit and is required to account for any sums subtracted from the deposit at the end of the lease. A landlord acting in bad faith can be liable for the full return of the deposit and (sometimes) punitive damages.

Other Things Worth Knowing about Renting a Home

Confession of Judgment Clause

Some leases include a *confession of judgment* clause—a bewildering provision that many people have never heard of, and few non-lawyers understand. Simply put, the clause takes away the tenant's right to contest (fight in court) any legal claim that the landlord makes under the lease.

By confessing judgment, the tenant pleads guilty to any civil claim that the landlord may make—from failure to pay rent, to doing excessive damage—regardless of the actual facts of the case. The clause was once an easy way for a landlord to evict a tenant without going through a formal eviction procedure. Many states have banned confession of judgment clauses in residential leases, although some older standard form leases in use may still have them.

A tenant should be wary of signing a lease that requires confession of judgment in any state where the clause is still enforceable.

Terminating a Lease

Unless the terms of a written lease provide otherwise, terminating a *month-to-month* lease requires thirty days' notice by either the landlord or tenant. There is one exception to this general rule: If the tenant fails to pay rent, the landlord can ask the tenant to vacate without any further notice. However, if the tenant refuses to leave, the landlord must go through the state's usual eviction procedures.

A landlord and tenant can mutually agree to terminate a *tenancy for years* at any time. This is called surrendering the lease. If more than one year of tenancy remains on the lease, the surrender must be agreed to in writing. If the landlord refuses to accept the tenant's surrender, the tenant can *abandon* the apartment by moving out. At that point, the landlord can do two things:

→ Accept the tenant's surrender of the apartment, thus terminating the lease. The tenant remains obligated to pay any past due rent and the cost of any damages that exceed the security deposit.

→ Make a good-faith attempt to re-rent the apartment. The tenant remains obligated for any months in which the apartment is empty, and for any shortfall in rent for the balance of the lease if the landlord is forced to re-rent the apartment at a lower monthly rental than in the original lease.

Subleasing a Rented Apartment

Most residential leases prohibit a tenant from *subleasing* a rental unit without the landlord's written consent. The obvious reason is that the landlord wants a say in who's living in—and caring for—an apartment.

Legally speaking, a *sublease* transfers *part* of a lease to a third party. For example, a sublease might convey the right to possess an apartment for three months of a twenty-four-month lease. By contrast, an *assignment* transfers *all* the rights and responsibilities of the lease to a third party.

For example, assume that one year into their lease, the Wises decided to move. They tried to assign their lease (which still had a year to run) to another person who would take over their rights and responsibilities under the lease. (They quickly discovered that Evan Slicker's lease also prohibited assignments without his permission.)

Keep in mind that a tenant who assigns or subleases a rental unit now becomes a landlord in his or her own right—and needs the protection of a written lease that includes the right of entry and makes provision for a security deposit.

When a Landlord Wants the Tenant Out

Let's turn the hypothetical around and assume that Evan grew tired of the Wises as tenants. Broadly speaking, a landlord can't interfere with a tenant's right of quiet enjoyment (*see* above), deny a tenant access to the apartment, or turn off the tenant's utilities if the tenant is living up to his or her responsibilities—and is paying rent on time. In many states, an *illegal lockout* (*unlawful eviction*) or other bad-faith behavior by a landlord virtually invites a judge to award punitive damages to the tenants.

If the Wises had behaved badly—say, by disturbing other tenants or by creating a fire or health hazard—or had repeatedly not paid their rent on time, Evan Slicker could have begun a legal proceeding to evict the Wises. In some parts of the country, eviction is a long, drawn-out procedure. But most states have a streamlined process—called *summary eviction* or an *unlawful detainer action*—that can remove a tenant in less than thirty days.

⊱⊰

BUYING (OR SELLING) A HOUSE

Fduring our lives represent the largest dollar-value transactions we'll make. That's obvious. But as you'll see in this chapter, buying (or selling) a house is also one of the most "legally active" things we do. Both buyer and seller take on a raft of complex and potentially expensive obligations during the lengthy transaction.

It's surprising then that so few buyers (or sellers) hire attorneys to shepherd them through the process. If you currently own a house, chances are that the transaction was handled by various real estate professionals—for example, real estate brokers, escrow company, and mortgage broker.

In many states, most (sometimes all) of the process can be completed without the participation of attorneys—although you can be sure that lawyers prepared the stack of standard forms that both parties cheerfully sign, often without any real understanding of their content. And in states where attorneys are required, it's usually just to deal with technical details at the end of the transaction—such as title searches and deed preparation.

This approach works well—if everything goes according to plan, if everyone involved is aboveboard, and if neither buyer nor seller has special requirements that don't fit standardized forms.

Mr. Dither Buys a Dream House

Once upon a time, Mr. and Mrs. Dither decided to buy their dream house. In truth, it was Agnes Dither's dream—Bob Dither worried that it was too expensive. And you guessed it; it was further down Elm Street. The seller was named Darren Deeds.

Bob Dither was determined to do things right—by himself. Being frugal, he wanted to understand the ins-and-outs of the transaction of buying a house—and do as much as he could by himself, without an attorney. The first challenge he ran into when he began his research was a long list of unusual words.

The Arcane Language of Property

The everyday law of real property has a legal language of its own that hearkens back to medieval England. For example, many new homeowners are baffled when they learn they will hold title to their house and land in *fee simple*.

Holding in "Fee Simple"

Fee simple is nothing more than an *interest in real property* (an *estate*) that lets the owner do anything with it that he or she wishes—the owner can sell it, give it away, mortgage it, live on it, plant trees on it . . . you get the idea.

The word *fee*—which has the same Germanic roots as *fief*—means "property or possession," whereas *simple* reflects the concept that ownership is unconstrained, that the owner has a "pure" right of possession, without complications or limitations.

Alas, there really is no such thing as a true fee-simple interest anymore (if there ever was). Today, local zoning, anti-discrimination laws, regulations issued by homeowners associations (*see* below), covenants attached to deeds (*see* below), the government's power of *eminent domain* (*see* below), and many other constraints impose significant limits on fee-simple ownership.

Nonetheless, fee simple still represents the highest form of ownership—the kind most owners want when they purchase a house.

Other Ownership Alternatives: "Condos" and "Coops"

Contrary to what many people think, *condominium* does not refer to a type of building or construction design. Rather it describes a form of ownership of real estate.

The owner of a *condo* owns the *interior space* of his unit in fee simple— the unit can be an apartment, a townhouse, or a detached house. In addition, he owner has an *undivided interest* (along with other condo owners) in the common elements of the condo development—grounds, walkways, hallways, parking areas, foundations, exterior walls, roofs, building lobbies, and recreational facilities.

Condominium units are considered real property, appear on tax roles as individual dwellings, can be bought or sold like other fee-simple properties, can be passed to beneficiaries in a will, and can be financed with a traditional mortgage.

A *cooperative*—common in New York City and a few other large cities—represents a significantly different mode of ownership. The owner of a cooperative apartment doesn't hold title to real estate; rather he or she owns shares in a not-for-profit corporation that is the legal owner of the building. The owner of the shares is granted a *proprietary lease* to live in a dwelling unit.

Because the owner holds shares rather than real estate, it can be difficult to finance the purchase of a cooperative apartment (conventional mortgages don't apply). Similarly, owners can't use the shares as collateral for a home-equity loan.

Moreover, the corporation may impose restrictions on the sale of shares—even blocking their sale to purchasers who don't meet specific requirements. Although the corporations must obey laws that prevent housing discrimination, they can invoke many other acceptability criteria based on financial resources.

Co-tenancies for Multiple Owners

Warning! This is a *different* meaning of the word *tenancy* from the one used in Chapter 8 to talk about renting a home. In legal-speak a *tenant* is one who holds or possesses lands. The word comes from the French *tenir*, "to hold."

A *co-tenancy*—or *concurrent estate*—describes the way in which real property is held by two or more people at the same time. For example, Bob and Agnes Dither want to be co-tenants in the ownership of their new house. There are three common kinds of co-tenancy:

1. *Tenancy in common*—Each party owns a separate and distinct share of the property. These shares, which can be different sizes, can be bought, sold, or passed to heirs or beneficiaries. The co-tenants can be related or unrelated; they all have a simultaneous right to possess the whole property.

2. *Joint tenancy with right of survivorship*—The two or more co-tenants, who must become owners of the property at the same time, via the same deed (transfer document), hold equal, proportionate shares of the property. Upon the death of any co-tenant, his or her ownership rights automatically pass to the surviving co-tenant(s)—*not* to the dead co-tenant's heirs or beneficiaries. Thus, the last surviving co-tenant becomes the sole owner of the property. You often see this tenancy labeled by its acronym: JTWROS.

3. *Tenancy by the entireties*—A co-tenancy that is applicable only to a husband and wife (and to the members of a *civil union* in some states). The two spouses are considered to be a single *legal person*, for purposes of property ownership. Upon the death of one spouse, ownership rights automatically pass to the surviving spouse. Some states have eliminated this tenancy, because JTWROS can achieve the same legal effect. One of the benefits of tenancy by the entireties is that the property is fully *exempt* from liens (*see* below) of creditors of one spouse (but not from creditors of both spouses).

The language used in the deed (*see* below) that conveys property to two or more people creates a concurrent estate. In many states, the specific clause that does this includes the words "to have and to hold"—this is called the *habendum* (Latin for "to have") clause. In states that recognize a tenancy by the entireties, a joint conveyance to a husband and wife automatically creates the estate unless the language says otherwise.

The "Deed" Is Done

A deed is the formal document that conveys title in real property from one party to another. The party transferring the property is called the *grantor;* the party receiving the property is called the *grantee.* To be effective, a deed must be *signed, sealed, and delivered.*

Deeds are *recorded* in an appropriate governmental recording office—typically by the *recorder of deeds* in the county where the property is located. Recording establishes a publicly available *chain of title* that shows the current owner and any liens (claims) against the property (*see* below). The process of looking through deed records to validate ownership—and find any "live" liens against a parcel of real property—is called a *title search.*

The formality of a deed begins with its language. The grantor *must* use *words of conveyance* that indicate his or her intent to convey property. They vary from state to state, but common words (and phrases) of conveyance are "I grant and convey," "I grant, bargain, and sell," "I sell and convey," and "I sell, convey, and confirm." Precise language is so important that many states have statutory deed forms. In any case, conveyancing is one area where an experienced attorney should prepare the paperwork.

Another aspect of deed formality is the requirement for proper execution. *Sealed and delivered* doesn't mean that sealing wax is involved. Rather, these words—that come after the grantor's signature, just ahead of any witnesses' signatures—are part of the *formula for the attestation* by which witnesses attest to the deed's validity.

A few states still want a deed to be witnessed before it can be recorded (typically by two witnesses), but most require *acknowledgment* by a notary. This is a certification by a notary public that the deed was signed—in the notary's presence—by the person whose signature appears on it as grantor.

WHY TITLE INSURANCE?

Because the deed recording system is not foolproof, it's possible, though not common, for titles to be defective (say, because of a forged signature that *sealed* a deed many years ago) and for valid claims against property (say, an uncollected lien—see below—that has amassed huge interest charges) to be missed. Consequently, title insurance was developed to indemnify (protect) an owner's or mortgage lender's financial interest in a property in the event of a faulty title or undiscovered lien. Most mortgage lenders require title insurance, which is typically paid for by the buyer/mortgage holder. (In some locales, sellers pay; but who pays is always negotiable.)

Over the years, many different kinds of deeds have been developed for different conveyancing purposes. Only a few are common in the everyday law of homeownership:

→ *General warranty deed*—This type of deed conveys all of the rights the grantor has in the property and warrants that the grantee's rights of possession and quiet enjoyment (*see* Chapter 8) will not be disturbed by any earlier claims against the property, and that all the *encumbrances* on the property (including *covenants* and *easements*, *see* below) have been revealed. In essence, the grantor asserts that he or she has good title to the property and that the grantor will defend the grantee should any unforeseen claimants appear. This is the kind of deed most house buyers expect to receive. Note that a general warranty deed doesn't replace title insurance, because the promise to defend the grantee doesn't mean anything if a grantor is dead or "judgment proof."

→ *Grant deed*—This is a kind of warranty deed (commonly used in a few states, most notably California) that incorporates fewer guarantees because it is typically written in conjunction with a title insurance policy (*see* above) that provides most of the buyer's protections.

→ *Trust deed*—Typically executed by home *buyers* at closing as part of the process of securing the mortgage loan used to finance the property, the trust deed conveys the *bare title* to property to an entity acting as a *trustee* (who will legally own the property until the buyer finally pays off the mortgage). This entity is often a division of the mortgage lender. The trust deed (or deed of trust) gives the trustee the power to sell the real property in case the buyers default on their mortgage loan. When the mortgage is paid off, the trustee conveys the property back to the home buyers.

→ *Quit claim deed*—This conveys any legal rights the grantor has or may have in real property, but it makes no warranty as to what the grantor actually owns. A quit claim deed—as its name suggests—states that the grantor gives up any interests in the property (known or unknown) that he or she has and will never make any future claims against the property. Why? Well . . . if one spouse owns a piece of property, a buyer will often require a quit claim deed from the other spouse to be certain that he or she can't raise any future claims. (The second spouse may have rights in the property even if it's titled in only one spouse's name.) Also, a quit claim deed is typically used to "erase" the other spouse's joint ownership when one spouse receives the family home as part of a divorce settlement.

→ *Fiduciary deed*—An *executor* or *trustee* (*see* Chapter 19) uses a fiduciary deed to transfer property to the beneficiary of a will or trust. This deed warrants nothing more than that the fiduciary has the capacity and authority to convey the property. It's sometimes called a *trustee's deed*, but don't confuse it with a *trust deed* (*see* above).

→ *Bargain and sale deed*—This type of deed is used by banks (after a foreclosure) and tax authorities (after a sale to recover unpaid taxes) to convey property to a new owner. The grantor releases its interest in the property to the grantee but makes no warranties of title.

Liens against Property

A *lien* is a claim or charge imposed on property to satisfy a debt or another obligation. The root of the word is the Latin *ligamen*, "to bind"—an apt description of what a lien accomplishes:

→ A lien will effectively bar the owner of the property from transferring title to the property until the lien is "lifted."

→ Some liens enable the claimant to force the sale of the property to pay the debt.

At the very least, a lien—which is recorded at the county recorder of deeds—creates a "cloud" on the title that waves a legal red flag at any potential buyer of the property and stops most potential sales dead in their tracks.

Liens against property can come from many different directions:

→ Second mortgages

→ Unpaid federal income taxes

→ Unpaid state property taxes

→ Unpaid child support (in some states)

→ Unpaid homeowners association (*see* below) fees and fines

→ Unpaid court-awarded judgments (called *judgment liens*)

→ Debts to workers and businesses whose efforts have improved the property (called *mechanics' liens*)

The Dithers Go House Hunting

Now equipped with a broader legal vocabulary, Bob and Agnes Dither went house hunting. As they drove along Elm Street, they saw a lovely house, a well-manicured front lawn, and a sign that read, FOR SALE BY SELLER. Bob was intrigued. With no real estate broker commission to pay, the price might be lower than comparable houses. Without further ado, Bob and Agnes met with Darren Deeds, toured the house, and quickly decided to buy it. Neither Bob nor Agnes gave any thought to the complexities of house buying—or to the fact that by acting completely alone, no *knowledgeable* person was looking out for their interests.

REAL ESTATE BROKERS AND BUYER'S AGENTS

A seller will typically hire a real estate broker to market a house. The broker is considered the seller's agent—this is true even if the buyer contacts a broker at a different agency who seems disconnected from the seller. A real estate agent who brings a buyer to the table becomes a subagent to the seller. Although the seller's *listing agent* must deal fairly with the buyer—and can't withhold material facts—he or she has a fiduciary relationship with the seller, can't reveal any confidential information, and must uphold the seller's interests.

Because of this, a savvy buyer may hire a *buyer's agent* to represent his or her interests. Whereas a selling agent can't wax poetic to a potential buyer about a house's potential drawbacks, a buying agent can—and can also help negotiate the best price and identify problems that the selling agent might choose not to emphasize. A buyer's agent is also likely to show you homes for-sale-by-owner. Most buyer's agents split the sales commission paid by the seller, so a buyer's agent doesn't necessarily increase the cost to the buyer. The agent fee is typically paid by the buyer—the commission is negotiated—for a buyer's agent who facilitates a "home for sale by owner" transaction.

Discrimination in Housing

One thing the Dithers were a tad concerned about was discrimination in housing, because they belong to a small religious sect whose members have often been the victims of discriminatory practices. The federal Fair Housing Act makes it illegal to discriminate in the sale or financing of property because of race, color, religion, sex, disability, familial status, or national origin. The statute forbids a seller from using these factors as the basis of a decision to do any of the following:

- Refuse to negotiate for housing
- Deny or refuse to sell housing
- Set different terms, conditions, or privileges for the sale of a dwelling
- Provide different housing services or facilities
- Falsely deny that housing is available for inspection or sale
- Deny anyone access to a facility or service (such as a multiple listing service) related to the housing sale

Federal law specifically exempts a single-family house sold by the owner—*unless* the owner uses the services of a licensed real estate broker to sell the house. In that event, the seller can't instruct the selling agent to impose any discriminatory limitations, terms, or conditions—or advertise that the property is available only to persons of a certain race, color, religion, sex, handicap, familial status, or national origin.

Many states have enacted fair housing statutes that are more comprehensive than federal anti-discrimination laws. They often add protections based on sexual orientation and gender identity, and strip away the "single-family house sold by owner" exemption.

I'm happy to report that Darren Deeds did—or said—nothing that even hinted at discrimination in housing. And so, Bob and Agnes signed the *home purchase contract* that Darren prepared.

The Home Purchase Contract

The *home purchase contract*—also called the *purchase and sale agreement*—is the key document in the transaction of purchasing a house. It is a binding contract; in fact, under common law, the buyer essentially owned the house after signing the purchase contract. He or she was considered the *equitable owner*—and could demand that the sale be completed by formally transferring the title.

More than one home buyer has been snookered by the apparent informality of the purchase-agreement signing—which often takes place in a real estate agent's office, or a housing development sales office, or even the buyer's living room. It's easy to overlook that signing this document is the heart of a home purchase transaction.

Despite its greater formality—often including the presence of two or three attorneys—the *closing* or *settlement* (*see* below) is largely an exercise in tying up loose ends. The final steps are essential and must be done correctly, but legally speaking, the buyer buys the house—and the seller sells the house—when they both sign the purchase and sales agreement.

My point is, no buyer should rush into signing a home purchase contract without understanding its terms—nor believe the flood of soothing comments ("Oh, those words make no difference," or "That clause is merely a minor technicality," or "The lawyers made us say that, but it really doesn't mean anything") he or she will sometimes hear.

Some states still require lawyers to handle closings (chiefly to make certain that the deed has been prepared properly and that title to the house is not clouded); yet few buyers or sellers involve attorneys before they sign purchase and sales agreements. Many end up wishing they had.

Most residential sales contracts begin as standard fill-in-the-blanks forms that were developed to comply with state laws. Some are provided by real estate agent organizations, others by companies that publish legal forms, and still others by Internet legal service providers. As with all standard forms, they typically don't cover special situations and may exclude protections and provisions that specific buyers and sellers need. Nonetheless, they implement the lion's share of home purchases every year. A home purchase contract typically does the following:

- → Describes the property
- → Identifies the seller and the buyer
- → Stipulates the purchase price of the property, the amount that the buyer intends to finance with a mortgage, and the percentage of the purchase price (*down payment*) the buyer will deliver when the transaction is completed
- → Specifies the deposit (*earnest money*) that the buyer will deliver upon signing the purchase contract as evidence of his or her good-faith intentions to complete the transaction. The earnest money will eventually become part of the buyer's down payment, unless the buyer breaches the purchase agreement (in which event the seller will keep it). The amount of earnest money typically depends on what's usual in the community; often a fixed figure (say, $5,000) or a small percentage (2 to 5 percent) of the price of the house. However, in a "buyer's market," the seller may have to accept a smaller deposit; and in a "seller's market," the buyer may have to come up with more front-end cash.
- → Provides that a seller will deliver good title for the home
- → Sets the date when title to the house will be transferred to the buyer (the *closing date* or *settlement date*)
- → Provides that the full amount of the purchase price (from the buyer and his or her mortgage lenders) is due at closing
- → Provides that the buyer will pay any utility costs, insurances, or property taxes that have been prepaid by the seller (through the closing date)

→ Specifies which if any "closing costs" (appraisal fee, financing "points," attorney(s) fee(s), deed recording fee, local real estate transfer taxes, and others) will be paid by the seller, and which by the buyer

→ Provides for the payment of real estate agent fees at closing

→ Provides details of how escrow will be managed if an escrow company is handling the closing (*see* below)

This list of provisions presumes a trouble-free transaction. But because many house sales run into problems, the purchase and sale agreement should also include provisions to deal with contingencies. A *contingency* is merely a legal what-if—something that might occur and force a change in the terms of the purchase contract. These are three common contingencies:

1. One provision terminates the agreement (and returns the buyer's earnest money) if the buyer can't obtain financing for the house (usually for a specified number of years at below a maximum interest rate) after making a good-faith effort to do so.

2. A similar contingency provision terminates the contract if the buyer can't arrange homeowner's insurance at a maximum price (especially in coastal regions that are risk areas for hurricane strikes).

3. One provision allows the buyer to have the home inspected (for both mechanical soundness and pest infestations), usually within a few days after the contract is signed, and specifies the seller's responsibility to repair defects or deficiencies.

What the Dithers Did Wrong

When Bob Dither saw Darren Deeds bring out a standard form contract, he assumed that it included all the *usual provisions*. In fact, several important items in the buyer's favor were missing or had been changed. Here are four that Bob didn't spot:

1. The inspection contingency clause didn't release the Dithers from the deal if the inspection revealed especially serious problems and deficiencies (few standard inspection clauses do); rather, it allowed the seller to ignore minor defects and repair serious problems in any way of his choosing that met acceptable standards of workmanship. The Dithers came to regret this vague phraseology.

2. There was no provision for a walk-through inspection before closing to allow the buyer to verify that necessary repairs have been made and that the house is in "broom clean" condition.

3. There was no *risk-of-loss* clause that assured that the seller would continue to have all the risk of loss (say from storm damage or a fire) until closing. In the Dithers' state—and in some other states—the absence of such a clause in the purchase contract transfers the loss of risk to the buyers.

4. There was no provision that required Darren Deeds to keep their earnest money in an escrow account until closing. Consequently, he was free to spend it—making it much more difficult for the Dithers to recover their deposit should the deal fall through.

Aside: Home Inspections

The buyer of a house will typically commission—and pay for—a home inspection and a pest inspection soon after he or she signs the purchase contract. Depending on the location of the house, the contract may also call for a septic-system inspection, a toxic mold inspection, and measurement of radon levels.

Buyers are often surprised to find out that local home inspectors may not be licensed or certified (currently only about half the states have license or certification programs for inspectors). Real estate agents sometimes recommend home inspectors they work with—which can lead cynical people like Bob Dither to suspect that their inspections are *seller friendly*.

Because the buyer ultimately relies on the inspector's diligence, it makes good sense (and costs no more) for a buyer to hire a completely independent inspector.

A home inspection is just that—an *inspection*. The inspector will only spot visible problems, not *buried deficiencies* (a sewer problem, for example). He or she typically can't tell if a heat pump that works today will fail three months from now—nor will the inspector certify the condition of the roof.

Many good inspectors focus their reports on *exceptions*: They say little about systems and components that work well, but zero in on defects that can damage the house (interior water leaks are notorious problems) and big-ticket items that need prompt attention, including these:

→ Health and safety issues

→ Extensive areas of rotted wood

→ Roofs with a short life expectancy

→ Furnace malfunctions

→ Foundation deficiencies

→ Water infiltration, moisture, and drainage issues

→ Obsolete or inadequate plumbing

→ Obsolete or inadequate electric wiring

→ Poorly maintained fireplaces and chimneys

→ Asbestos and lead paint in older homes

A wise buyer will accompany the inspector as he or she works—to get instant feedback on potential problems and to get a better sense of which defects are minor (and can be ignored) and which must be fixed by the seller. This can be important because it's usually impractical to demand that the seller correct every defect. Also, sellers are likely to propose a price reduction—say, $750—to compensate the buyer for the inevitable collection of small defects, such as a dripping faucet or two, a torn sliding door screen, and a chimney that needs sweeping. This is often easier for sellers than a last-minute repair campaign.

Aside: The Closing

The seller wants his money—from the buyer and the mortgage lender—before he transfers title to the buyer. The buyer wants her house when she pays the seller. The mortgage lender wants a secure interest in the house before it hands over any cash. The real estate agent wants his commission when the house changes hands.

Simply put, several things have to happen at more or less the same time to complete a home purchase transaction.

Over the years, an event called *closing* or *settlement* (or charmingly, *passing of papers* in some locales) was developed as the final step in the process of buying and selling real property. Interestingly, two different approaches to settlement emerged in the United States.

Round-Table Closing

This is the formal settlement procedure still popular in the eastern half of the country. All the parties involved in the transaction (including buyer, seller, real estate agent(s), attorney(s), and bank) sit together, sign the many different documents, and exchange checks.

The process is typically managed—getting the details right can require the skill of a symphony orchestra conductor—by an attorney or a *title company* (an organization that specializes in title searches and settlements). Immediately after the closing, the attorney or title company records the deed in the buyer's name at the local recorder of deeds.

One advantage of a round-table settlement is that it establishes a firm closing date—a deadline that everyone works toward. Another is that minor last-minute problems can be resolved on the spot.

A potential disadvantage is that everyone involved has to be in the room at the same time (or else must arrange for powers of attorney, so that documents can be signed in his or her name), which can pose a scheduling nightmare. Also, in theory (but rarely in fact), a crooked seller can leave with his money then sell his house to another buyer—before the first buyer has had an opportunity to record the deed.

Escrow Closing

This is a less formal closing procedure that's traditional in the western half of the country. There is no need for the parties to assemble at the same time and place; rather an *escrow company*—essentially a professional independent third party—handles the settlement details one at a time, over a long period of time, if necessary. The buyer and mortgage lender transfer money into the escrow company's trust account; it stays there until the seller has signed a deed and other parties have executed the many different settlement documents. When all the paperwork is complete, the escrow company re-verifies that the title is clear, records the deed in the purchaser's name, and makes sure that the current taxes have been paid. Only then does the escrow company send the seller his or her money.

Surprise: The Dithers Are at Risk

The common-law notion that a buyer becomes the *equitable owner* of a house when the purchase contract is signed meant that the buyer assumed the risk of any damage to the property at that point. Many states have statutes that keep the risk of damage on the seller (who presumably is protected by a homeowner's insurance policy) until title is transferred to the buyer at the closing.

Other states follow the common-law rule but presume that the buyer will demand a *risk-of-loss clause* in the purchase contract that transfers risk back to the seller. These clauses usually allow the buyer to terminate the agreement—and get his or her deposit money back—if the house is destroyed or so badly damaged that repairs will take a long time or leave the house a different dwelling after completion.

Because the contract Bob and Agnes Dither signed with Darren Deeds had no risk-of-loss clause they unknowingly assumed the risk of any damage to the property between the signing of the contract and the closing of title. The worst-case scenario would have been a fire that destroyed the house, but even minor damage—say, a wind storm taking down a tree, or an errant driver hitting the mailbox—would have cost them money.

A less-than-perfect alternative to a risk-of-loss clause is for a buyer to purchase homeowner's insurance effective on the date that the purchase contract is signed. This is less desirable than a risk-of-loss clause because it forces the buyer to take on the hassle of rebuilding or repairing the house.

Surprise: Darren Deed Refuses to Repair Some Faults

A provision to inspect a home doesn't mean much without a well-thought-out approach for dealing with problems identified during the inspection. The purchase contract that Bob and Agnes Dither signed gave Darren Deeds the discretion to determine how to fix serious problems and which defects were too minor to worry about. And so, when their inspector found a $300 plumbing problem and a serious roof glitch, Bob and Agnes really had no legal grounds to complain when Darren dismissed the first as "a minor problem" and hired the cheapest, least-experienced roofer in the county to fix the second.

A well-crafted inspection clause can be—and should be—a subject for negotiation before the purchase contract is signed. The fundamental challenge is coming up with a contingency outcome that satisfies both the buyer and the seller.

> → The buyer would like a clause that gives her the right to rescind the purchase contract if, in the buyer's opinion, the inspection report is unsatisfactory.

> → A seller, of course, prefers the kind of clause that Darren Deeds wrote—a provision that gives him the right to repair serious problems in any way he sees fit and that doesn't allow the buyer to back out of the deal.

The ideal compromise for most transactions is somewhere in the middle. There are many practical inspection clauses out there—one common variation sets a maximum value (say, $5,000) for repair costs.

> → If the home inspector finds problems that will cost less than this figure to repair, the seller can either make the repairs or reduce the price of the house accordingly.

> → If the inspection turns up problems that cost more than the magic number, the buyer has a right to terminate the agreement.

The everyday difficulty with this kind of clause is that most home inspectors typically don't estimate the costs of repairing the defects they identify. (To do that, the inspector would have to spend hours troubleshooting faulty items—and keep track of dozens of different contractor labor rates and hundreds of different material costs.) Consequently, totaling up the likely cost of repairs (to know whether or not to back out of the purchase) can involve a major effort for a home buyer.

Surprise: "Everything" Wasn't Included

Bob and Agnes assumed that *everything bolted down* came with the house. Their notion is generally correct: An item of *personal property* (*see* Chapter 11) that is firmly attached to real property (is nailed in place; bolted to a wall, floor, or ceiling; glued or cemented; or otherwise built in) is presumed to be a *fixture*—a permanent part of the house that will become the buyer's property after closing. Unfortunately, some expensive items that seemed permanently attached at first glance really weren't:

→ Light bulbs (Darren Deeds decided to keep the costly energy-saving fluorescent bulbs that he'd installed throughout the house)

→ Curtains that are merely pinned to drapery rods (the rods themselves are bolted to the walls; they are fixtures)

→ Carpets that may fill a room but which are not tacked or glued to the floor

→ Appliances that are not truly built in and can be easily unplugged (for example, the refrigerator, the kitchen stove, the washer and dryer)

→ Portable shelving and workbenches in a garage

→ Storage baskets and portable bins in closets, drawers, and pantries

But Darren had also added a clause that the Dithers ignored—he specifically excluded two pricey chandeliers from the sale of the house and reserved the right to remove them.

Bob and Agnes learned two lessons:

1. Make sure that the purchase contract clearly lists everything in the house (whether or not a fixture) that the buyer expects to receive.

2. Understand which fixtures are excluded from sale.

Surprise: There Were Undisclosed Defects

After the Dithers moved in, they discovered a troublesome leak around the picture window in the dining room that had caused significant water damage inside the wall. They also realized that Darren Deeds had repainted the wall in order to disguise the damage.

The traditional legal doctrine of *caveat emptor*—"let the buyer beware"—has been softened in home buying. In most states, the seller has an affirmative duty to disclose material defects that he or she knows about, increasingly by providing the buyer with a *defect disclosure* form (completed in some states under the penalty of perjury).

A *material defect* is any problem that will harm the property's market value, shorten the life of the house, or pose a health or safety hazard to occupants.

A typical defect disclosure form lists a home's major components and systems and, for each, requires the seller to acknowledge a defect or state that he or she is not aware of a defect. The form isn't equivalent to a warranty, but it does prevent the seller from saying that everything works when the house is actually a festival of problems.

An unscrupulous seller like Darren Deeds would generally be liable for damages (the cost of subsequent repairs and possibly the diminished value of the house) for two reasons:

1. He failed to disclose known defects.
2. He concealed known defects from the buyer.

A seller who fraudulently conceals a serious defect (one that would have caused a reasonable buyer to reject the house) runs the risk of a court rescinding the sale after closing—and forcing the full return of the buyer's money.

But much of the *caveat emptor* principle remains alive and well. In many states a buyer can't complain about the seller's lack of disclosure if he or she did not exercise *reasonable diligence* to find defects—for example, commissioning a home inspection.

Some states now impose a duty on real estate agents to disclose known defects to buyers. An agent is required to *competently inspect* a property before making statements about the house. However, this requirement can generally be met by the agent doing his/her own inspection. State laws don't require agents to inspect inaccessible areas of a house or commission an independent inspection.

NEGLIGENT MISREPRESENTATION

Sometimes, a seller will tell the buyer what he or she wants to hear—without really knowing the facts. "Sure, the heat pump is in great shape." If the heat pump is actually full of about-to-fail parts, the seller has negligently misrepresented an important fact. The buyer can sue the seller for the cost of replacing the unit, but the buyer will have to show that he or she *justifiably relied* on the statement (a tough burden to meet unless the seller was an expert in heat pumps whose judgment could be relied on).

Surprise: Darren Deeds Didn't Move Out at Closing

After the closing, the buyer has title to the house he or she just bought—but surprisingly, not necessarily the right of possession.

Think about it! Many people buy rental properties for investment purposes. They're usually happy to have tenants remain in possession of their apartment after the closing.

On the other hand, Bob and Agnes Dither were fiercely unhappy to find Darren Deeds in *their* house, along with most of his furniture. Moreover, several rooms of the dwelling were in need of an industrial-strength cleaning.

How did this happen? Simple—the purchase and sale agreement they signed didn't specify that the seller would vacate the house before closing and leave the interior "broom clean." Moreover, it didn't reserve the right for the buyer to do a final walk-through inspection before settlement.

Other Things Worth Knowing about Buying a House

Covenants, Conditions, and Restrictions

Developers who create subdivisions often establish restrictions on the use of land to control such things as the types of dwelling that can be built, the kinds of fences that can be erected, the minimum *set back* of dwellings from the street, the kinds of home-based businesses that can be established, requirements to keep grass mowed, limitations on storing boats and recreational vehicles—and other regulations that impact community "look and feel."

These are called covenants, conditions, and restrictions (CCRs); they are typically recorded on a deed or a *subdivision plat* (the map that carves the subdivision into lots and streets). Some CCRs have specified expiration dates, but they can also be written to never expire.

CCRs are contractual—not statutory—restrictions on the use of land, but they are binding on property owners (including subsequent owners). Adjacent property owners can bring a civil action against a violator to compel compliance with the restrictions, but many subdivisions have homeowners associations (HOAs) that actively monitor and enforce the local CCRs. HOAs are often able to levy fines against rule breakers—and in some states have the power to launch a foreclosure proceeding if the property owner doesn't pay up and to bill violators for the legal fees involved in enforcing CCRs and other regulations. On this point, an HOA may have the power to impose even stricter rules and regulations than CCRs—including restrictions on pets, flag displays, and even backyard vegetable gardens.

One recent estimate puts the number of HOAs in the United States at about 290,000—and that upwards of 60 million people live in subdivisions governed by HOAs.

A purchaser of a house—new or existing—should make certain he or she understands the nature of CCRs that "run with the land" and the power of the local HOA (if any) to limit ownership freedoms. It's particularly important to

→ get a copy of a development's restrictive covenants (typically from the real estate broker) before you make an offer on the property;

→ get a copy of the HOA's bylaws or other governing document.

Easements

Lawyers describe an *easement* as an "interest to use—for a specific purpose—real property that another person possesses." For example, the gas company may have an easement to run gas lines under your property, or your next-door neighbor may have an easement to use "your half" of the common driveway that serves both houses. (You have an easement to use "his half.")

An easement is granted by a property owner with the same formalities as a deed to real estate and can be recorded along with the deed. After that, a typical residential easement is an *encumbrance* on the title that binds subsequent purchasers of the property.

Eminent Domain

Eminent domain is the power of federal, state, and local governments to "take" (also called *condemn*) private property for a public use—even when the property owner objects. The Fifth Amendment to the U.S. Constitution requires that the owner be *justly compensated*, which usually means that he or she receives fair market value from the government.

Public use is broadly defined—it can mean anything from creating a reservoir, to building a new road, to redeveloping a blighted neighborhood. Condemned property can subsequently be conveyed to new private owners if there's a *public advantage* or *public purpose.*

In 2005, the U.S. Supreme Court expanded the ability of government to allow a private development corporation to take private land using the power of eminent domain. The public outcry at this decision prompted most states to enact laws that either restrict takings by private entities—or set limits on the use of eminent domain for purposes of local economic development.

If a Home Purchase Falls Through

The purchase of a house occasionally falls through because of a contingency in the purchase contract—for example, when the buyer can't arrange financing or if the home inspection revealed that the foundation needs a major and costly repair before closing. (Unlike Darren Deed's home-brew purchase agreement, most contracts to purchase a house usually define how serious problems found in inspection will be resolved.)

In the first case, a good-faith buyer can back out of the deal and get his or her deposit back; in the second, both buyer and seller will probably agree to terminate the agreement to avoid legal wrangling. Once again, the seller will return the buyer's deposit.

Occasionally, a seller or buyer decides not to go forward with no real justification—perhaps the seller really loves the house or the buyer experiences buyer's remorse.

If the buyer backs out, the seller typically gets to keep the buyer's deposit. (Many purchase agreements stipulate that the deposit will be considered *liquidated damages*—what the buyer owes the seller in the event of a default.) In theory, a seller can sue to recover other actual costs if the deposit isn't sufficient, but in practice the additional damages that might be won are usually not worth the costs of litigation.

The situation is considerably different if the seller backs out. The buyer's first option is to recover his or her deposit and other moneys expended—including inspection fees, mortgage loan application fees, title search, and attorney's fees related to the purchase. If the agreed-upon selling price of the house was considerably less than comparable houses in the neighborhood, the buyer may also be able to recover the cost difference from the seller. These are all remedies for *breach of contract* (*see* Chapter 2).

The buyer's other option is to seek an *equitable* remedy (*see* Chapter 1). Because real property is considered unique, a judge can apply the doctrine of *specific performance* and compel the seller to deliver the property to the buyer.

CHAPTER 10

NEIGHBORHOOD
DISPUTES

I T WAS KING SOLOMON, THE WISEST OF ALL BIBLICAL KINGS, WHO WROTE, "Do not plan evil against your neighbor, who dwells trustingly beside you." Proverbs 3:29 (English Standard Version). Three thousand years later, wise lawyers who deal with common legal issues will add, "Nothing can turn the American Dream of owning one's own home into a nightmare faster than an ongoing conflict with a neighbor."

Happily, few neighbors plan to do evil things intentionally. Nonetheless, the vagaries of personalities, plants, and pets (to list a few familiar culprits) can create remarkably sharp disputes among neighbors.

Long before America was founded, English common law honored the oft-repeated principle that "a man's house is his castle, and each man's home is his safest refuge." This idea has become part and parcel of homeownership, so it's not surprising that unneighborly actions may be perceived as an "attack" on our castle that demands an immediate response. That can mean a visit to an attorney and the filing of a lawsuit—despite the high cost (and stress) of fighting a lengthy legal battle over a perceived injury to one's rights by a next-door neighbor.

Most lawyers agree that court should be the last resort—it's better to talk than to litigate. This is because everyday law doesn't offer good remedies for many of the most common neighbor-against-neighbor conflicts. On the other hand, more than a few battles between neighbors have escalated into violent altercations that resulted in the death of one of the parties. If words can't resolve a dispute—suing is preferable to shooting.

One of the best approaches if both sides agree is mediation, a form of alternative dispute resolution (*see* Chapter 1). Mediation, accomplished with the help of a neutral third party, enables both parties in the dispute to work out a *win-win* situation—as opposed to a lawsuit that leaves a winner and a loser. Advocates argue that mediation of neighbor-versus-neighbor disputes works upwards of 70 percent of the time, and that given the opportunity, most neighbors will choose a reasonable solution. The prerequisite for success, of course, is that both parties must be willing to compromise—which may not be true if the atmosphere has been poisoned by a lengthy conflict.

Case in point: a neighbor on Elm Street.

The Case of the Odoriferous Compost Heap

We'll call him Mr. Scratch. He owns the house next to Bob and Agnes Dither on Elm Street. The two houses are "cheek by jowl" alongside each other— with Mr. Scratch's family room and back garden scarcely thirty feet away from Bob Dither's bedroom window. This proximity is problematic because Mr. Scratch has an extraordinary ability to infuriate Bob Dither, who considers his neighbor the *neighbor from hell*.

Mr. Scratch is an organic gardener—and as frugal a homeowner as Bob Dither. So Mr. Scratch created a huge compost heap in his back garden, a foot from the boundary fence, and placed an impressive quantity of horse manure and stall bedding (acquired from a local horse stable) atop the pile.

The "How to Build a Compost Heap" manual that Mr. Scratch read explained that composting reduces odors compared to merely spreading manure. Perhaps so—but the stench wafting into the Dithers' open windows soon became intolerable to Bob. He chatted with Mr. Scratch, who replied, "Be patient, Bob, there won't be any smell when the composting process is finished."

Bob went ballistic; neither party has fully recovered from the shouting match that ensued. And so, when Mr. Scratch made no move to remove the moldering compost, Bob paid a visit to his attorney, who clarified the situation.

The Concept of *Nuisance*

"This is one time when the legal usage of a word closely echoes its common meaning," his lawyer explained. "A *private nuisance* is a substantial interference with the right to use and enjoy one's land. The law doesn't define specific private nuisances. Rather—in a felicitous phrase that goes back centuries—a nuisance is 'anything that worketh hurt, inconvenience or damage.'

"Another way to think of private nuisance is to focus on the *right of quiet enjoyment* [*see* Chapter 8] that every property owner enjoys. Nuisance is a disruption of quiet enjoyment that rises to the level of an intentional tort [*see* Chapter 3]. Note that I keep saying 'private nuisance,' because 'public nuisance'—a crime in most states—covers many minor offenses against the health, morals, safety, comfort, convenience, or welfare of a community. Mr. Scratch may or may not be guilty of public nuisance—chances are he isn't—but his compost heap clearly represents a private nuisance."

The lawyer went on, "To get the attention of a judge, a private nuisance must be more than merely bothersome or galling. A true nuisance is an *unreasonable* or *unlawful* use of property that produces material annoyance, inconvenience, discomfort, or damage to another person. Here are a few examples of a private nuisance:

> → Allowing unsanitary and smelly garbage to accumulate on residential property
>
> → Operating powerful flood lights that illuminate a neighbor's house all night
>
> → Applying 'weed killer' that wafts next door and kills a neighbor's shrubbery
>
> → Allowing a large tree to overhang a neighbor's backyard and interfere with the use of his or her property (perhaps by blocking the sun)
>
> → Producing excessive noise (say by allowing a dog to bark continuously through the night)
>
> → Producing noxious odors (say from a manure compost heap)
>
> → Allowing dogs to run free and damage a neighbor's property"

Bob's lawyer continued, "Notice that there's nothing intrinsically unreasonable about owning a dog, having floodlights, growing trees, or even creating a manure compost heap—if each is done in the *right* time and place. These things become private nuisances when the people responsible stop thinking about their neighbor's rights.

"Nuisances are remedied by *abatement*—the process for putting an end to, or terminating, a nuisance. Nuisances are typically abated by the person responsible for them, but under old common law, an injured party could abate a private nuisance that had been created *by an act of commission*, without notice to the person who has committed the act. The abatement had to be limited to eliminating the nuisance; no *wanton or unnecessary injury* could be committed.

"However, modern courts frown on the practice of an individual taking questionably legal action (including trespass) to abate a nuisance, so I recommend that you *don't* sneak into Mr. Scratch's yard and tear down his compost heap."

Officer, Do Your Duty!

Bob checked the Elm Street homeowners association covenants (*see* Chapter 9), which seemed to allow small, backyard compost heaps but were silent on the subject of adding manure to the pile. He then went on to look at the city ordinances and found a directly relevant law:

> Composting of horse manure is allowed only on lots or parcels where horses are kept. Compost heaps shall not be closer than seventy-five feet to any building not owned by the composter.

Bob looked further and discovered that the city also had a general nuisance statute:

No person on private property shall engage in any activity or create any condition which unreasonably disturbs, or would tend to unreasonably disturb, a person of reasonable sensibilities on private property in the same vicinity . . . if the disturbing activity or condition can be eliminated or ameliorated with reasonable accommodation on the part of the disturbing party. An unreasonably disturbing activity or condition shall include the emission of harsh, prolonged or unusual lighting, the emission of unreasonably loud, prolonged or unusual noise, or the emission of noxious, foul or nauseating odors, vapors, smoke or fumes.

Aha! Mr. Scratch was obviously *unreasonably disturbing* his closest neighbors, and he was also doubly violating the specific compost heap ordinance: Horses were not kept on his property, *and* the heap was scarcely fifty feet from Bob's house.

Bob immediately called the police (on the non-emergency line!) and asked for an officer to stop by as soon as practical.

Officer Rick O'Shea arrived the next afternoon, a day when the wind was blowing away from the Dithers' house. He listened politely and patiently to Bob, then said, "I'm sorry, Mr. Dither, but this seems a civil dispute—a private nuisance—rather than a criminal matter. I don't smell much of an odor—and even if I did, I wouldn't know its source.

"I didn't bring a search warrant, and I have no reason to invade your neighbor's backyard to investigate a bad smell. However, if you gather evidence that Mr. Scratch is violating the law, you can file a criminal complaint with the District Attorney's office."

Counselor, What Do I Do Next?

"I'm not surprised by the police officer's reaction," Bob's attorney said. "Building a manure compost heap may be a onetime violation of a fairly obscure regulation. The cop probably thought about the stack of reports he'd have to write and decided that your olfactory bliss wasn't on his list of things to protect and defend."

"Then maybe I *should* file a criminal complaint."

"Keep in mind that the D.A. has the discretion not to prosecute—and I doubt that she will, unless most of the neighborhood complains about the stench. On the one hand, proving that Mr. Scratch is operating an illegal compost heap won't be easy; on the other hand, she knows that some judges will laugh the case out of court."

"Then I have to put up with the foul smell?"

"Not at all! You have several options—including filing a suit for private nuisance. But the *first* step is to write a firm but polite letter of complaint to Mr. Scratch. I'll do that on my letterhead, so that he knows an attorney is involved—and I'll attach a copy of the city ordinance he ignored: a gentle reminder that we can take further legal action."

Bob Dither was skeptical . . . but much to his surprise, "jawing" worked. Mr. Scratch never again created a manure compost heap in his backyard.

An Exquisite—Though Disturbing—Noise

Alas, Bob Dither's suffering returned when Mr. Scratch—who loves Italian opera—began to play the largest, most powerful, seven-speaker audio system in the county. Bob Dither swore that he could see his neighbor's windows shaking when Mr. Scratch turned up the volume. In any case, the sound had no problem penetrating Mr. Scratch's walls and making its way into Bob's bedroom. To make matters worse, Mr. Scratch often listened to opera into the wee hours—ruining Bob's sleep. Agnes solved the problem by wearing earplugs; Bob refused to stuff his ears as a matter of principle.

Bob concluded that Mr. Scratch was violating the city's nuisance statute. "An open-and-shut case," Bob said to his attorney. "But once again, Officer Rick O'Shea decided to drag his feet, even though he agreed that 'O Mio Babbino Caro,' the well-known aria from the opera *Gianni Schicchi* by Giacomo Puccini, was clearly audible on my property."

The lawyer responded: "The officer refused to write a citation?"

"You got it! He shrugged at me and said, 'It's an awfully pretty piece of music—and it doesn't seem that loud.'"

"'Trust me,' I replied, 'It's impossibly loud at two in the morning.'"

The lawyer nodded. "The police usually deal with complaints about noisy parties or cars equipped with mega sound systems that annoy a whole neighborhood. Rick's not used to opera music played loud—so once again he prefers to treat your annoyance as a civil issue."

"Well—not completely," Bob said. "The officer paid a visit to Mr. Scratch and suggested that he turn the volume down to maintain friendly relationships in the neighborhood."

"What happened?"

"I enjoyed two blessed nights of silence, but then Scratch returned to his wicked ways—sort of. He plays his stereo late at night, but no longer during the day."

The lawyer smiled. "I guess I'd better write another letter."

But this time, the letter had no effect. What's more, when Bob Dither spoke to the neighbor on the other side of his house, he learned that she too felt tormented by Mr. Scratch's operatic "concerts."

"Now we're making progress," the lawyer said. "The courts in this city begin to take notice when noise disturbs two or more people. It proves that the complaint isn't coming from an *unreasonably sensitive* person."

"Which court will we use? District court or small claims court? [*See* Chapter 1.]"

"The small claims courts in the state can't issue injunctions—they can't tell a defendant to do (or stop doing) something. That's true of the small claims courts in most states. But they can award money damages to a plaintiff who has been injured by a defendant. Paying money can be as strong a deterrent to bad behavior as a court order—in some cases even stronger. And, considering how difficult it can be to get a district court to issue an injunction, it makes more sense to begin in small claims court."

"How much money damages should I ask for?"

"That's an excellent question. What most people do in your situation is to come up with a reasonable figure for each night of ruined sleep."

Bob had developed a detailed log of the days and times that Mr. Scratch's sound system blasted his bedroom. The attorney used the log to compute a damage number. "The stereo has annoyed you for forty nights. Let's assign a value of $50 per night. We multiply that by forty, we get $2,000—a nice round number that will certainly get Mr. Scratch's attention."

The attorney helped Bob prepare his complaint, serve it on Mr. Scratch, and worked with Bob to develop an effective presentation of the facts (*see* Chapter 14).

"To win in small claims court, you'll have to prove the following:

→ The noise that annoyed you was both excessive and disturbing—especially at one in the morning—and has adversely impacted your right of quiet enjoyment.

→ Mr. Scratch acted unreasonably when he persistently repeatedly produced the noise.

→ You took several reasonable actions to reduce the noise, but Mr. Scratch ignored them all."

The lawyer owned an inexpensive decibel meter—a sound level measuring instrument he'd purchased at a local stereo-system shop. Bob used it to take sound readings outside his home; they proved that the "noise" produced by the stereo system was equivalent to the sound of a noisy machine tool in a factory. To further prove the point, Bob made tape recordings of the music both inside and outside his house. Bob prepared a large diagram that showed the proximity of the two houses. Finally, Bob arranged for his other neighbor to testify at the trial.

"A plaintiff in a noise-abatement lawsuit needs to be very well prepared," the lawyer said. "In essence, you have to prove that the nuisance is truly offensive—and impossible to live with. A court presumes that petty annoyances are part of everyday life—minor irritants that we have to tolerate."

The hard work paid off: Bob Dither won his lawsuit; Mr. Scratch was ordered to pay a $2,000 judgment plus costs. Most important of all, Mr. Scratch decided to purchase a set of headphones, which he uses to listen to opera late at night.

Other Neighborhood Disputes

In the years that followed, Bob Dither found himself involved in several more neighborhood disputes with Mr. Scratch. One of them began soon after "the lawsuit," as the loud music case came to be known. Mr. Scratch exacted a small revenge by complaining about the damage Bob and Agnes's dog—a friendly Airedale named Rosie—did by pooping on his lawn and uprooting his shrubbery. Also, for reasons that no one could explain, Rosie barked and growled at Mr. Scratch whenever he walked past the Dithers' front lawn. Consequently, Bob and Agnes never let Rosie roam unleashed and chained her only in the backyard where she could pose no threat to their neighbor.

Mr. Scratch, however, was not satisfied by these accommodations. He concluded that his personal safety required that he rebuild the fence that separated his property from the Dithers' land. Moreover, he decided that this was a perfect opportunity to "reclaim" all of his rightful property. His old fence had been built a foot inside his property line; the new one would be built *on* the line.

Unfortunately, in the spirit of frugality, he didn't hire a surveyor, but rather bought himself a pricey tape measure, found a copy of the subdivision plat (map), and used these items to establish his property line. Soon thereafter, he installed a new, more robust, fence—a fence that *encroached* on the Dithers' property.

Encroachment with a Fence

This is one of the more common sources of friction among next-door neighbors: One of them builds a fence that encroaches on the other's land. An *encroachment* is simply the intrusion on another's property rights. In this case, Mr. Scratch built his fence on the "wrong side" of the property line he shares with Bob and Agnes Dither.

Mr. Scratch made a duffer's mistake when he built his new fence on his supposed property line. He should have hired a professional surveyor to conduct an updated survey and establish an accurate boundary line. At this point, Bob Dither can

→ notify Mr. Scratch in writing about the encroachment and request that his neighbor move the fence;

→ bring an *action in ejectment* (a lawsuit to recover real property unlawfully held by another) and obtain a court order that will require Mr. Scratch to move his fence;

→ offer to sell Mr. Scratch the property on the other side of the fence.

A useful first step to any of these actions is for Bob to suggest that he and his combative neighbor split the cost of the professional survey. Faced with irrefutable evidence, Mr. Scratch—a frugal and intelligent man—will probably choose the first (and least expensive option): Move the fence to his property.

Water Runoff

Bob and Agnes Dither's property is slightly downhill of Mr. Scratch's property, so that during an intense rainstorm, water tends to run in somewhat hefty streams that carve natural channels in the Dithers' side yard. Bob grew tired of repairing the channels and so decided to erect a low cement "curb" along the side property line to keep "Mr. Scratch's water" on Mr. Scratch's land.

Bob was quite surprised when he received a pointed letter from his neighbor's attorney demanding that he remove the cement curb forthwith.

Bob immediately checked with his own lawyer, who once again explained the legal issues.

"The law in this—and a majority of—states is that the *downstream* property owner must accept *natural* water runoff from an *upstream* neighbor's property. In particular, the downstream owner can't block or divert ordinary drainage water.

"Practically speaking, you must tolerate and make provision for water that flows naturally from land above yours. You can't complain about the runoff from Mr. Scratch's land unless he does something (say regrades the land, paves his lawn with asphalt, or builds a new structure) that *unreasonably* concentrates or *unreasonably* redirects the flow of the natural runoff. In that case, you would have a valid cause of action to support a lawsuit."

Trees and Overhanging Branches

One of the large, old trees on Mr. Scratch's land is so close to the property line that Bob Dither feared that a branch overhanging his property might fall and do damage, or that the tree's enormous root structure might penetrate his home's foundation or sewer pipes. And so he approached Mr. Scratch and requested that the tree be removed.

Mr. Scratch refused (he told Bob that the beautiful tree was one of the reasons he bought his house years earlier), and he warned Bob not to damage the tree in any way.

Bob consulted his attorney, who said, "You have a right to prevent a neighbor's tree from encroaching on your property. In this state, as in many, you can prune tree limbs and remove tree roots that are over or under your property. But, you have to give Mr. Scratch advance notice of your intentions. *And*—and this is a big *and*—you can't injure the tree or ruin its appearance. I suggest that you have the work done by a professional tree surgeon."

"It's Mr. Scratch's tree—do I have to pay for the tree surgery?"

"You do . . . unless he has failed to maintain an obviously sick tree or planted a tree himself in a location that was likely to result in foreseeable damage to your property. But that particular tree was standing long before your house was built. Mr. Scratch isn't liable in this state for damage done by *natural forces*—including vegetation planted years earlier on land. After all, he has no way of knowing where the tree roots are or where they will travel."

A MESSY TREE

Like it or not, one practical nuisance isn't considered a legal nuisance under everyday law. A messy tree—one that sends leaves, nuts, pine straw, pine cones, fruit, acorns, and other tree debris onto an adjacent property—is considered a natural occurrence. The mess is *not* considered tree-related damage. However, the owner of the adjacent property can trim any branches extending over his property line (if the pruning doesn't harm or significantly deface the tree, and if the tree's owner is notified before the tree is pruned). Bottom line: A property owner can usually limit gravity-driven messiness but not windblown tree debris.

"It just doesn't seem fair! As I keep pointing out, it's not my tree."

The lawyer smiled. "Well, as far as courts and legislatures are concerned, you have a perfectly good remedy—the right of self-help that will completely eliminate the problem. There's no reason to provide additional remedies."

A Lack of Lateral and Subjacent Support

One summer, Mr. Scratch decided to add a wine cellar to his house and had a hole dug for the new foundation—the absolute minimum distance away from his property line. Before the cement could be poured, the earthen walls of the hole collapsed inward.

Immediately thereafter, Bob Dither spotted a nasty crack in his foundation and called an experienced contractor who diagnosed the problem: Digging an adjacent hole undermined the land under Bob Dither's house. In technical terms, the digging and subsequent collapse affected the lateral support of Bob and Agnes Dither's land. The law recognizes two kinds of support:

1. Lateral (sideways) support comes from adjacent property.

2. Subjacent (from below) support comes from the earth beneath it.

The owner of adjacent property has a duty to support neighboring land. This means that the owner is *strictly liable* (*see* Chapter 3) for damage to land and buildings if he or she removes lateral or subjacent support—say by digging a hole or creating a tunnel. (An especially common source of damage is excavating to create an in-ground swimming pool.)

Legally speaking, the duty to provide lateral and subjacent support applies only to adjacent land in its *natural state*. Mr. Scratch will argue that the neighboring property would not have shifted but for the weight of the Dithers' house. If he prevails, the Dithers won't be awarded damages unless they can show that Mr. Scratch acted negligently.

You've Ruined My View!

Mr. Scratch decided that he could not live without a large backyard barbecue—a brick and stone monster with a tall and wide chimney. He built it, after getting approval from the Elm Street Homeowners Association. Once again, Bob Dither went ballistic: The tall chimney ruined his view of the Elm Street Pond—the only visible body of water in the neighborhood.

Bob visited his attorney in a hopeful mood, but left feeling morose.

"Broadly speaking, property owners in our city don't have the right to a scenic view from their land unless it is granted in a subdivision covenant, or possibly an easement on neighboring properties. These are more common in oceanfront or mountain communities, where the view is an important factor in establishing property value.

"On occasion, some communities have adopted zoning rules to protect views or have enacted *view ordinances*. A backyard barbecue would probably violate neither—assuming that we had one, which we don't."

CHAPTER 11

PERSONAL PROPERTY AND GIFTS

FINDERS KEEPERS, LOSERS WEEPERS! Every child learns that simple maxim. The idea seems so logical: If I lose something that I own, it's no longer mine. If you find it, it's yours. What could be fairer than that?

In fact, everyday law takes a much more nuanced approach to lost and found personal property. The law recognizes that you found an item that used to be in my possession for one of three reasons:

1. I *mislaid* the item—I merely forgot where I placed it.
2. I *lost* the item—I unintentionally placed it where I might never retrieve it again.
3. I *abandoned* the item—I intentionally placed it where I will never retrieve it again.

As you'll soon see, "finders keepers" is absolutely true only in the case of property that I intentionally abandoned.

The Case of the "National Treasure"

The heroine of our tale is Mademoiselle Viola Take, a life-long resident of Fractal City, in the State of Chaos. (Although Viola's not French, she hates being called *Miss Take*.) Viola inherited her grand, old house on Ancient Lane (and everything in it) from her mother, who died two years ago.

The three-story Victorian—heavily decorated with gingerbread—was built in 1860. The Takes bought it in 1966. Before that it had belonged to members of the Outerluck family for more than ninety years.

Viola finally got around to cleaning out the huge attic a year after her mother died. Along with several dumpster loads of junk, she found a well-preserved violin case that contained a well-preserved violin.

By a remarkable coincidence, *National Treasure Road Show,* the popular TV program, was being produced in Fractal City that very week. When Viola showed her dusty violin to the antique musical instrument appraiser—and explained that she "came across it in her attic"—he identified it as a handmade Vladovarious worth more than $2 million.

One person who watched the show was Ebenezer Outerluck—grandson (and only living heir) of the couple who'd sold the house on Ancient Lane to Viola Take's parents. He immediately filed a lawsuit to recover the violin, arguing that his grandparents had obviously mislaid the violin and that he had inherited the right to possess it.

PERSONAL PROPERTY IN A NUTSHELL

Legally speaking, *personal property* is everything that can be owned that isn't classified as *real property* (land and things like buildings and trees that are attached to land). There are two major kinds of personal property. The first is *chattels* (also called *corporeal* or *tangible* personal property), including the vast array of products, cars, animals, jewelry, books—the list would fill a library of books. The second category is *intangible* (or *incorporeal*) *personal property*, including such things of value that can't actually be touched (for example, contract rights, stocks, bonds, patents, and copyrights). The paper certificate that a shareholder receives merely represents a portion of the corporation's assets.

You'll sometimes see the word *personality* instead of the term *personal property*. Although the usage sounds odd, consider that *reality* is often used in lieu of *real property*.

When Viola visited her attorney, he began by explaining an idea she hadn't heard before. "The laws involving found personal property are more complicated than most people realize," he said. "They have to be, because there are so many different ways that a chattel can become separated from its true owner. But the various laws are built atop a common foundation: Whenever possible, a lost chattel is returned to its owner; if that's impossible, the chattel goes to the person who has the greatest legal right to possess it."

Much like the ownership of real property (*see* Chapter 9), the ownership of personal property also gives you a *bundle of rights*, including the right to use and possess the chattel, the right to exclude other people from using or possessing it, and the right to transfer ownership to another person (most often by selling it or giving it away). An important point is that everyday law protects this bundle of rights; a claimant can file a lawsuit to recover personal property illegally possessed by another.

THE QUAINT LEGAL LANGUAGE OF PERSONAL PROPERTY LAW

Some states still use old English common-law terms for the lawsuit a plaintiff files to recover a specific item of personal property, or the cost of repairing it, or the cost of replacing it. An action in *replevin* asks for the possession of a chattel wrongfully taken by the defendant. An action in *trover* seeks the value of a chattel that the defendant has *converted* (treated the property as his or her own to such an extent that it's just to make the defendant pay for replacing the item). A claim of *trespass to chattels* is appropriate when the defendant has somehow interfered with the rightful owner's possession (possibly by damaging a chattel). The court will award damages to compensate the harm done to the plaintiff (for example, the cost of repairing the damaged chattel). See Chapter 3 for a discussion of *conversion* and *trespass to chattels*.

Who Is the True Owner?

One of the tricky aspects of personal property law is deciding who is the true owner of a specific item. Real property stays put, it can be mapped and measured, and governments routinely establish organizations that record real-property ownership—at the very least, so that they know where to send the tax bill. (Land surveyors, land records, and real estate taxes in ancient Egypt date back to around 3000 B.C.)

Many kinds of personal property have serial (or identification) numbers, but only a few circumstances does government record and keep track of the numbers and link specific items of personal property with specific people—motor vehicles, aircraft, boats, and (to some extent) firearms are examples.

With *most* personal property, *possession* is the best indicator of ownership. You may have heard the old legal proverb, "Possession is nine-tenths of the law" (sometimes "nine points of the law"). This means that he or she who actually possesses a disputed item has a much stronger legal claim to ownership than someone who merely says, "I'm the true owner."

Viola's rare violin illustrates the challenges of dealing with *movable* property. It has no serial number and no *provenance* (a documented history of ownership that frequently accompanies an artwork, antiques, or a rare book). The instrument might have belonged to the Outerlucks, *or* it might have belonged to Mr. and Mrs. Take. All we know for certain today—unless Ebenezer Outerluck can present other, more compelling evidence of ownership—is that the Vlad is currently possessed by Viola Take. Perhaps that's enough to declare her the true owner.

Even people who've experienced a theft of property from their homes can find it difficult to prove that recovered property is theirs. They're typically required to provide a complete description (can you *completely* describe a favorite piece of jewelry?) and serial numbers or other documentation proving ownership.

WHY LAW STUDENTS STUDY WILD ANIMALS

We're so used to the idea that we can own things that few of us think about the difficulties behind the simple question: *How do personal property rights begin?* To drive this point home, the first cases about personal property studied in many law schools focus on the ownership of previously wild animals—like fox and deer. No one can be said to own a wild animal in its natural habitat. But under rules created as part of common law, a person began to own a wild animal when he or she physically possessed it. This is called the *capture rule*: The first person to kill or capture a wild animal acquires legal ownership of it. Today, the idea of possession as the central aspect of ownership permeates the law of personal property.

Four Kinds of Found Property

To expand what was mentioned earlier in this chapter, personal property is *lost* if the owner parted with it *involuntarily* and doesn't know its location. The key point to remember is that an owner may be careless, but he or she never intends to lose a chattel. Consequently, lost property *continues to be owned* by the person who lost it. This means that the true owner has a greater right of possession than a person who finds a lost chattel.

By contrast, personal property is *mislaid* if the owner *intentionally* places it somewhere fully expecting that he or she will be able to find it again—but then forgets the property's location. The key point here is that property is never mislaid accidentally—although the owner may have been careless in not taking better note of the location chosen for the chattel. As with lost property, a mislaid chattel *continues to be owned* by the person who mislaid it. And the true owner has a greater right of possession than a person who finds a mislaid chattel.

Personal property is *abandoned* when the owner intentionally relinquishes all property rights. Abandoned property is *unowned* by anyone. The most common way to abandon a chattel is to throw it away. The law generally gives the right to possess and own an abandoned chattel to the first person who takes possession of it with the intent of claiming it as his or her own.

THE PROBLEMS WITH "FINDERS KEEPERS"

There are two common explanations for why courts don't apply the simple approach of "finders keepers" to lost and mislaid property. First, is the assumption that "finders keepers" would encourage some *finders* to steal personal property and then lie about how they acquired it. Second, "finders keepers" requires owners to chain themselves (at least metaphorically) to their personal property, because any item not in the immediate control of the owner would be "findable" (and available for possession) by another person.

A *treasure trove* is a special kind of found personal property that was neither lost nor mislaid. It consists of money, coins, or bullion that was hidden long-enough ago—typically under obscure circumstances—so that the identity of the true owner can't be determined. Treasure trove has been unearthed (literally!) by finders, discovered hidden in walls, and tucked into secret compartments in furniture. Most states treat treasure trove the same way as other found property—a trove belongs to the finder (because in the case of treasure trove, the true owner will never be identified). Critics of this approach argue that it invites trespassing by treasure hunters. Consequently, some states award treasure trove to the owner of the property where it is found. (In England, a statute grants title of the trove to the government, subject only to the claim of the true owner. However, the government typically pays substantial rewards to finders who turn in treasure troves.)

Greater and Lesser Rights of Possession

Found property also illustrates that while possession is a strong indicator of ownership, it isn't conclusive. This is because there are greater and lesser rights of possession.

Imagine that you've borrowed a DVD from a friend. You leave in possession of the DVD, but you know that your right to possess the disk is temporary, that you'll have to return it to its true owner in a few days. Now imagine that you mislay the DVD on a coffeehouse counter—and that the cashier takes possession of it, intending to return it to you.

She realizes instinctively that she has a superior right of possession than the man standing behind you who says to her, "Hey . . . that DVD you just picked up doesn't seem to belong to anyone. Can I have it?" But she also understands—as an honorable individual—that she has a lesser right of possession than you do. Note that the cashier doesn't know who *really owns* the DVD—she's based her decision completely on her observation that you had possession of the disk.

Later that same day, you return to the coffeehouse and say to the cashier, "I think I left 'my' DVD on the counter earlier today." She replies, "You certainly did. I locked it in our lost-and-found cabinet for safekeeping."

Who is in possession of the DVD right now?

She is . . . but the law recognizes two kinds of possession:

1. *Actual possession*—The possessor has direct physical control over a chattel.

2. *Constructive possession*—The possessor has the power and intent to control the chattel, but not direct physical control.

The cashier had actual possession when she picked up the DVD; she began to have constructive possession when she placed it in a locked cabinet that she controls.

Now, let's add another twist: You never do remember where you mislaid the DVD and finally admit to your friend that it's gone forever. Who has the right to possess the DVD if you never reclaim it? The cashier might decide to hang on to the disk, but in everyday law, her right of possession would continue to be subject to the claim of the DVD's true owner—the friend who lent it to you.

It's hard to care much about a lost DVD, but what if the borrowed item you mislaid was a solid gold fountain pen—a unique chattel worth a significant sum. You—and your friend—would probably feel differently if the cashier merely hung on to it or passively stored it indefinitely in a locked cabinet. Shouldn't she do something "active" to help restore the chattel to its true owner?

Duties of Finders

Most states (sometimes municipalities) require the finder of money or personal property having more than a negligible value to deliver the find to the local police department. Then, the police department—but surprisingly, sometimes the finder—has the duty to advertise the find in a local newspaper. (Where required, a finder who doesn't place the ad gives up his or her rights to eventually claim the property.)

In theory, the ad notifies the true owner that a lost or mislaid item of personal property has been found. In practice, most owners of valuable lost or mislaid property will contact the police themselves.

If the true owner doesn't come forward, the property is typically returned to the finder after a statutory time period—usually ranging from sixty days to six months. At this point, the property is considered the legal equivalent of abandoned, and the original owner forfeits any claim to its return.

Miss Take's Vlad

Does Viola face trouble from the Fractal City police for failing to report her find? Will Ebenezer Outerluck be able to prove that his grandparents once owned the old Vlad—and if so, will that make him the true owner? Will Viola learn to play the violin?

Probably not is the answer to all three questions. If need be, her attorney will argue that Viola didn't find anything; the violin is *her own* property. After all, she inherited all her mother's personal property, including her so-called junk in the attic. There's every reason to believe that the Take family owned the violin for decades—not recognizing its value doesn't indicate a lack of right to possess it. [Viola may have to consult an experienced estate lawyer to determine if She—her mother's executor (*see* Chapter 19)—will have to file amended federal and state estate-tax returns.]

The Generous Mademoiselle Take

The legal brouhaha surrounding the old Vlad evaporated when Viola discovered a sepia-tone photograph that showed Great Grandpa Take playing the violin some seventy years earlier. Ebenezer Outerluck reluctantly admitted that the Take family possessed the Vlad long before his grandparents sold the house to Viola's parents.

Viola immediately sold the violin and—true to her very generous nature—gave a series of monetary gifts to her nieces and nephews to help fund their college educations.

"I want to do things right," Viola said to her lawyer. "Is there anything I should I know about the everyday law of giving gifts?"

The lawyer smiled. "The truth is that few clients ever ask me about gifts—most of us have a gut feeling about what makes a gift. But I do remember what I learned in law school. Alas, the legal language of gift-giving seems to take away the sentiment, and the fun."

"In law, a gift is an immediate voluntary transfer of personal property from one individual (called a *donor*) to another person (called a *donee* or *recipient*), that is made gratuitously to the recipient."

"Oh dear," Viola began. "I thought I understood . . ."

"It's actually quite simple," the lawyer said. "Look at the different elements of the definition one at a time. Here's what a gift is:

➔ *A transfer*—The ownership of the chattel or money shifts from the donor to the recipient.

➔ *Made voluntarily*—If a gift giver is coerced or forced into giving a "gift," a court will likely allow the donor to revoke the transfer of ownership.

➔ *Immediate*—The transfer of ownership takes place when the gift is made.

➔ *Made gratuitously*—The donor doesn't receive any compensation, or *consideration* [*see* Chapter 2], or something of value in exchange for the gift (warm, cozy feelings don't count)."

A true gift is irrevocable; the donor can't demand his or her money or property back. Over the years, many legal battles have been fought by donors who wanted their money or property returned. Accordingly, courts (and legislatures) have developed ways to determine whether the requirements of gift giving are met. A judge who has to decide if a gift was actually made will look to see that three factors are present:

1. *Donative intent*—The donor actually desired to part with his or her property. Intent is usually reflected in the donor's words, but a court will also look at the circumstances of the purported gift, including how the donor and donee are related, the size of the gift in relation to donor's personal wealth, and how the donor behaved after giving the gift.

2. *Delivery*—The donor surrendered control of the property to the donee. This can be either *actual* (the donor gives the property to the donee) or *implied* (for example, the donor presents the keys to a car to the donee, rather than the actual car). Some courts also recognize a *symbolic* delivery (for example, the donor gives the donee a photo of a car).

3. *Acceptance*—The donee unconditionally agreed to take the gift at the time the delivery was made.

If any of these three things are missing, a court will determine that the donor did not make a gift to the donee.

Thus informed, Viola went on a spate of gift giving.

Double Take's Tuition

She handed her nephew Double a paper bag full of crisp $100 bills. "This should pay your college tuition for the next four years. Consider it my gift to you."

Double clutched the bag to his chest and replied, "Thank you, Aunt Viola."

Was this a valid gift? Yes! We can *hear* Viola's donative intent in her words and *see* actual delivery in her actions. Her nephew clearly accepted the gift.

Clever Take's Tuition

Viola rushed from Double's home to visit her niece Clever—but realized that she forgot to go to the bank and get another bag of money. "It won't make any difference," Viola said to herself, "I'll give her a check."

Viola handed Clever a personal check drawn on her bank account. Clever hugged her aunt and said, "Thank you. I'm delighted to accept the best gift I've ever received."

Was this a valid gift? Not quite! A gift of money made by a personal check is not complete until the donee has cash in hand (or in her bank account). This is because the donor can stop payment on a personal check until it clears the donee's bank.

Quick Take's Tuition

Because it was late in the day, Viola didn't want to drive across Fractal City to see her nephew Quick. So she called him up and said, "Quick, I'm giving you a gift of money that you can use to pay your tuition."

"Thank you, Aunt Viola. I can use every cent you give me."

Had she made a valid gift? Nope! Viola might, from her perspective, have had a heart full of donative intent, but there was no delivery because she hadn't surrendered control of any money to her nephew. Similarly, Quick had nothing to accept.

Fresh Take's Tuition

The very next day, Viola brought another bag of $100 bills to her niece Fresh. "I have a gift for you. If I figured right, it will pay your tuition and expenses for the next three years."

"Thank you, Aunt Viola—but the truth is, I've dropped out of college and joined the French Foreign Legion. I won't have any use for your money. Please take the bag with you when you leave."

Had Viola made a valid gift? Clearly not! Although she had donative intent and successfully completed delivery of the money, Fresh Take refused to accept the gift, so it was not completed.

Gifts Can't Be Conditional

A few weeks after Viola's visit, Double Take used his bag of money to purchase a new motorcycle and a wardrobe of biker duds. Viola immediately called her lawyer and asked, "Can I do anything more than merely complain about Double's misuse of my generous gift?"

"Not really, Viola," the attorney replied. "You gave the lad an irrevocable gift. Once he took possession of the money, it was his to spend as he chooses. Broadly speaking, courts don't allow completed gifts made between living people to be revoked by future events. This is because a donor who reserves the power to revoke a gift hasn't really given a gift at all."

Viola also wondered if it's possible to structure a gift so that delivery isn't complete until some condition is met. "For example," Viola said, "What if I'd told Double that I'd give him a gift when he graduates from college—enough money to repay all the tuition money he spent?"

The lawyer shook his head. "Although you think of your promise as a gift, you've actually made a *contract* [*see* Chapter 2] with Double. A valid gift becomes effective when it is made, not when some future event occurs.

"The general rule is that there are no *conditional gifts* between a living donor and a living donee—although conditional gifts are routinely made (and enforced) in wills and in gifts made in anticipation of the donor's death [*see* Chapter 19]. But like many legal rules, there's an interesting exception. Many courts treat an engagement ring as a conditional gift."

Engagement Rings as Conditional Gifts

He pops the question; *She* says, "I will." He gives her a diamond engagement ring. The scene repeats a myriad of times each day across the United States. Unhappily, as Shakespeare noted, "the course of true love never did run smooth." And so, He and She decide to break off their engagement.

Does she have to return the ring?

→   The No-sayers argue that He gave her an irrevocable gift—
      complete with donative intent, delivery, and acceptance.
      Consequently, He can't revoke his gift merely because they split
      up. She should keep the ring, no matter what.

→   The Yes-sayers counter; the gift of an engagement ring is
      actually a uniquely *conditional* gift—it is given presuming that
      a future event will occur. Specifically, He gives She the ring
      as a conditional gift made in contemplation of marriage. If the
      condition fails—if the marriage doesn't happen—the gift is not
      complete. He is entitled to get the ring back.

Many courts treat pricey engagement rings as the exception to the rule that gifts are irrevocable—often adding other requirements based on fault. Thus, if He broke off the engagement for a good reason, or She got cold feet, or He and She decide together to end the relationship—He can revoke his "gift" and get the ring back.

Gifts and Income Tax

A "true" gift is not considered income to a donee. None of the Takes needed to report their gifts on their tax returns. I emphasized *true* above because more than one taxpayer has tried to characterize a payment for work done as a gift.

On the other hand, what about Viola? Does she have to report her substantial gifts to her nieces and nephews and pay a federal gift tax? The answers are possibly *Yes* . . . and probably *No*.

If a single donor gives a single donee more than the *annual exclusion amount* ($13,000 in 2010), the donor has a reporting obligation. But the requirement to pay gift tax doesn't begin until the total of all gifts to the donee exceeds one million dollars (the *lifetime limit*).

Interestingly, Viola didn't take advantage of the unlimited exclusion for the payment of educational costs (the payments must be made directly to an educational institution). A similar unlimited exclusion exists for payments for medical expenses.

Anyone who makes really large gifts to family or friends should consult an attorney, accountant, or financial consultant who's experienced in gift taxation.

Other Things Worth Knowing about Personal Property

Temporary Possessors of Property

If you read the fine print on the back of a receipt from a valet parking facility, you're likely to see the word *bailment*, often in a disclaimer that attempts to deny that a bailment was created—or possibly in a statement designed to limit the effects of the bailment.

You also run into bailments when you rent a car, ship a package, check your bag at the airport, borrow a library book, leave clothing at a dry cleaner, bring a watch to a jeweler to have the battery replaced, leave your dog at a pet groomer, lend a garden tool to your neighbor, take possession of a lost or mislaid item— and in many other familiar situations where you take possession of someone else's personal property or allow another party to take possession of your personal property.

It's a safe bet that you've had the word *bailment* tucked into your wallet (or pocket) on countless occasions, but have little idea what it means. That's because the law of bailments is an aspect of everyday law that is simultaneously remarkably *common* and largely *obscure*.

Legally speaking, a bailment is a *temporary transfer* of the possession or custody of personal property for a limited period of time and for a specific purpose. (The word *bailment* comes from the old French *bailler,* "to place in charge of.") The *bailor* owns the property; the *bailee* takes exclusive possession.

The essential point is that ownership is *not* transferred by a bailment—only the right to possess and control a chattel. In many everyday bailments, the bailee doesn't have the right to use the chattel he possesses.

A good example is a parcel shipping service. You entrust the company with possession of your parcel for the specific purpose of moving it from Point A to Point B. You don't want—or expect—anyone along the way to use the item inside.

And when you use the valet parking service in front of a restaurant, you don't want—or expect—the attendant to drive your car anymore than necessary to park it safely. He or she has the right of possession for a few hours and a strictly limited right of use.

NON-BAILMENT CAR PARKING

Bailment parking used to be far more common. Today, you're likely to park your car in a parking facility yourself, choose your own parking spot, hang on to your car keys, retrieve your car without an attendant's help, and be issued a *parking ticket* that merely identifies the time you entered the facility. Under these circumstances, a bailment is not created, even if you pay a fee for the privilege of parking, because you don't transfer possession of your car to another party.

Most of us can safely ignore the law of bailment until

> → our chattel is damaged or stolen while in the possession of a bailee;
> → the bailee can't (or refuses to) return our property at the end of the bailment period.

A bailee is required to care for the personal property in his or her temporary possession. The level of care that the law demands depends on the type of bailment that was created. Although this can sound like one of the most arcane aspects of bailment law, the underlying principles are straightforward:

> → Some bailments are for *the sole benefit of the bailee*. For example, you borrow a book from the public library. In this circumstance, you—the bailee—must exercise a *high level* of care and return the chattel in its original condition. You are liable for the damage (or loss) caused by even slight neglect.

→ Other bailments are for *the mutual benefit of the bailee and the bailor*. For example, a car dealership takes possession of your car to perform routine service or a dry cleaner takes possession of your jacket to clean and press it. (A bailment to service or repair a chattel is considered a bailment for mutual benefit when the bailee is paid a fee to do the work.) In this circumstance, the bailee must exercise reasonable care and is liable for damage (or loss) caused by his negligence.

→ Still other bailments are for *the sole benefit of the bailor*. A free attended coatroom at a museum is a good example. This is also called a *gratuitous bailment*, because the bailee doesn't receive any compensation. In this circumstance, the bailee has to exercise only modest care; the bailee is liable for damages (or loss) caused by his or her gross negligence (*see* Chapter 4).

Regardless of the kind of bailment, the bailee is expected to return the chattel to the bailor at the end of the bailment. Consequently, bailees can be liable for the tort of conversion (*see* Chapter 3) if they use the chattel without authorization or unjustifiably refuse to return it.

Certain mutual-benefit bailees were traditionally held to strict liability standards if they failed to redeliver chattels in their care: these include *common carriers* (companies that transport people or goods for a fee), warehouses, and innkeepers. They are responsible for any loss or damage—although there may be statutory or contractual limits to the compensatory damages they're required to pay.

CHAPTER 12

+⟾ ⟾+

THE PRODUCTS YOU BUY

L
EGEND TEACHES THAT THE ANCIENT ROMANS APPLIED THE DOCTRINE
of *caveat emptor*—Latin for "let the buyer beware." The chief idea is that
a buyer must assess the quality of a purchase before making it. If the
product is defective or fails prematurely, the buyer has no recourse unless the
seller wrongly concealed the product's latent defects.

Bottom line: The unhappy buyer bears the entire loss of the purchase price.

In fact, the legend is a fable. Legal historians now know that Roman law
expected sellers to deal honestly and show good faith.

Nonetheless, *caveat emptor* became a cornerstone of English common law and
was made a rule of American law by the U. S. Supreme Court in 1817. Happily,
both England and the United States have moved away from the doctrine—
which many people consider primitive, dishonest, and unfair given the complexity of modern products. When you think about it, how can a buyer truly
assess in advance the quality of an automobile, or an iPod, or even a candy bar?

Although every purchase you make still requires a dollop of faith—and may
lead to buyer's remorse—everyday law gives you a range of remedies when a
product you buy fails to meet your expectations or proves to be dangerous.

The Case of the Abominable Appliance

You may have seen the recent news reports about Al Dente's lawsuit against the
Owch Appliance Corporation. As one reporter wrote: "The poor man feels he's
lucky to be alive after surviving the blast that destroyed his kitchen. 'Who knew,'
Al says, 'that a simple pasta maker could cause so much damage.'"

Al Dente's unusual story began when he purchased his first Pasta Phantom
at Big-Box Kitchen Store. He tried to make a batch of linguine and discovered
that the machine's pasta dough feeder rotated backwards—probably (he guessed)
because of a manufacturing defect.

Al brought the defective Pasta Phantom back to the Big-Box Kitchen Store and
exchanged it (under the store's fourteen-day exchange policy) for an identical unit.

The second machine produced flawless pasta for nearly a month, but then went
up in a whiff of smoke caused by an apparent electrical short circuit somewhere
in the innards of the appliance—probably another manufacturing defect.

This time, however, Big-Box Kitchen Store refused to exchange the contrap-
tion, explaining that after fourteen days, the customer must return a faulty
product directly to the manufacturer. And so, Al shipped the frazzled pasta

maker to Owch Appliance Corporation, who promptly sent him a *second* replacement machine.

When Al turned the new Pasta Phantom loose on a big batch of spaghetti, the machine exploded with sufficient *oomph* to cover his kitchen walls with pasta dough and send Al to the hospital. Paramedics were amazed that he lived to tell the tale.

As the reporter wrote in a follow-up story: "The victim's attorney—standing alongside his hospital bed—said, 'Mr. Dente intends to pursue appropriate legal action against Owch Appliances. The company clearly breached both *express* and *implied warranties*—and is also liable under the principles of *product liability*.'"

We'll look closely at these aspects of everyday law in this chapter.

Warranties—Express and Implied

A warranty is a promise—typically about a product's performance or quality—that the seller or manufacturer makes *expressly* (*explicitly*), or is *implied* (presumed to have made *implicitly*). Most express warranties are written (often on the box, or in a printed warranty certificate, or a statement in an advertisement). However, an express warranty can also be oral (for example, a statement or promise made by a salesperson). A buyer can ask the court (often a small claims court) to enforce a warranty whether it's express, implied, written, or oral against a seller (and usually the manufacturer) of a product. A breach of warranty may give the purchaser the right to recover the cost of the item—and other damages caused by that breach of warranty.

An express warranty doesn't have to include words like *warrant, promise,* or *guarantee*—any written or oral representation of fact or promise can be sufficient to establish an express warranty. Here are a few examples of express warranties:

→ "This van will hold eight passengers."

→ "This air conditioner will cool the average sized room."

→ "We will repair any manufacturing defects that become obvious during the first year of use by the purchaser."

Warranties You Get without Asking

The *Uniform Commercial Code* (UCC) is a comprehensive body of statutes that regulate all manner of transactions involving personal property. Every state has enacted the complete UCC—except Louisiana, which chose to let its existing laws govern sales (the subject of the UCC's Article II).

Before states passed the UCC, buyers of products could generally only rely on express warranties. One universal exception was the *implied warranty of title*, the unspoken promise that someone selling a product had the right to sell it.

Here and there, some courts honored other implied warranties—for example, that the sample of a product shown to a customer before a sale actually represented what the customer would receive. All *implied warranties* originate out of a buyer's reasonable expectations to receive "fair value for money spent" (to quote a well-known phrase from common law), not because the seller made an explicit promise.

The UCC formally defined two important implied warranties that can arise in consumer-product transactions. These are the *implied warranty of merchantability* and the *implied warranty of fitness for a particular* purpose. Both provide significant consumer protections. Today, products sold throughout the United States come with one—or possibly both—implied warranties unless the seller specifically disclaims them (a practice that some states refuse to allow). In legal speak, the implied warranties are said to *arise out of operation of law*, unlike an express warranty (which is basically a contract between the seller and buyer).

THE PUFFING DEFENSE

The salesman tells you, "This is the best widget in the world" and "It will last a lifetime." You purchase the gizmo, take it home, and discover that it's less effective at widging than other widgets you own—and will probably wear out before the really good widgets you own. Can you argue that the salesman made an express promise? Probably not—because he was really engaged in *puffing*. Everyday law tolerates exaggerations in selling that are little more than personal opinions. A reasonable buyer (like you) should recognize that "this is the best widget in the world" is probably not a factual statement. However, puffery can't include an outright lie or communicate apparent facts. Suppose the salesman said, "this widget weighs less and operates at a higher speed than any other widget you can buy." A court would likely consider the salesman's statement an express warranty—a legally enforceable promise.

Implied Warranty of Merchantability

The *implied warranty of merchantability*—says that the product, when used for its ordinary purpose, will reasonably conform to an ordinary buyer's expectations and meets the standard of quality *as passes ordinarily in the trade.* The buyer can also expect that the product be adequately packaged and labeled—and that it fulfills any promises made on the label:

→ A customer who buys a box of corn flakes can reasonably expect them to be intact within the box, resemble the photo on the box, and be edible.

→ A buyer who buys a movie on a DVD can presume he or she has purchased the film depicted on the label and that the disk will load and play in an ordinary DVD player.

→ A person who buys an ordinary bicycle can expect it to be ride-able on ordinary pavement and be capable of carrying a rider of average weight (but probably *not* a rider who weighs 400 pounds).

To *disclaim* this implied warranty, a seller must declare that the product is being sold *as is* or *with all faults*, or must specifically state that "no warranty of merchantability is made."

The implied warranty of merchantability only applies to a *merchant* (a person or company who makes a business of selling goods) who regularly sells the product in question—for example, the supermarket that sold the box of corn flakes I mentioned earlier. If you gave up eating corn flakes and sold the remaining box in your pantry to a neighbor, there'd be no implied warranty of merchantability.

Implied Warranty of Fitness for a Particular Purpose

The *implied warranty of fitness for a particular purpose* arises when the buyers rely on the seller to provide a product that can perform a specific, nonordinary purpose. For example, if a seller assured the heavyweight bicyclist (*see* above) that a particular bicycle would carry his weight, this would create an implied warranty of fitness for that purpose. If the bicycle subsequently failed, the customer could sue the seller for breach of implied warranty.

However, the implied warranty of fitness for a particular purpose requires that

→ the seller knows that the buyer intends a particular purpose;

→ the seller knows that the buyer will rely on the seller's skill and knowledge to furnish an appropriate product (often a good assumption when the seller is a specialist, such as an electronics retailer, antiques dealer, or a bike shop);

→ the buyer does, in fact, rely on the seller's skill and knowledge.

A seller can disclaim this implied warranty (in states that allow disclaiming) by expressly stating that "no warranty of fitness for a particular purpose is made." Also, the implied warranty doesn't arise if the buyer is as knowledgeable as the seller—or if the buyer gives the seller particular specifications for a product.

Keep in mind also that these implied warranties haven't eliminated a buyer's responsibility to be cautious—to make a reasonable inspection of a product before purchase. In fact, a customer's failure to check out a product before reaching for his or her wallet can be a defense in a suit brought to enforce the warranty.

How Long Do Implied Warranties Last?

In many states, the statute of limitations (*see* Chapter 2) for suing a seller for breach of an implied warranty is four years. This doesn't mean that an implied warranty will *last* four years, or that a seller promises that every product will work well or be trouble free for a period of four years.

Suing a seller for breach of the implied warranty of merchantability requires the buyer to show that the unspoken promise was breached *at the time of sale or delivery*—that the product the buyer received was not fit for sale (or for a specific purpose) when it was sold. Durability is one of the fitness factors that a court will consider; a product is expected to have *normal durability*—a characteristic that depends on its nature and price.

A Seller's Returns Policy

When Al Dente's first pasta maker failed, he brought it back to Big-Box Kitchen Store and exchanged the faulty appliance for another Pasta Phantom—an acceptable resolution to Al. Most states do not require that a retailer provide a cash refund for a defective item; the store can replace or repair a defective product, provide a credit, or exchange the dud for an identical item.

However, stores must post their *returns policy* conspicuously so a buyer can see it before he or she makes a purchase. Printing the policy only on the receipt—as some stores do—violates the *before purchase* notice requirement.

When his second pasta maker failed a month later, Al brought it back to Big-Box Kitchen Store, but the smiling lady at the customer-service counter refused to take it back. She politely told Al that the store had a straightforward returns policy: Any products that proved to be defective more than fourteen days after purchase had to be returned to the manufacturer for refund, repair, or replacement. Al grumbled a bit, but agreed.

Can the Retailer Shift the Responsibility?

What happened to Al Dente happens to countless other consumers—a store tells the purchaser of a defective product that its *returns policy* places the burden of dealing with the problem on the buyer's shoulders.

Is this legal? Probably not—in the sense that while few retailers offer their own express warranties for the products they sell, the buyer can sue the retailer under the seller's implied warranties (unless the retailer *conspicuously* disclaims the warranties, something most stores won't do, even where state law allows them to escape liability).

Lacking a valid disclaimer, an obviously defective product (say, an item doesn't work when brought home and taken out of the box) can be returned to the seller for refund or replacement.

Similarly, a product that fails prematurely was arguably defective when it was sold and can also be returned for a refund or replacement—*regardless* of the seller's posted returns policy to the contrary.

However, buyers prefer to avoid the hassle of launching a legal battle (even in small claims court) and often (like Al Dente) take the easy way out when faced with a seemingly ironclad returns policy. *They* send the product back to the manufacturer.

When Al did this, he realized that he was taking advantage of Owch Appliance Corporation's *written warranty.*

The Everyday Law of Written Warranties

When Al Dente's third Pasta Phantom arrived, he actually took a moment to scan the Express Warranty card that was tucked into the instruction manual. Once again—probably for the thousandth time—Al wondered why the words on this card were almost identical to other product warranties he'd perused (but not actually read). Is there one law firm that specializes in writing product warranties? Do manufacturers plagiarize each other's paperwork?

No. And *no.* The reason that written warranties are so similar is that they must comply with the Magnuson-Moss Warranty Act—a federal law enacted in 1975 that shapes *written* warranties on consumer products. (Magnuson-Moss doesn't cover oral warranties.) The act is administered by the Federal Trade Commission (FTC), which also issues appropriate rules and regulations about written warranties.

WARRANTY SUITS IN A FEDERAL COURT

Because Magnuson-Moss is a federal act, consumers can—in theory—sue manufacturers for breach of warranty in federal courts. In practice, though, the act requires that federal claims have an amount in controversy of more than $50,000 or be a class action involving more than one hundred claimants (a *class action* is a lawsuit brought by one plaintiff on behalf of many parties who all have the same complaint against a common defendant). Consequently, most unhappy customers sue in state courts. Magnuson-Moss also provides that consumers can recover court costs and reasonable attorney's fees—a strong incentive for manufacturers to resolve disputes out of court.

Magnuson-Moss Warranty Act

Magnuson-Moss doesn't require a manufacturer to provide a written warranty to buyers. However, customers have come to expect written warranties on all but the least expensive products—and so most manufacturers believe that written warranties are necessary to effectively market their products.

If a company does decide to provide a written warranty, FTC regulations and provisions of the Magnuson-Moss Act snap into action. For starters, a written warranty must be a single, clear, and easy-to-read document—available to customers *before* a sale is made—that contains specific information, written in language that won't confuse the average consumer. The required statements include many familiar topics:

- → Whether this is a *Full Warranty* or a *Limited Warranty* (*see* below)
- → Who's providing the warranty (who is the *warrantor*)
- → Who is covered by the warranty (possibly only the original purchaser)
- → The length of warranty (during what period the warrantor will perform its obligations under the warranty)
- → Products and parts covered by—or excluded from—the warranty (for example, batteries and other consumable components are often not covered by warranties)
- → What the warrantor will do in the event of a defect or malfunction (for example, repair, replace, provide an equivalent product)
- → What the buyer must do to take advantage of the warranty—such things as required documentation (for example, sales receipt), procedures for returning a product, locations of service centers, and costs (if any) that fall on the buyer
- → Any limitations on implied warranties (*see* below)
- → Any exclusions of—or limitations on—other remedies (such as claims for consequential damages caused by the failed product)
- → A brief statement of the consumer legal rights under state law

Third, the Act does not apply to warranties on services. Only warranties on goods are covered. However, if your warranty covers both the parts provided for a repair and the workmanship in making that repair, the Act does apply to you.

Magnuson-Moss covers only warranties on *consumer products* (specifically, "tangible personal property normally used for personal, family, or household purposes"). The act *does* cover warranties on products that become fixtures (*see* Chapter 9) when installed in a house, such as curtain rods or a dishwasher.

Full vs. Limited Warranties

A manufacturer can choose whether to provide a *full warranty* or a *limited warranty*. The FTC (and Magnuson-Moss) define a full warranty as follows:

1. There is no limitation of the duration of implied warranties.

2. Warranty services are provided to anyone who owns the product during the warranty period (for example, coverage is not limited to the first buyer).

3. Warranty services are provided free of charge (including such costs as returning the product or removing and reinstalling the product when necessary).

4. If, after a reasonable number of tries, the manufacturer can't repair the product, the consumer receives (at his or her choice) either a replacement or a full refund.

5. Consumers are not generally required to do anything as a precondition for receiving warranty service, except notifying the manufacturer that service is needed.

Any warranty that doesn't include these features—for example, buyers may be required to ship the product to a service center at their expense—becomes a *limited warranty* and must be labeled as such.

A manufacturer can create a warranty that is *full* for a defined period of time and then becomes *limited* for an additional period, or *full* for some parts of a product and *limited* for others. Either of these is called a *multiple warranty.*

Magnuson-Moss prohibits any manufacturer who offers a written warranty from disclaiming or modifying the implied warranties of merchantability and fitness for a particular purpose available in the state. The only exception to this rule is that manufacturers who offer a limited written warranty can restrict the duration of implied warranties to the same time period as the limited warranty.

No "Tie-In" Provisions

Magnuson-Moss also forbids most warranty provisions that tie warranty protection to future sales requirements. For example, the maker of an MP3 music player can't state in its written warranty that the warranty will become void unless the owner uses batteries sold by the manufacturer. Nor can a car manufacturer tie the validity of its written warranty to a requirement that routine maintenance be performed only by its own dealer network. However, a manufacturer can recommend that all service be performed by authorized service providers and can state that improperly performed maintenance will void the warranty. (Tie-ins may be allowable if a manufacturer can show that its parts or its factory service are uniquely required because of the special nature of the product.)

Informal Dispute Resolution

Magnuson-Moss allows manufacturers to require that customers use *informal dispute resolution* before launching a lawsuit. However, the Act defines resolution mechanisms that are considerably different than the *alternative dispute resolution* approaches you read about in Chapter 1. For example, the mechanism must

> → be adequately funded and staffed to resolve all disputes quickly;
>
> → be available free of charge to consumers;
>
> → be able to settle disputes independently—without influence from the parties involved;
>
> → follow written procedures;
>
> → provide each party an opportunity to present its side, to submit supporting materials, and to rebut points made by the other party;
>
> → issue non-binding decisions (either party must be free to take the dispute to court if dissatisfied with the decision), although companies may agree to be bound by the decision;
>
> → keep complete records on all disputes;
>
> → be audited annually for compliance with the rule.

Given the costs to the manufacturer of establishing such a mechanism, it's not surprising that few everyday written warranties include informal dispute resolution.

The Universal Legal Rights Statement

Finally, the FTC requires that every written warranty include a boilerplate statement to notify consumers that state law often impacts customer rights under warranty:

> This warranty gives you specific legal rights, and you may also have other rights which vary from state to state.

How true!

After the Third Pasta Phantom Exploded

Al Dente could have requested another replacement—possibly even a full refund—under the terms of the limited warranty that accompanied the Pasta Phantom. He and his lawyer took a different path: They filed a products liability lawsuit against Owch Appliance Corporation.

Products Liability

The doctrine of products liability imposes *strict liability* (liability for damages, without requiring proof of negligence; *see* Chapter 4) on a manufacturer who sells a product that causes injury when the product is used in a reasonable manner.

Al Dente, for example, used the correct pasta flour and followed every instruction in the user's guide when he tried to make spaghetti with his third Pasta Phantom. He did everything right—and apparently acted in a completely reasonable manner—yet the machine exploded.

Over a period spanning more than one hundred years, courts in the United States and other common-law countries moved away from the notion of *caveat emptor*—"let the buyer beware"—and adopted the principle that a manufacturer is liable for *latent defects* if products in their *original condition* cause injury when *used in their normal and proper way.*

A *latent defect* is a hidden defect that will cause a product failure but which a consumer can't be expected to find, even if he or she conducts a thorough inspection before purchasing the product. Latent defects are common today because the products we buy are complicated and made of unusual materials. An average consumer can't examine a product and determine whether or not it poses a danger. (In most cases, opening a product to thoroughly inspect its innards will void the warranty; and in others, a thorough inspection will ruin the product, as it has to be taken apart completely.)

A *product used in its original condition* means that nothing has been done to the product after it has left the manufacturer. This ensures that the defect that caused the failure that injured the user was not created by someone who modified the product after it was manufactured and shipped.

Used in the normal and proper way is a fairly obvious requirement. A manufacturer shouldn't be blamed for an injury if a product is knowingly used incorrectly. I emphasize *knowingly*, because—as we'll see—the manufacturer has a duty to anticipate common misuse of a product and warn against it.

The Stream of Commerce

I have written about the liability of manufacturers, but in fact, every party involved in the *stream of commerce* can be held responsible under the doctrine of products liability. This includes the manufacturer, distributor, and wholesaler, plus the retailer that actually sold the faulty product to the injured consumer. Some states, however, bar product liability suits against retailers, unless they somehow altered the product before selling it.

Products liability cases typically fall into one of three major categories:

1. Design defects
2. Manufacturing defects
3. Warning defects

Design Defect Cases

In design defect cases, a manufacturer designs a product in a way that creates unreasonable danger and risk of harm to the user. A truly simple illustration is a hammer that has a reinforced plastic handle. Imagine that a hammer maker introduces a new, cheaper model with a handle made of inexpensive *nonreinforced* plastic that can't withstand the stress of repeated hammer blows.

A customer buys a hammer; the flimsy handle shatters in normal use; the heavy steel hammer head injures the user. Clearly, the hammer left the factory as an *inherently dangerous* product: Its design wasn't appropriate for the hammer's intended use. Every hammer made according to this design is an injury waiting to happen.

Design defects are likely to appear soon after new products are introduced and widely sold.

PACKAGING DEFECTS

Packaging defects represent a subcategory of design defects. Consider the many different containers in your home designed to be childproof because they contain inherently dangerous items that cannot be made child-safe in themselves—prescription pharmaceuticals, over-the-counter drugs, pesticides, poisons, sharp blades, flammable liquids, and others. If a manufacturer fails to provide this simple precaution and a curious child is harmed, a jury is likely to decide that the risk of injury outweighed the small increased costs of secure packaging.

Another kind of design defect occurs when the manufacturer leaves out adequate protection against foreseeable injuries that are likely to occur. For example, because rear-end collisions happen so often, automakers have to design fuel tanks (and car bodies) so that routine accidents don't result in fatal fuel tank fires.

Similarly, a potentially dangerous power tool—a circular saw, for example—must be equipped with a blade guard to protect the user from accidental contact with a moving blade.

Manufacturing Defect Cases

A *manufacturing defect* is introduced—usually by accident—when a perfectly well-designed product is manufactured incorrectly. Think of our plastic-handled hammer again, but this time imagine that the designer specified a heavy-duty reinforced plastic for the handle. The company produced tens of thousands of good hammers, but then, a small batch of hammers is made with the wrong kind of plastic. They begin to fail—and cause injury to consumers. This is a classic manufacturing defect. Here, too, there's no way for a buyer to recognize the potential danger before he or she uses the product.

Warning Defect Cases

A *warning defect case* (also called a *marketing defect case*) is a products liability claim that alleges that a well-designed, well-manufactured product is unreasonably dangerous because of inadequate instructions, warnings, and labels. Consequently,

- ✦ purchasers are not instructed in the correct assembly and use of the product;
- ✦ purchasers are not warned of known sources of danger;
- ✦ purchasers are not warned of potential dangers if they misuse the product.

To illustrate these different problems, consider a children's swing set—the kind of playtime structure you'll find in millions of backyards. The typical swing set is purchased as a box of metal and plastic parts, several plastic pouches full of bolts, nuts, and other hardware—and the all-important sheet of assembly instructions.

First, imagine that the assembly instructions are written in such a confusing manner that a reasonable person might mix up several important bolts when putting the parts together—and create an unstable and unsafe swing set. This is a fairly common marketing defect.

Next, assume that the manufacturer of the swing set knows that if more than three children swing at the same time, there's a good chance that their combined weight could cause the unit to tip over. However, the instructions for use don't warn of this potential danger. This, too, is a marketing defect.

Finally, let's say that the metal eye bolts that support the individual swings are not strong enough to carry the weight of an adult—even though the swing seats are wide enough for adults to sit on. If the instructions (or warning labels) fail to warn that the swing set is dangerous when used by "swingers" above a certain weight, that would also be considered a marketing defect.

Some critics say that marketing-defect lawsuits illustrate the worst aspects of everyday law. Is it fair to blame the manufacturer of a folding chair because it collapsed when a large, heavy man—not warned of the obvious danger—used it as an ad hoc ladder? What happened to personal responsibility?

The answer is that personal responsibility is alive and well, but that the cost of providing warnings to foolish users—silly though they may seem to the rest of us—is negligible compared to the costs of the injuries that result from misuse of a product.

And so, the users' guides accompanying some firearms sold in the United States include the following caution, "WARNING: DO NOT TOUCH THE TRIGGER UNTIL YOU ARE ACTUALLY READY TO FIRE."

Products liability laws require that product warnings be conspicuous enough to catch the attention of an average user and must be written so as to be readily comprehensible to the average person. Many user guides and warning labels incorporate icons and key phrases in other languages because of the high likelihood that non-English-speaking people will use the product.

EXPRESS WARRANTIES AND PRODUCT LIABILITY

A manufacturer may be liable under the doctrine of products liability if it offers a misleading express warranty that is relied on by a user. For example, a bicycle maker advertises that its new trail bike can accommodate a 300-pound rider. If the bike collapses under the weight of a 290-pound bicyclist, a court will probably conclude that the bicycle is defective—even though the injured rider can't point to a specific design or manufacturing defect.

Defenses Against a Products Liability Claim

When a manufacturer faces a product liability lawsuit, the company can raise a number of defenses to show that the company isn't at fault:

→ The absence of prior accidents (for example, more than one million Pasta Phantoms have been sold; this is the first and only explosion). This *might* help to convince a jury that Owch has done everything possible to design and manufacture a safe product, that there were no design and/or manufacturing flaws, and that Al Dente must have done something to trigger the explosion.

→ The product was altered after leaving the manufacturer (for example, Al Dente "souped up" his pasta maker with a more powerful motor).

→ The product was unreasonably—and unforeseeably to Owch— misused by the plaintiff (for example, earlier that day, Al Dente had used his Pasta Phantom as a step ladder and cracked the housing, or he had employed the machine to mix up a small batch of concrete and gummed up the works).

→ The plaintiff understood the danger—but continued to use the product (for example, Al Dente knew that the Pasta Phantom was not operating properly when he made the "deadly" batch of spaghetti). Perhaps Al had seen smoke billowing out of the housing, or perhaps the machine had been making shrieking noises for several days—either symptom an indication that something was amiss inside the Pasta Phantom. Owch will argue that Al should not have used the obviously faulty machine to make that final batch of pasta.

Some of these defenses are stronger than others. A jury is much more likely to exonerate Owch if Al Dente modified or seriously misused his Pasta Phantom—two happenstances clearly out of the manufacturer's control.

CHAPTER 13

⊹⇒ ⇐⊹

BUYING A CAR

F OR MOST PEOPLE, BUYING A NEW CAR PROVIDES A PERFECT EXAMPLE OF mixed emotions. On the one hand, there's the excitement of choosing and acquiring a shiny new vehicle. On the other hand, there's the knowledge that many a car owner's initial elation transmutes into years of hassle-filled regret.

Everyday law doesn't offer a solution (or solace) if you choose the wrong vehicle for your needs, spend more than you can afford, buy from a dealership who doesn't provide the best customer service in town, let a sales manager talk you into a deal you come to regret, or give in to a sales pitch for accessories and add-ons you really didn't need.

But the law does provide a surprising range of protections against bad-faith practices by a car dealer. These take a big chunk of risk out of buying a new car. And there are some—more limited—protections when you buy a used car.

That is fortunate because, at the very moment your bank account recovered from the purchase of your large screen WowScreen 64 TV set (*see* Chapter 2), the new-car bug bit. And so, you went browsing at several dealerships.

The New Vehicle Window Sticker

Every new car and light truck you look at will have a sticker on a side window (or less often the windshield) that presents a wealth of information about the vehicle. You'll impress the salespeople you deal with if you call the document the *Monroney sticker,* as most knowledgeable professionals in the auto industry do. (It's named for "Mike" Monroney, a senator from Oklahoma who sponsored the Automobile Information Disclosure Act of 1958.) This is what the Monroney sticker must list:

→ Make and model of the vehicle

→ Standard equipment

→ Engine and transmission specifications

→ Warranty details

→ City and highway fuel economy ratings

→ Crash test ratings as determined by the National Highway Traffic Safety Administration

→ The manufacturer's suggested retail price (MSRP) for the base model

→ Optional equipment added to the vehicle (along with price)

→ Suggested retail prices of such dealer services or dealer-added options

→ The manufacturer's transportation charge

→ Additional dealer markup (additional dealer profit), if any

Federal law mandates that the Monroney sticker *not* be removed by a dealer—but only by the purchaser after the car or light truck is actually sold—although many dealers do remove it as part of getting the car ready for delivery. It's a good idea to tell the dealer you want to keep the sticker, because it provides a valuable reference if repairs become necessary and when you sell the car in the future.

A Written (Not Oral) Purchase Agreement

Once you've chosen your next car, the salesperson will encourage you to sign a *written purchase agreement*. The reason that car dealers typically press for your signature is that the Uniform Commercial Code—a uniform body of law, passed by most states, to control commercial transactions—includes a *statute of frauds* (*see* Chapter 2) that requires contracts to sell goods above a certain dollar value to be in writing and be signed. The threshold value in most states is still $500 but will increase in the years ahead. In any event, purchasing a new car will always trigger the provision.

This means that prices or promises you receive during a telephone call—or from an exuberant salesperson—are not binding until you get them in writing as part of a signed purchase agreement.

On the other hand, *don't* sign a purchase agreement—which is a *binding* contract—until you are ready to actually buy a car. There's never a reason during the negotiation phase to sign documents at a car dealership. In years past, some unscrupulous dealers would disguise purchase agreements, give them misleadingly benign names, and get not-quite-ready customers to commit themselves. Consequently, many states require a valid agreement document to be conspicuously identified (for example, MOTOR VEHICLE PURCHASE CONTRACT).

The Purchase Contract

The essentials of a purchase contract for a new motor vehicle are straightforward:

→ Names and addresses of the dealer and purchaser

→ An affirmation that the vehicle is new

→ The year, make, model, and vehicle identification number (VIN) of every vehicle involved in the transaction (the new vehicle and any trade-ins)

→ The total price due upon delivery, and all of the components of that total, including any charges for vehicle preparation, optional accessories not covered on the Monroney sticker, sales tax, licensing fees, and service fees

→ Verification that the manufacturer's new-car warranty applies to this vehicle

→ The anticipated delivery date

→ The financial terms of the purchase (cash, financing arranged by the dealer, or financing arranged by the purchaser)

→ Oral representations (promises), if any, made by salespeople

If the dealer has arranged financing, the purchase agreement must comply with federal Truth in Lending laws. Typically, the details of the loan must be *disclosed*—including the annual percentage rate of interest charges and the total amount of interest that the buyer will pay over the life of the loan.

Some transactions include *contingencies*—conditions that must be met as part of the transaction. For example, a vehicle taken in trade may have to pass an inspection when it's delivered to the dealer.

Many motor vehicle purchase agreements require binding arbitration in case of disputes (*see* Chapter 1) or require the buyer to waive certain legal rights. As a rule, none of these clauses are put there to benefit the purchaser. If times are tough, car dealers can be "encouraged" to delete them—although motor vehicle purchase contracts tend to be classic examples of "take it or leave it" *contracts of adhesion* (*see* Chapter 2).

Why the Car Buyer Signs First

In fact, calling the complex document you will be asked to sign a *purchase agreement* or *purchase contract* is somewhat misleading to anyone who has read Chapter 2 of this book. The confusing jumble of legalese is a *purchase order*—that is, an *offer* to buy a specific car—that becomes a contract when it is accepted by the dealer.

When you read the long document—as you should—you'll typically find a statement to the effect that a binding contract doesn't exist until the purchase agreement is signed by the dealer's authorized representative. Car salespeople rarely have authority to sign for the dealership; that power is usually reserved for a sales manager or vice president.

You can change your mind up to the point that the authorized representative adds his or her signature. After that time, the document binds both the dealer and the customer.

Can't I Cool Off?

Many car buyers mistakenly believe that the laws of their state provide a cooling-off period (say three days) to cancel a motor vehicle purchase agreement. *Not true*—at least for the purchase of a new car. A handful of states have brief cooling-off periods for used cars, car leases, and purchase contracts signed away from a dealership. But the general rule is, *when you sign, you buy*—unless the dealer has a cancellation clause in its purchase contract (some do, but may charge a fee for the privilege). The moral: Don't pick up a pen until you are ready to buy the vehicle in question.

New-Car Warranties

I explained the key details of the federal Magnuson-Moss Warranty Act in Chapter 12. Although it covers virtually all manufactured products, it's of particular importance to buyers of new cars. In fact, a driving force for passage of the legislation in 1975 was a perceived need to "clean up" the warranties provided with new cars. Even today, many people call Magnuson-Moss the *federal lemon law.* Note however that the Act doesn't apply to a vehicle you purchase *as is* (typical with many used cars) or to vehicles purchased from private individuals.

Under Magnuson-Moss, a vehicle manufacturer is not obligated to provide a written new-car warranty, but if it does, the following must occur:

- ✈ The warranty must be labeled "full" or "limited" (*see* Chapter 12)—or can be a multiple warranty (*full* for a defined period of time and *limited* for an additional period; or *full* for some parts and *limited* for others).

- ✈ The warranty's coverage must be described in a *single,* clear, easy-to-read document.

- ✈ You have a right to see the written warranty document before you buy the car.

- ✈ The warranty must explain what a purchaser must do to receive service.

- ✈ The manufacturer can't declare the warranty void if a car owner uses proper aftermarket parts (parts not made by the manufacturer) to repair or maintain the vehicle—or has the vehicle serviced at a nondealer.

- ✈ The manufacturer can't disclaim the state-imposed *implied warranties* of merchantability and fitness for a particular purpose (*see* Chapter 12). For example, a *merchantable* car is of *good and average quality* and can be operated on the streets and highways in its intended manner with reasonable safety. (Magnuson-Moss allows a manufacturer to limit the duration of implied warranties to the same time period as its limited warranty.)

A written warranty is an *express warranty*—its terms are stated explicitly. However, there are other ways for a vehicle manufacturer to create an express warranty. The most important of these is product advertising: A court will interpret an ad that promises a "fuel injected, turbocharged engine" as a promise that the vehicle you buy will be equipped with such an engine.

An unhappy car buyer can file a claim based on breach of express warranties, implied warranties, or a so-called extended warranty (a *service contract, see* below) that's sold by the manufacturer.

More recent clear-air act legislation added two emission warranties. The *defect warranty* requires car manufacturers to deliver a vehicle free of defects that would prevent it from achieving mandated emission levels over its useful life. The *performance warranty* requires that the vehicle maintain mandated levels of emission performance over its useful life. If emission levels exceed mandated numbers, the manufacturer must make necessary repairs at no cost to the owner.

Sometimes, dealers make promises about a new car that rise to the level of product warranties. (Perhaps the dealer has agreed to cover items, such as windshield wipers or brake pads, that the manufacturer's warranty excludes.) If so, make sure the promises are clearly described in the purchase contract, in writing. Magnuson-Moss doesn't apply to oral warranties.

Secret Warranties

A so-called secret warranty comes about when a manufacturer knows a widespread problem exists that impacts relatively young vehicles whose written warranties have expired. The manufacturer doesn't publicize the defect—or *recall* the vehicles (*see* below)—but rather issues a service bulletin to dealers and quietly agrees to pay some or all of the cost of the repair for

→ owners who complain loudly and repeatedly;

→ owners identified as good customers by dealers.

There's no federal law prohibiting secret warranties and only a few states require vehicle manufacturers to disclose their nonwarranty adjustment policies. However, relevant service bulletins can be ordered for a small fee at www.safercar.gov, a website hosted by the National Highway Traffic Safety Administration. Consumer advocates recommend checking for a service bulletin if an unusual, out-of-warranty problem arises and then becoming a "squeaky wheel."

State Lemon Laws

A typical express warranty promises that the manufacturer will repair the vehicle as required. But what if your new vehicle experiences numerous failures—or a single defect that causes a recurring major problem that no one can diagnose and correct? In other (more evocative) words, what if your car is a *lemon*?

Not too many years ago, your only solutions were to sell the lemon on the used-car market or use it as a trade-in for another vehicle. Today, all states have *lemon laws* that require the manufacturer to replace a car or light truck, or to refund your purchase price—and often other purchase-related expenses, such as licensing fees—when specific conditions are met. For example,

→ a major defect remains unfixed after four visits to an authorized service facility;

→ the car has spent a cumulative total of thirty days in service facilities—for repairs—during the first twenty-four months or 24,000 miles (routine maintenance or installation of accessories don't start the clock running).

Many lemon laws require non-binding arbitration (*see* Chapter 1) before an unhappy owner can initiate a lawsuit. If you should decide to sue the manufacturer, keep in mind that lemon-law litigation can be complex—you'll almost certainly need an experienced attorney to move ahead. For starters, the value of the suit will probably be too large for small claims court. Fortunately, most state laws—and Magnuson-Moss—allow a court to award attorney's fees to a winning plaintiff.

An essential requirement for success in court is thorough and *convincing* documentation. Be sure to keep four things:

1. All service-center work orders and receipts
2. Towing receipts
3. Copies of the letters you wrote your dealer or to the car's manufacturer
4. A detailed log that summarizes trips to the dealer, the number of days the car was out of service being repaired, and all discussions you had with service personnel.

Extended Warranties (Service Contracts)

A car dealer may call it an *extended warranty,* but legally speaking, Magnuson-Moss defines it as a *service contract* that provides repair and maintenance for a specific period of time. The big difference, of course, is that a true warranty is included in the price of a new vehicle—whereas the so-called extended warranty is sold separately for an additional price. The company offering the service contract can be the car manufacturer, the dealer, or an independent company.

Magnuson-Moss requires that the terms of the service contract be clearly disclosed. The FTC—the agency that administers the Magnuson-Moss Warranty Act—urges a buyer to understand the terms before paying the additional money. Specifically:

→ What's the difference between the coverage under the manufacturer's warranty and the coverage under the service contract? (Some extended warranties provide little expanded protection.)

→ What repairs are covered?

→ Who pays for the labor? Who pays for parts?

→ Who must perform the repairs? Can repairs be made elsewhere?

→ How long does the service contract last?

→ What are the cancellation and refund policies?

A manufacturer or dealer who sells a service contract for a vehicle can't disclaim the implied warranties that may be available during the life of the service contract—which may provide modest additional protection beyond the "four corners" of the service contract document.

Certain service contracts are classified as *insurance policies* under the laws of some states. The Magnuson-Moss requirements specifically don't apply to these contracts; they are regulated by state insurance law.

Unfair and Deceptive Acts and Practices

The old legal maxim *caveat emptor*—"let the buyer beware"—is still commonsense advice when you go car shopping. Attorneys who specialize in recovering money for plaintiffs who were treated unfairly by car salespeople recommend that car buyers watch out for these somewhat popular deceptive practices:

→ The sales manager—the only person who can commit to sell a car at a specific price—adds several hundred dollars to the price the salesperson quoted. (Few customers who have chosen a specific car will counter with "take it or leave it.")

→ Advertising a car for sale that is not available—unless the ad makes clear that the vehicle is not in stock.

→ Bait-and-switch—substituting a more expensive vehicle for an advertised car that's suddenly and mysteriously no longer available.

→ Selling a "new car" that's had an accident on the dealer's lot—or during a test drive—and was repaired and repainted.

→ Linking the availability of financing of a new car to the purchase of an expensive extended warranty.

→ "Yo-yo sale"—telling a buyer at the very end of the transaction that financing has fallen through, so that the dealer can offer new financing terms that are more advantageous to the dealer. (Some unscrupulous dealers have been known to "yo-yo" customers several times during a single sale.)

→ Trade-in reappraisal that lowers the value of the vehicle when the buyer actually delivers his or her trade-in. (A customer who falls for this trick clearly hasn't read his new-car purchase agreement. Besides committing the buyer to buy a new car, the agreement "locks in" the value of the car he's selling to the dealer. The value won't change unless the vehicle is damaged or driven an excessive number of miles after the agreement was signed.)

Some states allow an aggrieved buyer who has experienced any of these practices to file a lawsuit and recover triple damages, punitive damages, and attorney's fees.

Odometer Fraud

Some experts believe that the most serious deceptive practice committed against buyers of automobiles is still odometer fraud. By one estimate, upwards of half a million vehicles are sold each year with false odometer readings. (It can happen on supposedly new cars, when an unscrupulous dealer resets an odometer of a lightly used vehicle and sells it as new.)

On average, odometer fraud causes each victim to pay about $4,000 more than the vehicle he or she buys is actually worth—a total cost of overpaying by $2 billion per year. Odometer fraud continues even though altering the mileage reading on a motor vehicle is a felony under federal law and many state laws. The fraud can be perpetrated by

→ resetting an odometer;

→ operating a vehicle with the odometer intentionally disconnected.

Federal and state laws require the transferor of a motor vehicle (a dealer or private individual) to complete a *mileage statement* when the vehicle is sold. These forms vary from state to state, but all require the seller to certify that the mileage shown on the odometer is correct—unless the odometer failed, was replaced, or otherwise can't be relied on.

Buying a Used Car

You're delighted with your new car—so happy, in fact, that you forgive your son Junior for buying the Dazzle 600 game system without your permission. When he turns sixteen, you decide to buy him an inexpensive used car as a birthday present—and to congratulate him for earning his new driver's license.

What Is a Used Car?

Surprisingly, the answer depends on the context of the question: For purposes of state law, a common definition of a used car is a vehicle whose title has been transferred to an ultimate purchaser. This is clearly a *pre-owned* vehicle. But under federal warranty law, a used car is any vehicle—even an untitled car—that has been driven more than the limited number of miles necessary to move or road test prior to delivery to a consumer.

Federally speaking, a *dealer's demonstrator*—driven around town but never titled—is a used car, although many states will consider it a new car. In a worst case, the difference can impact the buyer's rights under the car's warranty. Moreover, it makes little sense to pay the price for a new car when the dealer actually delivers a used vehicle.

Used-Car Buyer's Guide

The Federal Trade Commission's Used-Car Rule requires that every used car sold by a dealer have a *Buyers Guide sticker* affixed to the window. The primary purpose of the Buyers Guide is to inform the purchaser about the written warranty—if any—offered with the used vehicle, and whether the dealer has disclaimed any of the implied warranties. This rule only applies to a used-car *dealer*, a person or enterprise who sells more than six cars each year. (This definition includes banks, rental car companies, auction companies, and insurance companies—along with traditional automobile dealerships and used-car lots.) The rule clearly does not apply to a private individual who sells a used vehicle. To quote the FTC:

> The Buyers Guide must tell you:
>
> - Whether the vehicle is being sold "as is" or with a warranty.
> - What percentage of the repair costs a dealer will pay under the warranty.
> - That spoken promises are difficult to enforce.
> - To get all promises in writing.
> - To keep the Buyers Guide for reference after the sale.
> - The major mechanical and electrical systems on the car (listed on the back of the Buyers Guide), including some of the major problems you should look out for.

– To ask to have the car inspected by an independent mechanic before you buy.

When you buy a used car from a dealer, get the original Buyers Guide that was posted in the vehicle, or a copy. The guide must reflect any negotiated changes in warranty coverage. It also becomes part of your sales contract and overrides any contrary provisions. For example, if the Buyers Guide says the car comes with a warranty and the contract says the car is sold "as is," the dealer must give you the warranty described in the guide.

If a used car is sold as is, a large box next to the *As Is—No Warranty* disclosure on the Buyers Guide must be checked. An as-is designation typically disclaims implied warranties (*see* above). Some states, however, don't allow as-is sales by used-car dealers. A few other states have used-car lemon laws that apply to dealers—typically for used cars that cost more than some statutory minimum price.

If a used vehicle comes with a written warranty, the Magnuson-Moss warranty rules (*see* Chapter 12) apply—the warranty section on the Buyers Guide must summarize the written warranty's terms and conditions:

→ Whether the warranty is *full* or *limited*

→ The percentage of the repair cost that the dealer will pay (for example, the dealer will pay 20 percent of the labor and 80 percent of the repair parts)

→ The components and systems that are covered by the warranty (for example, engine, drive train, frame, and brake system) and the warranty terms for each item (for example, "ninety days or 3,000 miles, whichever comes first"), and whether the dealer will impose a deductible

MANUFACTURER'S ORIGINAL WARRANTY

If a used vehicle is relatively young, the manufacturer's original warranty may still be in effect (assuming that the unexpired portion can be transferred to a new owner). This will be indicated in the "Systems Covered/Duration" section of the Buyers Guide.

You have the right to see a copy of the written warranty before you buy the vehicle. It will provide additional information, including how to get repairs under the warranty and who (the dealer or a third party) is responsible for fulfilling the warranty's terms.

Automotive Products Liability and Recalls

Many of the most notorious *products liability* (*see* Chapter 12) lawsuits involve motor vehicles—fuel tanks that catch fire during rear-end collisions, vehicles that tip over in sharp maneuvers, tires that shed their tread. The same three categories of products liability that encompass other products also apply to vehicles:

1. *Design defects*—for example, the car's fuel tank is in a location where it's likely to be crushed during an accident and cause a fire

2. *Manufacturing defects*—for example, the *pitman arm* (a critical steering component) is made of the wrong kind of steel and fails in use

3. *Marketing defects (failures to warn)*—for example, a manufacturer knows that a pickup truck, if heavily loaded in a specific way, might be likely to tip over, but fails to warn of the danger with appropriate labels and instructions

A vehicle manufacturer can be found strictly liable for these kinds of defects even though another negligent driver rear-ended the car, or forced the vehicle to swerve.

Vehicle Recalls

When a safety-related defect is recognized—perhaps because it was responsible for a number of accidents—the National Highway Traffic Safety Administration (NHTSA) will request a vehicle recall. The manufacturer must then attempt to notify owners and offer a free repair to correct the defect. (Defects in vehicles more than eight years old do not have to be corrected free of charge.)

Federal law doesn't require manufacturers to reimburse vehicle buyers who fixed the defect before the recall was announced, but most manufacturers do reimburse owners who acted on their own.

The federal law is silent about an owner's responsibility to respond to a recall notice. However, manufacturers must keep detailed response records; the NHTSA may request a manufacturer to renotify owners of motor vehicles or items of equipment who have not had recalled defects corrected.

CHAPTER 14

TRIALS IN SMALL CLAIMS COURT

THE SAME AMBROSE BIERCE WHOSE DEVIL'S DICTIONARY DEFINED lawsuit as "a machine which you go into as a pig and come out of as a sausage" also defined *lawyer* as "one skilled in circumvention of the law" and *love* as "a temporary insanity curable by marriage."

You get the idea: Ambrose was a tad biting and cynical. On the other hand, there's more than a little wisdom in his warning about full-blown lawsuits. It's best to avoid them whenever possible.

But not all legal proceedings have the grinding teeth of a sausage machine. When an uncomplicated legal dispute between two parties involves a *relatively small* sum of money, every state provides an easy-to-use *small claims court* process that generally functions without lawyers *or* complicated legal procedure. The relatively small upper limit varies from state to state—from as little as $1,500 to as much as $25,000. The lion's share of small claims trials involves disputes between landlords and tenants, minor automobile accidents, collection of personal debts, damage to property, and fights between customers and stores.

A trial in small claims court is straightforward and informal—with surprisingly simple paperwork, a minimum of legal language in the courtroom, and the kind of speed unheard of in traditional civil courts. Small claims suits often go to trial within two months of filing the complaint (and sometimes even more quickly). Lawsuits in trial courts of general jurisdiction typically take upwards of a year (and often much longer) to be heard.

Most of this chapter looks at small claims court procedure and trials; the "Other Things Worth Knowing . . . " section addresses the often difficult challenge of transforming a favorable small claims judgment into actual money in your pocket.

The Case of the Buckled Wood Floor

Veronica Vespa, a resident of the State of Play, decided to replace the forty-year-old orange shag carpeting in her basement playroom with a hardwood parquet floor. She visited Freddie's Fabulous Floorings—FFF for short—a local store in the Blackacre County Mall that specializes in wood flooring. Freddie Fortune himself helped Veronica choose the Outrageous Oak pattern and—on the basis of a sketch she brought—estimated that she'd need 400 square feet of flooring, at a price of $12 per square foot, which included installation. The total cost of her new floor would be $4,800.

When Veronica hesitated to spend that much money on a playroom, Freddie offered to reduce the price to $11 per square foot and remove the old shag carpeting for free. This seemed too good a deal to refuse. Veronica signed a purchase agreement for $4,400 that called for 50 percent of the total to be paid on signing. The balance was due ten days after the new floor was installed. Veronica contentedly wrote Freddie a check for $2,200.

A few days later, an FFF work crew removed the shag carpeting and installed the new wooden floor. Veronica—immensely pleased with the Outrageous Oak parquet—was about to send FFF her check for $2,200 when a bill arrived, announcing that the playroom actually required 420 square feet of flooring, that the total cost of the floor was $4,620, and that Veronica owed FFF a total of $2,420.

Before Veronica could even think about asking Freddie for clarification, she noticed that the edges of the wood parquet tiles had begun to curl. Her good friend Vinnie Vaughn made an immediate diagnosis: The FFF crew had used the wrong adhesive. It had caused the tiles to warp and pull away from the concrete floor. Vinnie had experienced a similar problem several years earlier.

Veronica called Freddie to her house. He took one look at the floor and said, "I'm sorry you're having difficulties, but we're experts at laying parquet floors and did everything right. There must be a problem with the concrete surface underneath. In any case, we installed the parquet tiles as promised—you owe us $2,420."

Needless to say, Veronica didn't send the second check. Instead, she took photographs of the warped tiles and then hired Heddie's Happy Handymen (HHH) to remove the parquet squares and scrape the floor clean of adhesive. HHH's bill came to $750.

Veronica was wondering what to do next, when a sheriff's deputy knocked on her front door, verified her identity, handed her an envelope, and intoned, "You're served."

Inside was a Notice of Claim, announcing that Freddie's Fabulous Floorings had filed a claim against her in small claims court for the sum of $2,420, plus $240 expenses related to the claim. The notice stated that trial was scheduled in twenty-seven days in the Small Claims Division of State of Play District Court, in Blackacre City. The notice went on to explain that if Veronica didn't appear at the trial, she risked having the judge enter a *default judgment* against her— automatically awarding the requested sum to Freddie, even though the judge didn't hear her side of the story.

Small Claims Procedure

Veronica had never been involved in any sort of lawsuit before—either as a plaintiff (claimant) or as a defendant. So she quickly fleshed out her understanding of State of Play small claims court regulations and procedures. The first thing she came across was an abundance of information published by the court, including easy-to-read "How to File a Small Claim" and "How to Defend Against a Small Claim" manuals. Also, the staff in the small claims court office (part of the local Clerk of Court office) were happy to answer procedural questions, although they couldn't provide specific legal advice about a claim.

This is what Veronica learned:

→ The *jurisdiction* of the Small Claims Division—the authority of the court to resolve disputes—is limited to disputes where the amount of money or the value of the property sought to be recovered is $5,000 or less. (Different states set different limits for their small claims courts, some as low as $1,500, some as high as $25,000.)

→ Some states *require* suits below a certain value to be brought in small claims courts—others, including the State of Play, leave the decision up to the claimant—although the significantly higher cost of a full-blown lawsuit encourages most claimants to keep small claims in small claims court.

→ The Small Claims Division can resolve most disputes *in law* and some issues *in equity* (*see* Chapter 1)—it can award money damages and in appropriate circumstances require a defendant to perform specific actions (many states limit their small claims courts to awarding money damages).

→ Individuals must represent themselves in Small Claims Division without the help of an attorney (some states require that business claimants or defendants be represented by an attorney). However, many claimants and defendants use lawyers to help them get ready for trial, including gathering evidence and planning the best ways to present their cases.

→ Small claims disputes are never presented to a jury in the State of Play; a judge (often a magistrate) hears the evidence and renders a judgment. (A few states allow a small claims defendant to request a jury trial, typically by paying an additional fee. Fewer still give claimants the option.)

→ The *burden of proof* (*see* Chapter 1) in a small claims court requires the claimant to prove his or her case by a *preponderance of the evidence*. The claimant must ultimately convince the judge that the defendant is liable for damages (has done something wrong that the court can remedy) and also prove the actual amount of damages that he or she is entitled to recover from the defendant.

→ Many judgments in small claims lawsuits are rendered immediately by the judge or magistrate. On occasion—if a claim raises complex issues—the judge may *take the matter under advisement* and notify the parties about the judgment by mail. (Some judges prefer to mail judgments to speed the flow of trials and to avoid after-trial discussions with upset parties.)

→ Most states allow appeals, although there's enormous variation among different states as to how appeals work. Most are not true appeals (*see* Chapter 1), because the appellate court typically doesn't look at what happened during the trial; rather, the higher court conducts a new trial—a *trial de novo*—from scratch. In some states, a losing party who has been ordered to pay a money judgment has to post an *appeal bond* when filing an appeal (a sum of money equal—or sometimes greater— than the judgment). This discourages appeals merely to delay paying the judgment. In other states, only a losing defendant can appeal the judgment—the claimant agrees not to appeal a loss when filing the original claim.

Small Claims Cases

Veronica also discovered that actions in small claims court typically involve contracts (*see* Chapter 2), intentional torts (*see* Chapter 3), negligent torts (*see* Chapter 4), and breach of warranty (*see* Chapter 12). These are the kinds of disputes most often heard in small claims court:

→ Recovery of money owed to a claimant

→ Recovery of personal property in the defendant's possession

→ Minor automobile accidents

→ Faulty repairs to a car or major appliance

→ A purchased item fails to perform as promised

→ Defective home repairs

→ Landlord/tenant disagreements—such as eviction proceedings when the tenant fails to pay rent, demands for return of the tenant's security or cleaning deposit, or claims to recover the cost of essential repairs paid for by the tenant

Small claims courts don't tackle divorce, spousal support, child custody issues, defamation, and disputes that must be resolved by federal courts (including bankruptcy, copyright infringement, and claims against the federal government). In addition, some states do allow suits against state government in small claims court.

Filing a Small Claim

The process starts with filing a relatively simple form—called a "Notice of Claim" in the State of Play—that clearly and briefly states the claim against the defendant and specifies the amount of money sought (or the property to be returned). The description must be sufficiently clear and specific that the defendant can fully understand the nature of the claim.

COMPLAINT FORMS

Some states have specific forms for different kinds of small claims: for example, money debt, breach of contract, or return of personal property. If the claimant uses the incorrect form, the defendant can request the claim be dismissed.

The claimant must also provide sufficient information about the defendant—name, address, telephone number—so that the defendant can be properly *served* with the notice (*see* below). *Service* is sometimes called *process service*; it notifies the defendant that he or she faces a claim, it summons the defendant to small claims court, and it establishes the court's jurisdiction over the defendant—its authority to resolve a dispute involving him or her. Accuracy is essential, because a small claims court can't grant a judgment against an improperly named defendant.

Properly naming the defendant can be tricky when suing a business. A corporation doing business inside a state will have the name and address of a *registered agent* on file (typically available on the Internet on the state's Secretary of State's website). The Notice of Claim should name the company and the registered agent; the registered agent is the person served with the complaint.

Partnerships are usually named in the Notice of Claim by naming all the partners individually as defendants and then the partnership by its correct legal name. One of the general partners can be served with the notice.

If the business is a sole proprietorship—a business owned by one person—both the business and the owner should be named as defendants in the notice, and the owner served with the notice. To find out who owns a business that operates under a name that's different from the owner's, check with the county's assumed names department (often part of the Register of Deeds office, Business Taxation office, or County Clerk's office).

If a small claim is based on a contract, an account statement, a purchase agreement, a written warranty, or some other document, most states require that a copy of the document be filed along with the Notice of Claim. This further ensures that the defendant will fully understand the claim against him or her.

Small claims court is inexpensive but rarely free. Filing fees—which vary from state to state—average less than $100 and usually include the cost of process service. If the claimant wins his or her case, the court will usually order the defendant to repay the filing fee.

The State of Play, like most other states, schedules the small claims trial date when the claimant files the Notice of Claim.

MANDATORY MEDIATION

Some states require that the parties in a small claim action attend one mediation session and try to resolve the dispute before a trial. If the parties can't agree, the court then sets a trial date and provides notice to each party.

Demand Letter

Some states require that the claimant send the defendant a *demand letter*—a formal letter requesting the payment of money owed or the return of disputed property—before the claimant can invoke the jurisdiction of small claims court to resolve the dispute. This can be worth doing even if not necessary, because a strong letter will often jog the recipient to correct the problem. Your attorney can send this letter even though he or she will not take part in the eventual small claims proceedings.

Statute of Limitations

Small claims courts typically must abide by the same *statutes of limitation* that apply to lawsuits brought in trial courts of general jurisdiction (*see* Chapters 2 and 3). The claimant can't file a claim if the statute of limitations has expired; neither can the defendant file a counterclaim if the statute of limitations has run out. (It's unlikely, but theoretically possible that a claim would be "timely," while a counterclaim would not be permitted.) In any event, claims in small claims courts are best filed as quickly as possible.

Service of Process

Service of process is one of the more formal aspects of bringing a claim to small claims court. It has to be done correctly to meet the constitutional requirements (in the Fifth and Fourteenth Amendments) that prohibit government from depriving any person of life, liberty, or property without *due process of law*. This means that a small claims court can't order a defendant to pay money *unless* the defendant

→ receives ample notice of the claim against him or her;

→ has an opportunity to confront the claimant and refute the claim;

→ receives a hearing before an impartial tribunal.

Broadly speaking, small claims court must honor the same constitutional mandates as other civil courts. Consequently, many small claims courts use the same service procedures as their trial-court siblings.

In the State of Play (and in many other states) there are three ways that the defendant can be served with a small claims Notice of Claim:

1. *Mail*—Service of process by registered or certified mail (with *restricted delivery* to a specific addressee) is usually the least expensive method. But a defendant who avoids the postman— or refuses to respond to the attempt to deliver notice—is not considered served. At that point, the claimant must switch to *personal service* (*see* the items that follow). Also, mail service of process is usually not permissible if the only available address for a defendant is at his or her place of employment; personal service is required.

2. *Personal service by a sheriff's deputy*—The Notice of Claim is hand-delivered by a sheriff's deputy to the defendant or to any reasonable adult member of the defendant's family at his or her *usual place of abode*. (Some states allow the deputy to *post* the notice on the main entrance of the usual place of abode if the defendant or other recipient can't be found.) The deputy then files a *proof of service* with the court; a copy is sent to the claimant.

3. *Personal service by a private process server*—The Notice of Claim is hand-delivered by a *private process server,* private individuals (licensed in some states) who often specialize in serving hard-to-serve defendants, people who have learned how to avoid service of process. The fees for private process service are usually higher than the other methods. After service, the private server files a sworn proof of process with the court.

Sending Subpoenas to Witnesses

The Small Claims Division enables parties to *subpoena* witnesses to testify at small claims trials. A subpoena is an order issued by the court that commands a person to come to court and testify. Or, a subpoena can compel a person to bring specific documents or other evidence to a trial. Subpoenas are typically used when an essential witness refuses to appear at a trial voluntarily. Although subpoenas are available when absolutely necessary, a subpoenaed witness often becomes an unfriendly witness, who may do more harm at the trial than good. Also, a witness responding to a subpoena is entitled to a nominal witness fee and travel expenses. For all of these reasons, the parties in small claims actions rarely subpoena witnesses.

Discovery

Discovery is the procedural process that allows one party to a civil lawsuit to request copies of documents, other evidence, and witness statements that are the heart of the other side's case. About the only things that aren't discoverable are privileged information (for example, discussions between parties and their attorneys), *work product* (for example, memos and research done by attorneys), and certain kinds of expert opinions.

Many people find it odd that each side of the dispute can be compelled to show "its best cards" to the other side. In fact, the purpose of fully revealing the strengths and weaknesses of the plaintiff's and defendant's cases is to encourage the parties to settle the case before trial—ultimately reducing risk and expense for both sides.

Many states don't permit discovery for small claims actions, but the Small Claims Division in the State of Play permits reasonable discovery in small claims court. This means that the judge has the discretion to grant requests for pretrial discovery that he or she considers appropriate.

Veronica's Answer and Counterclaim

In many states, a defendant in a small claims case need merely show up in court for the scheduled trial. In the State of Play and some others, the defendant is required to submit an *answer* to the claim to both the court and the claimant. This is typically submitted on a form provided by the court. Veronica knew how she would answer the claim against her: She would declare that the balance she agreed to pay FFF was $2,200, not $2,420. She would insist further that she didn't owe FFF the balance due under the purchase agreement (or court expenses) because FFF failed to install a functional wood floor.

When Veronica read the answer form provided by the court, she found that she could submit a two-part answer:

1. Her denial to FFF's claim for money

2. A claim of her own against FFF that arose out of the same circumstances as the original claim—FFF's installation of the floor. Specifically, this was her opportunity to recover her $2,200 deposit, plus the $750 she paid to remove the faulty flooring and the adhesive—a total of $2,950.

Veronica's claim is called a *counterclaim* (sometimes a *cross-claim*). Although it will be resolved at trial along with FFF's claim, the court will treat the counterclaim much like any other small claim. The same $5,000 dollar value maximum and two-year statute of limitations applies; the counterclaim must be written as clearly as the original notice of claim; and supporting documentation—in this case the receipt from HHH—must accompany the counterclaim.

State of Play small claims court rules require that the answer and any counterclaim be filed with the court at least ten days before the trial date set for the claimant's original claim. The court will send FFF a copy of Veronica's answer and counterclaim. (Due process requires that FFF have adequate notice of the counterclaim.)

REQUEST FOR REMOVAL

The small claims answer in some states can be used to request the *removal* of the claim to a trial court of general jurisdiction. This can happen if the defendant's counterclaim exceeds the small claims court dollar maximum, if the defendant wants a jury trial and the claim can be heard in a trial court, or if the defendant believes he or she will gain a strategic advantage by removing the case (the higher costs involved—including attorney's fee—may encourage the claimant to settle the case quickly).

In some states, a counterclaim can be filed as a separate small claims court case, if the defendant prefers a separate trial. In others, a cross-claim arising from the same transaction or incident as the original claim must be heard at the same trial. In those states, a defendant who fails to counterclaim loses his or her rights to file a separate claim against the original claimant.

Postponing the Trial

Delays go by many names, but if one or the other party in a small claims action can't make the trial date assigned by the court—or perhaps an essential witness won't be available—a party may request a deferral, a continuance, an adjournment, or whatever a postponement is called in his or her state. Most states require requests be made to the court several days in advance and that notice of a request be given to the other party.

Because it's widely accepted that delays in trying a case benefit the defendant, most small claims courts discourage postponements (court regulations may permit no more than one continuance). Merely asking for a postponement doesn't assure that one will been granted. Unless the court staff notifies the parties that the trial has been rescheduled, both sides should be ready to present their cases at the original date and time.

Veronica Tries to Settle the Case

Veronica was disappointed with FFF's performance, but she was also sensible. Everything she'd read about small claims court—including the State of Play's manuals for claimants and defendants—urges the parties to make a sincere effort to settle their dispute themselves. Veronica knew that the judge might not see things her way and that, even if she prevailed, she would have a hassle collecting the full judgment from Freddie. A fair settlement might well be the best result.

And so, Veronica called Freddie and asked if he would be interested in reaching an amicable settlement. She further explained that they could put their settlement agreement in writing and have the Small Claims Division approve it and enter it as the court's judgment. The lawsuit would be over in days—with nothing more to do and both sides happy.

Freddie heaved a sigh. "It hurts me to offer this," he said, "but I'm willing to agree to the following: You don't ask for any money from me, I won't ask for more money from you. Simply put, I'll keep your original deposit check and we both walk away."

Veronica managed to maintain her cool. "My idea of a *fair* settlement is that you return my deposit in full. I won't ask you to reimburse my costs to remove the faulty parquet floor you installed."

"I'll see you in court," Freddie said. He slammed down the phone before Veronica could say anything more.

Veronica Prepares for Trial

Because Veronica had no previous experience with small claims procedure, she decided to visit the Small Claims Division in Blackacre City and watch several trials. She chose the same courtroom that would be used for her trial, hoping that the same judge would preside over her case a week later. She guessed that Freddie had been to court on many other occasions and would have a definite advantage if she arrived "cold" for her trial. Watching the small claims process in action would even the playing field and build her confidence. She might even pick up a hint or two that could help her win.

She wondered if she would need permission to watch—but discovered that small claims court trials are open to the public. She walked into the courtroom and took a seat at the back. She'd brought a notebook to capture her observations and soon had made several notes to herself:

→ Everything happens much faster than the court shows on TV—
   I saw several trials that took less than five minutes each.

→ The claimants stood toward the left side of the judge's bench when viewed from the judge's perspective (on the right side as seen from the courtroom seats). The defendants stood on the other side. Witnesses stood next to the claimant or defendant— they didn't sit in the witness box.

→ The bailiff ordered everyone to turn off their cell phones and PDAs.

→ The judge didn't let anyone—claimant, defendant, or witnesses— ramble when he or she spoke.

→ The judge expected everyone speaking to direct comments to him—not to people on the other side of the case.

→ Everyone addressed the judge as "Your Honor."

→ The judge didn't let either party interrupt another person who was speaking.

→ The judge asked lots of questions—and expected brief answers. Many of his questions had to do with evidence, or the lack thereof. For example: "Do you have a photograph of the damage?" "Do you have a receipt for the money you spent?" "Did you get a written estimate of the cost of repairing the damage?" Note to myself: Be sure to bring a warped parquet tile to the trial as an item of *physical evidence*. And bring the HHH receipt to prove what you spent on repairs.

→ Several parties brought witnesses to testify about matters in dispute. Note to myself: Bring Vinnie to testify about the incorrect adhesive.

→ One claimant arrived in court late. The judge chewed him out, rescheduled the case for another day, and told the claimant to pay the defendant's additional travel expenses.

→ The judge became upset at one claimant who kept saying "Objection!" while a defendant was presenting her case. The judge explained that the *rules of evidence* are relaxed in Small Claims Division—and that he will decide what evidence to ignore or exclude without the help of someone "playing at being a trial attorney."

→ Some parties and witnesses were dressed in business suits; others were more casual. Everyone seemed neat and clean. The judge didn't seem to mind what kind of clothing people wore.

→ One of the claimants blew up at a defendant and started shouting at her. The judge yelled at him and threatened to throw him out or fine him for contempt of court if it happened again.

→ I'm not sure how I'll react when I see Freddie in the courtroom. I will try my best to be professionally polite. The judge knows that we disagree strongly—or else we wouldn't be facing each other in court.

→ I didn't expect to hear profanity or foul language—and I didn't. (The only exception was when one plaintiff testified to how the defendant replied when asked for a complete refund for an apparently faulty repair.)

→ A few people tried to read from prepared statements on paper. The judge interrupted them and insisted that they tell their stories using their own words. This seemed strange to me until I thought about it. The no pre-prepared statement rule ensures that parties don't have other people—lawyers, most likely—put words in their mouths.

→ I could tell immediately who had practiced their presentations to the court, and who hadn't. The judge seemed to react more favorably to parties who knew what they wanted to say—and said it clearly and confidently. A few people obviously hadn't thought about how to make their cases; they looked and sounded confused. Many of them ended up losing their trials.

The Rhythm of the Trials

After watching several of the trials, Veronica Vespa was familiar with the five-step pattern:

1. The trial opened with the judge asking the claimant to explain his or her claim and present evidence. All of the claimants testified on their own behalf and most showed receipts, purchase agreements, warranties, and other documents. Several claimants asked the defendants questions. A few claimants offered witnesses they had brought to court. After a claimant witness testified, the defendant had a chance to cross-examine him or her. Notes to myself:

   - Buy an inexpensive plastic portfolio to hold documents and photos I bring to court. More than a few parties dropped their evidence or had difficulty finding specific items when the judge asked to see them.
   - Think about what kind of witnesses Freddie will invite to bolster his case.
   - Brainstorm the kinds of questions he might ask his witnesses.
   - Figure out questions I can ask to counter their answers.

2. After the claimants made their cases, the defendants took over and testified in their own behalf, presented their evidence, and offered their witnesses. This time, the claimant had the chance to cross-examine defense witnesses. Notes to myself:

    - Practice my presentation to the court in front of a mirror.
    - Have the photos you plan to show as evidence blown up to 8-by-10 size; the judge didn't seem happy when parties gave him small snapshots to look at.
    - Figure out the questions you plan to ask Vinnie.
    - Explain to Vinnie the kind of information you want him to provide to the court.
    - Tell Vinnie what to expect when he testifies.
    - Think about the questions that Freddie might ask Vinnie to discredit the testimony he gives.

3. In three of the trials, the claimants asked to testify again—the judge called this *rebuttal evidence*—to challenge the evidence that the defendants had presented. The claimants weren't allowed to expand their original case; they could only respond to specific points the defendants had made.

4. The defendants were then invited to rebut the claimants' rebuttals. Only one of them did; the others said, "I have nothing more to add, Your Honor."

5. Each side may make a brief *closing argument* at the end of the trial. Only about a third of the parties were prepared to do this well. One claimant seemed to contradict what she'd said earlier; one defendant annoyed the judge when he insulted the claimant rather than stick to his case.

Veronica's Trial

On the day of the trial, Veronica drove Vinnie, her witness, to the courthouse in Blackacre City and arrived an hour early to give herself plenty of time to park. She also wanted to avoid any last-minute rushing around that would only increase the nervousness she felt.

Because of her previous visit to the courtroom, she knew where to sit and how to check in with the court clerk. Her trial was first on the *docket,* the list of small claims suits that would be resolved that day. Freddie—red faced and huffing—raced into court, tugging another man, an instant before the bailiff said, "All rise."

The court clerk called the case of "Fortune vs. Vespa." (It had that name because Freddie began the proceedings by filing a complaint against Veronica.)

Veronica led Vinnie to the defendant's side of the judge's bench; Freddie and his witness moved to the other side. The clerk administered an oath to tell the truth to the four people together. After this *swearing in,* the judge immediately invited Freddie to state his claim and offer his evidence:

FREDDIE: Well, Judge . . . this is a fairly simple case. The defendant refuses to pay the balance due she owes my proprietorship, Freddie's Fabulous Floorings. She signed a contract with FFF, agreeing to pay an installed price of $11 per square foot for a parquet floor in her basement playroom. Our estimate based on her sketch and measurements, I estimated 200 square feet of wood tile, for a total price of $4,400. She gave me a deposit of $2,200. We installed the floor promptly. When we did, we discovered that her playroom actually required 220 square feet of flooring. Our purchase agreement clearly explains that the final price may be 10 percent higher or lower than the estimate, if the estimate is based on customer measurements. The total price now became $2,620. We sent the defendant a bill for the balance due of $2,420. She refuses to pay it.

JUDGE: Mr. Fortune, do you have a copy of the purchase agreement the defendant signed and a copy of the demand letter you sent her?

FREDDIE: (*Fumbles*) Uh . . . yes . . . they're here somewhere. (*Wastes several seconds*)

JUDGE: Mr. Fortune . . . we don't have all morning.

FREDDIE: I have them. (*Hands papers to the judge*)

JUDGE : Mr. Fortune, do you have any evidence that the parquet floor in question was actually installed in the defendant's home?

FREDDIE: I visited her home after the installation was complete. She told me she was "immensely pleased with the floor," then she initialed the purchase agreement at the bottom to acknowledge that the job was done as promised.

JUDGE: Do you have anything else to add, Mr. Fortune?

FREDDIE: Oh yeah. I have a witness. Mr. George Grout. He's been a flooring installer for more than twenty years—twelve years working for me. There's nothing he doesn't know about wood flooring. In fact, he installed the wood floors in the offices on the upper floors of this building."

JUDGE: Very well. Proceed with your witness.

FREDDIE: George . . . you installed the parquet floor in (*points at Veronica*) her playroom—right?

GEORGE: Yep. A real smooth job.

FREDDIE: There were no problems with the parquet tiles when you finished?

GEORGE: Everything was perfect. Flat, even, all the lines between the tiles virtually invisible. The customer said she loved the new floor.

JUDGE: (*To Veronica*) You can ask Mr. Grout questions if you disagree with his testimony.

VERONICA: No thank you, Your Honor. Everything Mr. Grout said is true.

JUDGE: (*To Freddie*) Is there anything else you want to tell the court, Mr. Fortune?

FREDDIE: Only that I'm amazed that that woman didn't pay what she owes me.

JUDGE : Yes, well . . . let's turn to the defendant. Ms. Vespa, please tell the court why you refused to pay the claimant the sum of $2,420.

VERONICA: Thank you, Your Honor. I acknowledge that I signed the purchase agreement, that I gave Mr. Fortune a deposit check for $2,200, and that I initialed the agreement after the floor was installed. However, I never agreed to pay FFF a total of $4,620. I agreed to a full price of $4,400. Moreover, a few days after the parquet floor was installed, I discovered that FFF had used the wrong adhesive to install wood on concrete. As a result, the tiles curled . . .

JUDGE: Excuse me, Ms. Vespa . . . what are your qualifications to state that Mr. Fortune's company used the wrong adhesive? Are you a flooring expert?

VERONICA: (*A bit flustered*) Uh . . . no, Your Honor, I'm not. Vinnie Vaughn, my neighbor once had the same unhappy experience. I've brought him as a witness.

JUDGE: Okay. What will he testify about?

VERONICA: He'll explain that wrong adhesive was used to install the floor.

JUDGE: I see. (*Peers at Vinnie*) Mr. Vaughn—can you please tell the court your qualifications to testify about wood flooring. Are you a flooring installer?

VINNIE: No, Your Honor. I'm a dental technician. However, I've had the same problem with my floor that Ms. Vespa had with hers, and . . .

JUDGE: Be that as it may, Mr. Vaughn, you don't have the education, training, skills, or experience that makes you more knowledgeable about a particular subject than the average person. Consequently, I can't let you testify as an expert witness—although you can provide testimony about what you saw (*glances at Veronica*) if Ms. Vespa would find that useful in her defense.

Veronica caught her breath. She could tell that the trial wasn't going her way. Why hadn't she learned more about expert witnesses? What the judge said made perfect sense: Vinnie Vaughn *didn't* have the experience to talk about floor tile adhesive. Why hadn't she been clever enough to find a witness as skilled as Mr. Grout?

ABOUT EXPERT WITNESSES

Although many expert witnesses are highly educated professionals—physicians, dentists, and engineers—any individual with sufficient skills and experience in a specific area can qualify. This includes carpenters, electricians, plumbers, building contractors, real estate agents, beauticians, automobile mechanics, and flooring installers. Most expert witnesses expect to be paid for the time they spend preparing and testifying. You'll also have to reimburse their travel expenses.

Click!

Veronica suddenly had an idea: George Grout is here today. And he swore to tell the truth.

VERONICA: (*To the judge*) Your Honor, I would like to have Mr. Vaughn testify to what he saw in my home.

JUDGE: That's perfectly proper, Ms. Vespa. Proceed.

VERONICA: (*To Vinnie*) Mr. Vaughn, can you please tell His Honor what you saw when you visited my playroom a few days after FFF installed the parquet floor.

VINNIE: (*To the judge*) Well, Your Honor, I saw that the edges of almost every parquet tile had curled upwards. I poked at one of them, and it came loose in my hand. I tiptoed around the room and dislodged several more tiles.

JUDGE: (*To Vinnie*) You say you tiptoed. Were you able to walk on the floor?

VINNIE: No, Your Honor. I was afraid I'd trip on the warped wooden tiles.

VERONICA: Your Honor, I brought three of the tiles with me today. I also have a photograph that I took of the floor shortly after the edges began to curl. If I may, I'd like to present them to the court as evidence (*hands items to bailiff, who brings them to the judge*). Now, Your Honor, I have a specific question for Mr. Fortune.

JUDGE: Please ask it.

VERONICA: (*To Freddie*) Mr. Fortune, what did you do when I called and told you that there was a problem with my floor?

FREDDIE: I immediately visited your home and examined the floor. We pride ourselves on our customer satisfaction. I told you we had installed the parquet tiles properly and that there must be a problem with the surface of the concrete surface underneath the wooden flooring.

VERONICA: Thank you, Mr. Fortune. (*To Judge*) Your Honor, if I may, I would like Mr. Grout to testify as an expert witness.

FREDDIE: (*Shouts*) That's not fair! He's my witness!

JUDGE: (*Loudly*) I will decide what's fair, Mr. Fortune. You've had your opportunity to make your case. Now it's Ms. Vespa's turn.

FREDDIE: Sorry.

JUDGE: (*To Veronica*) Go on.

VERONICA: (*To Judge*) Your Honor, I'd like Mr. Grout to examine one of the warped floor tiles.

JUDGE: Certainly (*Hands tile to bailiff, who brings it to George*).

VERONICA: Mr. Grout, that is one of the parquet floor tiles that you installed. Based on your many years of experience, what could have caused the tile to curl like that and come loose from the floor after the parquet floor was installed?

GEORGE: (*Hesitates*) Um . . . well.

FREDDIE: (*Jumps in*) There was something wrong with the concrete floor.

JUDGE: Another outburst like that, Mr. Fortune, and I will have the bailiff remove you from my courtroom. You will not speak out of turn. Do you understand me?

FREDDIE: (*Sheepishly*) Uh . . . yes, sir.

JUDGE: (*To George*) Please answer the question, Mr. Grout.

GEORGE: (*Softly*) It's probably the adhesive.

JUDGE: I'm afraid I didn't hear you, Mr. Grout.

GEORGE: I said, it was probably wrong adhesive that caused the tiles to warp and lift.

VERONICA: Then you don't think the surface of my concrete floor is the problem?

GEORGE: (*Reluctantly*) No, there's nothing wrong with your floor.

VERONICA: Thank you, Mr. Grout. (*To the judge*) That's all the evidence I have, Your Honor.

JUDGE: Do you have any evidence in rebuttal, Mr. Fortune?

FREDDIE: No . . . er . . . Your Honor.

JUDGE: Fine. Then let's move on to the defendant's counterclaim. Ms. Vespa, please state your case.

VERONICA: Your honor, here is a copy of my canceled check for the sum of $2,200 paid to FFF as a deposit for a wooden parquet floor. And here is a receipt for $750, the cost of having the failed tiles removed and the remaining adhesive scraped off my floor. I had to call in HHH after Mr. Fortune refused to do anything about the floor. Here's a photograph of my playroom today. (*Gives to bailiff, who brings it to the judge*) Because the floor failed within days of installation, I ask for my deposit to be refunded and I ask to be reimbursed for the cost of removing the faulty floor. The total is $2,950.

JUDGE: Mr. Fortune, please tell the court why you believe that you don't owe Ms. Vespa the sum of $2,950.

FREDDIE: We installed the floor as promised. We didn't do anything wrong. The only sensible explanation for the slight tile deformation that she experienced is that something is wrong with the surface of the concrete floor. As I see it, she had no reason to spend money having the tiles removed.

JUDGE: Do you have any evidence in rebuttal, Ms. Vespa?

VERONICA: No, Your Honor.

JUDGE: Then we'll move on to closing arguments. The claimant will begin.

FREDDIE: We've installed hundreds of parquet floors—and we don't make amateur mistakes with adhesive. As I said, there must be something wrong with the surface of her concrete floor. Now, as for her statement that she did not agree to pay FFF $4,620, the purchase agreement she signed clearly states that when we base an estimate on a customer's measurements, the actual price may be as much as 10 percent higher. (*Glares at Veronica*) She owes me $2,420. There's no reason for me to refund her deposit or to pay for her floor removal. That's all I have to say.

JUDGE: Thank you, Mr. Fortune. (*To Veronica*) Please make your closing argument, Ms. Vespa.

VERONICA: Thank you, Your Honor. For starters, I don't think it's right that he tried to charge me more money than I agreed to pay. However, that seems besides the point. I don't know enough about installing wooden floors to be sure what Mr. Fortune's company did wrong. All I know is that within days of the installation, the tiles curled and the floor became useless—actually dangerous to walk on. I shouldn't have to pay anything for flooring I had to remove. I want my deposit back and the money I spent to remove the bad tiles. That completes my closing argument.

JUDGE: As Mr. Fortune said a few minutes ago, this is a somewhat simple case. The first issue is the correct total of the final bill. Here, I agree with the claimant. The purchase agreement does allow FFF to adjust the estimate by 10 percent when the actual room measurements are known. This is only fair. However, because the floor failed soon after installation—apparently because faulty adhesive was used—it would be wholly unfair to require the defendant to pay the claimant any more money. Therefore, I find that Ms. Vespa does not owe Mr. Fortune's company the sum of $2,420. Moving on to the counterclaim. Ms. Vespa did not receive the functional wood floor she contracted to purchase. Consequently, Mr. Fortune should return her $2,200 deposit. Moreover, the wooden tiles shown to the court and the witness's testimony that the failed floor could not be walked on safely convince me that Ms. Vespa could not leave the parquet floor as is. When Mr. Fortune declined to address the problem, Ms. Vespa had no choice but to have the floor removed. Therefore, I award Ms. Vespa $2,950, plus court expenses of $150—a total of $3,100.

Other Things Worth Knowing about Small Claims Court

Collecting a Money Judgment

Actually collecting the money judgment awarded at the end of a small claims trial can be even more challenging than bringing the case to court. Consequently, most states have sections in their small claims court manuals—or possibly additional documents—that explain the various available tools for collecting money judgments. All of them brim over with legal procedure, most involve more expense, many can take months to play out—and none are guaranteed to succeed.

Some *judgment debtors*—the people who have to pay money judgments—are judgment-proof (they literally can't pay what they owe); others are slippery enough to avoid collection efforts or hide the money and assets they own; a few may be driven into bankruptcy by the judgment (everyday money judgments typically become one more debt in the debtor's bankruptcy proceeding and may be discharged along with other debts). In any case, the chore of *enforcing* (collecting) the judgment ultimately belongs to the party who won the judgment—called, logically enough, the *judgment creditor.*

An Agreement with the Judgment Debtor

As with most other aspects of a legal dispute, it's preferable for the parties to agree between themselves about how the money judgment will be paid. Some judgment debtors can simply pay the full sum; others require that the award be split into weekly or monthly payments, usually with interest, to compensate the creditor for the time value of the money he or she has not received in a lump sum. Interest usually begins to accrue on the day that the judgment is entered.

The best time for the judgment creditor and the judgment debtor to reach an agreement is immediately after the judgment is announced. The agreement—often called a *stipulation*—can be put in writing, signed by the parties, and approved by the court, transforming it into a court order that the judgment debtor is required to obey.

At this point, the creditor may be willing to settle for a lesser amount of money. This can make good sense given the cost and hassle of collecting a judgment (for example, there are certain aspects of the collection process that may require an attorney's guidance—which will cost money the judgment creditor won't recover).

Judgment Collection Tools

If a judgment debtor refuses to reach an agreement and is otherwise uncooperative, there are several collection tools that a judgment creditor can use. All of them presume two things that I'll talk about first:

1. The debtor has assets.

2. The creditor knows—or can learn—the location and details of the assets.

Debtor Examination

One of the chief reasons why consumer credit applications ask for so much information is to simplify the chore of locating a debtor's assets in the event of a future lawsuit. Few of us have the luxury of asking questions before winning a money judgment, but most states have a mechanism for getting the information after the fact. It goes by different names, including a *debtor examination*, a *discovery hearing*, *interrogatory*, and a *supplemental examination*. The judgment debtor is called into court to answer questions—under oath—about his or her assets.

The individual is typically also required to fill out a form that asks for details of current employment, description of any real estate he or she owns, and location and account numbers of bank accounts. If the debtor avoids the hearing, the court can usually issue an arrest warrant to compel cooperation.

Please note that a debtor examination doesn't actually recover any money; it sets the stage for the next step: The court-approved *taking* of the debtor's assets.

Writ of Execution

A *writ of execution* is a court order that empowers a *levying officer* or *enforcement officer*—typically a sheriff's deputy or a marshal—to seize money or a specific item of property belonging to a judgment debtor. The court will issue a writ of execution upon a showing that the judgment creditor holds a valid money judgment, that the debtor has resisted other attempts to collect the judgment, and that the debtor owns specific assets that can be seized under the laws of the state.

This last point can be complex to navigate: Social security payments are *exempt*—they can't be seized. As a rule, neither can the portion of the debtor's wages that supports his or her family, the owner's equity in his or her house, household furniture, the car he or she uses to get to work, clothing and personal effects, and possibly the money in an individual retirement account (IRA). Few creditors can manage the subtleties without the help of an attorney.

Wage Garnishment

A *writ of garnishment* is a writ of execution that orders the judgment debtor's employer to withhold a portion of his or her wages each pay period until the money judgment has been satisfied. State laws usually limit the amount of wages that can be garnished—25 percent is the typical maximum, although the court may order less if most of the debtor's income is going to basic support, if the debtor is paying child support, if the debtor's wages have already been garnished to pay another debt, or if his or her income comes from public support (welfare) payments.

Wages paid to federal employees and military personal can be garnished, but the process can be long and involved. To begin, the creditor must complete Form OF-311—Application for Federal Employee Commercial Garnishment. The form and detailed information are available on the Office of Personnel Management website: www.opm.gov.

Attorneys who specialize in debt collection recommend garnishment as the simplest collection method—if the creditor knows the debtor's place of employment. This is because employers are likely to comply with garnishment orders. Moreover, the embarrassment of having his or her wages garnished is likely to prompt the debtor to work out a less-intrusive payment arrangement.

Till Taps and Keepers

If a judgment debtor is a retail business, some states allow a *till tap*, a writ of execution that authorizes the sheriff to take sufficient money out of the cash register to pay the judgment. A *keeper* is a related procedure; the enforcement officer stays inside the premises and collects the business's cash revenue for several hours (or even days).

Levying a Bank Account

Another possibility is a *bank levy*, a procedure that seizes the funds in a bank account—or withholds future deposits—until the judgment is satisfied. Broadly speaking, joint accounts—where one of the holders is not a judgment debtor—can't be levied. And funds from exempt sources (for example, social security, public support, and exempt wages) can't be seized, so the whole process can become quite complicated.

Real Estate Lien

The is a long-term solution that will test the patience of most judgment creditors. In many states, a judgment can be registered with the county land records office to create a lien against the debtor's current (and often future) real estate holdings. Some states prohibit small claims judgment liens; others limit the amounts that can be collected.

A lien doesn't have much effect until the owner tries to sell, transfer, or mortgage the property. The creditor typically doesn't see any money until the property is sold; then he or she is entitled to receive the judgment, interest (which can be substantial), and post-judgment costs.

Satisfaction of Judgment

When the creditor finally receives the full amount of the judgment, he or she should file a *satisfaction of judgment* form with the small claims court. This formally ends the collection process. Because creditors may not always follow through, it's important for a debtor to provide the form to the creditor, to make certain that the creditor signs it, and to ensure that the original is filed as required.

CHAPTER 15

═╪═ ═╪═

YOUR CONSTITUTIONAL RIGHTS AND FREEDOMS

KNOW MY RIGHTS!

We've all said that—perhaps with an emphatic gesture—to someone who challenged what we perceived to be one of our fundamental rights as an American. Trouble is, few people actually *know their rights.* Fewer still understand the limitations on the legal (or civil) rights we have as Americans. Rather, most of us have vague ideas based on oft-heard slogans and bumper-sticker wisdom: The Constitution makes this a free country. I can say anything I want to say. I can conduct any kind of religious ceremony that fits my beliefs. I can do anything I want to that doesn't hurt someone else. The police can't search my person without a warrant.

In fact, none of these statements are true without qualification. Most of the time, mistakenly believing these things are absolute rights causes nothing more than minor embarrassment (or a poor grade on a civics exam). But in some circumstances, acting on these notions can result in serious criminal jeopardy.

In this chapter, we'll look at such *personal rights* as freedom of speech, freedom of religion, the right to travel freely, the right to assemble peaceably, and the right to bear arms. You'll find a whole cluster of rights pertaining to criminal proceedings, including the well-known right to remain silent, in Chapter 17.

The Case of the Constitutionally Protected Cookies

Pleasantville is a small, pleasant city in the State of Grace. One of the city's cheerful traditions is Cookie Day, an annual event in Pleasantville Park. Various organizations in town set up tables and sell homemade cookies to raise revenue. Many different clubs, associations, societies, churches, and civic groups participate. Alas, at last year's Cookie Day a fight broke out between the parishioners of several local churches and the members of the Pugnacious Atheists of Pleasantville (PAP)—a highly vocal group opposed to all forms of organized religion. The scuffle began when PAP members

→ refused to take down an enormous sign that read, "People Who Believe in God Are Pinheads Who Make Us Toss Our Cookies";

→ refused to stop selling cookies in the shape of religious symbols (for example, crosses, doves, church steeples, Stars of David, and Buddhas) with "Don't Be a Pinhead!" written in vanilla icing.

This year, the City Council of Pleasantville decreed in a new ordinance that "no organizations supporting or opposing religion shall be allowed to participate in Cookie Day on city property. This will ensure the 'separation of church and state' in our fair city and also eliminate any opportunities for 'hate speech' directed at our citizens."

Many citizens thought the new rules made good sense. As an editorial in the *Pleasantville Gazette* put it, "Our local churches have many other ways of raising money, and we certainly don't have to provide a forum for kooky organizations with extreme views to sell nasty cookies that insult people. All in all, the new ordinance seems a reasonable exercise of governmental powers for the public good."

To everyone's amazement, two organizations immediately joined forces to protest the new ordinance:

1. The Pugnacious Atheists of Pleasantville—They claimed that the new ordinance is an assault on the rights of free speech and free assembly set forth in the Constitution.
2. The Community Church of Pleasantville—They opposed the new ordinance as an infringement of constitutionally protected freedom of religion.

The leaders of the two organizations—Eaton Sweets, the church's pastor, and Ima Hater, PAP's Fearless Leader—visited Noah Lott, a local attorney who was an expert in constitutional law.

Noah began by handing out copies of the First Amendment to the U.S. Constitution:

> *Congress shall make no law respecting an establishment of religion, or prohibiting the free exercise thereof; or abridging the freedom of speech, or of the press; or the right of the people peaceably to assemble, and to petition the Government for a redress of grievances.*

"It's no accident that these rights and freedom are in the first paragraph of the Bill of Rights," Noah said. "They are clearly among the *fundamental rights* we have as citizens of the United States."

It's hard to imagine a schoolkid in the United States who hasn't wondered why life, liberty, and the pursuit of happiness were listed as "inalienable rights" in the Declaration of Independence—and what that odd label really means. The philosophical concept that Thomas Jefferson wanted to get across is that individuals have certain "natural rights" (God-given rights) that can never be fully transferred to government.

FUNDAMENTAL RIGHTS

You won't find a full list of fundamental rights in the Constitution, although the Bill of Rights is a good start. And, although we consider them fundamental, new ones come to the fore and old ones seem to become less important in most people's minds.

Freedom of speech, religion, press, and assembly are explicitly spelled out. The right to privacy, the right to travel, and increasingly the right to be free of various kinds of discrimination are *implicitly* guaranteed (they are implied— and we consider them vital—but the specific words don't appear anywhere in the Constitution). On the other hand, few non-lawyers perceive the essential "freedom to contract" as a fundamental right; many more people did during the nineteenth century.

Some rights that people assume are fundamental aren't. For example, the Supreme Court has never labeled education as a fundamental right. The famed case of *Brown v. Board of Education* (its full legal name is *Brown v. Board of Education of Topeka*) decided in 1954 established that racially based "separate but equal" public schools were unconstitutional—but said nothing to prevent wealthier school districts from providing a better education than poorer districts.

Citizens of a country waive *some* personal freedoms so that people can live together more or less comfortably. For example, a person who pursues happiness by stealing someone else's property is likely to have his liberty taken away for a while by the government—but government can't arbitrarily decide to enslave people. The idea is that freedom is a natural (inalienable) right possessed by all people everywhere—a right that doesn't depend on local beliefs, customs, or laws.

Freedom of Speech

"It's often said," Noah continued, "that our belief that everyone should be free to say what he or she likes is put to the test when we run into speech that goes against everything we hold dear." He frowned at Ima. "I disagree with most of the words you speak, yet I will fight as hard as I can for your freedom of speech— because the First Amendment protects everyone, including those who express viewpoints that most people find obnoxious.

"Freedom of speech is an aptly named right. You are free to speak and to otherwise express yourself (in writing, broadcasts, recording, on the Internet, in other media, and *symbolically*) and say virtually anything you want—as long as you don't violate another person's rights or cause predictable immediate harm."

Eaton Sweets jumped into the conversation. "You lost me. How can I express myself symbolically?"

"By wearing a T-shirt that proclaims a message, by trampling a U.S. flag, by torching a book, by burning a cross (if the act doesn't communicate immediate threat or intimidation), and even by making insulting cookies in the shape of religious symbols."

"Absolutely!" Ima gestured triumphantly.

Noah talked on, "Several U.S. Supreme Court decisions extended free-speech protection to *symbolic speech*: The government can't ban these activities, even though the majority of other people in the community may find them repugnant.

"When we talk about free speech it makes sense to begin with the assumption that there are no rules—and then zero in on the few kinds of speech that governments can regulate. For example, there's a 'preliminary crime' called *solicitation* [*see* Chapter 17] that's committed when one person urges another person to commit a crime. A person charged with solicitation can't invoke his or her right of free speech as a defense.

"The other few restrictions to free speech that do exist are about balance—the goal is to balance an individual's right to speak freely against the government's responsibilities to prevent and redress harm to others."

STUDENT SPEECH

The U.S. Supreme Court said that students "do not shed their constitutional rights to freedom of speech and expression at the schoolhouse gate." However, public school officials can regulate certain types of student expression, including prohibiting speech that is disruptive, lewd, or interferes with a school's fundamental educational mission. A recent Supreme Court decision upheld a school principal's suspension of a student who displayed a banner that many interpreted as promoting the use of illegal drugs.

A Clear and Present Danger

"Every schoolkid learns," Noah continued, "that freedom of speech doesn't include the right to *falsely* scream 'Fire!' in a crowded theater. This is the classic example of speech that threatens the public interest with a *clear and present danger.* I've emphasized 'falsely' because the basic idea is that government can forbid speech that has no useful purpose of any kind and will create *real and imminent* danger. Another example is a speech that incites a crowd to riot. Not surprisingly, inciting to riot—or some variation on the theme—is a crime in most states.

"The requirement that the danger be *'present'* (imminent) is an essential requirement. Government can't forbid or limit speech that advocates lawless actions unless the speaker is trying to whip listeners into a frenzy that will incite lawlessness there and then."

Ima raised her hand. "So I can urge people not to pay their city tax bills next month to protest the tax exemptions given to churches?"

"Urge away," Noah replied.

Fighting Words

"*Fighting words* strong enough to provoke an angry reaction are a concept that's the cousin of inciting a crowd to riot. Fighting words aren't protected speech, because to quote the U.S. Supreme Court's explanation in *Chaplinsky v. New Hampshire*, a 1942 case, they 'by their very utterance inflict injury or tend to incite an immediate breach of the peace.' The Court went on to observe that fighting words are never an 'essential part of any exposition of ideas, and . . . any benefit that may be derived from them is clearly outweighed by the social interest in order and morality.' People who use fighting words are often arrested for *breach of the peace,* or some such crime. They often defend themselves by asserting their right of free speech—and they often lose.

"There are many different insults and epithets that qualify as fighting words." Noah smiled at Ima. "Calling someone a 'pinhead' is probably not strong enough."

WHAT ABOUT HATE SPEECH?

Hate speech has been defined as speech that demeans the race, sex, religion, color, creed, disability, sexual orientation, national origin, or ancestry of a person or group of people. Although hate speech is outlawed in some other countries, the U.S. Supreme Court has not provided a First Amendment exception for hate speech. And so, unless the speaker incites listeners to violence, delivers fighting words, defames someone, or spouts obscenity, his or her hateful words are constitutionally protected.

Defamation

"Speech that defames another person is not protected," Noah said (*see* Chapter 3). "*Defamation* is an untruth that damages a person's reputation. *Slander* is defamation by a spoken statement; *libel* is defamation in print. The law of defamation makes it extraordinarily difficult to defame a public official—which ensures that citizens (and the media) can criticize and complain about government and leaders to their hearts' content."

Obscenity

"Obscene speech (for example, selling or distributing pornography) is also not protected by the First Amendment. The Supreme Court's definition of obscene material tends to change over time. The current definition has three components:

1. The work depicts or describes sexual conduct in a *patently offensive way* (as determined by a "reasonable adult" who applies the contemporary standards held by people in the state).
2. The sexual conduct is specifically described in the state or local law that outlaws obscenity.
3. The work, taken as a whole, lacks serious value and appeals to a prurient interest in sex.

"This can be difficult to prove in court—and is highly situational—because it's tough to come up with a good definition for pornography that doesn't 'accidentally' encompass valid art, medical and scientific text books, and edgy literature, to name a few challenges. As the late Justice Potter Stewart famously said about obscenity in a case dating back to 1964: 'I know it when I see it.'"

Although state and local governments can attempt to ban the sale of so-called adult-oriented materials, the constitutionally protected *right to privacy* (*see* below) prevents government from making it a crime for adults to have these materials in their homes. This is not true of child pornography, possession of which is a serious crime in all states.

Freedom of Peaceable Assembly

"During the nineteenth century," Noah Lott said, "many legal scholars saw the right to assemble peaceably as part of the right to petition government. Simply put, people had the right to assemble in front of federal government buildings to *seek redress for their complaints*. But in the twentieth century, other kinds of public protests—such as picketing by union members, marches to protest discrimination, antiwar rallies, and public demonstrations to support different viewpoints—transformed the right of peaceful assembly into an important freedom of its own, a freedom that the U.S. Supreme Court has affirmed as a fundamental right.

Most of the U.S. Supreme Court's major peaceable-assembly decisions during the twentieth century are responses to state and local government attempts to stop assemblies by arresting the participants—typically on charges of *breach of peace* or *disorderly conduct*, because they violated statutes supposedly designed to prevent potentially violent gatherings. The Court said that the fear of a disorderly crowd doesn't justify banning a peaceful demonstration or cancel the right of peaceable assembly.

The only justification for restricting the right of peaceable assembly is our old friend *clear and present danger* or an *imminent incitement of lawlessness*. Consequently, courts have overruled local prohibitions and granted the freedom to assemble peaceably to groups that espouse racial and religious hatred. "As a federal judge noted in the famous Skokie parade case in 1977 (the court overturned a local ban that prevented a group of Nazis from parading through Skokie, Illinois, at the time the home of many Holocaust survivors), 'it is better to allow those who preach racial hatred to expend their venom in rhetoric rather than to be panicked into embarking on the dangerous course of permitting the government to decide what its citizens may say and hear.'"

NOT ALL ASSEMBLIES ARE PROTECTED

To gain First Amendment protection against undue governmental restrictions, an assembly must be a gathering to advance a common political, economic, or cultural interest. Courts have called this an *expressive association*. This is in contrast to gatherings that are intended for *leisure and diversion*—a dance, for example. Because social gatherings aren't protected, government can issue regulations designed to achieve any rational purpose. For example, in one U.S. Supreme Court case, a local government was allowed to restrict attendance at "young adult dances" to people between the age of fourteen and eighteen, thus preventing participants' association with older and younger individuals.

Reasonable Restrictions on Public Forums

"When I hear the terms *free speech* and *freedom of assembly*," Noah went on, "I think of a speaker standing on a soapbox in the town square, or a group of protesters parading down Main Street. Well, one group of U.S. Supreme Court decisions makes it unconstitutional for government to arbitrarily forbid access to public property—which can be an effective way to squelch free speech. On the other hand, government can ensure order by establishing reasonable restrictions on the time, place, and manner of access to *public forums*. As one Supreme Court decision comments, no one can 'insist upon a street meeting in the middle of Times Square at the rush hour as a form of freedom of speech.'

"However, the restrictions can't be used—as they often were in the past—to deny a group access to public places merely because the members advocate unpopular, even offensive positions.

"Government can require parade permits . . . insist that demonstrators remain in a designated area of a public forum . . . prevent protesters from blocking access to a public building . . . have demonstrators pay reasonable fees for policing costs. But none of this can be done selectively, based on the content of speech. A city can't charge a group who will deliver an unpleasant message more to parade than, say, the Girl Scouts."

Ima Hater sat up in her chair. "Or refuse space in Pleasantville Park for a 'kooky organization' that intends to sell 'nasty cookies that insult people.'" Ima cheered, "Let's hear it for the First Amendment."

THE AYES DON'T HAVE IT: THE PROTECTED MINORITY

The Equal Protection Clause grants every individual equal protection of the laws. This means that government can't limit a person's fundamental rights—including the freedoms of speech, religion, and peaceable assembly—even though most of the population is in favor of the limitation. In essence, the Constitution protects minority groups from "the tyranny of the majority," a phrase coined by Alexis de Tocqueville, the French political thinker who wrote *Democracy in America*. Without this protection, every minority group is in danger of losing fundamental rights—although members of the majority are frequently annoyed by court decisions that declare popular laws unconstitutional.

The Doctrine of Incorporation

"And also the Fourteenth Amendment," Noah said. "The rights I described cover your activities in Pleasantville Park because of the *Doctrine of Incorporation*, which by the way has nothing to do with starting a new business. Rather, it's a doctrine created by the U.S. Supreme Court that extends the fundamental rights and liberties set forth in the U.S. Constitution to prevent encroachment by state and local government.

"If this sounds unnecessary, consider that the *Bill of Rights* was added to the U.S. Constitution to protect the rights of citizens from *actions by the U.S. government*. Until late in the nineteenth century, the protections afforded by the Bill of Rights did not apply to state or local government. A state (even a city) could, for example, have more stringent limits on *free speech* than the federal government—and often did.

"A series of Supreme Court cases spanning more than fifty years interpreted the *Due Process* and *Equal Protection Clauses* of the Fourteenth Amendment—an amendment aimed squarely at states—to incorporate most constitutional protections.

"The bottom line: State and local governments can't encroach on most of the fundamental liberties spelled out in the Bill of Rights and elsewhere in the Constitution."

I'll Take It to the Supreme Court

"While we're peeking at the inner workings of constitutional law," Noah said, "let me call your attention to one other detail that few people think about. Specifically . . . *why* does the U.S. Supreme Court get to say whether or not federal, state, and local laws pass constitutional muster?"

Eaton shrugged. "Because it's the *supreme* court. We have a government based on *checks and balances*—clearly the courts have to be able to balance the power of the legislative and the executive branches."

"True enough—but nowhere on the pages of the Constitution will you find the phrase 'checks and balances' or a clause that gives the Supreme Court the job of reviewing laws passed by Congress, by state legislatures, or by local governments. However, this kind of *judicial review* may happen dozens of times each year, as the Court *strikes down* or *upholds* various laws, statutes, and ordinances—declaring them unconstitutional or constitutional.

"It's not too far-fetched to say that the Supreme Court *itself* invented judicial review. It happened in 1803, when, for the first time, the Court invalidated a federal law that conflicted with the Constitution. The Chief Justice explained that Acts of Congress that conflict with the Constitution are not law and the Courts are bound instead to follow the Constitution."

Freedom of Religion

"The third major personal right secured by the First Amendment," Noah said, "is freedom of religion. The Constitution proclaims that 'Congress shall make no law respecting an establishment of religion, or prohibiting the free exercise thereof . . . .' These are the two short clauses:

1. The *establishment clause* that, practically speaking, is the wall that separates church and state (to use Thomas Jefferson's famous

metaphor). Government can't establish an 'official religion' (like the Church of England), nor can it act in ways that interfere with religions, favor one religion at the expense of another, or hinder one religion to advance another.

2. The *free exercise clause* that prevents government from setting limits on how a person practices his or her religion unless it has a compelling interest (for example, government can ban polygamy and human sacrifice). However, a *neutral law of general applicability* that impacts the exercise of religion is acceptable (for example, a state may ban the use of peyote even though it's used in some religious ceremonies).

"When government puts limits on religion it may simultaneously limit speech—so several of the cases I use as examples seem similar to the free-speech examples I've already talked about."

The Broad Meaning of *Establishment*

Noah continued explaining, "Back in 1947, the late Justice Hugo Black authored a U.S. Supreme Court decision—*Emerson v. Board of Education*—that set forth an oft-repeated definition:

> The establishment of the religion clause of the First Amendment means at least this: Neither a state nor the federal government can set up a church. Neither can pass laws which aid one religion, aid all religions, or prefer one religion over another. Neither can force nor influence a person to go to or to remain away from church against his will or force him to profess a belief or disbelief in any religion. No person can be punished for entertaining or professing religious beliefs or disbeliefs, for church attendance or non-attendance. No tax in any amount, large or small, can be levied to support any religious activities or institutions, whatever they may be called, or whatever form they may adopt to teach or practice religion. Neither a state nor the Federal Government can, openly or secretly, participate in the affairs of any religious organizations or groups and vice versa.

"Although this list sounds extensive, there are circumstances when government can pass valid laws that concern religions. The U.S. Supreme Court provided a three-prong test—it's nicknamed the *Lemon Test* because it was announced in the 1971 decision *Lemon v. Kurtzman*—that specifies the requirements of constitutional legislation:

1. The government's action must have a secular legislative purpose.
2. The government's action must not have the primary effect of either advancing or inhibiting religion.
3. The government's action must not result in an *excessive government entanglement* with religion.

"The court has applied this principle to different situations and has come up with results that strike some legal scholars as inconsistent—a consequence of the difficulty of resolving First Amendment issues."

School Prayer

"Public schools can't require students to say prayers," Noah said, "listen to prayers read by teachers, or set aside a period for silent prayer. A school can't invite a clergyman to present an invocation before a school event, nor can it authorize (or allow a student body to authorize) student-led prayer. Any requirement that puts pressure on students—directly or from peers—is likely to be struck down."

Schools and Public Money

Noah went on, "State government can fund student transportation to schools— public, private, and parochial—because the applicable law applies to all citizens without regard to religious belief. However, a state can't pay part of the salaries of teachers at religious institutions, because that practice *excessively entangles* the state with religion.

"However, states *can* partially reimburse the parents of students who send their children to private schools, including religious schools. Public school districts can provide secular textbooks, school supplies, and other nonreligious assistance to religious schools. And, public funds can be used to support the construction of *nonreligious* buildings at religious institutions of higher learning.

"Finally, the U.S. Supreme Court has upheld the constitutionality of governments providing *school vouchers* to pay tuition at private and religious schools."

Religious Symbols in Public Places

"It's a violation of the Establishment Clause for a school district to require the posting of the Ten Commandments in every public classroom," Noah continued. "However, it's not unconstitutional to post the Ten Commandments in courtrooms and legislative chambers, or on state Capitol grounds—because since the earliest days of the nation's history, there's been an 'unbroken history of official acknowledgment by all three branches of government of religion's role in American life.'"

"Also, while the Ten Commandments are religious, they have 'an undeniable historical meaning.' (The U.S. Supreme Court made this point in a 2005 decision, *Van Orden v. Perry*.) The court has also noted that mere religious content does not run afoul of the Establishment Clause. Moreover, a city that has accepted a religious monument (for example, a Ten Commandments monument) is not required to accept other religious monuments. Simply put, the city is not required to give *equal time* to other faiths."

Religious Symbols in Public Holiday Displays

"Government can include religious symbols in public holiday displays—a Christmas crèche for example surrounded by secular holiday symbols—when the benefit to religion is merely *indirect, remote, and incidental*," Noah explained. "However, a strongly religious symbol that occupies a prominent position—for example, a Christmas crèche prominently displayed in a county courthouse that included the Latin phrase *Gloria in Excelsis Deo*—is unconstitutional."

Religious Use of Public Facilities

"The principle that government must not entangle itself in religion is violated when government tries to turn public places into *religion-free zones*. If public facilities are made available to secular groups, religious organizations can't be excluded merely because they advocate religion. In other words, constitutionally required *neutrality* toward religion is not *hostility* toward religion."

Eaton Sweets leaped to his feet. "So Pleasantville can't exclude churches from Cookie Day?"

"Not without a much, much better reason than the Pleasantville City Council has come up with so far," Noah said. "But before we reach conclusions, we have to examine one last First Amendment clause."

Your Right to Freely Exercise Your Religion

"To quote the U.S. Supreme Court, the Free Exercise Clause 'embraces two concepts—freedom to believe and freedom to act. The first is absolute, but in the nature of things, the second cannot be.' In other words, government can *never* tell you what—or what not—to believe, but it can establish rules that limit religious practice in certain situations," Noah clarified.

"For example, you can belong to a religion that advocates bigamy and polygamy—and proclaim the virtues of these practices to everyone you meet—as long as you remember that every state in the Union makes it a crime to have more than one spouse. All of these laws are constitutional.

"For many years, the U.S. Supreme Court allowed limitation on the exercise of religion only when government had a compelling interest. The Court subsequently announced a slightly *softer* rationale when it upheld that a criminal statute that impacted the practice of a minority religion but didn't target a specific religion (the peyote statute I mentioned previously, that makes the drug illegal although the ban *burdens* some religious practice). Over the years, a number of other well-publicized decisions have given shape to Free Exercise protections:

+ *1963*—A state *must* provide unemployment benefits to a Seventh Day Adventist who turned down a job that required work on Saturday (his Sabbath).

+ *1972*—A state *can't* require Amish students to attend school until the age of seventeen.

+ *1979*—A state *can't* enforce hunting laws against Native Americans whose religion requires that they hunt moose out of season.

+ *1986*—The U.S. Army *can* require an Orthodox Jewish officer to not wear a yarmulke (skull cap) on duty, as part of the military's ban on unconventional headwear.

+ *1988*—The federal government *can* construct a road through a national forest that certain Native Americans consider religious sacred ground.

+ *1993*—A state *can't* pass laws that target minority religious practices that most of the population disapproves of—in this case, animal sacrifice.

+ *2004*—A state *can* refuse to award college scholarships to students studying to fulfill a religious calling—in this case, a degree in devotional theology."

"What Will Happen on Cookie Day?"

Eaton Sweets and Ima Hater asked that question simultaneously.

"I'm confident," Noah answered, "that both of your organizations will participate in Cookie Day. For starters, I will write a letter to the City Council of Pleasantville explaining why the new ordinance violates both your freedom of speech and freedom of religion.

"A detailed explanation may be enough to bring about a change. If it isn't, we'll seek a *preliminary injunction* in federal court—essentially a court order that commands the City of Pleasantville to allow your participation in Cookie Day.

"Courts are willing to issue preliminary injunctions in First Amendment cases because the Supreme Court has stated that 'the loss of First Amendment freedoms, even for minimal periods of time, unquestionably constitutes irreparable injury.'"

Other Things Worth Knowing about Rights and Freedoms

Ima Hater's "Last Gasp"

Cookie Day came and went without any protests or fist fights. In fact, Ima Hater was feeling so good that she forgot that Pleasantville had recently passed another ordinance forbidding smoking in public. She lit up a small cigar and blew smoke rings at several people—including the policeman who eventually gave her a citation for committing an infraction (*see* Chapter 17).

People who believe they have a right to smoke in public generally make one of two arguments:

1. The right to smoke is a fundamental right to privacy (*see* below) that is protected by the U.S. and state constitutions.

2. Equal protection clauses in constitutions prevent the state from creating legislation that discriminates against smokers.

"Sorry Ima," Noah Lott said. "Smoking in public has never been declared a fundamental right; therefore state and city governments can limit smoking in public places if the legislation they enact has a rational purpose. Because anti-smoking laws can be justified by many plausible arguments—many related to government's interest in preserving the health of nonsmokers—courts typically *don't* find the restrictions unconstitutional."

Speaking of the Right to Privacy

Back in 1965, the U.S. Supreme Court declared unconstitutional a Connecticut law that prohibited the use of contraceptives—and, in the process, announced the existence of a constitutional *right to privacy.*

The Constitution does not explicitly mention such a right, but several of the Justices who wrote the decision noted that various amendments in the Bill of Rights create *zones of privacy* into which the government cannot intrude. Simply put, there are some highly private areas of our lives that should be beyond the reach of government control.

This is the central concept of the right to privacy as it has been developed in a series of more recent decisions, including *Roe v. Wade*, the controversial 1973 ruling that a woman's choice to have an abortion is a private decision reached by her and her physician.

Many critics of the right of privacy—including two Justices who wrote dissents of the original decision—argue that the so-called right to privacy doesn't exist, and that courts can now add new rights to the Constitution simply by labeling them privacy rights. In fact, courts have been reluctant to expand the *zones of privacy* much beyond intimate, highly personal activities—such as marriage, contraception, consensual sex, family relationships, and the rearing and educating of children.

As with other fundamental rights, government must have a compelling interest to invade the right of privacy.

Freedom of the Press

The First Amendment forbids the government to create any law that abridges the freedom of speech or of the press. Although these two freedoms are mentioned individually in the Bill of Rights, courts have treated both rights as different sides of a single coin: our fundamental right to express ourselves freely. Because freedom of the press is recognized as a fundamental right, it can't be limited unless government has a truly compelling reason to do so. The limitations on the press fall into two categories:

1. *Prior restraint*—Censorship laws prohibit newspapers and other media from publishing specific kinds of information (for example, government secrets).

2. *Post-publication*—Defamation laws (*see* Chapter 3) punish the media for publishing libelous statements.

Of the two, prior restraint is considered the most oppressive challenge to freedom of the press. As the U.S. Supreme Court said in *Nebraska Press Association v. Stuart*, a 1976 decision:

prior restraints on speech and publication are the most serious and the least tolerable infringement on First Amendment rights. A criminal penalty or a judgment in a defamation case is subject to the whole panoply of protections afforded by deferring the impact of the judgment until all avenues of appellate review have been exhausted. Only after judgment has become final, correct or otherwise, does the law's sanction become fully operative. A prior restraint, by contrast and by definition, has an immediate and irreversible sanction. If it can be said that a threat of criminal or civil sanctions after publication 'chills' speech, prior restraint 'freezes' it at least for the time.

Consequently, any government attempt at prior restraint of the press starts out with a strong presumption that it's unconstitutional. The government must prove that disclosing information will cause *direct, immediate, and irreparable damage to our nation or its people.*

A fairly common kind of prior restraint is called a *gag order*—an injunction issued by a judge who wants to stop the media from reporting on a current case. Appeal courts are reluctant to sustain gag orders unless the issuing court can make a strong case that pretrial publicity will make a fair trial impossible.

Your Rights When Out of the United States

It should go without saying, although I'll say it anyway, that a U.S. citizen in a foreign country, is subject to that country's laws and regulations—which may not afford the protections available under U.S. law.

As many Americans who commit crimes overseas find out each year, a traveler

→ can't invoke his or her rights under the U.S. Constitution when in another country;

→ doesn't have the same set of fundamental rights that Americans enjoy;

→ doesn't have the right to a jury trial (few foreign countries provide trial by jury) or all the other procedural protections Americans take for granted (*see* Chapter 17);

→ can be imprisoned for months of *pretrial detention*;

→ may face trials that involve lengthy delays or postponements;

→ typically must deal with criminal proceedings conducted in a foreign language.

Your Right to Travel Freely in the United States

Another fundamental right that is not mentioned explicitly in the Constitution is the right to travel freely. As one U.S. Supreme Court Justice wrote, the right to travel is "a virtually unconditional personal right, guaranteed by the Constitution to us all." Some legal scholars believe that the right to travel was considered so fundamental that the framers of the Constitution saw no need to include it in the Bill of Rights.

The right to travel has three aspects:

1. Every citizen has the right to travel freely between states.

2. A citizen of one state who enters another state enjoys all of the *privileges and immunities* (rights and benefits) available to the local residents. This is spelled out in Article 4, Section 2 of the Constitution.

3. A citizen who moves permanently to another state is entitled to all of the rights and benefits available to other citizens of the state.

Many of the right-to-travel cases that reach the Supreme Court involve challenges to *durational residency requirements*—laws that deny benefits to newcomers until they have lived in the state for specific periods of time. These benefits can range from acquiring a low-cost hunting license to paying in-state tuition at a community college.

Because some durational residency requirements may *penalize* people who exercise a fundamental right—or else deter people from exercising a fundamental right—courts will invalidate them unless they achieve a compelling governmental interest.

A state law requiring one-year residency before one could be eligible for welfare assistance was declared unconstitutional. So was a state law that set a durational residency requirement before a new arrival could register to vote.

However, a one-year residency requirement before a newcomer can file for divorce was upheld. And durational residency requirements that define when a student can receive lower in-state tuition at public colleges have also been ruled constitutional.

Your Right to Bear Arms

The Second Amendment of the Bill of Rights provides: "A well regulated Militia, being necessary to the security of the free State, the right of the people to keep and bear Arms, shall not be infringed."

Until 2008, legislators and courts were not certain if the second clause—*the right of the people to keep and bear Arms, shall not be infringed*—was simply a *collective right*, a necessary adjunct to the need to have a well-regulated militia. However, in 2008, the U.S. Supreme Court declared in *District of Columbia v. Heller* that the Second Amendment protects an individual's right to self-defense and gun ownership. It also noted that "the inherent right of self-defense has been central to the Second Amendment right."

The Court went on to say,

> Like most rights, the right secured by the Second Amendment
> is not unlimited. [It is] not a right to keep and carry any weapon
> whatsoever in any manner whatsoever and for whatever purpose.
> For example, the majority of the nineteenth-century courts to
> consider the question held that prohibitions on carrying concealed
> weapons were lawful. Nothing in our opinion should be taken to
> cast doubt on long-standing prohibitions on the possession of firearms
> by felons and the mentally ill, or laws forbidding the carrying of
> firearms in sensitive places such as schools and government buildings,
> or laws imposing conditions and qualifications on the commercial
> sale of arms.

The bottom line: There is a constitutional right to bear arms, but government can set reasonable rules for the kinds of weapons available, purchasing, ownership, possession, concealment, and use.

In a second landmark decision, *McDonald v. Chicago*, announced in 2010, the U.S. Supreme Court said that the Second Amendment applies to state governments and protects gun owners from overreaching regulations imposed by state and local laws. As before, local government can impose reasonable rules on gun ownership.

CHAPTER 16

EVERYDAY LAW ON THE JOB

NE OF THE MOST COMPLEX AREAS OF LAW IN THE UNITED STATES encompasses the alphabet soup of different state and federal laws that impact employees and employers: EEOC, ADA, COBRA, HIPAA, ERISA, OSHA, FLSA, FMLA—the list goes on and on. In all, there are many thousands of federal and state statutes, regulations issued by administrative agencies, and relevant judicial decisions. Together, they touch almost every aspect of the relationship between employee and employer. Most of the laws and regulations were put in place to *protect* employees—in the broadest sense of the word. The protections go beyond economic considerations, health, and safety to encompass an employee's dignity and self-worth.

Only a handful of employment law topics fit our definition of everyday law: legal questions that you and I are likely to ask . . . *every day.* These include issues related to the following:

- → Discrimination during the hiring process and later, when some employees are promoted, while others are not
- → Wage and hour regulations and overtime pay
- → Who is an *exempt employee*
- → Sexual harassment on the job
- → Wrongful termination of employment
- → Workers' compensation and unemployment insurance
- → Agreements not to compete with a current employer
- → Ownership of trade secrets, inventions, and copyrighted materials
- → An employee's *right to privacy* in the workplace
- → Health and safety issues in the workplace

We'll examine these issues in this chapter from an unusual perspective.

A Day in Human Resources

You've worked hard at Acme Corporation—and you were recently promoted to Director of Human Resources. When it comes to on-the-job personnel issues, the buck stops at your desk. A typical week can bring you many different challenges, all of them with significant legal implications. And so, every Monday morning you meet with Annie, your assistant; Zachary, a member of Acme's legal staff; and Chuck, Acme's corporate ombudsman, an independent manager who advocates the joint interests of employees and the company. This morning's meeting requires you to answer an unusual number of interesting legal questions.

A Tale of Three Job Candidates

An e-mail you received the other day explained that Eileen, Acme's Vice President of Public Affairs, had narrowed the selection for the plum job of Manager of Media Relations down to three candidates:

1. *Alex*: a white male with a master's degree in public relations and ten years of directly relevant experience in another media relations department quite similar to ours.

2. *Simone*: an African-American female who spent many years working as a nurse before she returned to college to complete a bachelor's degree in communications. She has worked six years in a nonprofit organization's public relations department, dealing mostly with media requests for information.

3. *Lenora*: an Asian-American female with a prosthetic leg, who has a master's degree in journalism, was a newspaper reporter for five years, and a media relations associate at a community college for five years.

Eileen explained that all three passed Acme's news-release writing test, have excellent references, and seem highly capable of doing the job. She added that the choice among the three was difficult, but that she finally gave the nod to Alex, because of his greater media-relations experience. But, she's concerned that not giving the job to Simone or Lenora might raise concerns about discrimination in hiring.

Annie chimed in first, "I'm not surprised that Eileen is unsure what to do. Our Public Affairs Department is widely considered a great place to work. We get dozens of applications each month—and tons more when we announce a job opening. You remember that we received complaints in the past that the department made hiring decisions on the basis of race and disability."

"One of them turned into a lawsuit that we eventually won," Zachary said, "but we don't want to go through that kind of hassle and expense again."

"You bet we don't," Chuck said. "But more important, we don't want a reputation as a company that breaks the law. I know it sounds corny, but Acme is really committed to do the right thing when we hire people."

"Well . . . our challenge today is to advise Eileen," you said. "I want to send her an e-mail this morning. What should I say?"

"As I've often pointed out to this group," Zachary said, "federal law generally leaves it to our business judgment to decide who we should hire or promote. Our decisions won't be challenged if we hire and promote based on job-related ability, as measured by uniform and consistently applied qualification and selection standards. In other words, to honor the anti-discrimination laws—to do the *right thing* when we hire people—the criteria we use to select new employees can't have a significantly discriminatory effect."

THE EQUAL EMPLOYMENT OPPORTUNITY COMMISSION

The U.S. Equal Employment Opportunity Commission (EEOC) enforces a series of wide-ranging federal laws that apply throughout the United States. They create a broad range of employee protections by barring discrimination based on race, gender, pregnancy, national origin, religion, disability, and age (for people older than forty). The laws don't apply to the smallest of small businesses, but any company with more than twenty employees must follow these laws in every aspect of the process of hiring a new employee—from creating advertisements to recruit potential employees, to designing tests designed to evaluate applicants, to coming up with the interview questions that short-listed candidates must answer. (Many other state and local statutes fill in gaps by forbidding employment discrimination by smaller companies, or on the basis of sexual orientation, marriage status, and body weight.) The EEOC tries to resolve—often through mediation—the charges of discrimination by employers, but if its attempts fail, the EEOC will authorize employees to file private lawsuits against their discriminating employers. The remedies for employee discrimination include hiring, promotion, reinstatement, back pay, attorney's fees, court costs, expert witness fees—almost anything required to make the claimant *whole* after being discriminated against. An employee can also be compensated for inconvenience and mental anguish. Moreover, in cases of obviously intentional discrimination, juries can award punitive damages (see Chapter 4). All of this makes on-the-job discrimination a highly expensive practice for companies. Consequently, intelligent companies do their best to avoid discrimination.

"Spoken like a true lawyer," Annie said. "I worked with Eileen to transform your legalese into simple English. We came up with a nondiscriminatory job description for Manager of Media Relations that specifies reasonable qualifications for the job. Our requirements are straightforward, including a bachelor's degree appropriate to media relations, a minimum of five years' experience dealing with various kinds of reporters, excellent writing and editing skills, and computer skills ranging from word processing to the Internet. We explained that the Manager of Media Relations will be expected to travel to different Acme facilities to gather information for news releases. We estimated four trips a month to locations throughout the United States. We also required all candidates to take a writing test that asked them to prepare three sample news releases based on hypothetical facts. We commissioned two journalism instructors at local universities to evaluate and critique the news releases that candidates wrote.

"Incidentally, I conducted the initial interviews with all the candidates. I agree with Eileen: Alex deserves to be offered the job."

BONA FIDE OCCUPATIONAL QUALIFICATION

One narrow exception to on-the-job discrimination laws is the so-called bona fide occupational qualification (BFOQ). In certain situations, employers may discriminate when a specific characteristic is a necessary requirement of the job. For example, airlines can require pilots to be younger than mandatory retirement age; film studios can require actors playing male roles to be men; advertising agencies can advertise for female models to wear women's clothing; a Christian university can require that its president, chancellor, and faculty be Christians (but probably not security guards, administrative staff, or maintenance personnel); and a gym can hire a female to oversee its women's locker room (but not require that front-desk greeters be of a specific gender).

"I have to ask a question," Zachary said, "although I'm confident that I know the answer. Was there anything about our employment ad, the interviews, our writing test, or any other part of the process that biased our selection on race, gender, age, religion, or national origin?"

"Absolutely not!" Annie said. "We have a thoroughly neutral applicant-evaluation process. For example, every candidate was interviewed by a diverse group of interviewers—current employees in different age groups, with different experience levels, and of different races. And of course, our employment application forms don't ask questions about age, race, religion, or national origin."

"Let's talk about Lenora," Zachary said. "How do you know that she has a prosthetic leg? I hope that no one asked her if she was disabled."

"Absolutely not!" Annie said, again, this time with a shake of her head. "We always follow your rule: Ask candidates about their abilities, but not their disabilities. I know that we are not allowed to ask prospective employees if they have disabilities that might impact their ability to perform the job. Instead, we have to focus on how they intend to meet the essential requirements of the job. That's how we handled Lenora's interview."

"I get it," Chuck said, "you talked about travel."

"Yep," Annie said. "The travel requirements are extensive—about one trip each week. Lenora pointed to her cane—it was obvious she had some sort of mobility issue—and said that frequent airline travel was no problem, but that she needed to get to the airport fairly early because her 'bionic leg,' as she called it, makes it difficult for her to run down corridors. She also said that she'd appreciate an office near an elevator."

"Both seem like *reasonable accommodations* [*see* below] to enable her to do her job," Zachary said. "Your question about travel invited her to talk about accommodations. But in fact, when you saw Lenora using a cane, you had a legitimate reason to assume that she had a disability and were free to ask her about accommodations."

"True," Chuck said, "but they won't be necessary. Based on everything I've heard, I think that Eileen can confidently offer the job to Alex."

"I agree," Annie said.

"Me too," Zachary added.

REASONABLE ACCOMMODATIONS

An employer must make a reasonable accommodation to the disability of a qualified applicant or employee if the accommodation will not impose an *undue hardship* on business operations. An undue hardship involves significant difficulty or expense when considered in light of factors such as an employer's size, financial resources, and the nature and structure of its operation.

"Good. That's what I'll tell Eileen," you said. "And we'll close the loop by sending Simone and Lenora personal letters explaining our decision to go with the candidate with the most relevant experience."

MEDICAL EXAMINATIONS AND CREDIT CHECKS

An employer may reject a candidate on the basis of medical examination—if the same examination must be passed successfully by all candidates for similar jobs. These examinations must be job related; they can't involve factors unrelated to the employer's business needs. An exception is testing for the presence of illegal drugs. An employer can reject a candidate on the basis of illegal drug use.

Employers face strict limitations when using credit checks to evaluate candidates for hiring—including specific disclosures to job applicants before and after the company performs the check. (Although critics argue that a credit check has little to do with a candidate's ability to perform a specific job unless the potential employee will handle the company's money, many employers routinely use credit checks as indicators of a candidate's personal responsibility, management skills, and ability to make sound decisions.) However, a negative credit check can never be used to automatically reject a candidate. The candidate must have an opportunity to explain the circumstances that led to a low credit rating, along with any recent changes in the management of his or her finances.

Can We Fire Lucy Jones?

"Our next issue this morning," you said, "concerns Lucy Jones, one of our website technicians. We've decided to outsource the work she does, so we plan to terminate her employment."

"Lucy's been with Acme for six years," Annie said. "She's not covered by a collective bargaining agreement with any of our unions, and we don't have a written employment contract with her. In other words, Lucy is one of our many *at-will* employees. She's good at what she does; she received excellent performance appraisals every year. Unhappily, the current economic situation makes it necessary for us to reduce costs. We trimmed our website budget by 10 percent, and we have to cut back our support staff."

Zachary raised a finger. "This is a great opportunity to review the *rules* for terminating at-will employees. The phrase *at-will* captures the idea perfectly. Either an employee or the employer can end at-will employment at any time—and for any reason—with or without advance notice. She's free to quit, and we can't complain; we're free to fire her, and she can't complain."

"However . . . " Chuck said, "these days, there are a few restrictions."

"Indeed there are," Zachary nodded. "Federal anti-discrimination laws apply to firings as well as hirings. For starters, discriminatory firings based on race, age, gender, religion, disability, or national origin are illegal. A wrongfully discharged employee can file a complaint with the EEOC and may be authorized to file a lawsuit against the company.

"Moreover, the traditional at-will employment doctrine has been *softened*, if you like, by laws in many states and by various court decisions. Consequently, terminations that violate the so-called public-policy exception to the at-will doctrine aren't permitted in most states. For example, an employee can't be terminated because he or she objected to do something illegal . . . or was a whistle-blower who reported improper conduct or unsafe working conditions . . . or refused to vote his or her shares of company stock in a specific way . . . or took time away from the job to serve on a jury.

DISCRIMINATION IN PROMOTIONS

Federal (and often state) law requires that employees not be refused promotions—or receive demotions—on the basis of race, gender, religious beliefs, disabilities, national origin, or other characteristics we've talked about in this chapter. A discriminated-against employee is entitled to promotion (or reinstatement) along with the pay he or she would have received. Courts can also award lost benefits, damages for emotional suffering, punitive damages, and attorney's fees.

"There can also be limitations caused by *implied contracts* with employees. In years past, company employee handbooks sometimes declared that employees will be terminated only for *just cause*—in other words, because of employee wrongdoing. Courts found that these handbooks established employment contracts that prevented at-will terminations."

"Do we face any of these issues with Lucy Jones?" Annie asked.

"I don't see any," Zachary said, "unless there's some aspect of the termination that might suggest *bad faith and unfair dealing*. This is a catchall limitation that courts have interpreted in many different ways. It generally means that a company intends malice when it singles out an employee to be fired."

"Quite the opposite," Annie said. "We juggled budgets for several days before we decided that we had no option except to shrink staff."

"Then we're all agreed?" you said. "We can terminate Lucy Jones." You watch everyone nod.

Does Nora Nelson Deserve Overtime Pay?

"This is a fairly unusual issue for us," you said. "However, because Nora Nelson brought her complaint to Chuck, I think it's best if he explains the problem."

"Nora is one of our company nurses," Chuck began. "She has a fairly irregular schedule—she's available to work during different days and for different numbers of hours each week. So when Acme hired Nora two years ago, we worked out a per-hour rate. We pay her for the actual number of hours she works each week—most weeks about thirty-five hours, but a few weeks fifty or more hours.

"Nora came to see me the other day. She believes that she is entitled to overtime pay—time-and-a-half her usual rate—when she works more than eight hours during any day."

"This may be an unusual issue for us," Zachary said, "but it's fairly common at other companies. The federal Fair Labor Standards Act (FLSA) is the law that sets the federal minimum wage and also establishes the requirement that employers pay overtime to employees who work more than forty hours each week. The FLSA also requires that male and female employees receive similar pay for doing similar work, and includes *child labor* provisions that restrict the kind of work children can do, when they can work, and the minimum age for employees.

"Note that I said that *forty hours a week* is the threshold for overtime. This is the magic number—not eight hours per day. Working one, two, even three long days per week doesn't qualify an employee for overtime. The FLSA focuses on the hours each week that an employee works. Consequently, Nora *might be* eligible for overtime during every week she works more than forty hours.

"*Might be* raises many questions that are often hard to answer. This is because all employees are covered by the FLSA unless they are considered *exempt* because they fall into a specific exemption category. Many companies run into problems because they are *over-inclusive* when they categorize employees as exempt for wage and hour purposes.

"We've obviously categorized Nora Nelson as exempt—that's why she hasn't received any overtime pay. Our challenge this morning is to determine whether or not she really is an exempt employee."

"Whoa!" Annie said. "I'm the one who decided that Nora is exempt. I thought long and hard before I made my decision."

"Okay," Zachary said, with a grin, "tell us why Nora is exempt under the FLSA."

"Well . . . as I understand the law, employees who hold executive, administrative, and professional jobs, certain employees who work with computers, and outside sales employees are exempt. As a registered nurse, Nora qualifies as a professional. What's more, we pay her a lot of money each month."

"Your statement of the basic law is correct," Zachary said, "although applying it to a particular employee can be complex, because the law requires that an employee's job pass certain specific tests involving the nature of their job duties to be considered exempt. But I think you're right—I've no doubt that Nora will be considered a professional under FLSA."

"I knew it!"

"However," Zachary went on, "the FLSA *also* requires that an exempt professional employee be paid a salary that exceeds a minimum set by the FLSA. *Salary* is another tricky word. A salary is paid *free and clear*. This means

- → it's paid regularly (weekly or less frequently);
- → it won't be reduced because of variations in the quality or quantity of the work performed;
- → it's paid in full for *any week* in which the employee performs any work."

"Oh, oh . . . ," Annie frowned. "That's not the way we pay Nora. We consider her to be an hourly employee."

"In that case," Zachary said, "even though Nora is a professional who receives 'lots of money,' as you put it, she should receive overtime pay because she's paid on an hourly basis. Nora is right—she is entitled to back pay for any overtime hours she worked. Specifically, anytime she worked more than forty hours in a week, she began accruing overtime pay."

Ted Johnson's Religious Accommodations

"Our ombudsman has a second issue for us this morning," you said. "Ted Johnson, a member of the information technology staff, has requested that we accommodate his religious practices."

"For starters," Chuck began, "let me say that Ted has followed proper procedure in making his request. He carefully explained to his supervisor the nature of the conflict between his religious needs and the company's work rules. He also gave us enough information to understand the kind of accommodation he needs and why it's made necessary by a religious practice or belief."

"Okay!" Zachary said. "That puts the ball in our court. We all know that federal law prohibits employment discrimination on the basis of religion. A less well-known aspect of federal law requires an employer to *reasonably accommodate* an employee's sincerely affirmed religious practices. A religious accommodation is an adjustment to the employee's work environment that allows him to practice his religion. Most minor adjustments are considered to be reasonable accommodations unless they create undue hardship on our legitimate business interests. Some examples of undue hardship are accommodations that do the following:

- → Significantly increase our administrative costs
- → Diminish efficiency or productivity in other jobs
- → Infringe on other employees' job rights or benefits
- → Reduce workplace safety

→ Force other employees to do the accommodated employee's hazardous or burdensome work

→ Conflict with government laws or regulations

"To echo the U.S. Supreme Court, we don't have to conform our business practices to an employee's religious practices—but we do have to make accommodations that are reasonable. What does Ted Johnson have in mind?"

"He's asked for three accommodations," Chuck explained. "The first involves his faith's dietary requirements. There's a refrigerator in the employee lounge on his floor. Ted would like us to assign a shelf in the refrigerator to him, and to any other employees with the same beliefs.

"Second, Ted wants to shift his work schedule so that he begins an hour later every morning and ends an hour later every afternoon. This will allow him to attend a morning service before he comes to work.

"Finally, Ted wants to attend a week-long religious retreat every spring. And so, he's asked to schedule one week of his vacation far in advance."

"None of that sounds like an *undue hardship on business interests*," Annie said.

"I agree," Chuck said.

"And so do I," Zachary said. "Reasonable accommodation often includes flexible scheduling, job reassignments and transfers, modification of grooming and dress requirements, and other minor modifications of workplace policies and procedures."

Les Simpson's Disability

"Our next issue involves a request for a different kind of on-the-job accommodation," you told the group, "this one for an employee with a disability. Les Simpson has worked in the engineering department for more than fifteen years. Three months ago, a brain injury he suffered during a car accident left him *legally blind*. His corrected vision is less than 20/200. We've been discussing possible accommodations with Les for several weeks. In fact, we took the initiative."

"Good," Zachary said. "The Americans with Disabilities Act (ADA), the chief federal law that protects employees from discrimination based on disability, recognizes that a disabled employee can be a *qualified employee* if an employer makes reasonable accommodations. Broadly speaking we have the responsibility to engage in good-faith, interactive, give-and-take dialogue with a disabled employee when we consider what kind of accommodations might be reasonable under the circumstances. We have to begin the discussion process even if the employee doesn't request a specific accommodation. Moreover, we can't simply reach a one-sided conclusion that accommodating the employee will cause undue hardship to the company, or that a possible accommodation won't enable the employee to perform his or her job properly. Finally, the expense of making reasonable modification may *not* be passed on to the disabled person who requests the accommodation."

"Some companies use letters and e-mails to facilitate the interactive discussion," Chuck said, "but it's preferable to hold them face to face, so that the employee can contribute fully."

"Yep!" Annie said. "Les Simpson made some great suggestions about practical accommodations. Here's what accommodation plan includes:

- ➜ A modified meeting room in the engineering team's offices that makes the space more accessible and easier for Les to navigate

- ➜ An extra-large computer monitor for Les to use

- ➜ Accessible computer features—including screen magnifier software

- ➜ Text-to-voice software that will read e-mails and documents aloud

- ➜ Voice recognition software so he can do most of his work without using the keyboard

- ➜ Audio book versions of reading materials, whenever available

- ➜ Approval for Les to use a service dog if he decides to get one (to tie up loose ends, we specifically excluded service animals from our no-pets policy, even though a service animal isn't a pet)."

Monitoring Neal Mason's Computer

"A new employee wrote to me the other day," you said, "and asked Human Resources to clarify Acme's policy on electronic monitoring of employee computers and company-provided mobile phones. His name is Neal Mason; he works in corporate finance. He knows that we do some monitoring but isn't sure about the full extent."

"I'm sure you'll get lots more queries in the months ahead," Chuck said. "Employee monitoring has become a major privacy issue—many people inside and outside companies are concerned that companies may abuse their legal right to monitor their employees' workday use of e-mail services, Internet access, and certain aspects of telephone and mobile phone communications."

Zachary nodded. "Although federal and state laws are being challenged on many fronts, a company like Acme currently has the right to intercept and monitor most employee communications that were made with—and stored inside—the information systems that we own. That includes our land-line telephone system, our company voicemail system, our computer networks, and to some extent company-owned mobile phones.

"Our computer monitoring software—installed on the desktop and laptop computers we provide to our employees—can capture individual keystrokes, can let us see what is on the screen, and can give us access to files stored on hard disks. We can also keep track of idle time, when employees who should be using their computers aren't. And of course, we can monitor Internet usage such as web-surfing and the contents of e-mail messages that arrive in our network—even messages from private individuals outside the company that are sent to our employees.

"We can't monitor text messages sent to Acme-paid-for mobile phones, because they are stored outside the company, on equipment owned by the cell phone network. And, although we can't listen in on mobile phone discussions, we receive a list of all telephone numbers dialed on company-provided mobile phones."

"Those seem awfully broad and invasive capabilities," Chuck said. "Do we really need that much access to our employees' telephone and Internet communications?"

Zachary shrugged. "Well . . . like many other aspects of everyday law, we have to balance competing interests. On one hand, employees feel they have a right to privacy—and they certainly do, but to a much lesser extent than most people realize. On the other hand, courts give us the power to monitor our systems for these reasons:

- ✦ We own the equipment.
- ✦ Employees use our equipment in our place of business.
- ✦ We have a strong interest in overseeing employee activity to ensure their productivity and the quality of their work.
- ✦ We have the right to protect our significant information technology (IT) investments from theft, fraud, and misuse.
- ✦ We have a duty to protect other employees from abusive or harassing e-mails and telephone communications.
- ✦ We have a responsibility to safeguard confidential information provided by clients and customers."

"Is there a way for an employee to minimize monitoring," Chuck asked, "say by erasing e-mail messages and voicemails quickly, or by turning off 'cookies' in a web browser?"

"Not really," Zachary said. "E-mails, voicemails, and logs of website visits are stored in our systems even if deleted on the user's computer, telephone, and mobile phone."

"Moreover, it doesn't do any good to mark an e-mail as *private,* or to encrypt messages and documents with company provided encryption software. Our IT people have the means to access *protected* information."

"I understand the logic," Chuck said, "but it seems odd that I lose so much of my right to privacy when I arrive at my job."

"So far, courts have concluded that employees have a *limited* expectation of privacy when on the job," Zachary said. "After all, employers routinely ask *personal* questions on employment applications, do credit checks on applicants, and may also perform criminal background checks. An employer can search an employee's desk or locker and even frisk employees when necessary. So it hardly seems excessive that employers also have the right to monitor the company's information systems."

"However, employers' rights are not wholly unlimited:

→ A few state courts have held that companies can't listen to personal voicemail messages beyond the point necessary to determine that they are not business-related.

→ Different state laws provide narrow privacy rights for employees.

→ Certain union contracts limit an employer's right to monitor employees' electronic communications.

→ Companies are increasingly recognizing the need to notify employees that monitoring does take place."

"We introduced notification three years ago," Annie said. "Our employee handbook explains that we monitor communications—and an explicit warning about monitoring appears every time an employee logs onto our company network. We might want to expand our warning so that it covers the full extent of our monitoring capabilities."

"Warnings are always good," Zachary said. "But with or without warning, a wise employee will assume that everything he or she types on a company-owned computer will be monitored—and that every telephone call he or she makes on a company telephone or company-provided cell phone will be logged."

Tom Blanchard's On-the-Job Injury

"Everyone here knows Tom Blanchard," you said. "He operates the A/V equipment in our central auditorium. He fell the other day and broke his leg. He won't be able to work for about six months. He's getting ready to apply for workers' compensation, but he's concerned that he may not be covered, because the accident occurred outside our headquarters building—actually in an industrial park on the other side of town."

"The plot thickens," Zachary said. "Was Tom on a *detour and frolic* of his own?"

"On a detour and *what?*" Annie shouted.

"*Detour and frolic* is a charming legal term that we inherited from English common law. A *detour* means that Tom temporarily stepped away from his role as an Acme employee to perform a *frolic*—an act on his own, outside the supervision of Acme Corporation—perhaps a personal errand. In any case, a *frolicker* who has *detoured* is not considered an employee at work, because he or she is acting outside the scope of employment. Injuries sustained during a *detour and frolic* aren't covered by workers' compensation."

"Oh boy!" Chuck said. "Tom won't like that."

"Let's not jump to conclusions," Zachary said. "We need to look at all the facts of the situation—and at our state's scheme for workers' compensation."

"I sense another lecture coming on," Annie said.

"Only a short one, because *workers' comp* is a straightforward idea." Zachary took a deep breath. "Before states put workers' compensation systems in place, an injured employee was rarely compensated for his or her injuries. Although the employee could sue the employer in state court—typically alleging negligence [*see* Chapter 4] or some kind of intentional tort [*see* Chapter 3]—he or she had little chance of winning. Other employees were unlikely to testify to what happened; moreover, negligence defenses such as *assumption of risk* often gave employers the winning edge at trial.

"New York State was the first state to enact a workers' compensation law that established an administrative process to compensate employees for on-the-job injuries. In time, all of the other states enacted workers' compensation laws.

"Workers' comp provides payments to workers who are unable to work temporarily (have suffered temporary disabilities), pay for retraining for employees whose injuries make them physically unable to return to their prior jobs, and provide long-term payments for severely injured workers who can no longer do any job (have suffered total disabilities). Workers' comp also pays medical benefits for treatment of work-related injuries, and death benefits to the families of workers killed in job-related incidents.

WORKPLACE HEALTH AND SAFETY

There are many different federal and state laws in place to reduce on-the-job injury and disease. They impact all manner of workplace hazards—from computer mice (which can cause wrist injuries), to potentially dangerous machinery, to hazardous materials, to excessive noise. Most laws place the burden of creating a safe and healthy workplace on employers.

The most familiar federal law is the Occupational Safety and Health Act of 1970. The Act is administered by the Occupational Safety and Health Administration—OSHA to most people—part of the U.S. Department of Labor. OSHA issues occupational safety and health standards and performs inspections to ensure that standards are applied. Violators can face civil and even criminal penalties. OSHA claims that since the agency was created in 1971, occupational deaths have been cut by 62 percent, and injuries have declined by 42 percent.

"Employers fund the workers' comp system in some states by making mandatory contributions to pay the state-run workers' compensation insurance fund. In other states, businesses purchase workers' comp insurance from private insurance companies. In some states, companies are allowed to self-insure.

"The advantage of workers' comp to employees is that they will be compensated for accidental on-the-job injuries, regardless of who is at fault. The advantage to employers is that employees are typically barred from filing lawsuits against them. Injured workers are usually also prevented from suing the fellow employees who might have been legally responsible for causing the accident.

LAWSUITS AGAINST THIRD PARTIES

Although injured employees are typically barred from suing their employer and coworkers, they can file lawsuits against third parties who are legally responsible for their injuries. For example, a factory worker (we'll call him Fred) is hurt while operating a defective machine tool. Fred can collect workers' comp benefits, can't sue his employer or coworkers, but can sue the manufacturer of the machine tool seeking an award of damages under products liability (see Chapter 12).

"Economists point out that the cost of workers' comp insurance becomes one more cost of doing business—and so the cost of each product 'bears the blood of the workman' (the cost of worker injuries suffered to manufacture the product).

"It's a fairly basic principle of workers' comp that benefits are available only if an injury is work-related. As you'd expect, most work-related injuries are suffered at work—on an employer's premises, during working hours.

"Many years ago, courts worked out the *going-and-coming* rule. The idea is that most injuries suffered while coming and going to work—say, in a traffic accident while commuting—are not eligible for workers' compensation benefits. An important exception to this rule is that outside salespeople—injured traveling to and from meetings with customers—can collect workers' comp benefits. This is because traveling to customer locations is part of their everyday work.

"The notion of *detour and frolic* includes the same exception. If Tom Blanchard was doing company business when he traveled to the other side of town, he wasn't frolicking and he didn't detour."

Annie chimed in, "I know for a fact that Tom went to an A/V distributor to purchase a light bulb for one of our digital projectors."

"Doesn't sound like a frolic to me," Chuck said.

"Not at all," Zachary said. "He deserves to receive workers' comp benefits."

Roger Lapin Promised to Keep Our Secrets

"Roger Lapin joined Acme two years ago as an engineer in our technical development department," you explained, "a position that gave him access to much of our proprietary information. Simply put, he has learned many of our trade secrets. As a condition of employment two years back, we asked Roger to sign three agreements:

→ an agreement never to disclose any of the trade secrets he learned;

→ an agreement that any *intellectual property* he developed, including new inventions and copyrighted written materials belonged to Acme;

→ an agreement never to compete directly with Acme should he decide to leave the company.

"Well . . . I just learned that Roger has accepted a marketing position at Wiley Coyote Industries—a corporation that we believe is trying to develop a line of products similar to ours. Coyote will benefit greatly if Roger shares his knowledge with them. Consequently, I want to understand the validity of the agreements we have with Roger."

"Let me tackle the trade-secrets issue first," Zachary said. "Acme's technological trade secrets represent some of the most valuable assets that Acme owns. We made that fact clear to Roger Lapin when we hired him, and he affirmed his understanding when he signed his original agreement to protect our trade secrets. Should Roger disclose our trade secrets to Coyote, we can sue both Roger and Coyote to recover the profits earned by exploiting our confidential information. The same thing is true should Roger give Coyote our customer and client lists; these also represent valuable trade secrets.

"Now, it's important to note that Roger gained new knowledge and skills during his two years at Acme. None of these are considered to be 'our' trade secrets. We can't complain if Roger's enhanced capabilities as an engineer benefit Coyote.

"However, we probably should remind Roger at his exit interview that he committed to keep secret the know-how and techniques that give Acme its edge in the marketplace. A good way to do this, is to get a copy of the original trade-secret agreement and ask him to sign a simple document that indicates he is aware of his commitment to protect our trade secrets, and understands his obligations when he works for another company."

"But our secrets are in his head," Annie said. "How can he help but use them for Coyote's benefit?"

"That's an interesting point," Zachary said. "Our state is one of many that applies the *inevitable disclosure* doctrine, which presumes that an employee performing a similar job at a new company will inevitably make use of his old company's trade secrets. Consequently, a court will be willing to enjoin—prevent—the employee from doing a similar job at another employer for a reasonable period of time, so that the trade secrets in his mind will *age* and lose their value.

NEW COMMITMENTS MADE DURING AN EXIT INTERVIEW

Companies sometimes require an employee leaving a company to sign an exit agreement that involves new commitments— possibly a noncompete clause. These new clauses are often *not* enforceable because the departing employee has received no *consideration* (see Chapter 2) for the fresh commitment. Merely paying a laid-off employee a severance payment established by company policy or a retirement pension that he or she is entitled to doesn't represent additional consideration. However, if the departing employee receives an extra payment, a pension increase, or another bonus of some kind, a court will probably find sufficient consideration to enforce the new commitments.

"This isn't an issue with Roger Lapin, because he'll perform a different job at Coyote."

You speak up, "Roger also signed an agreement that says Acme owns all the intellectual property he developed."

"That was two years ago" Chuck laughed. "We now have new employees sign an intellectual property agreement that actually makes sense."

Zachary added, "The 'all' is much too broad. If Roger spent his evenings writing a romance novel, the copyright wouldn't belong to Acme. The general rule is that any intellectual property—inventions or copyrights—that Roger created as part of the scope of his employment belongs to Acme. That would include an invention for a new Acme product that grew out of a brainstorm Roger had while trout fishing in Montana or while taking his morning shower." Zachary paused. "Again, this is something to talk about at his exit interview. We want to be sure that he's properly documented anything he invented and that we have copies of any copyrighted materials he developed during his years at Acme."

"That brings us to the *noncompete agreement* that Roger signed," you said.

"More than one employee has told me that he or she really didn't want to make that kind of commitment," Chuck said. "I don't know how Roger feels about it."

"Agreements not to compete," Zachary said, "also called *covenants* not to compete, are commonly used when one company (I'll call it *Company A*) buys an existing business (*Company B*). Company A doesn't want the former owner of Company B to launch a new business—*Company C*—that competes with the one he just sold. And so, Company A may require an agreement not to compete as part of the sales transaction.

"Courts generally enforce reasonable agreements of this kind, but they become more reluctant when an employer seeks to prevent a valuable employee from working for a competitive company. After all, the restrictions in such an agreement interfere with the employee's right to make a living as he or she sees fit.

"However, courts will generally enforce a noncompete agreement if

→ the employer restricted the employee's rights in order to protect a legitimate business interest—such as safeguarding the company's confidential trade secrets, or to prevent a competitor from exploiting the company's *goodwill* among clients and customers;

→ the agreement is not overly restrictive—the limitations imposed on the employee are appropriate to protect the employer's business interests and are reasonable in terms of time, activity, and geographical area;

→ the noncompete agreement is supported by consideration.

"When an employee signs a noncompete agreement prior to beginning employment, his or her new job is sufficient consideration for a promise not to compete in the future. (However, noncompete agreements made during employment or during exit interviews need additional consideration.)

"If we decide to ask a judge to enforce Roger's noncompete agreement—which would prevent him from beginning his new job—the second issue (the reasonableness of the restrictions) will be the battleground in court. In this case, a court might well find that Roger's new marketing position at Coyote is sufficiently related to the kind of work he did at Acme that it represents a directly competitive activity. The judge might be willing to enjoin him from beginning the job for a reasonable period of time—perhaps six months to a year—but certainly not *forever.*

"The obvious question is: Should we enforce the agreement? That's a business decision more than a legal decision. If Acme management believes that Roger Lapin's presence at Wiley Coyote Industries will dull our competitive edge in the marketplace, we can probably keep Roger out of his new position for a reasonable period of time."

The Unfortunate Incident in the Data Center

"Our last question this morning is an especially unhappy one," you said. "Melissa Adams, one of our data analysts has charged Norm Frasier, her supervisor, with sexual harassment."

Once again, Zachary explained the law: "Many people think of sexual harassment as an intentional tort," Zachary said, "a legal wrong [*see* Chapter 3]. The truth is more complex. Although sexual harassers often commit the intentional tort of battery—an unwelcome touching—legally speaking, sexual harassment is a form of sex discrimination that violates a section of the federal Civil Rights Act of 1964. The EEOC investigates and responds to harassment claims.

"Sexual harassment occurs when conduct directed toward an individual explicitly or implicitly affects an individual's employment, unreasonably interferes with an individual's work performance, or creates an intimidating, hostile, or offensive work environment. The term *hostile environment* means just that. According to the EEOC, 'sexual flirtation or innuendo, even vulgar language that is trivial or merely annoying, would probably not establish a hostile environment.'

"But if *mildly* unwelcome conduct persists over a long period of time, it can become illegal harassment—particularly if the victim has announced that he or she finds it offensive, and/or has complained to an appropriate manager.

"The conduct can involve *unwelcome* sexual advances, *unwelcome* requests for sexual favors, and other *unwelcome* verbal or physical conduct of a sexual nature. I've repeated *unwelcome* because to be sexual harassment, the harasser's conduct must be unwelcome by the victim.

"Over the years, the EEOC has responded to different kinds of sexual harassment:

↪ There are male and female victims and male and female harassers (the victim and the harasser don't have to be of the opposite sex).

↪ Victims may be harassed by coworkers, by their direct supervisors, by supervisors in other areas of the company, and by nonemployees.

↪ The victim doesn't have to be the person who is actually targeted by the harasser—anyone affected by the offensive conduct is potentially a victim of sexual harassment.

"It's not unusual for a victim of sexual harassment to be fired before he or she can complain; however, unlawful sexual harassment can occur without the victim being discharged or suffering any other economic injury."

Chuck said, "Our corporate training program designed to prevent sexual harassment advises victims to tell the harasser that the conduct is unwelcome—and ask them to stop. If that doesn't work—if the harassment continues—the victim can use a variety of complaint mechanisms. In this case, Melissa came to me. I immediately notified Human Resources."

Annie shook her head. "Frankly, I was astonished when Chuck called, because we have such an extensive prevention program at Acme. Our online training makes it crystal clear to every employee, every year, that sexual harassment will not be tolerated. And we make the same point again and again in our employee handbook, and in the training that our supervisors receive."

"Sexual harassment cases can be difficult to investigate," Zachary said, "because they often involve shades of gray rather than unwelcome conduct that's black-and-white illegal. We often have to unravel 'he said, she said' claims. In the end, it often comes down to which party's story seems more credible."

RETALIATION IS UNLAWFUL

Federal law prohibits retaliating against an employee who complains about sexual harassment, who testifies about harassment, or who participates (in any way) in an investigation, company proceeding, or lawsuit. Retaliation exposes the company to a fresh lawsuit under EEOC regulations.

"I'm sorry to say," Annie said, "that in this case, I spoke to three other employees who corroborated Melissa's story. Two of them are in direct knowledge of the alleged harassment; a third said that Norm had also harassed her, but she'd never reported it to management."

"I don't think there's any doubt about what happens next," Chuck said.

"As I said, this is an unhappy question," you said. "It has an even unhappier answer. I'll begin to process Norm Frasier's termination from Acme."

CHAPTER 17

CRIMINAL LAW AND PROCEDURE

For most of us—happily—getting arrested for committing a serious crime is anything but an everyday occurrence. However, it's not unlikely that you and I will have to deal with these things:

→ Traffic stops and driving-related offenses

→ Policemen who want to search our cars (or even our persons)

→ Law enforcement personnel who ask us questions

→ The task of bailing out a friend or relative

These are a few of the everyday aspects of criminal law I'll explore in this chapter. It goes without saying (but I'll say it anyway) that you need the help of an experienced criminal attorney the moment you move beyond the simplest issues of criminal law. The reason is that even *minor* criminal charges can pit the person involved against the formidable resources of his or her state. The *People v. Whomever* is a one-sided battle; the defendant needs an advocate on his or her side who understands both criminal law and criminal procedure.

Few of us do this in advance, but it's a good idea to identify a good criminal attorney in your community whom you can call upon as "my lawyer" should you ever find yourself needing one—for yourself or for a relative. Keep his or her name and phone number in your mobile phone's address book. Some criminal lawyers produce business cards with polite but forceful statements on the back. They proclaim your right to an attorney (and other rights) should you be questioned or arrested by the police.

What most people refer to as *criminal law* actually consists of two closely related bodies of law:

1. *Substantive criminal law*—These are the government's penal code, statutes, common law, and regulations that define what conduct is considered illegal.

2. *Procedural criminal law*—These are the rules (sometimes codified in laws, sometimes created through judicial decisions) that determine how the substantive laws will be enforced.

For example, substantive criminal law declares that committing an armed robbery is a crime and defines the appropriate punishment (typically a long stay in prison). Procedural criminal law specifies how the police can interrogate a person suspected of committing an armed robbery, guarantees the suspect's right to an attorney, and defines how the person will be brought to trial.

Substantive criminal law changes relatively slowly as new conduct is made illegal (for example, identity theft) and some formerly prohibited behavior is decriminalized (for example, adultery). However the "biggies"—murder, manslaughter, larceny, burglary, and others—have remained essentially unchanged for hundreds of years.

By contrast, procedural criminal law raises many constitutional issues and continues to evolve and change as time passes. What's permissible today may be prohibited tomorrow. This is why criminal procedure can be more difficult to get a hold on than substantive criminal law. We'll look at crimes and criminal law first, then examine criminal procedure.

Crimes and Criminal Law

The Case of Sticky-Fingered Aunt Edna

Your whole family knew that Aunt Edna had "sticky fingers." Relatives often joked about her *cashless shopping expeditions* to the local mall, so it wasn't all that surprising when you got the call one evening that Edna—a resident of the nearby State of Denial—had been arrested for shoplifting at Sacks First Avenue in Denial City. She'd been arrested at the same store about three years ago, but Sacks had decided not to prosecute. This time, the store filed criminal charges against Edna.

What Is Crime?

A *crime* is the breach of a law enacted by government. Some crimes involve the *commission* of acts forbidden by law (theft by shoplifting, for example) while other involve the *omission* of duties required by law (failure to pay taxes, for example). The key point is that crime is defined by individual governments. Consequently, different countries around the world, different states in the United States, and different municipalities in those states often ban (or require) different behaviors.

Some kinds of acts are made criminal in virtually all societies because they are considered inherently evil, or because they involve *moral turpitude*. These are called *malum in se* acts—"evil in themselves." Murder, theft, rape are obvious examples.

Other acts and omissions are made criminal because government has decided—for many different reasons—that they interfere with the public good. These are called *malum prohibitum* crimes—"wrongs because society prohibits them." Driving more than sixty-five miles per hour on a specific section of Interstate 95 in Virginia is not inherently evil behavior, but it will be punished by fine (and possibly loss of driving privileges). Other examples are prohibitions against allowing dogs to run loose in a park, a ban against roadside littering, and the requirement for stores to collect sales taxes from customers.

Making the distinction between *malum in se* and *malum prohibitum* offenses can be tricky these days, because we've come to consider some crimes as more serious and others as less serious, regardless of the moral turpitude involved. Aunt Edna's offense illustrates the problem. Shoplifting (a form of theft) was traditionally included among *malum per se* crimes in most states, yet many people view it as a *less serious* crime because no one is physically threatened or injured by Aunt Edna's sticky-fingered behavior. Consequently, it's become less useful to rank crimes on the basis of their alleged *moral wrongness*.

The Seriousness of Crimes: Felonies and Misdemeanors

Crimes are commonly arranged according to their relative threat to society (as determined by Congress or by a state legislature) using three—or possibly four—categories:

1. *Felonies*—These are the most serious crimes that are punished by more than one year in prison (and even death in certain cases and some states). While the list of felonies varies from state to state, the following are felonies everywhere: murder, manslaughter, kidnapping, sexual assault, robbery, burglary, aggravated assault, and arson.

2. *Misdemeanors*—These are less serious crimes that are typically punished by less than one year in a jail. Shoplifting and simple battery are misdemeanors in many states.

3. *Petty offenses* (in federal criminal law and in some states)—This category consists of minor violations that can be punished by jail terms of six months or less (and sometimes only with fines). Some examples are disorderly conduct and minor disturbances in federal buildings.

4. *Infractions*—Violations of civil laws rather than criminal laws are infractions, which are punished by fines and administrative sanctions (for example, committing the traffic infraction of speeding may lead to the Department of Motor Vehicles suspending the person's driver's license). Being convicted of civil infraction doesn't create a criminal record, although states keep records of infractions for administrative purposes.

Most state criminal statutes (often known as *penal codes*) assign every crime to a specific *class* of felony, misdemeanor, or petty offense. In turn, each of these crime classes is defined in terms of the punishment a court can (or must) impose.

A *wobbler* is a crime that can be either a misdemeanor or felony, depending on the specific circumstances of the offense. For example, in some states stealing an inexpensive item is a misdemeanor, while stealing an expensive item (say, worth more than $1,000) is a felony. In other states, a first offense of some crimes (say, driving while intoxicated) will be prosecuted as a misdemeanor, while subsequent offenses may *wobble* into a felony.

PRISON VS. JAIL

Prisons are facilities designed for long-term incarceration and are typically operated by a state, while jails are facilities designed for short-term sentences and to hold arrested people until their trials are complete. Jails are often operated by county and municipal governments.

Infractions and Citations

Because even the most law abiding of citizens is likely to receive a citation or two during their lives for minor parking and traffic violations, it's worth pausing a moment to consider exactly what a *citation* is in everyday law. There are actually two ways to look at the piece of paper the state trooper or sheriff's deputy hands you:

1. A *summons* prepared and issued by a law enforcement officer that calls you into court—typically a short proceeding before a magistrate—to answer the allegation that you committed a civil infraction. If you so choose, you can acknowledge the violation by mail and pay a predefined fine in lieu of appearing at a hearing.

2. The actual penalty for committing the infraction—a preset fine that was imposed by the law enforcement officer who wrote the citation. You can pay the fine by mail or you can choose to request a hearing and challenge the officer's determination that you committed the infraction.

Different states view their citations differently, but either approach makes it possible for a law enforcement officer to send you on your way with a piece of paper to ponder, rather than arresting you on the spot for an alleged violation. Most states require the recipient to sign the citation. This isn't an admission of guilt, but either proof that he or she received the citation or, equivalently, a promise to appear at a hearing. Refusing to sign gives the officer a reason to arrest the recipient and have his or her car towed.

Here's an important point that most non-lawyers overlook: By definition, a *civil infraction* is not a crime. Consequently, the state doesn't have to prove the commission of an infraction *beyond a reasonable doubt.* Rather, the state has the much lighter civil burden of proof: a *preponderance of the evidence.* At most infraction hearings, the judge will ask him- or herself if it's more likely than not that the law enforcement officer's version of the story is correct. Most often, the judge's answer is "yes." This is why it can be difficult to beat a traffic ticket in court.

Another source of confusion is that some traffic tickets are summonses for alleged violations of misdemeanors, rather than infractions. These tend to be serious offenses in most states, such as driving while intoxicated, driving without insurance, or driving without a license. Although the tickets may look the same, a misdemeanor citation is a criminal complaint and typically requires the accused to appear in court. Be sure you understand any ticket you receive.

The Crime of Shoplifting

Back to Aunt Edna's sticky fingers. Every state's criminal statutes are available on the Internet (or at your county's law library). A bit of research leads you to the State of Denial's penal code statute for theft by shoplifting:

A person commits *theft by shoplifting* by knowingly taking merchandise from a retail establishment, in which merchandise is displayed for sale, through any of the following means:

→ Concealment

→ Altering or swapping price tags

→ Transferring from one container to another

Theft by shoplifting is a *Class 4 Misdemeanor* when the value of the merchandise is $800 or less. Theft by shoplifting is a *Class K Felony* when the following occurs:

→ The value of the merchandise exceeds $800.

→ The person takes property with a total value of $500 from three different stores in the same county within seven days.

→ The shoplifting offense is the person's fourth one, even if the value of the merchandise is $200 or less.

After a bit more research, you discover that the penalty for a Class 4 Misdemeanor is between one and six months in jail, whereas the penalty for Class K Felony is one to five years in prison. You also learn that trial judges have discretion to impose fines and probation instead of incarceration for these kinds of crimes.

You realize that Aunt Edna's eccentric behavior has finally caught up with her. She is in serious trouble.

The Elements of the Crime

For someone to be convicted of a crime—declared guilty of committing the crime in question—the government must prove the *elements of the crime*. There are two kinds:

1. *External elements of the crime*—the prohibited conduct. The legal Latin term for this is *actus reus* (which means the "guilty act"). Simply put, the government must present solid evidence that the crime actually occurred.

2. *Internal element of the crime*—the fault element. The legal Latin term for this is *mens rea* (which means "guilty mind"). This is the accused's intent to commit the prohibited conduct.

In the State of Denial, these are the external elements of theft by shoplifting:

→ The defendant takes possession of the property of another.

→ The property consists of merchandise on display in retail establishment.

→ The property has value more than $800 (if the defendant has been charged with felony shoplifting).

The internal element of theft by shoplifting is that the defendant intended to *convert* the property to his or her own use (*see* Chapter 3) without paying the purchase price.

The internal element—the defendant's intent to carry out the criminal act—is critical. Accidentally (or carelessly) concealing merchandise in a store is not shoplifting, although it will certainly get the attention of the store's security personnel.

An age-old principle of criminal law is that a prohibited act can't be a crime if done without a guilty mind. Like many legal principles, this one can be tricky to apply. Someone who starts a fire next to a house may not have had any intention of burning the house down, but intentionally starting the nearby fire is sufficient *guilty mind* to earn a conviction for arson.

In criminal law, most crimes require both an external element and internal element. This means that thinking about committing a crime is not a crime if no action is taken—no matter how guilty a mind the person has. You really can't go to jail for what you're thinking, if all you do is think.

Similarly, committing the external elements—the prohibited conduct—without the required fault element is also not a crime. For example, if someone accidentally started a fire by dropping a lit cigarette, he might be negligent—but not guilty of arson.

How does Aunt Edna fit into this definition of criminal wrongdoing? Well, she has a track record of intentionally converting merchandise on display for her own use by concealing it. Although evidence of prior criminal conduct generally can't be used in court to show that the defendant acted criminally in the present case, a savvy state's attorney probably won't have much trouble proving both elements of theft by shoplifting when he prosecutes Aunt Edna.

"Almost Crimes" That Receive Real Punishment

While you are researching shoplifting in the State of Denial, you run across a curious label: *inchoate crimes* (or preliminary crimes). These involve conduct that's considered criminal, even before actual harm is done.

An example is the crime of *conspiracy*—an agreement between two or more people to commit a crime in the near future. Like other crimes, conspiracy has its two elements—external and internal:

1. *External*—Two or more people agree to commit a crime *and* moves the agreement ahead by completing an *overt act*.
2. *Internal*—Each party intends to commit the underlying crime.

You immediately recall hearing about Aunt Edna's Wednesday Afternoon Canasta and Shoplifting Club, four close friends who supposedly compare notes about the best retail targets in their communities. Last Thanksgiving Day, cousin Erma, Edna's daughter, told you how the four coordinated their efforts so that they wouldn't "hit" the same stores on the same day during Christmas shopping season. Moreover, they modified four topcoats, adding especially deep inside pockets that were perfect for concealing merchandise.

You never thought of Edna as a *conspirator*, but the district attorney in Denial City almost certainly will consider her one of a group of four. Each of them intended to commit the crime of theft by shoplifting; they took a step toward that goal by completing the overt act of transforming their topcoats into shoplifting *tools*. At that point, their conspiracy was complete. There's no requirement that they actually steal anything.

And then you read the explanation of *solicitation*—another preliminary crime. These are its elements:

→ *External*—counseling, advising, urging, inciting, or persuading another person to commit a crime

→ *Internal*—the intention that the solicited person actually perform the prohibited act

You wince. A while back, Edna tried to talk you into "visiting" the Denial Mall with her, because the mall's security personnel had begun to recognize her. She offered to split everything she "acquired" with you.

You realize that Edna was guilty of solicitation, even though you refused to do anything wrong. In the words of an old legal maxim, the crime of solicitation is *over with the asking*. The solicitation *itself* is the offense, regardless of its eventual consequences.

AN ACCOMPLICE TO A CRIME

An *accomplice*—sometimes called an *aider* or an *abetter*—is a person who is complicit in the commission of crime. Most often, an accomplice actually helps to perform the illegal act in some way, from acting as a lookout, to acquiring the tools needed to commit burglary, to driving a getaway car, to luring the victim to the perpetrator. In some states, merely encouraging the commission of a crime is sufficient to be considered an accomplice. Conspirators (see above) become accomplices when a crime is actually committed. An accomplice is usually considered as guilty as the person who actually commits a crime—and is punished as severely.

The last of the "big three" preliminary crimes—typically the most common—is *attempt*. Because the external element can be confusing, it's best to reverse the order when explaining attempt.

> ✦ *Internal*—The person has the intent (the guilty mind) required to commit a particular crime.

> ✦ *External*—The person has not fully performed the guilty act that defines the particular crime, but has gone far enough to have crossed the line of *mere preparation*.

How far is *far enough* behavior? The answer is, "That depends." Whether or not an attempt has occurred can only be assessed by carefully considering the facts of the individual situation.

For example, a person shoots a pistol at another with the intention of killing him, but misses and strikes a nearby tree. That is attempted murder. But if the shooter had aimed at the tree and wounded the man by mistake, he could not have attempted murder, because the required fault element—a guilty mind—was absent when he aimed the pistol and pulled the trigger. In many states, the punishment for attempt is less severe than for the corresponding completed crime—which seems to reward the shooter for his bad aim or good luck, but chiefly acknowledges the less serious consequences of an unsuccessful attempt.

Let's use Aunt Edna as an example one last time. Imagine that she'd stashed a pricey chemise inside her special topcoat, then immediately had a change of heart that prompted her to return the garment to its proper shelf. Has she committed *attempted* theft by shoplifting?

Probably. Although her temporary *possession* of the chemise might not be sufficient to complete the actual crime of theft by shoplifting, her short-term concealment seems close enough to qualify as attempt.

Oh boy! It's a good thing, you decide, that the state's attorney doesn't know Aunt Edna as well as you do. With luck, he or she won't find out about the *many* inchoate crimes that Edna seems to have committed.

Keeping Pace with Criminals

There's a widespread notion that law is stodgy, that it remains the same for decades. In fact, everyday law must evolve to keep pace with the way that people live—and the challenges they face. Criminal law for example needs to change in step with the ingenuity of criminals. Not too many years ago, most people (including Aunt Edna) agreed with Iago—one of Shakespeare's nastiest villains—when he said (in the third act of *Othello*):

> Who steals my purse steals trash . . . but he that filches from me my
> good name robs me of that which not enriches him, and makes me
> poor indeed.

Alas, these days, filching a good name can be exceedingly enriching to the thief who does it. As a result, *identity theft* (also known as *identity fraud*) is estimated to touch upwards of ten million law-abiding Americans each year. The essential ingredient of identity theft is the wrongful obtaining and use of an individual's personal information in a way that enriches the thief. There are several common variations on the theme:

→ *Credit card fraud*—For example, a thief acquires your credit card number and uses it to make a purchase, or completes a pre-approved credit card application in your name, but has the card sent to a different location.

→ *Bank fraud*—For example, a thief uses fraudulent identity information to cash a check stolen from your mailbox or to access your bank account.

→ *Loan fraud*—For example, a thief uses stolen personal information to take out a loan in your name or purchase an expensive item on credit.

→ *Illegal use of a valid ID*—For example, a criminal uses your ID to purchase a firearm.

Identity theft grew along with the use of electronic systems to manage financial transactions, because a computer has only three ways to know who you are:

1. *What you know*—a password, a user name, driver's license number, your social security number, or some other identifying phrase or number

2. *What you have*—a paper check, driver's license, passport, a credit card equipped with a magnetic stripe or embedded chip, a phone located in your house (with a known telephone number), or some sort of security token

3. *What you are*—a thumb print, a *voice print*, a photograph, or another form of biometric identification

Because biometric identification is still relatively expensive—and difficult to implement across large populations of hundreds of millions of people—the items that are relatively easy to steal (facts you know and things you have) are the principal characteristics used by computers to authenticate you (determine that you are who you say you are).

And so, identity thieves cheerfully engage in these things:

→ "Shoulder surfing" to watch you enter PIN numbers in a cash machine

→ "Dumpster diving" to recover bank statements and other documents with personal information

→ Network "sniffing" to capture passwords you enter on financial websites (many travelers have regretted accessing their retirement accounts using laptop computers connected to nonsecure public networks—especially wireless networks)

→ "Phishing" with fraudulent websites that look like legitimate banking sites, but actually steal your personal information and authentication data

States have responded by making identity theft a heavy-duty crime. Here's the wording of a comprehensive statute (this one from Florida):

> Any person who willfully and without authorization fraudulently uses, or possesses with intent to fraudulently use, personal identification information concerning an individual without first obtaining that individual's consent, commits the offense of fraudulent use of personal identification information, which is a felony of the third degree.

The offense becomes a felony of the second degree (more serious) if the criminal perpetrates a fraud that exceeds $5,000, or has used personal identification information from ten or more people. Large-scale perpetrators commit first-degree felonies and face mandatory ten-year sentences.

The Florida identity theft statute includes other provisions that prohibit use of counterfeit IDs or the wrongful obtaining of personal information by people who misrepresent themselves as law enforcement personnel, bank employees, credit card company employees, and others. The law also allows the victim to recover his or her out-of-pocket costs and other expenses involved with restoring his or her credit history.

Criminal Procedure

You haven't heard from Aunt Edna yet, but you suspect that she'll call and ask for help the first chance she gets. You use this lull before the storm to get an overview of criminal procedure in the State of Denial. As you presume, Denial has typical processes in place for arresting and bringing to trial defendants suspected of committing serious crimes (such as felony theft by shoplifting).

Ouch! It's hard to think of rosy-cheeked, blue-eyed, silver haired Aunt Edna as a defendant, but that's what she is—or will soon be.

You also discover that Denial—like most states—has a simpler procedure for dealing with people accused of committing misdemeanors. This is because a defendant charged with a misdemeanor has fewer legal rights and safeguards than a defendant charged with a felony.

THE PROSECUTOR

Every state has legal professionals who prosecute the government's case against an individual suspected of breaking the law. They go by different titles in different states: County Attorney, Prosecuting Attorney, County Prosecutor, State Attorney, State Prosecutor, Commonwealth Attorney, and (most familiar of all to the watchers of legal shows on TV) District Attorney. The State of Denial calls its criminal prosecutors District Attorneys.

For example, a misdemeanor defendant who will not be sent to jail if convicted has no right to an attorney during the trial. Nor is there a requirement to establish *probable cause* that a misdemeanor trial is warranted by holding a preliminary hearing or through an indictment by a grand jury (*see* below).

Step 1: Aunt Edna Is Arrested

The first major milestone in Denial's criminal justice process is the arrest of the criminal suspect so that he or she can be formally charged with a criminal offense. In many criminal cases, important things happen before a person suspected of committing a crime is formally arrested. The police may ask the suspect questions, possibly the police will search his or her house or car, maybe the suspect will be asked to participate in a lineup (all of these possibilities will be discussed, below). However, being arrested is a truly major milestone because, although the person is not yet a criminal defendant (that happens when a suspect is formally charged with committing a crime), he or she experiences a major reduction of his or her freedom, at least for a while.

Aunt Edna was first detained by Sacks First Avenue's manager, who immediately notified the police. When a police officer arrived, the manager indicated that Edna had concealed a chemise worth more than $900. This gave the officer *probable cause* to believe that Edna had committed a felony—specifically, theft by shoplifting involving more than $800 worth of merchandise. And so, the police officer notified Edna that she was under arrest. He probably also *read her her rights*, by giving her the well-known Miranda warning:

> You have the right to remain silent. If you give up the right to remain silent, anything you say can and will be used against you in a court of law. You have the right to an attorney present during questioning. If you cannot afford an attorney, one will be appointed for you before police questioning. Do you understand these rights?

THE MIRANDA RULE

The Miranda rule, put in place by the U.S. Supreme Court, ensures that a suspect can take advantage of his or her Fifth Amendment right against self-incrimination. Many people are intimidated when police ask questions. The Miranda warning reminds people in custody that they don't have to answer questions and that they have the right to be advised by an attorney. If police fail to give the warning—or keep asking questions after a suspect has expressed the desire to consult an attorney—the statements made by the suspect are usually not admissible, although *suppressing* them after the fact is rarely easy to do.

Had the evidence indicated that Edna committed the lesser offense of misdemeanor shoplifting, the officer would have issued a citation to Edna, requiring her to appear in court at a later date.

Probable Cause for Arrest

In the State of Denial, and most other states, there are three circumstances when a police officer can arrest someone:

1. The officer witnesses the person commit a misdemeanor or a felony.
2. The officer has *probable cause* to believe that the person has committed a felony.
3. An *arrest warrant* (*see* below) has been issued for the person.

These three *arrest triggers* reflect the U.S. Constitution's prohibitions against arbitrary, baseless arrests. An arrest is justified if a law enforcement officer sees someone commit a crime (circumstance 1) or else has *probable cause*—the reasonable belief supported by facts or evidence that would lead a reasonable person to believe that a serious crime has been committed and that the person arrested is responsible (circumstance 2).

The officer can also make an arrest if he or she is executing a valid arrest warrant (circumstance 3). An arrest warrant is a legal document issued by a magistrate or other judicial officer who has concluded there is probable cause that the suspect has committed a crime. The warrant empowers law enforcement officials to arrest the named person so that he or she can be formally charged with a criminal offense.

The magistrate typically evaluates probable cause to arrest by considering a *complaint* filed by the victim of a crime or the police officer who investigated the crime. The complaint details the substance of the accusation against the suspect and often contains allegations of fact to establish probable cause that a crime was committed. To move ahead and issue the arrest warrant, the magistrate must find that the totality of the circumstances would lead a reasonable person of ordinary care and prudence to entertain an honest suspicion that the person to be arrested is guilty of a crime. This rule, which appears in countless court decisions (often with minor variations), was first defined in 1983 by the U.S. Supreme Court in the case of *Illinois v. Gates*. *Probable cause* is an easy standard of proof—much less rigorous than *proof beyond a reasonable doubt* or even *preponderance of the evidence* (the standard used in civil trials).

The prosecuting official—the District Attorney in Denial—usually reviews and approves a complaint before it is presented to a magistrate. In Denial, as in most other states, District Attorneys have considerable discretion to choose whether or not to bring criminal charges—and arrest suspects.

WHAT HAPPENED TO THE
PRESUMPTION OF INNOCENCE?

The concept of *probable cause* seems to fight the often-heard statement that every defendant is presumed innocent until proven guilty. In fact, *presumption of innocence* is another way of saying that the prosecution has the burden of producing evidence that convinces the *fact-finder* (typically a jury at a criminal trial) that the defendant is guilty of a specific crime beyond a reasonable doubt. This requires that the government compellingly prove the elements of the crime—that the defendant performed the required *guilty act* and possessed the required *guilty mind*. However, this procedural *presumption of innocence* doesn't reflect what people think about the defendant. The police who arrested the defendant clearly believe that he or she is guilty; so does the District Attorney who prosecutes the case.

Book Her, Danno!

Legally speaking, a person is in police custody in any situation where a reasonable person would not feel free to leave. There's no requirement that a police officer say, "You're under arrest." However, an arrest that begins the process of prosecuting a criminal suspect typically involves several formalities.

These days, the police usually handcuff a suspect in custody and search for weapons—even if he or she has not been accused of a violent crime—then bring the person to a police station for *booking* or *processing*. Several things happen when a suspect is booked. Police will do the following:

→ Fingerprint Aunt Edna and, if considered necessary, collect samples of her hair, voice, handwriting, and even DNA

→ Photograph Aunt Edna

It's common knowledge that the police will fingerprint an arrested suspect, but many people are surprised to learn that the police can also require suspects to provide *exemplars* of their handwriting and voice, along with samples of blood, hair, and even DNA. Making these things available to police is not considered *self-incrimination* under the Fifth Amendment, any more than the common practice of providing fingerprints. The U.S. Supreme Court has held that individuals do not have an *expectation of privacy* that prevents police from determining their personal characteristics.

CHEMICAL TESTS FOR DRIVING WHILE INTOXICATED

A person taken into custody for driving while intoxicated can initially refuse to provide a breath, blood, or urine sample for chemically testing his or her blood alcohol level. However, in most states, any person who operates a motor vehicle is presumed to have given *implied consent* to a chemical test if arrested for driving while intoxicated. Consequently, a driver who refuses to take a chemical test of the officer's choice usually faces loss of license and other mandatory penalties. At this point, an officer can usually obtain a search warrant quickly and compel a driver to provide samples for chemical testing.

Here's what the police will also do:

→ Catalog (and temporarily confiscate for safekeeping) the personal property found on her person

→ Prepare an arrest report, explaining why the officer went to Sacks First Avenue and why the officer arrested Aunt Edna

→ Describe the alleged offense and evidence in a probable cause affidavit

→ List the items of evidence recovered from the crime scene— possibly the shoplifted items that Edna is accused of concealing

→ Retrieve her prior criminal record, if any

→ Place Edna in a holding cell at the police station or in a nearby jail

Step 2: Bailing Out Aunt Edna

The call from Aunt Edna arrives! She giggles a bit, explains that she's in a bit of a bother, and asks you to get her released on bail.

The first request that most incarcerated suspects make is, "Get me out of here!" Unless a suspect has been charged with an extraordinarily serious crime, is perceived to be a significant danger to the community, or represents a substantial *flight risk*—he or she can usually

→ gain release by paying money *bail*;

→ be released on his or her "own recognizance."

Release from custody is typically conditional. The first and foremost condition is the promise to appear in court for all future proceedings, including (to list a few) the *bail hearing, preliminary hearing, arraignment,* and *trial.* We'll look at all of these, below. Other release conditions may include not leaving the county or state, depositing the suspect's passport with the court, and wearing some sort of electronic tracking device. Violating any condition of bail or personal recognizance will result in the suspect being taken back into custody.

Money Bail

Money bail is a guarantee—a kind of "insurance"—that a suspect will keep his or her promise to return for future proceedings. Some states have predefined bail schedules that specify the amount of bail for many common offenses. A suspect can *post bail* for some offenses with a jailer, sheriff's deputy, or other law enforcement official authorized to *set bail* for incarcerated suspects. These offenses typically include misdemeanors and *bailable felonies* (less serious felonies). In other states, bail must be set by a magistrate or other judicial officer.

State of Denial criminal procedure requires that a magistrate determine bail for suspects in custody alleged to have committed any felony, and that such suspects shall be taken before a magistrate without undue delay for a release decision. And so, a magistrate is on duty most days at the Denial City lockup to hold a quick *bail hearing.* The magistrate may also advise Edna of her Fifth-Amendment right to counsel, by re-reading the Miranda warning and making certain that she understands it.

Also on duty—directly across the street from the lockup—are several bail bondsmen. Because few suspects can afford to post bail themselves, a bail bondsman provides a service that many suspects need. The suspect—more likely the suspect's friends and family—pays 10 percent of the bail amount to the bondsman as a nonrefundable fee; the bondsman then posts the total bail amount to the court. When the case is over and the suspect is either free, in jail, or on probation, the bondsman gets 100 percent of his money back. If the suspect fails to appear, the bondsman will lose his money and try to recover it by suing the suspect—although, the bondsman will probably hire a bounty hunter to track down the missing suspect before the bail is forfeited. Consequently, bail bondsmen pay close attention to a bailed-out suspect's whereabouts.

Aunt Edna Gets Out of Jail

You know that posting a cash bond—using your savings—will be the easiest, most economical way to bail Aunt Edna out of jail, so you are delighted that Edna's criminal attorney will be at the lockup to argue for a low bail amount, or for a release on personal recognizance. After all, Aunt Edna has lived in Denial City for most of her sixty years, owns her own home, has numerous family ties, and is not the sort of person who would jump bail and flee the state. But just because you believe in completely eliminating the risk of failure when you deal with new situations, you get a list of bail bondsmen from the Internet and from your telephone directory.

In many states it's possible to use real estate and other noncash assets as *surety* for bail. Doing so can be a complicated process that invariably lengthens the time a suspect remains in custody. The bail system *runs* on cash bonds. It's not unusual for suspects in big cities to be released within an hour or two of being booked.

In recent years, several states have eliminated the traditional bail bondsman system by allowing suspects to post a 10 percent cash bail themselves—10 percent of the amount set by a magistrate. At the end of proceedings, suspects receive a full 10 percent back, except for a small administrative fee. States that have made the switch in belief that the promise of a nearly full refund acts as further encouragement for suspects to show up for later court appearances.

Good news! The magistrate released Aunt Edna on her own recognizance. The District Attorney didn't argue for money bail, but he requested the court impose the additional requirement that Edna stay away from Sacks First Avenue during the criminal proceedings.

Step 3: Aunt Edna's Preliminary Hearing

Being a criminal suspect is not a fun experience. Even though Edna was released on her own recognizance, she suffered the embarrassment of arrest and booking, and she faces a trial, the possibility of prison, and the likelihood of significant lawyer's fees. Are the authorities confident that it's fair to put Edna through Denial's criminal justice process?

This is the key question that will be answered at Aunt Edna's *preliminary hearing*. The judge (or more likely a magistrate) will confirm that sufficient evidence exists to justify

- ✦ Edna's arrest without a warrant;
- ✦ trying Edna for the crime of felony theft by shoplifting.

The District Attorney doesn't need to present extensive evidence at her preliminary hearing, and Edna's lawyer won't present any. The magistrate will be satisfied with a showing of *probable cause* to believe that a crime has been committed and that Edna committed it. *Probable cause*, as I said earlier, is an easy standard to meet. Nonetheless, if the magistrate doesn't see sufficient evidence to support a criminal charge—an unlikely happenstance—Edna will be released. The judicial officer can also adjust bail if necessary.

The preliminary hearing would happen in a few days at most if Edna were still in jail. But because she's been released, State of Denial law allows the hearing to be scheduled as many as thirty days after her arrest.

An Important "Unless"

Most felony suspects in the State of Denial get a preliminary hearing because, in each case, a judicial officer must determine that there is probable cause to move ahead with a full-blown trial. The exceptions are prosecutions that are initiated by a *grand jury*. This is a panel of citizens—as many as twenty-three in some states— who listen to a presentation of evidence by the District Attorney and determine (often by a simple majority vote) whether there's sufficient probable cause to warrant filing formal charges against a suspect. If so, the grand jury returns an *indictment* against the suspect (the full, if antique, legal term is *true bill of indictment*)—a formal written accusation that the suspect committed a criminal offense. If not, the grand jury returns a *no bill*—a refusal to indict the suspect.

The U.S. Constitution requires that grand juries return indictments in serious federal criminal cases. States can choose if and when to use grand juries. The State of Denial (and many other states) reserve grand juries for complicated, high-profile cases that involve lots of investigation.

The alternative to a grand jury indictment that is used in the lion's share of state felony prosecutions is a two-step mini-process:

1. A preliminary hearing where a judicial officer verifies probable cause and clears the way for filing formal charges against the suspect.
2. An *information* prepared by the District Attorney—a written accusation that details the formal charges. The defendant typically receives the information at his or her *arraignment* (*see* Step 4, below).

Step 4: Aunt Edna Is Arraigned

The next event is Aunt Edna' *arraignment*—a public hearing before a Denial Superior Court judge (Superior Court is Denial's trial court of general jurisdiction; *see* Chapter 1). This is when Edna stops being a *suspect* and becomes an official *defendant* in the State of Denial's legal system.

You're not surprised when the judge begins by reading aloud the District Attorney's *information* (*see* Step 3, above). This is in keeping with the requirement in the Sixth Amendment of the U.S. Constitution that defendants shall "be informed of the nature and cause of the accusation against them." The judge gives Edna a copy of the information and then asks her to enter a plea.

She can plead guilty, not guilty, or *no contest* (*nolo contendre* in Latin) if the court allows this alternative plea. In effect, the defendant doesn't contest— deny—the state's allegations. No contest (or *nolo*) is equivalent to a guilty plea, with one significant legal difference: The defendant doesn't actually admit his or her illegal conduct. This can be important if the defendant expects to be sued for damages in a civil-court tort lawsuit. A guilty plea can be offered at a civil trial by the plaintiff as an admission that the defendant committed a legal wrong. By contrast, a no contest plea forces the civil plaintiff to prove the defendant's tortious behavior during the civil trial.

You expected Edna to plead not guilty—and she does.

The judge accepts her plea, sets a date for her trial, and also explains her Sixth Amendment right to be represented by counsel during the trial—a right which didn't become significant until this point in her journey through criminal procedure. (Only now is it certain that Edna will be tried and that she has been charged with committing a felony.) This right to counsel at trial is different than her Fifth Amendment right to have an attorney present during police interrogation, which provides protection against self-incrimination. Counsel during a trial ensures that Edna will be able to "do battle" with the District Attorney and mount an effective defense.

Step 5: Aunt Edna's Pretrial Activities

The four-month interlude between Edna's arraignment and her trial turned out to be a surprisingly busy time for Susan, Edna's criminal defense lawyer, and the District Attorney.

Discovery

Discovery is the exchange of information between the prosecutor and the defendant before a criminal trial begins. The goal is to eliminate surprises that puts a defendant at a serious disadvantage during the trial. Keep in mind that the state has enormous investigatory resources. Investigators can find and interview witnesses and crime scene technicians can gather forensic evidence from the crime scene. And, the police who arrested the defendant can be powerful witnesses at trial, so it's essential for a defense attorney to know what they learned about the defendant during arrest and possible interrogation.

Every state (and the federal government) has rules for criminal discovery. One of the most basic rules—established by a U.S. Supreme Court decision—is that the prosecutor must provide the defense with any *exculpatory information* that it has acquired. This is information that will help the defendant's case by raising reasonable doubt about the defendant's guilt. Common examples are statements from people the police interviewed that contradict witnesses that support the state's case, and forensic evidence (say, unexplainable fingerprints from a third party) that suggest an unknown person rather than the defendant committed the crime.

Here's what most states also require a prosecutor to disclose:

→ The names and addresses of prosecution witnesses who will testify at the trial

→ Any *real evidence* (as opposed to witness statements) the police gathered during their investigation—such as the pricey chemise that Aunt Edna was alleged to have shoplifted (Susan has a right to inspect the chemise.)

+ Photographs taken by the police

+ Results of any scientific tests

+ Written or recorded statements prepared by the police that contain relevant information, including statements made by the defendant, the victim, witnesses who will testify at trial, and other people who provided information to the police

Turnabout is fair play. The District Attorney can discover the details of a defendant's *alibi defense*, including the names and addresses of alibi witnesses. The defendant is also required to list other witnesses and provide any statements they have made.

Neither side can request *attorney work product*—a lawyer's private notes that captures his or her impressions, conclusions, strategies, opinions, or ideas.

What happens if one of the other side drags its discovery feet? The attorney who wants the information can *file a motion for discovery* with the court and ask the judge to compel disclosure.

All of this applies to Aunt Edna because the police seized an important piece of real evidence: the chemise that Edna was alleged to have shoplifted. Its value is at issue, because the State of Denial must prove that Edna shoplifted items worth more than $800 for the jury to find her guilty of a felony.

When Susan examined the chemise—and read a discovered statement the store's manager had given the police—she spotted a crucial inconsistency and pressed the District Attorney. He acknowledged that although the chemise's price tag read $949, the sweater was on sale that day, and that purchasing it at the cash register would have cost only $699.

The District Attorney insists that in Denial, the number on the price tag is the price of the stolen item—but Susan believes that the price that counts is the stolen merchandise's retail value at the time of the shoplifting. Consequently, evidence of the sale price may be crucial at Edna's trial.

Pretrial Motions

The defense attorney and the prosecutor are likely to disagree on several matters related to the upcoming trial. They can file *pretrial motions* that ask the court to resolve the issues before the trial begins. One of the most common disputes involves challenges to the *admissibility* of statements made by the defendant before the police explained his or her Miranda rights. In this event, the defense attorney would file a pretrial motion asking for the state to be suppressed (excluded from the trial). Many pretrial motions claim that evidence against the defendant was collected through unconstitutional methods such as *search and seizure* (*see* "Other Things Worth Knowing about Criminal Law" below).

Aunt Edna's defense attorney, Susan, seeks to suppress a statement that Edna made a few seconds after the police arrived at Sacks First Avenue. A police officer smiled at Edna and asked, "What are you wearing under your topcoat?" Edna replied, "Oops. That's not my chemise." The District Attorney sees this as an admission that Edna *converted* the sweater to her own use.

THE EXCLUSIONARY RULE

We've all read and seen reports of an accused criminal being set free because of a so-called legal technicality. Chances are, this happened when a judge applied the *exclusionary rule,* which allows the *suppression* of incriminating evidence collected by unconstitutional methods. This means that the prosecution can't present the evidence during a criminal trial—which may make it impossible to prove the defendant's guilt beyond a reasonable doubt. Faced with this likelihood, the district attorney may simply drop the charges. The purpose of the exclusionary rule is to discourage police misconduct and encourage investigators to follow all the rules pertaining to search warrants, warrantless searches, arrest, and interrogations (*see* "Other Things Worth Knowing about Criminal Law" below).

Susan doesn't dispute that Aunt Edna made the statement; rather, she argues that the police officer should have "Mirandized" Edna before interrogating her.

In return, the District Attorney insists that Edna was not yet in custody when the police officer asked the question—consequently Edna didn't have *Miranda rights* at the time she made the statement.

You're not surprised that the judge agrees with Susan rather than the District Attorney. The judge rules that Edna had been detained in the manager's office, was not free to leave, and reasonably felt she was in custody when the police arrived. As the judge explains, *Cops + Custody + Questioning = Miranda rights.*

Bottom line: The prosecutor won't be able to present the supposed confession at Edna's trial.

Aunt Edna's Upcoming Trial

A trial is the central event that comes to mind when we hear the term *criminal justice.* It is an iconic clash of adversaries, the people versus the defendant, in a carefully orchestrated battle to determine the truth of the allegations against the defendant.

As contemporary legal words go, *trial* is not especially old. The use of the word to mean examining and deciding a case in a law court goes back to the late sixteenth century, although long before that people suspected of crimes *proved* their innocence in trials by fire or trials by water.

Criminal trials in most states follow a pattern well known to moviegoers and TV watchers:

1. The prosecution makes an opening statement.
2. The defense counters, with its opening statement (the defense can postpone the statement until after the prosecution *rests*).
3. The prosecution makes its case by presenting witnesses and evidence—and then *rests.*
4. The defense presents its witnesses and evidence.
5. The defense presents a closing argument that summarizes why the prosecution has failed to meet its burden of proof that the defendant committed the crime beyond a reasonable doubt.
6. The prosecution offers the final closing argument, summarizing the proof against the defendant.
7. The trier of fact deliberates and returns a verdict.

Evidence at Trial

Evidence used at a trial is categorized in variety of different ways:

→ *Direct evidence* seeks to prove truth or falsity of a fact in issue without the need for making an inference—for example, a witness testifies that he saw Edna slip into the chemise then don her topcoat.

→ *Circumstantial evidence* invites the trier of fact (the jury at a criminal trial) to infer the truth or falsity of a fact in issue by considering a collection of pieces of direct evidence—for example, one witness testifies that Edna's fingerprints were found on the hanger that used to hold the missing chemise and also on the security device that used to be attached to the chemise; another testifies that a bit of fiber clinging to the lining of Edna's topcoat came from the missing chemise.

→ *Physical evidence* is evidence in the form of a physical object—for example, the sweater that Edna was alleged to have shoplifted, her fingerprints found on the hanger, and the bits of fiber found on her topcoat lining.

→ *Testimonial evidence* is oral testimony (spoken statements) made at the trial by a witness—for example, the testimony of the person who saw Edna put on the chemise.

→ *Opinion evidence* is testimony as to what a witness thinks, believes, or infers about facts in dispute. Because forming opinions and reaching conclusions is the job of the trier of fact (the jury), most witnesses are not allowed to give opinion evidence; their testimony must reflect their personal knowledge.

→ *Expert evidence* is testimony provided by an expert witness, someone whose training, experience, and/or education gives him or her greater knowledge in a specific area. Courts allow expert witnesses to provide opinion evidence if their opinions will help resolve facts in issue. For example, an expert in clothing fibers might testify that in his opinion, the only way that fibers could have become attached to the lining of Edna's topcoat was to wear the coat over the chemise.

→ *Hearsay evidence* is testimony about a statement made by a person not in the courtroom. For example, the store's security guard testifies that an unidentified man leaving the store told him that Edna had shoplifted the chemise. The judge won't allow this testimony to be used as proof of Edna's guilt, because the "man" (whoever he is and whatever he saw) is not available for cross-examination by Edna's lawyer. But not all statements made by *third persons* are considered hearsay. If the security guard was asked, "Why did you aim the security camera at Edna?" an allowable answer would be, "A man leaving the store told me that a tall lady was behaving suspiciously in the Senior Boutique department." This statement merely explains the guard's decision to fire up the security camera.

Jury or No Jury?

Although felony defendants have the right to a jury trial in most states and in federal courts, a defendant can opt for a *bench trial*, where the judge decides the facts (including the guilt or innocence of the defendant) as well as determining matters of law and procedure. The prosecutor has to agree to a bench trial, though most are happy to accommodate the defendant's wishes, because bench trials are often quicker and simpler.

Should Edna Testify?

The Fifth Amendment right against self-incrimination means that there's no requirement that a criminal defendant testify at his or her trial. The judge usually instructs the jury to ignore the defendant's decision not to testify and especially not to treat it as evidence of guilt.

Many defendants want to testify to show the jury they have *nothing to hide.* However, defense attorneys often recommend that the defendant *remain silent,* because jurors may interpret minor slips in a defendant's demeanor or responsiveness as evidence of lying. Furthermore, when a defendant testifies, he or she opens the door to a tough cross-examination by the prosecutor.

After the Verdict

If the jury (or judge in a bench trial) *acquits* the defendant (finds him or her not guilty), the case is over, because a prosecutor can't appeal the acquittal.

However, if the trier of fact convicts the defendant (finds him or her guilty) the defendant can ask the judge for a new trial (a rarely granted request) or can appeal the conviction in appellate court.

In most states, a person convicted in a criminal trial has the absolute right to appeal the conviction once. Defendants are sometimes granted new trials because the judge made a significant error during the trial (such as giving the jury incorrect instructions about the elements of the crime), or because the judge failed to exclude evidence collected by unconstitutional means, or because the prosecutor withheld exculpatory evidence. However, if a defendant pleads guilty, about the only justification for an appeal is that punishing him or her would represent manifest injustice.

Win or lose, the protections against double jeopardy guaranteed in the Fifth Amendment ensure that *most* defendants can't be prosecuted for the same offense again. I highlighted "most" because the Fifth Amendment doesn't prevent two different governments from prosecuting one defendant. Consequently, it's possible for the state government and the federal government both to bring criminal charges against a person for the same criminal conduct, if the conduct is prohibited by both state and federal laws.

Aunt Edna's Plea Bargain

But there *won't* be a trial for Aunt Edna.

A week after the flurry of pretrial motions, Susan and the district attorney work out a *plea bargain* that settles the case. Both sides agree that Aunt Edna will plead guilty to the reduced charge of misdemeanor shoplifting and that the district attorney will recommend a punishment consisting of a fine of $500, a six-month term of probation, and eighty hours of public service.

At first, you aren't sure what to think. On the one hand, you've never liked the idea of a criminal being able to cop a plea. On the other hand, you're delighted that Aunt Edna won't face a prison sentence and won't have a felony criminal record.

Susan explains to you that plea bargaining has become an essential tool in the criminal justice system. Without it, the trial courts of virtually every state would be overwhelmed by guilty defendants pleading not guilty. There simply aren't enough prosecutors, judges, court rooms, and juries to deal with the full total of criminal prosecutions. Plea bargaining—reducing the severity of the charge in exchange for a guilty plea—gives many defendants an incentive to admit their guilt.

"That's why," Susan explains, "close to 90 percent of the criminal prosecutions in the State of Denial are resolved with plea bargains. The chief exceptions are violent crimes. Our criminal rules of procedure prevent plea bargaining for the most serious felonies."

Despite these practical benefits, many critics of plea bargaining feel that it's unfair to allow criminals to get off easy. Advocates counter that argument by pointing out that bringing an accused person to trial doesn't guarantee a conviction. Neither the district attorney nor defense counsel can ever be certain what a particular jury will do during a trial. To an extent, both sides roll the dice by trying the case. Consequently, plea bargains bring a measure of certainty to an *iffy* process.

"The term *plea bargain* is actually misleading," Susan continues. "Although the district attorney and the defendant (through his or her lawyer) reach a bargain, the judge is under no obligation to impose the agreed-upon fine or prison sentence. The judge can choose to give the defendant the maximum punishment allowed by state sentencing guidelines. However, unless the defendant has a lengthy criminal record—or the crime is especially serious—the judge will probably honor the terms of the agreement."

That's what happened in Aunt Edna's case.

Other Things Worth Knowing about Criminal Law

Criminal Statutes of Limitation

The traditional argument behind establishing a *criminal statute of limitations* (*see* "Statute of Limitations" in Chapter 4, which explains the statute of limitations for civil actions) is that it's unjust to bring charges against someone many years after he or she committed the alleged wrongdoing. Thus, in some states, lesser felonies can't be prosecuted if more than a specific number of years have passed.

Advocates for statutes of limitations insist that it's unreasonably hard to defend against a charge from the past because the memory of witnesses may have faded and essential evidence may have been lost. Opponents, though, ask why a criminal should escape punishment merely because an arbitrary period of time has passed? They point out that the prosecution—who carries the burden of proving guilt beyond a reasonable doubt—is harmed more than the defense by aging witnesses and evidence.

The give and take has produced a patchwork quilt of statutes of limitations that apply to state and federal crimes—a collection of laws literally too complex to outline in this book. Some states have criminal statutes of limitations that vary for different crimes—one or two years for misdemeanors; five, six, or seven years for felonies. Other states have virtually eliminated all statutes of limitations. In states that still have them, however, major crimes—murder, for example—don't have statutes of limitation, and new exceptions are created every year.

The bottom line: The protection once provided criminals through the passage of time has become much less certain.

The Tale of Aunt Edna's Interrogation

When you drive Aunt Edna home after her release on personal recognizance, she tells you about her arrest and subsequent interrogation at the police station.

"When I think about it, I really feel foolish but I made that silly comment to the nice police officer who arrested me. My only excuse is that I was flustered at the time.

"It all began when the manager of Sacks First Avenue escorted me into her office. I was bold enough to ask her why she thought the store had the right to detain me. She smiled and said that their security camera had captured several minutes of video that showed me slipping into the most expensive chemise in the Senior Boutique department, putting my coat on, then doing up the buttons.

"She asked me to take my coat off. I reminded her that she had no right to search me. She shrugged and invited me to sit down and wait for the police. I shrugged back, because I doubted that the store would go to all the trouble of having me arrested.

"I was wrong.

"The police officer arrived a few minutes later. I felt flabbergasted—and also hot, bundled up in my coat. Without thinking, I undid the buttons. When the officer saw the chemise, she asked me if it was mine. That's when I said, "Not really. I'd never buy a chemise like this one." She immediately began to scribble in her notebook. She obviously made a slight mistake when she tried to write down my exact words.

"Anyway, the police officer arrested me—Miranda rights, handcuffs, backseat of the squad car, and all. It was really quite interesting, just like a mystery novel. And the booking process was also fascinating.

"By then, I'd calmed down. I began to remember everything that I knew about criminal procedure, so that I didn't feel nervous at all when the cops began to interrogate me. The police officer who asked me questions was a pinch-faced, plain-clothes sergeant who scowled when he spoke.

"'You're in a world of trouble, Edna,' he said. "'We have all the evidence we need to convict you of felony theft by shoplifting. You could spend several years in prison, even though this is only your first offense. Things will go lots better for you, if you cooperate fully with me.'

"I smiled at him—as prettily as I could. I knew how to handle the cops.

"Susan, my attorney, recently spoke at a meeting of my Wednesday Afternoon Canasta and *Whatever* Club. We invited her to give us a lecture about everyday criminal procedure, although we never explained why we were interested.

"'Rule Number One,' she said, 'is to keep your mouth tightly shut if the police ask you questions without an attorney present.'

"'Rule Number Two is to invoke your constitutional right to counsel. Tell the police you want a lawyer present while you are being interrogated.'

"I intended to demand that Susan be present, but I was amused by what the sergeant was doing. I didn't want to switch him off cold. I decided to ask my own question instead of answering his. I made a soft whimper and tried to look as if I was about to cry.

"'Evidence?' I said, with a halting voice. '*Wh* . . . what evidence?'

"The sergeant peered at me like a cat sizing up a cornered mouse. 'Our crime scene technicians have collected fingerprints from the chemise and the racks in the store, fiber evidence from inside your coat, and statements from witnesses who saw you shoplift the chemise. We have a mountain of conclusive evidence against you.'

"I had to struggle not to laugh in his face. Anyone who watches as much TV as I do, knows that it takes many hours for a busy crime lab to analyze evidence. But even more telling, he didn't mention the videotape—the really significant item of evidence against me.

"I realized that the good sergeant was lying to me. He was guessing about the true extent of the evidence against me. I might have been shocked, if Susan hadn't explained to us that the U.S. Supreme Court has held that police can be untruthful during an interrogation.

"I added a sigh to my whimpering and did my best to look frightened.

"The sergeant tried to look concerned and compassionate. 'I know that stealing the chemise wasn't your idea. I hate to see you go to jail when the person who thought up the crime goes scot-free. If you tell me who else is involved, I'll make sure that the prosecutor and the judge knows that you cooperated. With luck, you'll end up with a slap on the wrist.'

"*Ah ha!* Now I knew what the sergeant was after. Two of my canasta-club friends had gone. . . *er*, shopping with me that afternoon. The store's security personnel must have seen us together, but didn't know who they were. The police wanted me to turn in my friends.

"The sergeant touched my hand. 'I'll tell you something that I'm not supposed to. The captain is interviewing one of your friends right now. She told us that shoplifting from Sacks First Avenue was your idea—but I don't believe her.' He smiled a phony smile at me. 'Why don't you tell me what really happened and who is responsible.'

"I decided that I'd heard enough falsehoods for the day. 'Thank you for your concern, Sergeant, but I won't answer any questions until my attorney is present.'

"'Why would you need a lawyer?' he said. 'Only really guilty people ask for lawyers.'

"I'd anticipated that response. As Susan had explained, the presence of a lawyer in the room effectively ends an interrogation, so police officers may try to convince you that you don't need an attorney. That's the time when you really do need a lawyer. The police have lots more experience asking difficult questions than you have answering them.

"'I repeat, Sergeant,' I said, 'I won't answer any questions or say anything more until my attorney is here.'"

When Federal Agents Ask Questions

Many criminal lawyers point out that one of the most important times to invoke the Fifth Amendment right to counsel is when being questioned by a federal agent. Few people realize that lying to a federal agent—even when not under oath—is a federal crime that can send the wrongdoer to prison. Several of the most publicized federal prosecutions in recent years—including Martha Stewart's—involved knowingly making a *materially false, fictitious, or fraudulent statement or representation* to federal government agents. The quoted words are from the relevant federal statute: 18 United States Code Section 1001. The statute also explains that the lie must be about a matter *within the jurisdiction of the executive, legislative or judicial branch of the United States* but that encompasses an enormous range of topics. The lie in question doesn't have to be made to a federal law enforcement official or even a federal government employee; contractor personnel can be agents of the federal government.

Because it is all too easy to be panicked into telling a lie, defense attorneys advise people to politely decline requests to be questioned by federal agents. Rather, get the agent's business card and say, "My attorney will be in touch with you," or "I want to discuss the matter with an attorney." Don't promise that you'll talk to the agent when your attorney is present; your lawyer may ultimately advise you not to be interviewed.

Searches and Seizures

Law enforcement officials look for evidence of guilt by searching for it in houses or other premises, in vehicles, or on people. They then take possession of the evidence they find by seizing it.

The Fourth Amendment of the U.S. Constitution says:

> The right of the people to be secure in their persons, houses, papers,
> and effects, against unreasonable searches and seizures, shall not
> be violated, and no Warrants shall issue, but upon Probable Cause,

supported by Oath or affirmation, and particularly describing the place to be searched, and the persons or things to be seized.

These protections originally applied to only federal searches and seizures, but U.S. Supreme Court decisions expanded them to searches and seizures made by state officials. Note that searches and seizures by private persons—a private detective, for example—don't violate Fourth Amendment rights unless the private individuals are acting in the capacity of agents of the government. (However, *private searches and seizures* may break criminal statutes and also be intentional torts.)

Your Expectation of Privacy

Over the years, many U.S. Supreme Court rulings have put flesh on the Fourth Amendment's bones. Broadly speaking, a search without a search warrant issued on probable cause is unconstitutional if it violates the reasonable expectation of privacy. Thus, a search is an *invasion* by an agent of the estate into an area that is reasonably seen to be private and protected. And a *seizure* is a meaningful interference with an individual's right to possess something or to his or her own freedom. This can never be a fixed standard.

We have a much greater expectation of privacy in our homes than we do in our cars, and more in our cars than our business premises (because they're often highly regulated by administrative agencies that can require unannounced inspections). We also have definite expectations of privacy when walking on a public street, but these can reasonably fluctuate depending on our behavior. For example, a person who commits a crime in public can't really complain if searched and seized by a police officer who observes the illegal act.

Searches and Seizures in Your Home

In most circumstances, law enforcement officers can't search a person's home without obtaining a search warrant first. The warrant, issued by a magistrate or judge on a showing of probable cause that a crime took place and that items involved in the crime are likely to be found inside the home, must specify two things:

1. The items the police are searching for
2. The locations inside the home where they're likely to find them

Once inside the home, authorities can't go on a "fishing expedition" and search for unspecified items or look for listed items in reasonable locations. For example, if the authorities are searching for a stolen motorcycle, it's unreasonable to search for it inside a kitchen cabinet or to browse through the files on a laptop computer.

Home is broadly understood. A home can be a house, apartment, a trailer home, even a tent erected on private property. All are *residences* that generate an expectation of privacy. However, the few cases dealing with this issue have treated live-aboard boats and parked *motor homes* as vehicles rather than private residences.

Once inside a home, a police officer does not have to avert his eyes and avoid seeing stolen, illegal, or contraband items in plain view. For example, an officer looking for a stolen motorcycle who spots a stash of illegal drugs on a shelf in a suspect's garage can seize it as evidence of a crime. However, should the officer see a stereo receiver sitting on another shelf, he can't turn the receiver around to check serial numbers and verify that it's stolen property.

The *plain-view exception* also applies in circumstances where there is no search warrant. There's no expectation of privacy for anything visible to a person of ordinary, unenhanced vision—and no Fourth Amendment protection. The person who leaves stolen, illegal, or contraband items where other people can see them can't complain when law enforcement officers spot them. This can include items lying in a yard, discarded in curbside garbage, or visible through windows by passersby. *Unenhanced vision* means that the viewer doesn't need binoculars, telephoto lenses, night vision goggles, or other vision-improving devices to see the item.

There are a few situations where law enforcement officers do not need a search warrant to search a home. These fall under the heading of sufficiently exigent circumstances. For example:

→ A person screams for help from inside your home.

→ The police follow a fleeing suspect into a home.

→ Unless the police enter a home immediately, without a warrant, it's likely that evidence will be destroyed.

The police must justify these warrantless searches after the fact or any evidence they gathered will be excluded (*see* "The Exclusionary Rule" above).

The general rule is that law enforcement officials must knock on the door and announce their purpose before entering a home under the authority of a search warrant. The court can authorize a *no-knock warrant*—allowing authorities to simply break down an entry door—if knocking will increase the danger to officers (say, if the residents are armed) or if there is significant risk that the sought-for evidence will be destroyed (a common problem during drug raids). Most states also recognize a *sufficiently exigent circumstances* exception (*see* above) that allows police to enforce an ordinary search warrant without knocking in emergency situations.

Finally, a person living in the home can agree to a warrantless search. Defense attorneys point out that this can be a risky thing to do because police are not required to explain in advance the consequences if they find any stolen, illegal, or contraband item inside the home. It can be very difficult to suppress evidence seized after the owner permits a warrantless search.

Searches and Seizures in Your Car

One of the memorable sequences from the classic movie *The French Connection* shows New York police impounding a sedan parked on the street then virtually disassembling it in a search for illegal drugs. Interestingly, in a situation like this—if the police have probable cause to believe that an automobile contains contraband—they do not have to obtain a search warrant before searching the vehicle.

The general rule is that authorities can conduct a warrantless search based on probable cause that a vehicle contains contraband, the fruits of a crime, the *instrumentalities* used to commit a crime, or other evidence of a crime. The vehicle can be

→ stopped while traveling on public road;

→ parked on a public road;

→ parked in a nonresidential location, such as a public parking lot or gas station.

This so-called automobile exception to the requirement that police have a search warrant recognizes that cars are *readily mobile* and may be in another state long before a search warrant is issued. It doesn't apply to a car that is inside someone's garage, on blocks in a backyard, or is incapable of driving away. These are three examples of probable cause:

1. The vehicle was seen leaving the scene of a crime.
2. A narcotics sniffing dog *alerted* to the car.
3. The officer sees evidence of the crime in plain view.

The great majority of automobile searches occur when a car is pulled to the side of the road for a routine traffic stop. Something gives the police officer reasonable suspicion that the driver has committed a crime—the smell of burning marijuana, inconsistent answers to the officer of questions, possibly the sight of a firearm on the front seat. The officer can now search the vehicle's interior, including the glove box, without a search warrant. However, the officer can't search the vehicle's trunk without probable cause that it contains contraband or other evidence of criminal activity.

If a police officer arrests a motorist and impounds his or her vehicle, it can be searched to inventory the contents. Any contraband or instrumentalities of a crime found during the inventory can be seized and used as evidence.

Searches and Seizures of Your Person

A person is *seized* when a law enforcement officer restrains his or her liberty by means of a physical force or show of authority. People are seized when they are

→ arrested;

→ physically restrained;

→ ordered to stop while walking on the street for questioning or to be frisked;

→ taken into custody and brought to a police station for questioning;

→ ordered to pull off the highway (for example, to receive a traffic citation);

→ stopped by a roadblock while driving.

A law enforcement officer can detain any person reasonably suspected of participating in criminal activity. This is called a *Terry stop*. At that point, the officer can conduct a *Terry frisk*—a limited pat-down of the person's outer clothing to make sure that he or she is not carrying a hidden weapon. (The U.S. Supreme Court approved both of these actions in a significant 1968 decision called *Terry v. Ohio*.) The police officer can also *frisk* any purses, bags, or other items that might hold a weapon.

If the officer feels a solid object that might be a weapon, the officer can reach in and remove it. However, the officer cannot seize items that bear no resemblance to a weapon—even if the officer suspects they are contraband items such as illegal drugs. The officer needs a warrant to search any further.

The law changes if a law enforcement officer arrests a person (say, because the officer witnessed the person commit a crime). In the event of a lawful arrest, the police can search the suspect and his or her *wingspan*—the area within the suspect's reach. They can seize weapons and other items that may be used as evidence.

As with other warrantless searches, a person not under arrest—or the subject of a Terry frisk—can consent to a search that a police officer requests. Most defense attorneys recommend against anyone waiving their Fourth Amendment rights.

Mental Competence and Insanity

For a fleeting moment, Susan, Aunt Edna's defense attorney, wondered if she should question the elderly lady's mental health. There are two ways that the state of Edna's mind might impact the criminal process:

1. Her mental competence to stand trial

2. Her sanity at the time of the alleged offense

A criminal prosecution is an adversarial legal battle between two evenly matched opponents. America's notions of fundamental fairness require that a defendant be able to comprehend the nature and consequences of the proceedings that he or she faces *and* that the defendant is able to assist properly in his or her defense. For example, a defendant can't *assist properly* if unable to reveal information that might support innocence, or if he or she behaves incoherently throughout the trial.

Susan quickly decided that none of this is true about Aunt Edna. She's a bit *flaky*, but certainly possesses the mental competence to stand trial.

The State of Denial, like many states, applies the so-called substantial capacity test as the yardstick to measure a defendant's mental health at the time that the alleged crime was committed. The defendant is not criminally responsible for an act if he lacked the mental capacity needed to understand the wrongfulness of the act or to conform his behavior to the law.

Susan knows that only defendants suffering serious mental illnesses will meet this standard. Edna doesn't come close.

Habeas Corpus Proceedings

Most of us first come across the Latin words *habeas corpus* in high school social studies class. It is the first really hard-to-understand phrase in the U.S. Constitution (it appears in Article I, Section 9):

> The Privilege of the Writ of Habeas Corpus shall not be suspended, unless when in Cases of Rebellion or Invasion the public Safety may require it.

Habeas corpus means "to have the body." A writ of habeas corpus is a legal demand for a jailer (or other responsible official) to deliver an imprisoned person to a court for the purpose of determining whether or not the person is lawfully imprisoned and, if not, whether he or she should be released. In most contemporary habeas corpus cases, the person remains in prison while his or her attorney files motions that challenge the legality of the imprisonment in an appropriate court.

The writ of habeas corpus goes back to medieval England—to pre–Magna Carta days—and is one of the fundamental protections of individual freedom. It provides an avenue of relief if government arbitrarily imprisons someone without proper due process. The writ is most commonly used in the United States by people convicted of crimes when they have run out of direct appeals.

Imagine that Cyrus is found guilty of armed robbery by a jury in the State of Denial. He first files an unsuccessful motion for a new trial with the trial judge, and then he appeals his conviction—also unsuccessfully—to the Denial Court of Appeals.

His last bite at the appeals apple in Denial is to ask the Supreme Court of Denial to review the case. The Supreme Court declines. At this point, Cyrus has no more direct criminal-appeal options.

Cyrus's new lawyer now files a motion for writ of habeas corpus in Denial Superior Court claiming that Cyrus received *ineffective assistance of counsel* at his trial and citing specific errors that his defense attorney made. The motion asks that Cyrus be granted a new trial.

Ineffective assistance of counsel is a difficult assertion to prove; it rarely succeeds unless the attorney was truly incompetent (say, he kept dozing off during the trial or appeared in court never having discussed the case with Cyrus). It's not ineffective counseling to suggest defense strategies that didn't work—if they were based on the attorney's reasoned judgment.

Other common claims made in habeas corpus motions are that the trial judge imposed an illegally harsh sentence, that the prosecutor was guilty of serious misconduct, or that the conviction represents a fundamental miscarriage of justice (perhaps newly discovered DNA evidence proves his innocence). Many defendants seek a new trial; others ask for a change in sentence or an outright release.

If state habeas corpus proceedings fail to earn Cyrus a new trial, his lawyer might launch a habeas corpus proceedings in Denial Federal District Court (*see* Chapter 1). As a rule, federal courts won't consider motions for writ of habeas corpus until all possible state appeals have been exhausted.

+≒= ≒+

HEALTH-CARE LAW

THE FIRST CASE THAT COUNTLESS LAW STUDENTS ENCOUNTER IN LAW school involves heath care. It involves a lawsuit against a physician in New Hampshire who promised a young burn victim that he would give him a "one hundred percent good hand" by performing a skin graft. Not only did the doctor *not* remove the scars on the boys hand but, because the graft used skin from the patient's chest, the palm of his "repaired" hand became hairy.

Surprisingly, the case—decided in 1929, by the New Hampshire Supreme Court—doesn't illustrate medical malpractice but rather a question of contract law: what sort of *expectation damages* were appropriate because the doctor failed to deliver a "one hundred percent good hand" as he had promised.

Because the decision makes the point that "[t]here was evidence that the defendant repeatedly solicited . . . the opportunity to perform this operation, and . . . sought an opportunity to 'experiment on skin grafting,' in which he had had little previous experience," many students find themselves thinking about malpractice when they read the decision. I certainly did—and so did my friends in my study group.

Because medical malpractice springs to mind when most of us combine the words *law* and *health* in a single sentence, I'll start this chapter with a hypothetical malpractice scenario—then I'll quickly move on to the right of *patient self-determination*, a health-related everyday law issue that most of us deal with at some time during our lives.

Iatrogenic? What Does That Mean?

Most of us have never heard the word physicians invented to describe something that should never happen to a patient. *Iatrogenic* comes from *iatros* (Greek for "physician") and *genic* (a suffix that means "producing" or "generating"). An *iatrogenic disease* is an ailment that is *physician-induced*—a health problem inadvertently caused by medical treatments or procedures. Recent studies suggest that hundreds of thousands of people in the United States die each year from medical errors—many of which qualify as medical malpractice.

Although I've used (and will keep using) the words *physician* and *medical,* iatrogenic disease can be caused by medical doctors, nurses, anesthesiologists, physical therapists, dentists, podiatrists, psychologists, pharmacists—by every flavor of health-care provider, including alternative health-care practitioners and advisers. Among the major causes of *iatrogenic events* are medical accidents, medication errors, infections that originate in hospitals, and adverse reactions to prescribed medications.

Malpractice is a highly visible—highly controversial—aspect of everyday law. Some critics argue that malpractice lawsuits have created a national crisis by making health care unaffordable and forcing some providers to stop providing services. Others insist that the threat of malpractice litigation has driven marginal physicians out of practice and has encouraged good physicians to improve the quality of care they provide.

Interestingly, there seem to be many more iatrogenic events than medical malpractice lawsuits, which means that most patients who are the victims of medical accidents don't sue their physicians, hospitals, or pharmaceutical companies. Lots of these are cases of true malpractice but result in no permanent damage to patients.

Fiona Feelgood's Heart Problems

Frannie Feelgood—a lifelong resident of the State of Art—never thought much about medical malpractice until her mother Fiona died. Fiona had suffered chest pain and immediately went to the emergency room at the local hospital. A staff cardiologist ordered tests that discovered a partially blocked artery in Fiona's heart. She subsequently underwent a routine *balloon angioplasty* procedure that opened the blocked artery and immediately improved blood flow.

Fiona felt fine for a day or two, but then began to experience occasional sharp, stabbing chest pains that she described as "different," because they radiated downward. The pains increased whenever she took a deep breath, but went away when she sat upright or leaned forward. She began to feel lightheaded, even dizzy.

She called her cardiologist, whose appointment schedule overflowed that week. He squeezed her in the following week, but told her not to worry—that she was merely experiencing "routine discomfort after the procedure."

A few days later, when Fiona's symptoms had all become worse, Frannie took Fiona to the emergency room. A different staff cardiologist soon diagnosed that Fiona was suffering from *cardiac tamponade*—a buildup of fluid in the space between the heart muscle and the outer sac that covers the heart. Fiona was scheduled for corrective surgery the next day, but died of heart failure before it could be done.

Frannie knew that upwards of 7,000 people die every day in the United States. Consequently, the great majority of patients who suffer *bad outcomes* after medical treatment are not victims of careless physicians. But she was bothered by what happened to Fiona; the whole business didn't seem right. And so, Fiona visited an attorney who specializes in medical malpractice.

"It's not easy in the State of Art to bring a claim for malpractice," the attorney began. "For starters, I have to file an affidavit with the court declaring that I've consulted with a qualified medical professional who concluded that there's a *reasonable and meritorious cause for filing of such action.* I have to include the professional's report with my affidavit. The point is, the courts are not interested in hearing frivolous claims—which harm health-care providers."

"Well, perhaps my gut-feeling is wrong."

"Perhaps, . . . although what happened to your mother points to three *events* of possible malpractice:

1. The vascular surgeon performing the angioplasty accidentally perforated an artery and caused the cardiac tamponade.

2. Her original cardiologist failed to make a timely diagnosis of the cardiac tamponade, leaving Fiona untreated for several critical days.

3. Once diagnosed, an improper additional delay in beginning treatment led to cardiopulmonary arrest—and Fiona's death.

"These events represent the two kinds of medical malpractice that I see most often. The first kind is *improper treatment*—a physician chooses the wrong treatment or administers the right treatment incorrectly. In Fiona's case, the questions to ask are, "Was balloon angioplasty the appropriate treatment for her?" and, "Was the procedure performed competently?"

"The second kind of malpractice is *failure to diagnose*—a physician fails to make a timely diagnosis of the patient's ailment, setting the stage for a poor medical outcome. In Fiona's case, we want to examine whether a competent cardiologist should have diagnosed her post-operative problem as cardiac tamponade."

The attorney then explained that medical malpractice is actually a kind of *negligence* (*see* Chapter 4) that has much in common with that tort. To win a damage award from the *defendant* (the heath-care provider), the *plaintiff* (the injured patient) must prove four things:

1. The physician had a *duty* toward the patient. Broadly speaking, this legal duty is established whenever the health-care provider agrees to treat a patient. At that point, the patient has the right to expect that the physician will apply competence and skill that meets generally accepted professional standards.

2. The physician breached his or her duty of care. This is usually shown by having expert witnesses (typically other physicians and nurses) testify as to what comprises *proper care*, according to generally accepted professional standards. The expert witnesses will then go on to contrast this standard of care with what the defendant actually did. This is evidence that the defendant failed to follow generally accepted professional standards.

3. The defendant's breach of duty was the *legal cause* (or *proximate cause*; *see* Chapter 4). This means that what the physician did—or didn't do—actually caused the harm that the patient suffered. For

example, if Fiona had died when her ambulance was hit by a truck on the way to the hospital, the truck driver's negligence might be the proximate cause of her death—but not failure to follow generally accepted professional standards.

REGIONAL STANDARDS OF CARE

Many states (though fewer than half) put an interesting spin on *generally accepted professional standards*—they add *in this state* or *in the patient's community,* or *with similar training and experience.* This was done decades ago to ensure that resource-poor rural physicians wouldn't be held to the same standards as big-city health-care providers who were backed by large hospital and laboratory infrastructures. The trend is moving malpractice toward a uniform professional standard that all physicians are expected to meet, no matter where they practice.

4. The harm the patient suffered caused compensable damages (*see* Chapter 3). These can be *direct damages* (also called *special damages*) that compensate out-of-pocket losses, such as lost wages, for example, or *indirect damages* (also called *general damages*) that provide compensation for such things as emotional distress and pain and suffering. Courts can also award punitive damages if the physician's conduct demonstrates the intentional or wanton omission of proper care.

Informed Consent

The attorney went on: "Closely related to a physician's duty to provide competent care is the duty to warn a patient of the known risks associated with a recommended medical procedure or course of treatment. This information makes it possible for the patient to give *informed consent* for his or her treatment—a go-ahead based on this knowledge:

→ The likelihood of success and failure of a competently performed procedure

→ Significant risks posed by the procedure or treatment—including major complications—even when administered according to accepted professional standards

➔ If (and how long) the procedure or treatment will incapacitate the patient

➔ Available medically acceptable alternative treatments

➔ The benefits and disadvantages of these alternatives

➔ The persons who will perform the procedure or administer the treatment

"A patient who has not given informed consent—perhaps because the physician didn't disclose significant risks or potential complications—and is subsequently harmed by a procedure or treatment can file a malpractice lawsuit. Simply put, in virtually every state, a patient has the right to weigh the risks and elect whether or not to undergo the procedure or begin the course of treatment.

"Merely signing a consent form typically doesn't prove the patient gave informed consent. Because informed consent is based on informed decision-making, a physician must actually discuss serious risks, complications, and alternatives with the patient—in *plain language* that enables true informed consent.

"Your mother's case raises an interesting issue. Were the cardiologist and vascular surgeon required to disclose the slight risk of cardiac tamponade? Well . . . expert witnesses are likely to disagree, but here the risk of the complication was so small—fewer than one patient in a thousand—that we can probably conclude the following:

➔ Most competent physicians would warn their patients about other, more likely risks and complications and not bother with cardiac tamponade—a rare outcome.

➔ A *normal patient* with the same medical history and conditions as your mother would not have changed her mind about receiving a balloon angioplasty if she'd been warned about the remote possibility of cardiac tamponade.

EXCEPTIONS TO INFORMED CONSENT

Physicians don't need consent to perform life-saving procedures during medical emergencies. And patients are presumed to consent to routine procedures—drawing blood and taking X-ray images, for example—when they ask for advice or diagnosis from a health-care provider.

However, a physician can't make nonemergency treatment decisions for a patient who is intoxicated, under the influence of drugs, in extreme pain, or only partially conscious.

"These are the two standards that courts in different states use to evaluate whether a patient has received sufficient information to make an informed consent. The State of Art uses the first—expert witnesses testify as to what (or what not) information other competent physicians would have provided to the patient.

"The bottom line: I don't see an informed consent issue in Fiona's case."

One Malpractice Claim Moves Forward

Frannie's attorney—and the qualified medical professional he worked with— eventually came to these conclusions:

→   The vascular surgeon who performed the angioplasty did *not* breach his duty of care to Fiona. Cardiac tamponade is a rare complication, but it does happen, despite the best efforts of the surgeon not to perforate an artery.

→   The second cardiologist (and the vascular surgeon he consulted) applied generally accepted professional standards when they decided that Fiona's corrective surgery could wait until the next day.

"However . . ." the attorney said to Frannie, "in my opinion, the staff cardiologist who originally treated Fiona really let her down. Her complaints after the angioplasty should have raised an immediate red flag. A very small percentage of balloon angioplasties develop the kind of complication your mother did, but a cardiologist who meets accepted professional standards should be aware of the possibility—especially given all of her unexplained symptoms.

BINDING ARBITRATION IN HEALTH CARE

Some physicians, hospitals, managed care organizations (for example, HMOs), health insurers, and nursing homes require patients to agree to *binding arbitration* to resolve any patient-care disputes, including malpractice claims. The benefits and problems I talked about in Chapter 1 apply here, too. (Sometimes, binding arbitration clauses are hidden in the fine print of the form that a patient completes during the first visit to a doctor or when he or she is admitted to a hospital.) Courts will generally enforce these clauses, so patients should look for them—and at least make a careful decision before signing. In some states, physicians and hospitals are required to treat patients—especially those with medical emergencies—even if they refuse to sign a contract with a binding arbitration clause.

"Again, in my opinion, the standard of proper care required the physician to see her immediately and order additional tests—for example, an echocardiogram—which might have revealed the cardiac tamponade days earlier."

Other Patient Rights

The last time you were in a hospital—either as a visitor or patient—you may recall seeing a "Patient's Bill of Rights" on a poster or in a brochure. This may be an *official* legal notice required by law in your state, or it may be a broadly accepted list of principles created by the American Medical Association and honored by many hospitals. Every state has enacted some kind of *patients' rights* legislation, but specific *rights* vary from state to state. All patients have the right to informed consent that I described above, and also these rights:

→ Non-discriminatory care

→ Complete and current information concerning his or her diagnosis, treatment, and prognosis in terms that the patient can understand—including the right to see your own health records (unless it's not medically advisable to give such information to the patient, because knowledge of the diagnosis might cause emotional harm)

→ To refuse treatment to the extent permitted by the law

→ Privacy concerning his or her own medical care program

Many states, physicians, hospitals, and institutions add to this list these rights:

→ Choosing health-care providers

→ Participating in health-care decisions

→ Enjoying a fair and efficient process for resolving disputes and complaints

→ Receiving a detailed explanation of the bill

→ Knowing when a specific proposed procedure or treatment is part of a scientific experiment or trial

Patient Autonomy

Many of these rights are actually aspects of what everyday law considers the single most fundamental of patient's rights: the right to make your own decisions about receiving or rejecting health-care services. This is called *patient autonomy* or *patient self-determination*. The U.S. Supreme Court recognized this right in 1990, when it decided that every mentally competent person can make the decision to refuse life-sustaining medical treatment.

The central idea is that a competent patient has the right to *self rule* his or her health care—to choose among different proposed procedures and treatments. Patients also have the right to forgo treatment of any kind. Obviously, patient autonomy demands the full disclosure of relevant information about the nature of an illness, the prognosis, the chance of recovery, different available treatments, and the likely consequences of each treatment.

OPTING TO LEAVE A HOSPITAL

A mentally competent patient can refuse further treatment and leave a hospital at any time; although, the hospital will probably ask him or her to sign a waiver that releases the institution from any liability if the person's condition worsens or complications develop.

In theory, patient autonomy is a partial two-way street. Health-care professionals have a duty to treat a patient according to the patient's desires, within the bounds of accepted treatment. However, while patients can ask for specific kinds of treatment, the health-care professional ultimately gets to decide if the requested treatment is acceptable.

Advance Directives for Health Care

There's an obvious problem with patient autonomy. How can a patient decide what treatment to choose—or even to forgo treatment—if an illness renders him or her unable to express a choice of medical care, or even to consider the available options? A person may be unable to take advantage of his or her rights at the very moment they become most significant.

The everyday legal solution is an *advance directive for health care*—a carefully drafted and witnessed *legal instrument* (a document that grants rights or powers), prepared when you are mentally competent, that speaks for you when you can't speak for yourself.

In many states, a single, hybrid advance directive is sufficient, but in a few states you still need two separate documents:

1. *A living will* (also called a *health-care declaration*) that communicates the end-of-life medical care you want—or don't want—to receive if you can no longer convey your wishes. In essence, you predetermine and specify the kind of care you will receive.

2. *A durable power of attorney for health care* (also called a *health-care proxy*) that empowers another person to make medical decisions for you should you become unable to exercise patient autonomy because you're unconscious or otherwise mentally incompetent.

It takes both instruments—or a hybrid that covers both unpleasant contingencies—to express your wishes and see that they are followed. A living will (its oxymoronic name reflects that it takes effect while the creator is still alive) switches on only when there is no hope for recovery. By contrast, a durable power of attorney for health care springs into action whenever you're unable to make health-related decisions—say, during surgery from which you are expected to recover.

DO NOT RESUSCITATE ORDER

A *do not resuscitate* (DNR) order is a third kind of advance directive—a request that asks hospital staff not to give you cardiopulmonary resuscitation if your heart stops or if you stop breathing while a patient. You can incorporate a do not resuscitate order into a living will or make your wishes known to your physician when you enter the hospital. In either case, a DNR order will be added to your medical chart. In the absence of such an order, personnel will typically provide a *full code*—full advanced cardiac life support protocol—response, including all possible measures to revive the patient and sustain life.

Your Living Will

A living will, as I've said, expresses a patient's wishes for end-of-life medical care when the *declarant* (the person who created it) is terminally ill—or possibly permanently unconscious—and unable to speak for him- or herself.

Don't confuse a *living will* with a *living trust,* a popular technique to avoid probate after death. And note that a living will is not a *testamentary will* that disposes of personal property after death. (*See* Chapter 19 for details of living trusts and testamentary wills.)

Living wills typically authorize the withholding of life-prolonging measures from a patient who is terminally ill or in a persistent vegetative state (that is, a sustained complete loss of self-awareness). These measures may include mechanical respirators, artificial nutrition or hydration, or other techniques that delay a natural death. However, a living will can also request that life-prolonging measures be employed, if that is your wish.

A living will is not *fixed in concrete*. You can change your mind and revoke the instrument at any time, in writing or by oral declaration, typically without regard to your physical or mental condition.

It's a good idea to provide detailed guidance in a living will—and completely spell out your wishes. Although a health-care declaration can't compel your physician to deliver care that is medically or ethically unwarranted, health-care providers generally must follow requests detailed in a living will—even if those requests are opposed by family members (and possibly also by physicians and nurses).

THE PATIENT SELF-DETERMINATION ACT OF 1990

Many people—perhaps you—have entered health-care facilities for minor medical procedures or treatment for non-life-threatening illnesses, and found themselves reading ominous forms and brochures that asked unexpected questions about advance directives and explained their rights to self-determine treatment should they become incapacitated.

More than one confused patient has thought about dashing for the nearest exit.

In fact, the facilities in question were merely complying with The Patient Self-Determination Act of 1990, a federal law that requires hospitals, assisted living facilities, nursing homes, home-health agencies, and other health-care institutions that receive Medicare and Medicaid funding (but not individual physicians) to inform every adult patient of his or her right to accept or refuse medical treatment and to execute an advance directive. If the patient has an advance directive, the institution will place it in the patient's medical record.

It's also a good idea to inform family members of your wishes, because they may be surprised by a living will that requests an end to life support—and might possibly try to challenge your declaration. For this reason, you should also discuss your preferences with your physicians and ask them to record your wishes in your medical record.

A living will is an inherently flexible instrument and can be tailored to accommodate many different terminal illnesses and circumstances. Every state has its own laws that control living wills; however, most states recognize living wills created elsewhere unless some provision violates local law.

Many people have used purchased standard forms, Internet-based form services, even forms provided in state living-will statutes to create their health-care declarations. While you don't absolutely, positively need a lawyer, there are some formalities that have to be done right—including witnessing and notarizing requirements (these vary from state to state). If you *do it yourself,* make certain the standard or Internet form you use also guides you through these important state-specific details.

PHYSICIAN-ASSISTED SUICIDE

The U.S. Supreme Court's ruling that patients have the right to refuse life-sustaining medical treatment was subsequently followed by another decision that rejected the claims that patients have the constitutional *right to die* and/or a fundamental liberty to choose *physician-assisted suicide.* Consequently, states are free to permit physician-assisted suicide, or to treat them as crimes. At the time of writing (2010) only Oregon and Washington have laws on the books that allow patients *of sound mind* to request prescriptions for lethal medications. Early in 2010, the Montana Supreme Court held that physician-assisted suicide is lawful.

The Oregon and Washington laws establish carefully limited circumstances:

The patient must make an oral request and a written request followed by a second oral request at least fifteen days later.

Two physicians must certify that the patient has a *terminal disease*—defined as an incurable, irreversible disease that will cause death within six months.

Two witnesses to the patient's written request must attest that the patient is capable, acting voluntarily, and is not being coerced to sign the request (at least one witness must be a nonrelative and someone who won't receive any of the patient's estate after death).

The patient may rescind his or her request at any time and in any manner without regard to his or her mental state.

Durable Power of Attorney for Health Care

You'll sometimes see the name shortened to *durable power of attorney*, but this can cause confusion. In legalese, a *power of attorney* is any legal instrument in which one person (the *principal*) names another person (the *agent*) to act on his or her behalf in a legal or business matter. Adding *durable* out front means that the instrument has been designed to remain in effect even if the principal is no longer mentally competent (unlike an ordinary power of attorney).

A *durable power of attorney for health care* (sometimes abbreviated DPAHC) is a *limited* instrument that empowers the agent to make *medical* decisions—and typically *only* medical decisions. Moreover, the power of attorney is typically further limited so that it takes effect only when the principal is unable to make his or her own decisions. Here's what your agent will be able to do:

→ Review your health records with physicians

→ Refuse (or consent to) medical tests, procedures, and treatments

→ Request second opinions

→ Direct the withholding of life-prolonging measures

→ Act in your stead to choose treatment facilities and individual health-care providers—including changing physicians and transferring you to a different facility

→ Make decisions about autopsy and organ donations

→ Make choices in your best interest whenever your living will doesn't provide specific wishes

One of the most important uses of a DPAHC is to empower a friend or unmarried partner—a person closely related in all but the legal sense—to make health-care decisions for the principal, have rights of visitation, and have easy access to medical records. More than half of the states have *surrogate consent acts*, which give specific family members—typically the spouse, then parents, then siblings—the power to make health-care decisions if a patient can't speak for him- or herself. Your valid DPAHC will overrule the consent act in your state.

Drafting a DPAHC can become complex when it makes provisions for alternative agents (in the event that one can't—or chooses not to—serve), or if the principal wants two people to serve jointly as agents (to provide a check and balance to each other). In these circumstances, have an experienced attorney draft your DPAHC.

If you create two advance directives—or a single hybrid document—think about the relationship of your health-care wishes (the living-will side) to the decision-making powers you grant to your agent. Do you want your agent to be bound by your instructions, or do you want your proxy to act according to his or her interpretation of your preferences and best interests? You can give your agent as little or as much authority to speak for you as you wish. Also, try to avoid conflicting instructions in both documents. Here again, an attorney can minimize ambiguities and prevent conflicts that can spawn legal battles.

Registering Your Advance Directives for Health Care

If you don't tell your relatives and friends about your advance directives for health care, they may be overlooked—or more likely, not found—at the very moment you want them to take effect. One estimate suggests this happens with upwards of a third of living wills and durable powers of attorney for health care. This is another reason for discussing your wishes—and the instruments you make—with family, friends, and physicians.

Lawyers recommend that you store copies of the documents with other important papers *at home*—not in your safe-deposit box (which may not be accessible if you become incompetent)—and also give copies to your lawyer and your physician.

A convenient storage alternative is to upload your advance directives to one of the Internet-based private registries that record living wills and DPAHCs. An increasing number of states offer equivalent state-sponsored online registries. Private or public, you carry a wallet-sized notification card that announces that you've stored advance-directive documents in the registry. The registries protect your privacy by limiting access to those health-care providers who you (or your family) authorize.

CHAPTER 19

LEGAL ISSUES AT THE END OF LIFE

THIS CHAPTER IS ABOUT WILLS, TRUSTS, AND ESTATES—BUT MY FOCUS is to help you understand the issues and the language rather than transform you into an accomplished estate planner. I've taken this approach because this is an aspect of everyday law that causes much confusion—and even worse, generates a slew of inappropriate fears.

There are excellent reasons for preparing a will, taking steps to avoid probate, and doing some estate planning with an eye toward reducing estate taxes—but most people (according to some estimates, seven out of ten) do none of these things. Contrary to the popular misconceptions we'll deal with shortly, their families survive the much-feared probate process, estate properties are eventually distributed among legally determined heirs, and few (if any) of their survivors experience the grim events of Charles Dickens's *Bleak House* (where the only people to benefit from a disputed estate were the lawyers who worked many decades for the various heirs).

The Case of Your Three Favorite Uncles

If you have to "go," there are few better ways to go than what happened to your three favorite uncles: Huey, Dewey, Louie. They died at age 87 while climbing Mt. Everest, when a meteor the size of a school bus struck their base camp. The trio were residents of the State of Uncertainty (and to keep things simple, everything they owned is located in the State of Uncertainty). Finally, the three were modestly well-off—not wealthy, but reasonably *moneyed*. However, they had significantly different views about estate planning.

> ✦ Huey thought it was unlucky to write a will: He died without one.

> ✦ Dewey didn't like lawyers: He prepared a straightforward will using an Internet legal document service.

> ✦ Louie hated the thought of paying lawyers, courts, or tax collectors one more cent than absolutely necessary: He, his attorney, and his financial adviser worked out a comprehensive estate plan to avoid probate that was based on a *revocable living trust* (*see* below). He also gave his intended heirs annual gifts while he was still alive, to reduce estate taxes.

WHY *LAST WILL AND TESTAMENT?*

In classic legalese, a *will* is a legally effective declaration (typically in writing) of a person's wishes for the disposition of real property (*see* Chapter 9), whereas a testament disposed of personal property (*see* Chapter 11). Thus, a *last will and testament* took care of both kinds of property. This legal nicety is rarely observed today; most people talk about their will, although the full name may appear on the top of the document.

Huey—The Uncle Who Died Intestate

In legal-speak, a person who dies without a *valid* will is said to die *intestate* (literally, without a testament). The chief difference between dying without a will and dying *testate* (with a *valid* will) is that the *decedent's* (the dead person's) property will be distributed according to a distribution scheme established by state law.

Contrary to popular misconceptions (I'll use that phrase a lot in this chapter), the fact that Huey never prepared a valid will doesn't mean that his *estate*—the property he owns, less his debts and liabilities—automatically goes to the State of Uncertainty. This will happen only if no next of kin—no matter how remote—can be found. This is also true in most other states: The state becomes the final beneficiary if no legitimate *heir* of the decedent can be identified.

SPLITTING HEIRS

Strictly speaking, an *heir* is a person who receives an intestate decedent's property, whereas a *beneficiary* receives property under the terms of a valid will. However, you'll often see the terms used interchangeably. I'll do that throughout this chapter.

Here's a summary of Uncertainty's intestate distribution scheme:

1. Decedent is survived by spouse and living children: All marital property plus one-half of separate property (*see* Chapter 5) goes to the surviving spouse; the other half of separate property is split equally among the children.

2. Decedent is survived by spouse (no living children): All property goes to the spouse.

3. Decedent is survived by living children (no spouse): All property goes to the children.

4. Decedent is not survived by living children or a living spouse: All property is split equally among the decedent's *issue* (grandchildren, great-grandchildren, and others, if there are any).

5. Decedent is not survived by a living spouse, living children, or living issue: All property is split equally among the decedent's parents.

6. Decedent is not survived by a living spouse, living children, or living issue, or living parents: All property is split equally among the issue of the decedent's parents (his or her brothers and sisters, then nieces and nephews, etc.).

   a. If none, then all goes to the decedent's grandparents.

   b. If none, then all goes to the issue of the decedent's grandparents (his or her aunts, uncles, and cousins.

   c. If none, then all goes to any issue of any predeceased spouse (the decedent's stepchildren).

   d. If none, then all goes to the decedent's next of kin.

7. If none of the above parties exist, then all of the decedent's property shall *escheat* (revert) to the State of Uncertainty.

Although at first glance you seem fairly far down the list, it's not unusual for an estate to be distributed to an elderly decedent's nieces and nephews—and even his or her cousins. But, a ne'er-do-well grandchild might receive everything, despite Huey's preferences that his property pass to heirs that he actually liked.

This is a significant result of dying without a *valid* will: The state intestate distribution scheme may give property to people not on the decedent's preferred gift list. And because a limited list of relatives receive property, the process almost surely will ignore people that Huey might have wanted to remember.

State intestate distribution schemes vary in subtle ways that non-lawyers often don't understand; so even though Huey chose not to write a will, he would have been wise to consult an attorney merely to make certain that the State of Uncertainty's plan didn't do something he found truly objectionable.

The Probate Process

You may wonder why I emphasized *valid* whenever I mentioned *will*. The estate of a person who dies with an invalid will is handled as if he or she died intestate. The legal entity who decides whether or not the decedent has a valid will is called the *probate court* in many states (and the surrogate court or orphans court in others). Some states have specialized probate courts; others have a probate division in a court of general jurisdiction (for example, superior court; *see* Chapter 1).

The word *probate* comes from the Latin *probare*, "to prove." It originally meant the legal process of proving the validity of a last will and testament. Today, the term encompasses four essential steps:

1. The court appoints a *personal representative*—the person (or sometimes institution) who will oversee the many activities that must be performed. An *executor* is a personal representative who has been named in a will; an *administrator* is a personal representative appointed by the probate court (in the event of no will, or if the named executor can't fulfill the responsibilities).

2. The personal representative takes control of and inventories all of the decedent's property and identifies the decedent's creditors (if any).

3. The personal representative pays the decedent's debts, the expenses of administration, and estate taxes (both state and federal). If necessary, the personal representative can sell property to raise money to pay debts and taxes.

4. The personal representative will distribute the remaining money and property to the beneficiaries of the decedent's will or the decedent's heir(s) under the state's intestate distribution scheme. This is called the *final settlement* and is usually accompanied by an accounting prepared by the personal representative (or more likely the estate attorney assisting the administrator or executor).

The probate process is a highly technical area of everyday law, dripping with unusual language, and full of complex paperwork. As a rule, all but the simplest estates require a personal representative to have the advice and counsel of an experienced attorney.

The Representative's Other Chores

Most personal representatives have a host of other responsibilities as part of the probate process. Here are typical jobs (which depend on the decedent's age):

→ Paying funeral bills

→ Gathering all of the decedent's papers (for example, unpaid bills, credit cards, income tax returns, birth certificate, naturalization papers, adoption certificate, marriage certificate, divorce decree, stock and bond certificates, deeds, mortgage paperwork, title insurance policies, automobile title and registration, veterans records, and more)

→ Arranging for the interim support of the surviving spouse and minor children, if any (this may require permission of the probate judge)

→ Submitting life insurance claims

→ Terminating subscriptions and other home-delivered items (such as periodically delivered medical supplies)

NO, YOU CAN'T TAKE AUNT IRMA'S BROOCH RIGHT NOW

In many states, an executor named in a will can take action to protect valuable property even before being appointed by the court. This is because he or she has the right to *control* the property for the purposes of probate as of the time of the decedent's death. (The named executor can also follow the decedent's written instructions relating to the disposition of his or her body and funeral arrangements.)

Consequently, the named executor should take commonsense precautions to safeguard valuables (and perishable property), including moving jewelry and other *tempting* items to a safe location, rekeying door locks, and possibly hiring a guard during the funeral (a funeral announcement is also a declaration to thieves that a house will be unprotected for several hours).

The future administrator of an intestate decedent's property doesn't have as much flexibility; however, wise relatives will band together to protect assets, prevent *premature takings,* and explain that a judge will determine if *Aunt Irma's promise last summer* means that her brooch belongs to Cousin Frances.

A personal representative is entitled to compensation for his or her efforts—paid out of estate assets. Typically, friends and relatives who take on the responsibilities waive compensation.

Because many personal representatives are inexperienced, they (along with spouses) can be the victims of *postmortem cons*. Two of the most common are attempts to collect nonexistent debts and deliveries of merchandise that the decedent didn't order.

A TIP FOR REPRESENTATIVES: ORDER LOTS OF DEATH CERTIFICATES

One of the details that surprises inexperienced personal representatives (and also people helping bereaved family members) is the number of different organizations that require a certified copy of the decedent's death certificate—the document issued by the Registrar of Vital Statistics (or other county records agency) that confirms the date, location, and (possibly) cause of a person's death. A certified copy is embossed with an official seal.

Death certificates are required by banks, insurance companies, brokerage firms, pension administrators, retirement account administrators, the Social Security Administration, and the Department of Veterans Affairs. Most keep the copies they are sent.

Consequently, it makes sense to order a sheaf of copies at the earliest opportunity. Ordering certified copies one at a time lengthens the probate process (the local records agency may take a week or two to prepare them) and ends up adding to the cost (agencies usually charge less for additional copies ordered as part of a batch). Ordering a dozen certified copies is a good starting point, unless the decedent had an unusually large number of bank, brokerage, and retirement accounts.

Property Not Subject to Probate

When Huey's personal representative tallies the personal property Huey owned, he or she will find that a hefty chunk is *not* subject to probate. This is because the law recognizes the new owner without the need for a formal probate process. Property not subject to probate includes: life insurance (policies typically have a defined beneficiary), retirement plans and other *death benefits* (they also have beneficiaries), jointly owned bank accounts, jointly owned brokerage accounts, jointly held real estate (*see* Chapter 9), and property held in trust (*see* below).

In marital property states (*see* Chapter 6), the decedent's half of marital property doesn't automatically go to the surviving spouse unless the property is owned in joint tenancy with right of survivorship or as *tenants in the entirety* (*see* Chapter 9), a form of joint ownership available only to married couples.

Similarly, in most *community property* states (*see* Chapter 6) the surviving spouse doesn't automatically own the decedent's half of community property unless the couple took title to the property as *community property with right of survivorship.*

A few states recognize *community property agreements,* wherein a married couple declare all of their marital property to be community property that goes to the surviving spouse without probate.

Small-Estate Probate

Because many everyday estates involve relatively small amounts of property subject to probate, most states have established *small-estate probate* processes that dramatically simplify the task of probating these simple estates. In some of them, an affidavit filed by the people entitled to receive the decedent's property replaces the traditional legal paperwork filed with probate court. Typical small-estate probate processes require the following:

- → Probated property below a statutory threshold (as low as $15,000 in one or two states, as high as $100,000 in others)
- → No real property to be transferred
- → All debts owed to be listed in the affidavit (creditors will be paid before estate assets are distributed)
- → In the event the decedent died intestate, enough family detail in the affidavit so that the legal heirs are clearly identifiable
- → All the beneficiaries or legal heirs agree and swear to the affidavit (if any aspect of the transfer is contested, the estate must be probated as usual)

Preparing a satisfactory small-estate affidavit can be more complex than it seems—particularly for an intestate decedent. Consequently, many states urge that it be done by an experienced attorney.

Dewey—The Uncle Who Wrote a Will

As I told you earlier, the majority of people in the United States agree with Uncle Huey—they don't have wills either. But this is one time when the majority is dead wrong (pun intended). Uncle Dewey was in the wise minority—he recognized the many advantages of having a valid last will and testament to direct the disposition of his property. (Dewey also recognized the value of having a living will—*see* Chapter 18—to express his wishes for end-of-life medical care.)

The Advantages of Having a Will

There are several important reasons to invest the time and (reasonably modest for most people) legal fees involved in creating a valid will:

→ The *testator* (the man writing the will) or the *testatrix* (the woman writing the will) determines who gets what.

→ A married testator or testatrix can give all separately owned property to his or her spouse. (This can prevent the awkward situation of having to sell property items *split* between a surviving spouse and surviving children.)

→ The testator/testatrix can leave property to people who are not relatives—including his or her stepchildren (who aren't included in the state distribution scheme unless they were adopted by the decedent).

→ The testator/testatrix can leave property to churches and charitable organizations.

→ The testator/testatrix can include a clause that allows his or her personal representative to act without a bond to compensate any loss to the estate caused by his or her dishonest acts. (The cost of this bond—paid out of estate assets—often exceeds the cost of preparing a will.)

→ If the testator/testatrix has minor children, he or she can nominate a person to be their guardian. A court will ultimately appoint a guardian in the children's best interest, but judges typically try to follow the parents' wishes.

Guardianship

The last item on the list—guardianship—is often the most important reason for young testators/testatrices to create a will. He or she can nominate one person to be *guardian of a child's person* (the caregiver; the person who raises the child) and another to be *guardian of the child's estate* (the person who manages the child's inheritance and financial affairs)—or the maker of the will can combine both roles in a single *personal guardian* nominee. Here's what attorneys advise clients to do:

→ Discuss guardian nominations with potential nominees and get their agreement—never *surprise* someone with a request of this magnitude.

→ Name an alternate guardian to step in if the first choice can't serve.

→ Make financial provisions to support the child—via a trust (*see below*) and/or an insurance policy—nominees may refuse guardianship if they can't afford to care for a child.

Three Kinds of Wills

When most of us hear the word *will*, we conjure up an image of a document printed on legal-size paper dripping with signatures and stamped with embossed seals. This is the first—and most preferable—of the three kinds of wills that can be valid in different states.

Attested (Formally Witnessed) Will

An *attested will* is a written document (neatly typed or, these days, produced by on a computer and desktop printer) that is signed by the testator/testatrix and attested to (witnessed) by at least two competent witnesses (a few states require three witnesses). This is the kind of will an attorney—or an Internet legal-document website—will prepare for you. It is the only type of will that plays an important role in everyday law. I'll talk more about attested wills after I briefly describe the other two varieties.

Holographic (Handwritten) Will

A *holographic will* is a will written in the handwriting of the testator/testatrix and signed by him or her. A holographic will is not witnessed and is typically expressed in informal language (that often introduces unforeseen legal problems). Only about half the states will probate a holographic will—after a close examination to eliminate the possibility of fraud.

Broadly speaking, a holographic will should contain *only* the handwriting of the testator/testatrix. A "holographic will" written by someone else other than the testator isn't holographic—or valid. Probate judges may hiccup if they see dates added with rubber stamps, minor additions written by another hand, or typed-in details.

Many people confuse things when they add handwritten content to *standard* will forms, inadvertently creating a *partially* holographic will. If the additional portions are clearly in the testator/testatrix's handwriting and represent a valid will in their own right, a court may interpret them together and ignore the printed matter. More likely, the modified will form will be declared nonvalid.

Some states add the requirements that the holographic will be found among his or her *valuable papers*, in a safe deposit box, or in the custody of a person or organization who was given the will by the decedent for safekeeping.

Holographic wills were once popular ways to save money, but the high risk of rejection by a probate court makes a holographic will a foolish economy these days—even if you live in a state that will probate a handwritten will document.

Nuncupative (Oral) Will

A *nuncupative will* is an oral testamentary declaration spoken to two (or in some states three) witnesses by a person during his or her *last sickness* or other imminent peril of death, and who doesn't survive the peril. *Nuncupative* comes from the Latin word *nuncupo*, "to declare." Nuncupative wills must be *reduced to writing* by the witnesses (usually within a specified time) and signed.

Think of a nuncupative will as an *emergency will*—a stopgap for someone whose condition or circumstances make it impossible to draft a written will and see to the formalities. The testator/testatrix must be *in extremis*—at the point of death. Some courts have invalidated oral wills dictated several days before dying.

Currently, only a minority of states allow nuncupative wills—and the trend is to abandon them. Even in states that still honor oral wills, the following may happen:

→ They may be limited to serving members of the armed forces.

→ They can be difficult to probate—even more so if it contradicts an existing attested will document.

→ They can't be used to bequeath real property.

→ There may be a dollar-value-maximum on the amount of personal property that can be given.

A GIFT *CAUSA MORTIS*

This is a gift of personal property (see Chapter 11) made *on the occasion of death*, that takes effect when the *donor* delivers the gift to the recipient. If, however, the donor unexpectedly recovers or otherwise survives, the gift is automatically revoked—and must be returned. Gifts *causa mortis* are given by people who want to make absolutely certain that their most prized possessions go to specific people—*if* they actually die. As with any gift, the donor must intend to give the gift, the donor must deliver the gift, and the recipient must accept it. However, the donor can change his or her mind—and demand the item back—before his or her death.

Creating an Attested Will

Each state has specific attestation requirements—one of the reasons that many people rely on a experienced attorney to prepare a will. If you create a will using a standard will form or via an Internet legal-document website (as Uncle Dewey did), make certain that you have complete attestation instructions for your state. Three common requirements prevail:

1. The testator/testatrix must sign the document with the intent to create a last will and testament.
2. The testator/testatrix must announce to the witnesses that the document is his/her last will and testament.
3. The testator/testatrix must sign the document in the witnesses' presence or else affirm his or signature (if he/she signed it previously).

The Reason for Legalese

One reason that wills prepared by lawyers tend to be full of legalese that dates back to old England is that using tried-and-true language ensures that the document precisely communicates the intentions of the testator or testatrix. (By this point, judges and attorneys know precisely what every venerable word means.)

However, most states do not require specific words written in a specific way to create a will. A document that communicates the maker's intention to convey property to specific beneficiaries when he or her dies will *usually* be interpreted as a last will and testament. I emphasized *usually* because if a probate judge finds the language ambiguous or unclear, he or she may be forced to consider the will invalid. This is one area of everyday law where *neatness of language* counts.

SELF-PROVING ATTESTED WILL

Although not required by most states, it is a good idea to sign and witness an attested will in front of a notary public. His or her seal and signature on a simple *self-proving affidavit* attached to the will declares that the document is a will and that it was properly signed and witnessed according to state law. Probate judges will typically accept the affidavit in lieu of having the witnesses testify to the will's authenticity. This may be difficult for survivors to orchestrate if witnesses have moved, and impossible if they have died.

The Problem with Pre-prepared Wills

Because the language of a will is so important, be extra cautious if you use a *will form,* will software package, or an Internet legal-document service that creates a document full of language you don't understand. It's all too easy to properly sign a valid (but wildly inappropriate) will that does something you don't want done. A probate judge will have no choice but to follow your instructions, even if you gave them by accident. Even a *plain English* will can offer subtle legal twists and turns. Take the time to read—and understand—your will.

Will Formalities

We occasionally see news reports on TV about properly crafted *celebrity* wills that distribute estates worth hundreds of millions of dollars. Picture yourself as the judge in charge of such a proceeding, and you'll quickly understand why probate courts want to make certain that the testator/testatrix has followed to the letter of the requirements mandated by state law:

> → *Minimum age*—Most states require the testator or testatrix be eighteen years old to make and sign a will; some states allow people under eighteen who were married to make wills.

> → *Sound mind*—This isn't measured by a *sanity test* (assuming that such a thing existed); rather it means that the testator/testatrix has the mental capacity required to make a valid last will and testament. This is a fairly easy legal hurdle to pass: The maker of the will must know what property he or she owns, the identities of the people (usually family and close friends) who *have claims to his or her remembrances,* and how the will he or she created distributes the property.

> → *Properly signed*—The will document needs to be signed by the testator/testatrix in his or her own handwriting (or by another person at the testator/testatrix' specific direction), typically at the very end.

> → *Properly witnessed*—The will needs to be attested to by two or three witnesses, typically in their presence (but not necessarily in their simultaneous presence), as I describe above.

No matter who prepares your will, review the preliminary draft thoroughly (before the final document is produced) to make certain that the words accurately reflect your wishes and intent. In theory, routine spelling mistakes, simple grammar problems, and minor typographical errors that don't alter the obvious meaning aren't important—in practice, anything that *might* cause confusion should be eliminated from the draft. Again, the word processing programs available for all computers (and their built-in spell-checkers) make it easy to produce *clean* documents. It's especially important that your beneficiaries are fully, properly, and clearly identified.

There Are Things You Can't Give Away

Although you may be filled with the spirit of generosity when you prepare your will, keep this in mind:

+ You can't give away property that is jointly owned with someone else if the ownership *tenancy* (*see* Chapter 9) transfers the property to the other owner in the event of your death. (If you own property with someone *in common* you can bequeath your share of the property to someone else in your will.)

+ You can't give away property that is controlled by a contract. The proceeds of an insurance policy, the money in your retirement account, and various other death benefits will go to the beneficiaries you defined—regardless of what you say in your will.

+ Similarly, other property not subject to probate—a living trust and various kinds of joint bank accounts, to name two kinds—will also go to defined beneficiaries, even if you attempt to *modify* the recipients in a will.

+ Finally, although you can bequeath your pet (a chattel) to a beneficiary, you can't bequeath gifts to your pet, because an animal is not legally competent to hold title to money or property. (In most states, however, you can establish a trust to care for a pet. Doing it right is legally complex; you need a lawyer's assistance.)

A Will Can Be Contested

It's been said by many humorists that "where there's a will, there's a relative . . . who's unhappy." In fact, most will contests during probate—fights that challenge a will's validity—are likely to involve very large estates. However, large or small, will contests are difficult to win if the challenged wills meet all of the state's formalities.

For starters, a will can't be contested by anyone who thinks the property dispositions are unfair. In most states, only two groups of people can contest a will:

1. Beneficiaries actually included in the will (who typically fight for more money or property)

2. Heirs who would receive the decedent's property under the state's intestate distribution scheme if the will was declared invalid (they typically contest the will because they were left out and not named as beneficiaries)

Broadly speaking, a will can't be challenged merely because someone believes it's *unfair*. A testator/testatrix of sound mind can leave his or her property to anyone he or she chooses. After all, that's the whole idea of a will. Probate courts are reluctant to overturn the decedent's plan for distributing his or her property without a compelling reason. These are compelling reasons:

→ The maker of the will was not of sound mind when he or she created the will (or when he or she modified it at a later date).

→ A beneficiary exerted undue influence on the maker when the will was written (say that a caregiver *isolates* a testator/testatrix in failing health and convinces him or her to write a new will in the caregiver's favor).

→ The maker was coerced into making a specific provision, or else was the victim of fraud (a family member might pressure an ailing testator/testatrix to revise a will, increasing his or her bequest, or else make fraudulent representations about current beneficiaries that accomplish the same end).

Some testators/testatrices try to prevent will contests after their death by adding *no contest* provisions to the clauses that leave gifts to beneficiaries. These specify that any beneficiary launching a will contest will forfeit his or her bequest. Because they're meant to frighten beneficiaries who might otherwise seek bigger shares of an estate, they were once labeled *in terrorem* (in fear or warning) clauses. Broadly speaking, courts won't enforce these clauses if a will is contested in good faith, with probable cause to believe that the will is invalid.

Joint and Mutual Wills

A *joint last will and testament* is a single document signed by two people—typically a husband and wife, although gay and lesbian couples and domestic partners can also create a joint will. To illustrate the concept, imagine that Jack and Jill—the testator and the testatrix—create a joint will:

→ If Jack dies first, all of his property will go to Jill.

→ If Jill dies first, all of her property goes to Jack.

→ When the surviving member of the couple dies, his or her estate goes to the designated beneficiaries chosen by Jack and Jill when they created the will.

The one joint document must make two trips through probate court—once when the first party dies, and again when the survivor dies.

Joint wills were popular several decades ago, but most estate attorneys recommend *mutual wills* instead:

→ Jack signs a will that leaves all of his property to Jill, with the provision that if Jill is dead the property goes to designated beneficiaries.

→ Jill signs a will that leaves all of her property to Jack, with the provision that if he is dead the property goes to designated beneficiaries.

Although joint and mutual wills achieve the same property dispositions, individual mutual wills are more convenient to handle, must only survive one journey through probate (documents have been known to be lost or made unreadable during probate), and are easier to modify should one party change his or her mind.

How to Change a Will

A will should be a living document that reflects the testator or testatrix's current wishes for the disposition of his or her property. Unfortunately, people tend to make wills then forget about them for years. This, of course, results in *old wishes* determining property distribution should the maker die.

Knowing this, some testators/testatrices try to modify their attested wills by scribbling notes on the pages, by crossing out clauses, by changing the name of beneficiaries. In some states, these additions will *revoke* (cancel) the entire will; in others, the law requires the probate judge to ignore changes made after a will is signed and witnessed.

For hundreds of years, the appropriate way to modify a will was to prepare a *codicil*—essentially a separate document that became an add-on to the original. The codicil changed a provision or two, added or deleted a beneficiary, or disposed of a recently acquired item of property. To be effective, a codicil must be signed and witnessed with all the formalities necessary for a complete will.

Codicils made sense back in the days when legal documents were painstakingly written out by hand or slowly typed on manual typewriters, but they have been made obsolete by computers and word processing software that can crank out an updated will in seconds. It's just as easy to produce, sign, and witness a *brand new*, freshly revised will as a codicil, and there's a significant advantage to *starting from scratch*: Adding a codicil makes a will more difficult to interpret; the court must read the original, read the codicil, and then determine how the codicil changed the original. The situation becomes even cloudier—and the interpretation even more difficult—if a probate judge must interpret a series of codicils prepared over many years, often by different attorneys. Not surprisingly, the various codicils are often mutually inconsistent.

Whenever you create a new will, you should revoke all previous wills by including this or a similar statement upfront: "I revoke all wills and codicils that I have previously made." You'll also reduce potential confusion for your personal representative—not to mention the volume of his or her stomach acid—if you destroy all the copies of any earlier wills.

It's also possible (although few people find it necessary) to revoke a will without creating a new one. In most states, a will is revoked when the testator/testatrix intentionally rips it up, burns it, defaces it, or otherwise destroys it.

The Impact of Marriage and Divorce

In many states, the marriage of a testator/testatrix after he or she makes a will revokes the will. In a few states, so does a divorce. In most states, a divorce (or annulment) acts like a partial revocation—a probate court will ignore any provisions that concern the testator/testatrix's former spouse. This includes bequests to the former spouse and clauses that appoint the former spouse as executor—unless the will expressly provides that the clauses shall apply in the event of a divorce. In any case, marriage and divorce are such significant life events that the maker should create a new will when either occurs.

Disinheriting a Family Member

If a will lets a decedent *speak from beyond the grave,* the ability to disinherit a family member allows the maker of a will to scream vengeful insults.

Disinheritance is the legal mechanism by which a testator/testatrix prevents a share of his or her estate from passing to the person who would otherwise have the right to inherit under the state' s intestate distributions scheme—typically an estranged child or grandchild. The point is, the maker of a will can't *disinherit* a close friend or business colleague (who has no right of inheritance under state law).

The surest way to disinherit a child is for the maker to include a statement like the following in his or her will: "It is my specific intention not to provide for my son John, born on March 15, 1980, in this last will and testament."

Some estate attorneys advise including an explanation of why this child is not a beneficiary (for example, "I choose not to provide for John because we have been estranged for more than ten years"), while others argue that no explanation is necessary, and that including one will give John an opportunity to contest the validity of the will by attempting to prove that there was no estrangement.

At one time, it was common to leave a nominal gift—say $1.00—to a disinherited heir to further indicate the maker's intent (along with his or her scorn). Most estate attorneys recommend against the practice because it transforms the person into a named beneficiary—and gives him or her more legal weapons to challenge the will (or, at the very least, bedevil the executor and delay the probate process).

Incidentally, merely not mentioning a child in a last will and testament invites the presumption that the maker forgot to provide for the child when the document was drafted. A probate judge who reaches this conclusion is likely to award the left-out family member the share of the estate he would have received if the testator/testatrix had died without a will.

CAN A SPOUSE BE DISINHERITED?

The short answer is *No*—unless the spouse has agreed, in a valid prenuptial agreement, not to *take against the will*. *Taking against the will* is the right (given by law in every state) for a surviving spouse to receive a share of the decedent's estate— typically one-third to one-half of the decedent's property.

Bequests to Minor Children

Broadly speaking, minor children under the age of eighteen can't control property themselves. Consequently, when a minor child inherits property under a will, the probate court must appoint a court-supervised *guardian of property* (also called a *conservator*) to manage the assets until the *ward* (as the minor child is known) reaches age eighteen. Although the process seems straightforward, estate attorneys often warn of two shortcomings:

1. Court supervision can become cumbersome: The appointed guardian must file detailed annual accountings with the court— and also get the judge's permission to sell assets.

2. Unless the appointee is a close relative, he or she will likely receive a fee for serving as guardian. The person will also be required to buy a *surety bond* to insure the managed property against theft, fraud, or waste. These costs are paid out of the child's bequest and can significantly reduce the beneficiary's assets when he or she comes of age.

An increasingly popular way to avoid these problems is for a testator or settlor to take advantage of the Uniform Transfers to Minors Act that is the law in most states. A person writing a will or establishing a living trust can specify a *custodian* who takes charge of bequeathed property for a named minor beneficiary.

The custodian is not under court supervision, nor does he or she have to post a surety bond to protect. This can be simpler and less expensive—but poses a risk of loss to the beneficiary should the named custodian prove to be unreliable.

You Were One of Uncle Dewey's Named Beneficiaries

You were pleased when Uncle Dewey's lawyer told you that he'd named you as a beneficiary in his will and that you would receive a substantial monetary bequest.

The process of probating Dewey's will in the State of Uncertainty took fourteen months. The seemingly long delay surprised you, because you received a *first installment* of your share of your third uncle's (Uncle Louie's) estate less than three months after the meteor struck.

Because you were curious, you checked with Uncle Dewey's executor—one of his granddaughters—and learned that no one challenged Dewey's will and there were no other legal complications.

"Everything went smoothly," she said, "but it took more than a year to dot all the 'i's' and cross all the 't's.' You know me—I'm persnickety because I hate making mistakes."

Still curious, you also chatted with the grandson who helped "wind-up" Uncle Louie's estate. You know that he served as Uncle Louie's *successor trustee*—although you're not sure what the label means.

"It's really quite simple," he explained. "Louie set up a revocable living trust [*see* below]. When he died, I took over the management of the trust. I distributed the assets to the beneficiaries.

"Everyone knows that winding up a living trust is faster than going through probate," he said. "Louie ran his personal affairs by the book, so I felt sure there weren't any hidden land mines in his estate. You know me—I don't waste time. I distributed some of the assets as quickly as I felt appropriate."

Louie—The Uncle Who Avoided Probate

You're impressed by the apparent advantages of avoiding probate, so you look more closely at how it's done. Your family attorney gives you a quick introduction.

"Your Uncle Louie was a great believer in *estate planning*. That's the development and implementation of a legal strategy that bequeaths assets to intended beneficiaries, while maximizing the value of the property they receive by

→ avoiding probate—and thus reducing legal fees, personal representative's fees, court costs, and other estate administration costs;

→ reducing estate taxes.

"Most of my clients—people who are *well off* but not wealthy—avoid probate (more accurately, they *simplify* probate) by creating a revocable living trust. And, they reduce estate taxes by giving gifts while they are still alive. There are other ways to reduce taxes that may be used more widely if estate tax rates increase in the years ahead. One of these is the *life-insurance trust* (a trust that makes the proceeds of a life-insurance policy nontaxable; life-insurance proceeds are typically considered a taxable part of the decedent's estate). They are not really part of *everyday law* today."

How to Avoid Probate

"There's really nothing magical about avoiding probate," your lawyer went on. "The idea is to transform as much of the decedent's property as possible into property that's not subject to probate—simply put, property that will go to a specific beneficiary. This happens automatically with such things as certain joint bank accounts, retirement accounts, death benefits, and real estate that's jointly owned with a right of survivorship.

"Think of a revocable living trust as a *container* for a person's property that

→ enables the *settlor* of the trust (also known as the *grantor,* although I'll use the more familiar label *settlor, see* below) to name beneficiaries for certain items of property—say a family heirloom, a valuable stamp collection, or a vacation home;

→ allows the settlor to name beneficiaries who will receive a specific percentage of the value of other real and personal property (that will be sold after the settlor's death);

→ survives after the settlor's death and immediately transfers title to the property in the trust to the named beneficiaries, without court approval or the usual probate process (the *successor trustee*—rather than a probate judge—carries out the settlor's wishes for the distribution of his or her property);

→ and—this is a really important *and*—leaves the settlor fully able to use, control, and manage the property while he or she is alive—with an owner's rights to sell anything at any time, for any reason.

"The seemingly complex name—*revocable living trust*—conveys two key concepts: First, that the trust can be revoked (and modified) by the settlor at any time; this feature gives a living trust its great flexibility. The second concept is that the trust exists during the settlor's lifetime—as opposed to trusts that go into operation when the settlor dies.

"The chief advantage of having a revocable living trust is the way it shortcircuits the probate process. Consequently, a living trust

→ *may* reduce costs;

→ *may* accelerate the distribution of property to beneficiaries;

→ *doesn't* reduce estate taxes (the property in a living trust is subject to the same state and federal estate taxes as assets distributed by a probated estate);

→ keeps *who-got-what* private (as opposed to a will, where the inventory of the decedent's assets is open to the public);

➔ is a simpler way of dealing with real property in several states (if distributed by a will, each piece of property would be transferred by a local probate court, in a separate proceeding)."

What Is a Trust?

"Before I talk more about revocable living trusts," your attorney said, "let's take a brief look at *trusts*, in general. A *trust* is a three-way legal relationship in which

➔ a *settlor* (the original owner of some property) turns the property over to . . .

➔ a *trustee*—who controls the property and performs various *duties*, all for the benefit of . . .

➔ a beneficiary.

"Many traditional trusts are established by testators and testatrices when they write wills. For example, imagine that your Uncle Dewey—the uncle who prepared a will—had a daughter, Daisy, who was still a teenager. He wants to leave her his stock portfolio, but worries that she might be too young to handle so much money wisely. And so, he (the settlor) adds a clause to his will that creates a trust for Daisy (the beneficiary), wherein his bank (acting as trustee) will control the stock portfolio until she reaches age twenty-one. The bank's duties under the trust are to

➔ manage the portfolio conservatively with an eye toward maintaining its value;

➔ use the stock dividends to pay Daisy a monthly allowance;

➔ transfer the stock to her when she reaches age twenty-one.

"The law recognizes that the trustee (the bank) has a *fiduciary responsibility* toward Daisy (the beneficiary). This means that the bank must act with complete loyalty toward Daisy—acting honestly, in good faith, solely for her benefit, with no conflicts of interest. Failure to meet this high standard makes the trustee liable for damages in a court of equity [*see* Chapter 1]."

Wearing Two Hats: Settlor and Trustee

"Most people who establish a revocable living trust serve as both the settlor/ grantor and the trustee—with the trustee having full use and control of the property in the trust. Both jobs continue during the settlor's lifetime because newly acquired property must be brought into the trust. This is called *funding the trust*—it can represent one of the tedious aspects of having a living trust.

"Keep in mind that a living trust can only distribute property that has been placed into it. Funding a trust requires transferring the legal title of property to the trust. Current property must be transferred when the *document of trust* is created; newly acquired property must be added in a timely manner. The transfer procedure varies with the kind of property involved:

> → *Real estate*—A new deed must be executed and recorded (which may involve the payment of significant fees and taxes).

> → *Bank and brokerage accounts*—The names on the accounts must be changed to the name of the trust.

> → *Stock and bonds*—The transfer agent for the issuing company must reissue certificates in the name of the trust.

> → *Most other personal property*—Ownership is transferred to the trust by preparing a straightforward written declaration called an *assignment*.

"My point here is that a living trust requires that the settlor's estate plan be actively managed. You can't set up a living trust and pretend it's finished."

A "Pour-Over" Will

"Despite claims to the contrary," your lawyer continued, "a revocable living trust seldom eliminates *all* aspects of probate when the settlor/grantor dies. Most individuals with living trusts also require a last will and testament to

> → revoke any earlier wills that might conflict with the terms of the living trust;

> → nominate guardians for their minor children;

> → 'pour over' recently acquired assets (or other assets not transferred to the trust) into the living trust, so that they can be distributed along with trust assets;

> → appoint an executor (typically the successor trustee) to deal with any other aspects of the decedent's estate.

"If most of the decedent's property is inside the living trust, the rest of his or her estate can often be probated using the state's small-estate probate process."

The Joys (and Disadvantages) of Avoiding Probate

"Okay!" your lawyer said with a smile. "A revocable living trust will allow you to avoid probate—but do you really want to avoid probate?

"The much-maligned probate process actually has its share of virtues. To begin with, probate is supervised by an experienced judge—who may do a better job of protecting the interests of heirs and beneficiaries than a successor trustee. Another plus is that the decedent's assets are transferred in an orderly (and open) manner, not via a backroom process. (When property has gone through a probate process, the validity of title is never in question.)

"Also, the probate court will resolve—during the probate process—any questions and disputes about the validity of the will or about the distribution of the decedent's estate.

"Finally (and perhaps most important of all) creditor claims against a probated estate can only be made for a limited period of time—typically two to four months after the *notice to creditors* is published, depending on state law.

"Conventional wisdom says that these benefits carry too high a price tag—and that probate routinely spans too many months (unreasonably delaying the distribution of property to beneficiaries).

"But that's not necessarily so.

"The costs associated with probate must be balanced against the total costs of creating and funding a living trust. Depending on the size of the estate and the nature of the assets, probate often does cost more than a living trust—but surprisingly it may also cost less (especially if a relative or friend serves as executor without receiving a fee, and if you live in a state that has *reformed* and simplified its probate process).

"My point is that you and I, as your attorney, should do a comparative cost analysis before you assume that a living trust is inevitably less expensive.

"And as for excessive time . . . the lengthiest parts of the probate process are gathering and appraising the decedent's assets, waiting for and paying creditor claims, preparing state and federal estate tax returns, and then waiting for federal and state tax *releases*. Only then will the probate judge approve the executor's final plan for distributing the estate property.

"However, in most states the estate assets are not *frozen* during probate. Once the executor is sworn in by the probate court, he or she can make early distributions to beneficiaries. *But* . . . wise executors prefer to be sure that all debts and taxes are paid before they start making major distributions.

"The successor trustee of a living trust must also gather assets, pay creditor claims, and pay taxes. If the trustee immediately distributes part or all of the assets to beneficiaries, he or she takes the very same risk that our hypothetical executor tried to avoid: that there won't be enough assets left to pay a late-arriving creditor claim or a revised tax bill. Consequently, a cautious trustee may take just as long to distribute the decedent's property as an executor."

Minimizing Estate Taxes

Your attorney sighed. "There's so much uncertainty today about the future of estate taxes in the United States, that I advise my clients to focus on the other basics of estate planning: ensuring that your wishes for the disposition of your property are followed, and that the process for distributing assets to beneficiaries is carried out as quickly and efficiently as possible.

"Regardless of the estate tax rates and exemptions that are put in place in the years ahead, the *early distribution* of the estate via annual gifts to beneficiaries will continue to be the most important tax reduction technique for people of average wealth. Properly planned gifts [*see* Chapter 11] can avoid gift taxes and reduce the size of the estate, which reduces estate taxes.

"Although an ordinary living trust doesn't reduce estate taxes, it's possible to create a modified living trust—called an *AB living trust*—that takes maximum advantage of the estate-tax exemptions available to a husband and wife.

"In essence, the property of the first spouse to die remains in trust for the second spouse. He or she never takes legal title to the property—and never *uses up* the first spouse's tax exemption. When the surviving spouse dies, the beneficiaries can apply both spouses' tax exemptions to reduce estate taxes.

"The only downside is that the surviving spouse can't use (or sell) the first spouse's assets as he or she pleases—although the survivor can spend any income generated by the property and has limited access the principal to pay for health care and support."

Elder Law

The increasingly popular term *elder law* may make you think that it's a new legal specialty. While there are lawyers who focus their practices on elderly clients, this area of everyday law mostly gathers together familiar legal issues of special importance to older people, among which are the following:

- → The legal rights of elderly patients to choose their own treatments when seriously ill or incapacitated
- → Estate planning
- → Guardianship law (the law that defines the roles and responsibilities of legal guardians—people who take on the job of guarding the financial interests and general well-being of an elderly person who can no longer make sound decisions)

I've covered the first two topics earlier in these pages; I'll complete this chapter by discussing the third.

Guardianship

We often describe parents as the guardians of their children. This means that a parent has the power and obligation to care for children, who are considered incapable by virtue of their youth of managing their own affairs. But the concept of guardianship does not depend on age: A court can appoint a guardian for an adult ward who can't look after his or her own interests. A fairly common example: A grown child files a guardianship action when a parent becomes incapable of caring for himself or herself.

Some states split guardianship into two areas:

1. *Guardian of the person*—This person oversees the well-being of the ward's physical person (including providing food, housing, clothing, and other necessities of life and making health-care decisions).

2. *Guardian of the property* (also called a *conservator*)—This person oversees the ward's property and financial assets.

Unless the ward has an usually large estate, a single, court-appointed guardian fulfills both roles, with the *full guardian* having all the powers and duties of a typical parent—although the guardian's ward is a legally incapable adult.

It is usually possible for an elderly person to eliminate the need for future guardianship by creating a *durable power of attorney for health care* (along with a *living will, see* Chapter 18) that empowers a trusted individual to make health-care decisions, and another *durable power of attorney* that transfers financial decision-making to the same (or other) responsible person.

Representative Payee

A legal guardian usually becomes the ward's *representative payee*—the party authorized by the Social Security Administration or the Department of Veteran Affairs to receive and manage public benefits on behalf of someone who is incapable of doing so. The representative payee collects the person's government benefits, manages them, and makes sure they are spent for the person's welfare.

An incapable person without a court-appointed guardian can be represented by any adult concerned with his or her welfare—a spouse, child, even a friend—or by an appropriate organization, such as a nursing home, homeless shelter, or nonprofit agency.

CHAPTER 20

PERSONAL BANKRUPTCY

C HARLES DICKENS CREATED A "HALE FELLOW WELL MET" CHARACTER named Wilkens Micawber for his novel *David Copperfield.* Micawber gave David a famous piece of advice:

Annual income twenty pounds, annual expenditure nineteen pounds nineteen and sixpence—result happiness. Annual income twenty pounds, annual expenditure twenty pounds and sixpence—result misery.

Micawber was apparently modeled after John Dickens, the author's father, who spent eight months in Marshalsea, the English debtor's prison known for its horrific treatment of inmates.

Although the framers of the U.S. Constitution did not outlaw debtor's prison, they did include a provision for federal bankruptcy laws. Article I, Section 8 gives Congress the power "to establish . . . uniform laws on the subject of bankruptcies throughout the United States."

Bankruptcy is a proceeding in a federal court, after which

→ an insolvent person's *estate* is largely liquidated and distributed to creditors, and most of his or her debts are *discharged* (the debtor is relieved of further liability) *or* . . .

→ the person begins the scheduled repayment of some restructured debts without giving up most of his or her assets.

Bankruptcy has become an essential aspect of everyday law—a means for people to get out from under impossible-to-repay debt. Today, federal and state laws ban the kind of debtor's prisons that are sometimes labeled as *Dickensian* (a few state constitutions specifically forbid debtor's prison), but Americans are routinely imprisoned for fraudulent debts and for failure to pay child-support debts, alimony debts, tax debts, and court-imposed fines.

Historically, there are a few recurring reasons why people run into money problems severe enough to drive them to bankruptcy:

→ The long-term loss of a job (often during a severe economic downturn)

→ Excessive credit card debt

→ A catastrophic illness leading to massive medical expenses that exceed (or are not covered by) health insurance

→ Out-of-control gambling or other personal problems

→ Other severe financial setbacks—a natural disaster (for example, a hurricane or tornado), the failure of a small business, a costly divorce, an expensive lawsuit and/or a large adverse money judgment, or (as many recently experienced) the loss of savings because of financial institution fraud

Unhappily, these things often occur together and pile on a hopelessly crushing financial burden that only bankruptcy can remove.

Imagine the Worst

For the rest of this chapter, think of yourself as someone who has the following profile:

→ Just lost a well-paying job and has few prospects of finding another that pays as well

→ Owns a large house with an equally large mortgage—and no equity because house prices have plummeted in your neighborhood

→ Has several "maxed out" credit cards and can't send more than the minimum payment each month (if that!)

→ Used a store credit plan to acquire a pricey home theater setup (big-screen TV, sound system, reclining seats) two months before you lost your job

→ Has a large student loan (you used the proceeds to earn an MBA five years ago)

→ Is responsible for monthly child-support payments

→ Owes the IRS money for last-year's taxes

→ Recently learned that your old health insurer has refused to pay a hefty medical bill that you thought would be covered in full

→ Has been threatened with mortgage foreclosure and has lost count of harassing letters and calls from collection agencies

→ Has absolutely no way to significantly reduce your mountain of debt in the foreseeable future

Alternatives to Bankruptcy

You might have been able to deal with one or two of your financial setbacks, but together they are simply too overwhelming to handle. But, before you thought seriously about bankruptcy, you tried alternative ways to reduce your debt. For example, you did the following:

- → Negotiated with your creditors in an attempt to reduce your monthly payments (but the reductions they offered weren't enough to make a real difference each month)

- → Found a personal financial manager who will keep you on a tight budget until your finances are back in order (although the imposed financial discipline eliminated new spending, it won't make much of a dent in your existing debt for several years)

- → Talked to a nonprofit credit counseling group (alas, your debts are so large that they couldn't propose a solution)

- → Looked into a debt consolidation loan (unfortunately, your sorry credit rating and lack of any equity in your house discouraged potential lenders)

You've come to the conclusion that you need a fresh start. And so, you swallow hard, ignore the stigma of bankruptcy that you perceive in your own mind, and file a bankruptcy proceeding in federal bankruptcy court.

Actually, the word *court* is misleading. Most of the bankruptcy process that a typical debtor sees is administrative rather than judicial. It is overseen by a *trustee*, who operates in an office, not a courtroom. In fact, many debtors never appear in court at all. (A bankruptcy trustee is often a local private attorney, who's appointed by the local bankruptcy court.)

FEDERAL BANKRUPTCY LAW VS. STATE BANKRUPTCY LAW

Bankruptcy proceedings take place within the federal court structure and are governed by federal laws that have two goals: achieve the fairest possible outcome for creditors (by allowing them to recoup at least part of the money they're owed) and give an overwhelmed debtor a fresh start. State bankruptcy laws play an important role in determining what—and how much—property is *exempt* from distribution to creditors. Consequently, where an individual lives can make a significance difference in the impact of bankruptcy—and can even sway the decision to file for bankruptcy.

You almost certainty reached the decision to seek bankruptcy *voluntarily*—as do the great majority of other people who file for personal bankruptcy. (It's possible for creditors to force an individual into personal bankruptcy, although *involuntary personal bankruptcy* is somewhat unusual because the process is complex and creditors can face significant penalties if the court decides that the creditors acted in bad faith when they tried to drive the creditor into bankruptcy.)

Should You Do It Yourself?

You can download all of the forms required to file for bankruptcy from the U.S. Courts website: www.uscourts.gov/bkforms. And, there are many *bankruptcy kits* and other do-it-yourself bankruptcy resources available on the Internet. All of these resources prompt the obvious question: Do you really need an attorney to shepherd you through the proceeding? Well . . . once you check out the forms and instructions on the U.S. Court website, you'll probably conclude that you need the guidance of an experienced lawyer—especially if you have a complicated debt situation and own a typical amount of personal property.

Another consideration is that bankruptcy law drags in many other fields of everyday law. To do a bankruptcy well, an attorney needs to deal with bankruptcy law and procedure—and also aspects of contract law, real estate law, divorce law, tax law, even criminal law at times.

I said "probably conclude" above because some debtors are able to navigate the complexities and manage their own bankruptcies. However, it's probably also true that some do-it-yourselfers didn't take full advantage of the protections available under the law—and ended up wasting more money than they saved by not finding an experienced lawyer.

Mandatory Credit Counseling and Debtor Education

Within 180 days before you file for bankruptcy, you must complete a *pre-bankruptcy counseling session* with a nonprofit budget and credit counseling agency that's been approved by your local bankruptcy court. This will probably last sixty to ninety minutes and can be done in person, online, or over the telephone. Here's what the session will include:

→ Review and evaluation of your financial situation
→ Discussion of the alternatives to bankruptcy
→ Creation of a personal budget plan

The nominal counseling fee ($50–$75) will be waived if you can't afford to pay. At the end of the session, the counseling organization will issue a certificate of completion that you will submit when you file your bankruptcy petition. (Most organizations can provide more extensive credit counseling, but one session is all that's required by the bankruptcy code.)

When your bankruptcy proceedings are moving ahead, you are required to take a *debtor education course,* also from a court-approved provider. This will be a longer session—typically about two hours—and will probably cost more than mandatory credit counseling (you can request a fee waiver, if necessary). The course is designed to teach the debtor how to develop a budget, manage money more effectively, use credit wisely, and employ other financial management resources. This course can also be done in person, online, or over the telephone. The bankruptcy trustee can't discharge your debts until you submit a certificate of completion.

Bankruptcy: The "Nuclear Option"

Many bankruptcy attorneys call their specialty "the Nuclear Option"—a step to be taken only when all other means of escaping crushing debt are gone. This is because most debtors find going through bankruptcy a wrenching experience—and the fact that bankruptcy may adversely impact their lives for the next ten or twelve years.

You know that your bankruptcy will be reported on your credit report (*see* below), making it likely that banks and stores will deny you credit or charge much higher interest rates. Moreover, as a bankrupt debtor, you may find it difficult to lease an apartment, arrange a car loan, obtain a mortgage for a house, and maybe even land a new job. Although job discrimination against a bankrupt job seeker is illegal (*see* below), it's difficult to prove, and the plaintiff has to pay his or her own attorney fees, often making a lawsuit impractical.

Despite these harsh realities, bankruptcy is often the best—and most realistic—alternative for a debtor who faces the kind of grim scenario I outlined above. As the U.S. Supreme Court wrote in *Local Loan Company v. Hunt,* a 1934 decision, "It [bankruptcy] gives to the honest but unfortunate debtor . . . a new opportunity in life and a clear field for future effort, unhampered by the pressure and discouragement of preexisting debt."

Automatic Stay of Creditor Collection Efforts

Speaking of being "unhampered by the pressure of preexisting debt" . . . more than one debtor who has filed for bankruptcy finds that the single most important benefit is the temporary automatic stay of collection efforts. These include:

→ Phone calls and letters from collection agencies

→ Foreclosure proceedings

→ Evictions

→ Attempts to repossess cars and other personal possessions

> → Garnishment of wages

> → *Attachments* (or levies) of bank accounts

> → Utility shutoffs

> → New and ongoing lawsuits begun by creditors

The automatic stay leaps into action at the moment the bankruptcy petition is filed with the bankruptcy court—and lasts as long as the bankruptcy case is pending. Creditors sometimes seek relief from automatic stays before the bankruptcy proceedings are completed. Two common examples: A finance company may want to retrieve a car in the debtor's possession before it suffers additional depreciation, and a bank wants to foreclose on a mortgage now rather than later.

However, the automatic stay doesn't stop government actions to collect taxes, demands for alimony or child support, and divorce actions (although the divorce court will not be able to divide *marital property* (*see* Chapter 6) without the permission of the bankruptcy court).

Two "Chapters" of Personal Bankruptcy

Title 11 of the United States Code is the body of federal law that covers bankruptcy. The title includes provisions for several different kinds of bankruptcy proceedings—each in a separate chapter. Not surprisingly, each proceeding is commonly referred to by its corresponding chapter. Two of them are commonly used in personal bankruptcies:

1. *Chapter 7—straight bankruptcy*—distributes an individual's (or married couple's) *nonexempt assets* (*see* below) to creditors and discharges most of the debtor's debts.

2. *Chapter 13—reorganization* or *wage-earner bankruptcy*—allows a debtor with a regular source of income to repay some of his or her debt over a period of three to five years. A Chapter 13 debtor keeps most personal property—and collateral on which the debtor can make the usual payments.

Both chapters have advantages and disadvantages to debtors and creditors—along with specific regulations that define when each can be used. But, a debtor typically chooses Chapter 7 when he or she

> → has little or no hope of repaying debts;

> → has debts without co-signers (a debtor's Chapter 7 bankruptcy doesn't relieve a co-signer's responsibility);

→ owns personal property that is *exempt* (beyond the reach of the bankruptcy trustee, *see* below);

→ doesn't qualify for Chapter 13.

By contrast, a debtor may choose Chapter 13 when he or she

→ will earn an adequate income in the years ahead, but needs breathing room to get a handle on excessive debt;

→ is seriously behind on home mortgage payments—or owes a large amount of money for back taxes—and needs a respite from other payments to catch up;

→ owns significant nonexempt assets that will probably be liquidated under Chapter 7 (*see* below);

→ has debts with co-signers (the *Automatic Stay* under Chapter 13 prevents creditors from seeking to collect a *consumer debt* from any party who is liable along with the debtor);

→ has a strong personal feeling against walking away from debt;

→ doesn't qualify for Chapter 7.

Chapter 7 Bankruptcy

A Chapter 7 bankruptcy is the classic "wipe the slate clean" proceeding for a person with few assets and comparatively high debt. In a Chapter 7 bankruptcy, the trustee takes over the debtor's *nonexempt assets* (*see* below), typically sells them for cash, then distributes the proceeds to the unsecured creditors, who may only receive a few cents on the dollar in repayment. The debtor then receives a discharge, relieving him or her from liability for these debts. Any wages the debtor subsequently earns are beyond the reach of former creditors.

Chapter 7 bankruptcy is fast and relatively simple for most debtors. In fact, most Chapter 7 cases involving individual debtors are *no asset cases*. This means that the bankrupt debtors have no nonexempt property to surrender to the trustee.

Chapter 7 Abuse and the Means Test

Over the years, many creditors argued that Chapter 7 invited bankruptcy abuse because a complete discharge made it too easy for debtors to walk away from their obligations. A new bankruptcy law passed in 2005 tightened up the rules and established a *means test* for Chapter 7 eligibility. Simply put, if a debtor has sufficient resources to make minimal payments to creditors, he or she is required to seek a Chapter 13 bankruptcy plan.

The means test is fairly strict. The first factor is whether or not the debtor's "current monthly income" is lower than the *state median income* (half of the workers in the state earn less than the median income; half earn more). If so, the debtor can file for a Chapter 7 bankruptcy. If his or her income is higher than the median, the bankruptcy trustee will perform a complex calculation involving the debtor's "aggregate current monthly income over 5 years," a list of statutorily allowed expenses, and his or her unsecured debt. If the debtor's "disposable income" is above $186 per month, his or her Chapter 7 petition is converted to Chapter 13 with the debtor's permission, or will be dismissed. The bottom line: These days, many debtors who might have chosen Chapter 7 bankruptcy must repay a portion of their debts as part of a three-to-five-year-long repayment plan.

Debts Discharged in a Chapter 7 Bankruptcy

Once again, imagine yourself in the position of the hypothetical debtor I described above. The grim last statement on the list—you have "absolutely no way to significantly reduce your mountain of debt in the foreseeable future"— makes you a likely candidate for Chapter 7 bankruptcy.

Not *all* your unsecured debts will be discharged after a Chapter 7 bankruptcy. Broadly speaking, you'll have no further liability for credit card debt, unsecured personal loans, most auto accident claims and other claims of negligence, unpaid medical bills, civil or private judgments, personal loans from family and friends, and residential and automotive leases. However, you will still be responsible *after* bankruptcy for any of the following:

→ Unpaid taxes

→ Government-imposed fines and/or penalties

→ Student loans

→ Spousal support (alimony) and child support

→ Auto accident claims involving driving while intoxicated

→ Claims and judgments involving "willful and malicious" legal wrongs

→ *Luxury goods* worth more than $1,000 that you purchased within sixty days of filing a petition for bankruptcy

→ Cash advances of more than $1,000 that you withdrew within sixty days of filing a petition for bankruptcy

These last two items are designed to prevent a debtor from "maxing out" a credit card knowing that he or she is likely to file for bankruptcy.

Another important detail: If you have secured loans—a home mortgage, a car loan, a secured home-furnishings loan—you won't be liable after discharge for unmade payments up to the date that bankruptcy was filed. However, the secured creditor retains the right to repossess or foreclose upon those assets unless you bring the accounts up to date (by making those past payments) and keeping the accounts current in the future.

You may choose to *reaffirm* certain secured loans. This means that you remain liable for each reaffirmed loan and agree to keep making payments despite filing for bankruptcy. Reaffirmation can make financial sense when an asset pledged as collateral for a loan is worth significantly more than the outstanding balance of the loan, or if you have an especially low interest rate on a home mortgage. You have to reaffirm a secured loan within forty-five days of a key bankruptcy milestone: the *341 Meeting* with creditors (*see* below).

Exempt Property in a Chapter 7 Bankruptcy

Although your creditors would like all your property to be up for grabs during a Chapter 7 bankruptcy proceeding, much of it is exempt. The list of exempt property is different in every state but typically includes the following:

→ Social security payments

→ Pensions and retirement accounts

→ College savings plans

→ Alimony and child support

→ Life insurance policies

→ Tools and equipment necessary for employment (up to a statutory value)

→ Personal jewelry (up to a statutory value)

→ The equity in vehicles (up to a statutory value)

→ Household goods and other personal property (up to a statutory value)

Each item of exempt property is assigned the dollar value it would have if sold during the bankruptcy proceeding—a value typically much less than the original purchase price. Moreover, the statutory value limits are usually doubled if a husband and wife file a joint petition in bankruptcy. For both of these reasons, most debtors who file for Chapter 7 bankruptcy keep virtually all of their personal property.

A Common Question: Can I Keep My House?

I have to answer this question by first asking a question: Do you own your house? In the hypothetical scenario I outlined above, the debtor (you) lives in a heavily mortgaged house—it's likely that you will lose possession (when the mortgage holder forecloses on the loan), unless you can catch up on past missed payments and begin to make timely payments in the future.

The outcome *may* be different—you may retain possession after a Chapter 7 bankruptcy—if your house is not mortgaged. This can happen, for example, when an individual who has paid off the mortgage suddenly faces catastrophic medical expenses or has allowed his or her credit card purchases to spiral out of control.

Whether or not a house will be sold to satisfy creditor claims as part of a Chapter 7 proceeding depends on the specific *homestead exemption* that the bankruptcy trustee applies. The Chapter 7 debtor will keep the home if the homestead exemption is greater than his or her equity in the house. This sounds simple, but it can be remarkably complex because homestead exemptions vary *enormously* from state to state—from several thousand dollars all the way up to virtually unlimited—and are subject to various federal time-period regulations. This is one area where most debtors need the guidance of an experienced bankruptcy attorney.

Chapter 7 Collateral Redemption

Chapter 7 bankruptcy offers petitioners the opportunity to *redeem* property used as collateral for a secured loan—typically a family car and other vehicles—at the fair market value (*retail value*). This most often happens with cars, when the outstanding balance on a car loan is more than the car is actually worth.

As an example, imagine that the current retail value of your car is $10,000, but the *payoff value* on your secured car loan is $18,000. You can petition the bankruptcy court to authorize a redemption, which will require the loan company to release its lien on the car (give you unencumbered ownership) for a lump-sum payment of $10,000—a significant savings compared to the total of remaining monthly payments.

I can hear the gears in your mind turning: Where do *you*, a debtor filing a Chapter 7 bankruptcy, get $10,000 for the lump-sum payment? In fact, there are finance companies that specialize in making redemption loans. Also, you may be able to borrow money from an exempt asset, such as a retirement account.

Creditors typically prefer that you reaffirm debts and may challenge your efforts to redeem assets.

Chapter 13 Bankruptcy

These are the two most important differences of Chapter 13 bankruptcy for you as a debtor:

1. You don't surrender your nonexempt property to the trustee— rather, you retain possession of all your property. (Of course, your home mortgage can be foreclosed—and collateral, such as a car, can be repossessed by creditors—if you can't keep up the monthly payments.)

2. In exchange, you agree to make scheduled partial repayments of unsecured debt—and catch up on the missed payments of secured loans—according to a court-approved repayment plan (the remaining unsecured debt is discharged when you complete the plan).

In essence, a Chapter 13 repayment plan is an arrangement that enables you to pay your creditors as much as you can.

You'll pay some debts completely—but over a longer period of time, with smaller monthly payments. You'll pay some debts partially—the sum of your monthly payments called for by the plan will be less than the total you owe.

The length of your repayment commitment depends on your financial resources. If you earn less than your state's median monthly income, you'll usually be required to make payments for three years. If your monthly income is higher, you'll be required to make payments for five years. No Chapter 13 repayment plans span more than five years. During this period, creditors are barred from starting or continuing collection efforts.

When you complete the repayment plan—make all the promised payments during the repayment period—the bankruptcy court will release you from all debts covered by the plan. This means that creditors must be satisfied with the partial payments they received. On the other hand, if you fail to make the required payments, the court will not discharge your debts, leaving creditors free to begin new legal actions to collect them.

As advocates of restructuring often point out, the discharge under Chapter 13 is slightly broader than a Chapter 7 discharge. Specifically, loans used to pay tax obligations, and debts arising from property settlements in divorces or separations, will be discharged by the court.

All Disposable Income

The bankruptcy court will expect you to commit all of your *disposable income* during the plan period. This is income above and beyond what is *reasonably necessary* for the support of you and your dependents. Simply put, most Chapter 13 debtors live on exceedingly tight budgets.

Federal law establishes limits on the amounts of secured and unsecured debt a debtor can hold to be eligible for Chapter 13 bankruptcy. The numbers are large enough to include the great majority of debtors who seek protection under Chapter 13. The limits change from time to time; you can find the current numbers by visiting www.uscourts.gov/bankruptcycourts/bankruptcybasics/chapter13.html

You propose the repayment plan; the bankruptcy trustee (and later the bankruptcy judge) will review your proposed plan to ensure that it's feasible, was made in good faith, and repays creditors to the maximum extent possible. Among the factors they will consider are these:

→ How much of each debt you intend to repay

→ Your recent employment history

→ Your earning capacity in the years ahead—including whether you will have stable earnings that will provide disposable income

→ Whether your plan adequately reflects factors that may impact your financial situation (such as age or health-related problems)

→ Your honesty and sincerity in your filings and at hearings

Your proposed repayment plan usually must provide for the full payment of so-called priority claims. These are liabilities that have special status under bankruptcy law:

→ Unpaid taxes

→ The costs of the bankruptcy proceeding, including attorney's fees

→ Missed mortgage payments

→ Missed car payments

→ Unpaid alimony and child support

Unhappy creditors sometimes challenge a proposed repayment plan, arguing that they will receive less money than if your nonexempt assets were liquidated and that your repayment plan failed to commit all of your projected disposable income to debt repayment. Ultimately, the bankruptcy court will decide if your plan is reasonable given your specific financial circumstances.

Once your repayment plan is confirmed by the bankruptcy judge, the Chapter 13 trustee will distribute money according to the plan. Most debtors send a monthly payment check to the trustee; in some cases, the debtor's employer will forward the appropriate portion of the debtor's monthly pay directly to the trustee.

As you can imagine, circumstances can change during a five-year-long plan period. It's not unusual for debtors to find themselves unable to make the required monthly payments. A debtor typically has two options:

1. Ask the bankruptcy court to approve a modified repayment plan.

2. File for Chapter 7 bankruptcy.

However, a Chapter 13 debtor isn't allowed to create his or her own adverse circumstances. A debtor can't take on any new debt that may impact his or her ability to make regular payments without the trustee's permission.

Chapter 13 "Cramdown"

Cramdown in Chapter 13 is the cousin of Chapter 7 *redemption*—a procedure that allows a secured debt (typically, automobile loans) to be reduced to reflect true retail value of the collateral used to secure the loan. However, Chapter 13 doesn't require *you*, the debtor, to pay a lump sum. Instead you can include monthly payments as part of the three- or five-year repayment plan.

However, Chapter 13 cramdowns can only be done to cars purchased more than two and a half years before filing a petition and to other kinds of personal property purchased more than one year before filing. Currently, home mortgages can't be crammed down.

Comparing Chapter 7 and Chapter 13

The chief advantage of Chapter 7 compared to Chapter 13 is that the process is over—your debts are discharged—in a few months at most. You get a fresh start and need have no further dealings with the bankruptcy trustee.

The chief advantage of Chapter 13 compared to Chapter 7 is that you will keep more of your personal property, can restructure secured debts (other than a mortgage) by extending them over the three- to five-year period, and can repay missed mortgage payments slowly. Consequently, a well thought out repayment plan can help save your house from foreclosure.

Another difference worth noting is that a Chapter 13 bankruptcy will taint your credit longer than a Chapter 7 bankruptcy. This is because the fact that you filed for a Chapter 7 bankruptcy will typically be noted on your credit report for at least *ten years* after the *last action* in the bankruptcy proceeding, while your filing for a Chapter 13 bankruptcy will be reported for seven years after the last action. Consequently, a Chapter 7 bankruptcy will be around for ten years plus several months (the time between filing and debt discharge). But, a Chapter 13 bankruptcy will linger for seven years plus the three to five years of repayments for a maximum of twelve years.

Which method is better? I'll let you decide.

Other Things Worth Knowing about Bankruptcy

A Single or a Joint Petition?

Married couples are frequently uncertain if one spouse should file a single petition in bankruptcy or the two spouses should file a joint petition. The answer is to choose the approach that erases the most debt and leaves the couple in possession of the most property after the bankruptcy. This strategy is easy to talk about but hard to achieve. The decision can be sufficiently complex that it may require an attorney's advice. Here are a few considerations:

→ If the couple has amassed joint debts (as most couples do), a single petition will leave the nonbankrupt spouse liable for his or her share (typically half)—and open to harassment and legal action from creditors. In this situation it often makes sense to file a joint petition.

→ Husband and wife still remain separate debtors for their nonmarital debts, even though thei: *estate* is treated as one entity. This creates two-for-one pricing in bankruptcy court: A joint petition costs half as much as two separate filings.

→ One spouse may have considerable *separate property* (*see* Chapter 5), perhaps a recent inheritance or family heirlooms acquired before marriage. In this situation it may make sense for the other spouse to file a single petition—especially if there's not a lot of marital debt.

→ In a *community property state* (*see* Chapter 6), the bankrupt spouse's *estate* includes his or her separate property and *all* of the couple's marital property. All of the nonexempt property may be taken by a bankruptcy trustee and sold to repay creditors. Filing a joint Chapter 7 petition may double the exempt property limits and let the couple keep more of their marital property.

→ In some *equitable property distribution states* (*see* Chapter 6), certain jointly held marital property—notably a house owned as *tenants by the entirety* (*see* Chapter 9)—is excluded from a single petitioner's Chapter 7 bankruptcy estate. Here, a single petition may keep the house off the auction block.

→ Many bankruptcies are triggered by debts incurred by one spouse before (and sometimes after) marriage. In this event, a single Chapter 7 petition may be more appropriate than a joint petition.

→ The bankruptcy trustee will look at total household income—the combined income of both spouses—even if only one spouse files a Chapter 13 petition.

→ If a marriage seems to be headed for a divorce, a joint bankruptcy filing may not be appropriate.

Filing for Bankruptcy a Second (or Third) Time

Some debtors amass new liabilities after their debts are discharged—and have to file for bankruptcy again . . . and (occasionally) again. Legally speaking, you can have many bites at the bankruptcy apple, but there are statutory time limits as to how often debts can be discharged. The periods depend on the kinds of bankruptcies involved:

→ Eight years must pass between *filing for* a Chapter 7 discharge and *filing for* another Chapter 7 discharge.

→ Four years must pass between *filing for* a Chapter 7 discharge and *filing for* a subsequent Chapter 13 reorganization.

→ Two years must pass between *filing for* a Chapter 13 reorganization and *filing for* another Chapter 13 reorganization.

→ Six years must pass between *filing for* a Chapter 13 discharge and *filing for* a subsequent Chapter 7 reorganization.

I've emphasized "filing for" because the time periods are measured between the original and subsequent petition filing dates.

Your 341 Creditors Meeting

An important procedural formality after you file either a Chapter 7 or Chapter 13 bankruptcy petition is the *341 creditors meeting*. It's usually scheduled three to five weeks after you file your petition. This meeting is required by Section 341 of the federal bankruptcy code, hence its everyday name. You are required to attend, but few if any of your creditors are likely to actually show up.

Your 341 meeting will probably be over in a few minutes. There's no judge present, and it's not in any sense adversarial. The stated purpose of the meeting is fact-finding—an opportunity for creditors to ask questions about your assets (including your exempt property), your secured and unsecured debts, what factors drove you so deeply into debt that you need bankruptcy protection, and your proposed repayment plan (if it is a Chapter 13 proceeding).

After you are sworn to tell the truth, the trustee—the official who will conduct the meeting—will likely ask you questions on these same topics, and in addition will

→ verify your name, social security number, and home address;

→ make certain that you signed various bankruptcy submissions by yourself after you saw and read them;

→ ask if anything in your financial situation has changed since you filed your petition.

You (and your attorney, if you have one) are also free to ask questions in return. What you say will be tape-recorded and preserved for two years from the date of the meeting.

Fraudulent Property Transfers

One of the mistakes that some people contemplating bankruptcy make is to *protect* their most valuable assets—vehicles, boats, jewelry, even real estate—by transferring title to relatives or close friends prior to filing the petition. These "sales" are made for little or no money, with the expectation that the true owner will buy the assets back after the bankruptcy proceeding.

This strategy doesn't work, because every debtor must disclose asset transfers made within a year of filing for bankruptcy. (Some states have laws that bar transfers more than a year earlier.) The trustee can cancel transfers that did not yield the true value of the asset and recover the property for the bankruptcy estate.

This is the good news. The bad news is that a transfer made with the intention of concealing assets and defrauding creditors is illegal (a stiff federal offense) and is likely to stop the bankruptcy proceeding dead in its tracks.

Another no-no is called a *preference*. This is an attempt to protect a *friendly* creditor—say, a local small business—by paying off your debt a short time before you file for bankruptcy. The trustee also has tools to recover preferences so that all of your creditors are treated equally.

The point is . . . don't try to keep any debts or any assets out of your bankruptcy.

CHAPTER 21

EVERYDAY IMMIGRATION LAW

I MMIGRATION LAW—THE CORNER OF EVERYDAY LAW THAT FOCUSES ON gaining residence and citizenship within the United States—can be a dauntingly complex legal specialty. For example, there are *dozens* of different kinds of *visas* that give *immigrants* (people who want to live permanently in the United States) and *nonimmigrants* (people who are in the United States to study, for tourism, or for another time-limited purpose) the right to enter the United States. One federal court complained about "the labyrinthine character of modern immigration law—a maze of hyper-technical statutes and regulations." Another court described immigration law as "second in complexity only to the tax code."

As you'll see in this chapter, the fundamental principles are not difficult or abstract. Immigration law is a perfect illustration of the popular proverb: The devil is in the details.

It's still possible for a legal immigrant who holds a valid *Green Card* to apply for *naturalization* (U.S. citizenship) without the help of an attorney. But, because most other immigration issues involve complicated procedures, frequently changing regulations, and oft-time the risk of deportation (or criminal charges), anyone dealing with questions about immigrant status should be represented by an experienced lawyer.

THE NOT-SO "GREEN CARD"

The so-called Green Card, which goes by many names—*Form I-551,* the *Permanent Residence Card,* the *Alien Registration Receipt Card*—was once a green, laminated plastic card. Today's machine-readable I-551s aren't green—but the original nickname is so entrenched in the language of immigration that even government bureaucrats (and federal websites) talk about *Green Card*s.

The Case of the Innovative Immigrant

Myles Tugo is an exchange student from abroad who spent a summer in your home fifteen years ago. The last time you checked, Myles was happily living in his native country: Grosse Fenwick. But then—a few days ago—you received a telephone call from Myles. He surprised you by announcing that he has decided to relocate to the United States—preferably to a city not far from you in the State of Bliss—and eventually become a U.S. citizen.

Myles asks you to research the "whole immigration business." He explains that he has become a cuckoo clockwork guru. (Grosse Fenwick is one of the world's leading producers of cuckoo clocks!) He's earned a bachelor's and master's degree in clockwork engineering from the Royal Fenwick Institute of Technology, holds several patents in the field of alarm clock automation, is single, in good health, does not have a criminal record. You also note that he speaks flawless English.

You agree to help—and you begin your quest.

Immigration Law

A quick Internet search tells you that immigration is controlled by *federal law*— specifically the Immigration and Nationality Act (INA) that represents the basic body of U.S. immigration law—including the means by which *aliens* (*see* below) can gain permanent residence in the United States and eventually become *legally naturalized* citizens.

You also learn that the first step in the process of becoming a U.S. citizen is for an *alien* to become a *lawful permanent resident.* This is a person who is not a citizen of the United States, but who can reside permanently in the United States as a *legally recognized and lawfully recorded* immigrant. He or she may also be known as a *permanent resident alien,* a *resident alien permit holder,* and (to most of us) a *Green Card holder.*

Typically after five years as a lawful permanent resident (three years if the alien entered the United States as the spouse of a citizen), he or she can go through the naturalization process (*see* below) and become a naturalized citizen.

Immigration vs. Emigration

Although few people other than English teachers take offense when the words are misused, an *emigrant* leaves his or her country to move to another, while an *immigrant* enters another country to become a citizen (or permanent resident). Thus, Myles Tugo is an emigrant from Grosse Fenwick who will become an immigrant in the United States.

Confusion often reigns, because depending on context, Myles can be said to have emigrated (from Grosse Fenwick) *and* immigrated (to the United States). Incidentally, the similar sounding words are both rooted in the Latin *migrare,* "to migrate."

Who's in Charge of Immigration

You vaguely remember that a federal agency called the INS was the overseer of immigration law—including *visas* (*see* below) and naturalization. A bit more searching tells you that the Immigration and Naturalization Service—established early in the twentieth century—shut its doors in 2003, when managing immigration became one of the key responsibilities of the new Department of Homeland Security (DHS). Two DHS agencies (they were once called *bureaus*, but the label was dropped) handle the bulk of immigration-related matters:

> → *U.S. Citizenship and Immigration Services* (USCIS) is in charge of all aspects of *legal immigration* to the United States—everything from issuing visas to managing the naturalization process.

> → *U.S. Immigration and Customs Enforcement* (ICE) operates the *Office of Detention and Removal* (DRO), which identifies, apprehends, and removes illegal aliens, fugitive aliens, and criminal aliens from the United States.

Who Are You Calling an Alien?

The word *alien* sounds harsh to many people's ears, but from the standpoint of everyday immigration law, an alien is merely a person who is not a *citizen* or a *noncitizen national* of the United States.

A *citizen* is either born in the United States or born to U.S. citizens abroad, or else becomes a citizen through the *naturalization process. Noncitizen national* is a term that was used much more in the past; it refers to a person born in an *outlying possession of the United States* (for example, American Samoa). As the U.S. Department of State explains, a *national of the United States* is a person—a citizen or noncitizen—who owes permanent allegiance to the United States.

Aliens can be categorized four ways:

1. *Resident* and *nonresident*—those who live in the United States; and those who don't

2. *Immigrant* and *nonimmigrant*—those who reside in the United States permanently; and those who are here for a specific short-term purpose (for example, for a vacation or to attend college)

3. *Refugee* and *asylee*—those who fled from his/her home country to seek safe refuge in the United States; and those aliens who once in the United States (typically as nonimmigrants) declared themselves refugees and were granted *asylum* (the right to remain permanently in safety)

4. *Documented* and *undocumented*—those possessing documents that give them permission to enter and reside, at least temporarily, in the United States (for example, a passport from their own nation and a valid U.S. visa); and those who have entered the United States without permission as *illegal aliens*.

Most people who call themselves Americans are citizens *and* nationals. A *resident immigrant documented alien*—a label that would apply to someone who legally acquired a Green Card, lives in the United States, but hasn't become a naturalized citizen—is not yet a U.S. *national*. He or she is still a national of another country.

Visas

Broadly speaking, an alien citizen of a foreign country must acquire a visa before he or she can enter the country. The word *visa* comes from the Latin *visus*, "seen." The USCIS will issue an appropriate visa after examining an alien's documents and other particulars (for example, some visas require that health records and criminal records be checked)—all with an eye to verifying that he or she meets statutory and regulatory requirements to enter the country. There are dozens of different visas in two broad categories:

1. *Nonimmigrant visas*—These are granted for a temporary stay; for example: *B-1* (business travel), *B-2* (pleasure travel or medical treatment), *F-1* (students), *P-1* (athletes and members of entertainment groups), and *H-2A* (temporary or seasonal agricultural workers).

2. *Immigrant visas*—These are for permanent residents; for example: Green Card (Form 1-551 Lawful Permanent Resident Card), *IR-1* (spouse married to a citizen for more than two years), *CR-1* (spouse married to a citizen for less than two years; is conditional until two years pass), *K-1* (fiancée), *IR-3* (child adopted abroad; *see* Chapter 7).

The Visa Waiver Program for Visitors

The *Visa Waiver Program* enables nationals of certain countries to travel to the United States for tourism or business for stays of ninety days or less without obtaining a visa. These are countries that have machine-readable passports; that maintain high levels of counter-terrorism efforts, law enforcement, border control, and document security standards; and that share security-related data with the United States. U.S. citizens have reciprocal no-visa travel privileges in participating countries.

The list of participating countries changes from time to time; the last change occurred in 2010 when Greece was added to the list. The 36 countries in the program as of 2010 are Andorra, Australia, Austria, Belgium, Brunei, Czech Republic, Denmark, Estonia, Finland, France, Germany, Greece, Hungary, Iceland, Ireland, Italy, Japan, Latvia, Liechtenstein, Lithuania, Luxembourg, Malta, Monaco, New Zealand, Norway, Portugal, San Marino, Singapore, Slovakia, Slovenia, South Korea, Spain, Sweden, Switzerland, The Netherlands, and United Kingdom.

Canada and Bermuda are not participating countries, but are covered by the Western Hemisphere Travel Initiative. Most travelers from these countries don't require a visa. Travelers from Mexico must have a nonimmigrant visa or Form DSP-150 Border Crossing Card (also known as a *laser visa*).

Getting Myles His Green Card

During your next telephone chat with Myles, he says, "Obviously, the next thing I need to know is, how does a Fenwickian like me get a Green Card?"

"I anticipated your question," you say, with a chuckle. "There are five chief paths that lead to the issuance of an immigrant visa for foreign nationals:

1. Sponsorship by a relative who is a U.S. citizen or lawful permanent resident
2. By virtue of the foreign national's occupational skills and qualifications, or through sponsorship by a U.S.-based employer
3. Winning a Green Card in the annual *diversity visa lottery*
4. Making a significant investment in the United States
5. Having refugee status or by gaining asylum

"As you'd expect, sponsorship by family members accounts for the majority of Green Cards issued each year—more than 60 percent. Employment-related immigration comes next—roughly 16 percent."

Sponsorship by a Relative

U.S. immigration law favors the reunion of families. Consequently, a U.S. citizen can petition for the issuance of a Green Card to any *immediate relative*—the sponsor's spouse, parents, or unmarried children under age twenty-one. (For purposes of immigration law, a valid marriage is a marriage between a man and a woman for which authorities have issued a civil marriage certificate.)

Visas for immediate relatives are immediately available; there's no limit to the annual number that can be issued each year.

A U.S. citizen's other close relatives—brothers and sisters, children over age twenty-one, or younger married children—are considered *preference-category relatives* rather than immediate relatives. A limited number of Green Cards are issued each year to preference-category foreign nationals; the waiting list can be upwards of eight to ten years long.

A lawful permanent resident—the holder of a Green Card—can also petition for immigrant visas for his or her spouse and unmarried children. However, all the relatives of an immigrant not yet a naturalized citizen are considered *preference-category relatives*—and typically have to wait several years for their Green Cards. Note that unlike a citizen, a Green Card holder can't request an immigrant visa for a married child.

Whenever a U.S. citizen or Green Card holder sponsors a foreign national, the sponsor must file an *affidavit of support* that demonstrates sufficient income to support the new immigrant until he or she has become self-supporting—which is defined as having paid forty qualifying quarters into the Social Security System. The required support must reach or exceed 125 percent of the U.S. poverty level. This is a ten-year support commitment at a minimum, and it's enforceable by a court. If the sponsor doesn't have sufficient income to make such a commitment, a co-sponsor must also file an affidavit of support.

Sham Marriages to U.S. Citizens

It's the stuff of movies and novels—a foreign national eager to acquire a Green Card enters a sham marriage with a U.S. citizen and quickly becomes a lawful permanent resident. The USCIS also knows the plot—studies show that as many as 30 percent of spousal petitions for Green Cards may be based on sham marriages. Consequently, USCIS typically requires the newly married couple to provide extensive evidence that their relationship is genuine and may conduct rigorous interviews of foreign-national spouses.

Moreover, when a Green Card is issued less than two years after the couple marries, the immigrant is considered a *conditional resident.* His or her Green Card expires automatically two years after it is issued, unless the couple files a joint petition to remove the conditional status and make the Green Card permanent.

If USCIS discovers that the parties entered a sham marriage to commit immigration fraud

- → both parties can be charged with committing a federal crime;
- → the foreign-national spouse will be deported;
- → the foreign national is permanently barred from obtaining a valid Green Card.

Nonetheless, marriage (real or not) to an American is one of the few ways an illegal alien—usually an individual who has overstayed a student or tourist visa—can acquire a Green Card. (Illegal aliens are typically deported and banned from entry into the United States for ten years.) Many of the reasons a person might be ineligible for an immigrant visa (*see* below) can be waived for spouses—for example, long periods of illegal presence in the United States—making sham marriages especially attractive for individuals trying to circumvent immigration law.

Employment-Related Green Cards

U.S. immigration law sets aside 140,000 Green Card "slots" each year that enables foreign nationals to petition for permanent residence status based on the work they will do when living in the Unites States. The petition for the foreign national also includes his or her spouse and children. The lion's share of employment-based petitions for Green Cards is filed on behalf of foreign nationals by U.S. employers.

USCIS divides employment-based immigrant petitions into four preference groups:

1. Priority workers whose *extraordinary abilities* have led to significant accomplishments and recognition:

    - Foreign nationals of extraordinary ability in the sciences, arts, education, business or athletics
    - Foreign nationals who are outstanding professors or researchers
    - Foreign nationals who are managers and executives subject to international transfer to the United States

2. Professionals with *exceptional ability* in the sciences, arts, or business who will substantially benefit the national economy, cultural, or educational interests or welfare of the United States

    - Foreign nationals of exceptional ability in the sciences, arts or business
    - Foreign nationals who are advanced-degree professionals
    - Qualified physicians who will practice medicine in an underserved area of the United States

3. Skilled or professional workers

    - Foreign national professionals with bachelor's degrees (not qualifying for a higher-preference category)
    - Foreign national skilled workers (minimum two years training and experience)
    - Foreign national unskilled workers who can perform labor for which qualified workers are not available in the United States

4. Special immigrants

- Employees and former employees of the U.S.
  government abroad
- Foreign nationals who are members of a religious
  denomination that has a nonprofit religious organization in the
  United States, and who will be working in a religious vocation
  or occupation at the request of the religious organization

The categories are further divided into *set percentages* (to use USCIS's term) for different countries. This has created an especially long backlog of petitions from countries that send many emigrants to the United States (India, for example) in the *skilled or professional workers* category—sometimes upwards of four to seven years.

Green-Card Lottery

The *Diversity Visa Program*—popularly called the *Green Card lottery*—makes available 50,000 immigrant visas every year to foreign nationals from countries with low rates of emigration to the United States. The program is managed by the U.S. Department of State rather than USCIS. Each year, 50,000 winners are randomly selected from upwards of 10 million applicants.

Low-emigration countries have sent fewer than 50,000 of their nationals to the United States during the previous five years under other immigration programs. The list of allowable countries changes from year to year, but the nationals from the following countries are rarely eligible to enter the diversity lottery. Brazil, Canada, China, Columbia, Haiti, India, Mexico, Pakistan, Philippines, Poland, South Korea, United Kingdom (except Northern Ireland), and Vietnam.

To actually receive a Green Card, foreign nationals chosen in the random drawing must meet all immigration eligibility requirements (*see* below). Winners are authorized to live and work permanently in the United States and also to bring their spouses and any unmarried children under the age of twenty-one.

Although it's not necessary to be sponsored by a U.S. employer or supported by a relative, lottery winners must provide evidence that they will not become *public charges* in the United States. This is typically done by showing that they will be able to find a job because of their education and/or work experience. The requirements are modest: a high school education (or its equivalent) or two years of work experience within the past five years in an occupation requiring at least two years of training or experience to perform.

Another Path to a Green Card: Investment

There's actually a fifth employment-based preference immigrant visa category. USCIS will issue a Green Card to a foreign-national investor or entrepreneur who creates (or helps to grow) a commercial enterprise that benefits the U.S. economy. These are the requirements:

→ Establish a new commercial enterprise or invest in an existing business that was created or restructured after November 19, 1990.

→ Invest $1 million ($500,000 for investments made in a targeted employment area) in the United States.

→ Use money that came from a *lawful source of funds.*

→ Participate actively in the business.

→ Create full-time employment for at least ten U.S. workers.

Some critics have called the process *buying a Green Card,* but advocates claim that meeting the requirements are sufficiently difficult that only a small fraction of the 10,000 immigration visas available each year under the program are actually issued—and those go to genuine investors and entrepreneurs.

Refugees and Asylum Seekers

A *refugee* is a person living outside his or her native country who is unable or unwilling to return because of well-founded fear of persecution on account of

→ race;

→ religion;

→ nationality;

→ membership in a particular social group;

→ political opinion.

A refugee living abroad can apply for refugee status in the United States. If granted, the refugee will be brought to the United States for *resettlement and integration* into the country. The United States denies requests for refugee admission from the following individuals:

→ Those who are *firmly resettled* in another country (that is, have received an offer of citizenship, permanent residency, or some other permanent status from a foreign country)

→ Foreign citizens who have become disillusioned with their homeland and seek to take temporary refuge within the United States

An individual present inside the United States—typically a person who entered as a tourist, a student, or a businessperson—who fears returning to his or her homeland for the reasons listed above can apply for asylum within one year of arriving in the United States. An *asylee* has the same status as a refugee and can resettle in the United States.

A person in the United States who has been a refugee or an asylee for at least one year can apply for a Green Card and have his or her status changed to *lawful permanent resident*.

Persons Not Allowed to Enter the United States or Immigrate

The U.S. Code (specifically, Title 8, Chapter 12, Subchapter II, Part II, Section 1182) is a long block of complex text that lists innumerable reasons why aliens may be ineligible for visas or admission. (This statute is also known as Section 212 of the Immigration and Naturalization Act.) Many ineligibilities are permanent; others are lifted after a period of years has passed; some can be waived if the individual (or his or her sponsor) files an appropriate petition. Here are a few:

- → Health-related grounds (including drug addiction, having HIV/AIDS or another serious communicable disease, having a serious mental disorder, and not providing proof of vaccinations)

- → Crime-related grounds (including espionage, terrorism, drug trafficking, child abduction, aggravated felonies, and crimes involving moral turpitude)

- → Submitting fraudulent documents to immigration authorities

- → Overstaying a previous visa

- → Coming to the United States to practice polygamy

- → Advocating the overthrow of the U.S. government

- → Being unlawfully present in the United States for six months or more

- → Being previously removed (deported) from the United States

- → Being an *alien smuggler* (any noncitizen who helps or encourages another noncitizen to try to cross the border illegally)

- → Using fraudulent means to obtain a visa or admission to the United States, including marriage fraud

- → Being a stowaway to the United States

- → Being likely to become a public charge

REMOVAL (DEPORTATION)

Removal—once called *deportation*—is the expulsion of a noncitizen from the United States after he or she violates immigration or criminal laws. Most of the reasons for inadmissibility can be grounds for removal of a foreign national— even a Green Card holder—if the acts are performed after the foreign national is in the United States. Removal is managed by U.S. Immigration and Customs Enforcement.

Removal proceedings take place before an immigration judge. Aliens have the right to legal representation (but not an attorney paid for by the government), the right to notice of the charges against him or her, the right to examine the evidence against him or her, the right to cross-examine government witnesses, and the right to appeal.

Rights of Lawful Permanent Residents

The U.S. Supreme Court has recognized the power of the federal government (as a matter of national sovereignty) to set immigration policy—and its related power to exclude and remove foreign nationals. The Court has also determined that removal (deportation) is not criminal prosecution or punishment. Consequently, aliens facing removal don't have a right to a jury trial or a right against self-incrimination.

However, outside the narrow boundaries of immigration law, permanent residents have extensive rights in the United States. The Constitution only limits a few rights to citizens—for example, voting in federal elections and holding certain national offices.

The Supreme Court recognized more than a century ago that the language of the Fourteenth Amendment—"No state shall deprive any PERSON of life, liberty or property without due process of law"—applies to all *persons* in the United States, including noncitizens.

Green Card holders generally enjoy most First Amendment rights (*see* Chapter 15), protections during criminal proceedings, the right to travel freely, to earn a living, to access the courts, to own property, and to receive government benefits—although some of these rights are restricted compared to those available to citizens. For example, permanent residents

→   must notify the USCIS when they change their address (a limitation on their right of travel and, possibly, right of privacy);

→ can (rarely) be deported for certain activities that are protected
   under the First Amendment when engaged in by citizens, for
   example, holding membership in certain organizations opposed to
   the U.S. government;

→ can be excluded from holding certain positions in state
   government (including state troopers and probation officers).

In exchange, Green Card holders have most of the obligations of U.S. citizens, including paying state and federal taxes and being drafted into the Armed Forces in times of war.

Myles Tugo's Immigration Decision

"It's not really a hard decision at all," Myles says to you. "I must acquire an employment-based Green Card. Clearly my advanced degree in clockwork engineering will qualify me as a 'professional with *exceptional ability* in the sciences.' All I need is an employer who will petition in my behalf."

"Hmmm . . . ," you reply. Rather than tell Myles you're skeptical that importing a cuckoo clockwork guru will substantially benefit the national economy, you say, "I'll check around." You also add, "It might also make sense for you to enter the diversity visa lottery—and maybe even think of falling in love with an American tourist who visits Grosse Fenwick."

Naturalization

Naturalization is the administrative process by which a foreign national gains U.S. citizenship. These are some general requirements:

→ A period of continuous residence and physical presence in the
   United States (typically five years; three years for the spouse of
   a U.S. citizen)

→ The ability to read, write, and speak English

→ A knowledge and understanding of U.S. history and government

→ Good moral character

→ Attachment to the principles of the U.S. Constitution

→ Favorable disposition toward the United States

The first three requirements on the list may be modified or waived for certain applicants (such as spouses of U.S. citizens).

The Immigration and Naturalization Act provides a streamlined process for naturalizing immigrants who serve in the military. An immigrant who is serving honorably on active duty during wartime is eligible to file for immediate citizenship.

An immigrant who served honorably during peacetime can apply for citizenship after one year in the Armed Forces. He or she must file an application while still in the service or within six months of separation.

Many Green Card holders have remained in the United States their whole lives without becoming naturalized citizens. They have most of the rights enjoyed by U.S. citizens (*see* above). One potentially risky aspect of applying for citizenship is that, on rare occasion, the USCIS will discover an unsuspected ineligibility that makes the individual subject to removal from the United States.

INDEX

ABOUT THE AUTHOR

RON BENREY holds a juris doctor degree from the Duquesne University School of Law, where he was Associate Editor of the Duquesne Law Review. He is a member of the Bar of the Commonwealth of Pennsylvania.

Ron also earned degrees in electrical engineering and management. The breadth of his formal education helped him build a career writing easy-to-understand words that explain hard-to-understand subjects. He has published nine non-fiction books on topics ranging from computers to theology, has authored more than a thousand bylined magazine articles, and has written hundreds of speeches delivered by senior executives at major corporations. Ron and his wife, Janet, have worked together to write nine published mystery novels.

When he's not writing, Ron enjoys sailing, traveling, and cooking. He and Janet live in North Carolina.

Please visit Ron at his website, www.benrey.com, or send him an e-mail message at rmb@benrey.com.